Reinventing Poland

The end of communism, and accession to the European Union, have had a huge impact on Poland. This book provides an overall assessment of the post-1989 transformation in Poland. It focuses in particular on four key themes: economic transformation and its outcomes; the heritage of the past and national identity; regional development in Poland including the implications of EU accession for regional development; and political developments both before and after EU accession. In addition the book shows how changes in all these areas are related, and emphasises the overall common themes. The book is in memory of George Blazyca, of the University of Paisley, whose work on the political economy of transition in Poland is highly regarded, and who did a great deal to support the work of Polish academic colleagues and to promote the work of young scholars.

Martin Myant is Professor at the University of Paisley Business School, UK. His publications include five single-authored books.

Terry Cox is Professor of Central and East European Studies at the University of Glasgow, UK. His publications include five authored or co-authored books on Eastern Europe.

BASEES/Routledge Series on Russian and East European Studies
Series editor: Richard Sakwa
Department of Politics and International Relations, University of Kent

Editorial Committee: Julian Cooper, Centre for Russian and East European Studies, University of Birmingham; Terry Cox, Department of Central and East European Studies, University of Glasgow; Rosalind Marsh, Department of European Studies and Modern Languages, University of Bath; David Moon, Department of History, University of Durham; Hilary Pilkington, Department of Sociology, University of Warwick; Stephen White, Department of Politics, University of Glasgow

Founding Editorial Committee Member: George Blazyca, Centre for Contemporary European Studies, University of Paisley

This series is published on behalf of BASEES (the British Association for Slavonic and East European Studies). The series comprises original, high-quality, research-level work by both new and established scholars on all aspects of Russian, Soviet, post-Soviet and East European Studies in humanities and social science subjects.

Reinventing Poland

Economic and political transformation
and evolving national identity

Edited by Martin Myant and Terry Cox

Routledge
Taylor & Francis Group

LONDON AND NEW YORK

First published 2008 by Routledge
2 Park Square, Milton Park, Abingdon, Oxon OX14 4RN

Simultaneously published in the USA and Canada
by Routledge
711 Third Avenue, New York, NY 10017

Routledge is an imprint of the Taylor & Francis Group, an informa business

First issued in paperback 2011

Typeset in Times New Roman by
RefineCatch Limited, Bungay, Suffolk

British Library Cataloguing in Publication Data
A catalogue record for this book is available from the British Library

Library of Congress Cataloging in Publication Data
    Reinventing Poland : economic and political transformation and evolving national identity / edited by Martin Myant and Terry Cox.
        p. cm—(Basees/Routledge series on Russian and East European studies)
    Includes bibliographical references and index.
    1. Poland—Politics and government—1989– 2. Poland—Economic conditions—1990– I. Myant, M. R. (Martin R.) II. Cox, Terry, 1947–
    JN6760.R45 2007
    330.9438—dc22
                                                2007035795

ISBN10: 0–415–45175–2 (hbk)
ISBN10: 0–415–67484–0 (pbk)
ISBN10: 0–203–93045–2 (ebk)

ISBN13: 978–0–415–45175–8 (hbk)
ISBN13: 978–0–415–67484–3 (pbk)
ISBN13: 978–0–203–93045–8 (ebk)

In memory of George Blazyca 1952–2005

Contents

Figures

Tables

Notes on contributors

Terry Cox is Professor of Central and East European Studies at the University of Glasgow and Editor of *Europe–Asia Studies*. His research interests include the politics and sociology of economic change in East Central Europe and the changing character of social policy in the region. Recent publications include *Communication and Consultation in Public Space* (2002) (with Jolan Ronta and Laszlo Vass); 'Democratisation and social policy in East Central Europe', in Y. Bangura (ed.), *Democratisation and Social Policy* (2007); and 'Democratization and state–society relations in East Central Europe: the case of Hungary', *Journal of Communist Studies and Transition Politics*, 23, No. 2, 2007.

Mike Danson is Professor of Scottish and Regional Economics at the University of Paisley. He has a strong academic and applied interest in comparative regional and rural economic development. He has acted as adviser to the European Commission and to various Scottish, UK and local governments and organisations. He directed the first ever research for the Scottish Parliament. He is Treasurer and Vice Chair (Scotland) of the British Academy of the Social Sciences and Fellow of the Institution of Economic Development.

Adam Drobniak teaches at the University of Economics in Katowice, Department of Strategic and Regional Science. His main fields of interest include local and regional programme evaluation, strategy implementation, evaluation of the EU funds and new concepts of local and regional development. He has published in Polish and English on themes relating to Silesian regional development.

Marian Górski is Professor and Head of the Banking and Financial Markets Department at the Warsaw University School of Management, where he was dean of faculty in 1990–96. His research interests focus on the financial and banking sector, monetary policy and comparative economics. Recent publications include *Architektura systemu finansowego gospodarki* [The architecture of the financial system of the economy] (2005), and *Rynkowy system finansowy* [The market financial sector of the economy]

(2007). From 1991 to 2005 he was the Chairman of the Board of the Wielkopolski Bank Kredytowy (WBK SA), a state bank privatised in 1993 with the Allied Irish Bank as strategic investor.

Krystian Heffner is Professor and Head of the Department of Spatial Economics at the University of Economics in Katowice. His interests focus on regional policy, problems of the spatial development of cities and villages, development of rural areas and foreign migration. He has published in English and Polish on regional competitiveness, regional development and migration.

Ewa Helinska-Hughes teaches at the University of Paisley Business School. She has conducted research and consultancy work on Polish regional development in the context of EU accession and has published in such journals as *International Journal of Entrepreneurship and Small Business, Public Policy and Administration* and *Journal of East–West Business*.

Michael Hughes is Head of the Aberdeen University Business School. His research on international business has included work on inward investment and business development in the economies of East Central Europe. He has published in such journals as *International Journal of Entrepreneurship and Small Business, Public Policy and Administration* and *Journal of East–West Business*.

Jowanka Jakubek is a Ph.D. candidate and also teaches in the Institute of Political Science, University of Warsaw. She has worked for Polish government administration as the spokesperson for the General Inspectorate of Road Transport and has also worked for *Polityka*, the biggest Polish weekly magazine. Her research interests cover issues in Polish government and in EU integration.

Eamonn Judge is Professor of Economics and Spatial Policy and Director of the Doctoral Programme in the Faculty of Business and Law at Leeds Metropolitan University and also Visiting Professor at the Polish Open University in Warsaw. His research interests cover transport economics, planning and policy. He is the author of several articles in English and Polish on environmental and economic issues in transport development in Poland.

Ewa Kokoszycka is a doctoral candidate in history at the European University Institute in Florence. She has received scholarships from the Polish Ministry of National Education, Herbert-Quandt-Stiftung and Constanz University, Germany. In her Ph.D. thesis she analyses ethical consumption in the late nineteenth and early twentieth centuries, taking the vegetarian milieu in Berlin as a starting point. She has published several articles in Polish, both in academic publications and in the popular press, on issues within the social and cultural history of the nineteenth century and gender history, which are her long-term interests.

Tadeusz Kowalik is Professor of Economics and Humanities at the Institute of Economics, Polish Academy of Sciences and at the Warsaw School of Economics. His interests cover the history of social and economic thought and comparative economics. Recent publications in English include the edited volume *Economic Theory and Market Socialism: Selected Essays of Oskar Lange* (1994). He has recently written on controversies over the third way and on the effects and defects of reform.

Clare McManus-Czubińska is a Lecturer in the Department of Central and East European Studies at the University of Glasgow and the Reviews Editor of *Europe–Asia Studies*. Her research interests focus upon the states and societies of the East Central European (ECE) states, especially Poland, and their process of integration with the European Union. Her recent publications include 'The misuse of referendums in post-communist Europe' (with W. Miller, R. Markowski and J. Wasilewski), in D. S. Hutcheson and E. A. Korosteleva (eds), *The Quality of Democracy in Post-Communist Europe* (2006) and 'Mass higher education in Poland: coping with the "Spanish Collar" ', in T. Tapper and D. Palfreyman (eds), *Understanding Mass Higher Education: Comparative Perspectives on Access* (2005).

Frances Millard is Professor of Comparative Politics in the Department of Government at the University of Essex, where she specialises in communist and post-communist politics. Her books include *Elections, Parties, and Representation in Post-Communist Europe* (2004); and *Polish Politics and Society* (1998). She has written numerous articles on parties, elections and social policy in Poland.

William Miller is Professor of Politics at the University of Glasgow. His interests are in political behaviour and public opinion in Eastern and Western Europe (including Britain) and East Asia, with particular reference to voting, elections and the media; democratic values, civil rights and corruption; immigration, ethnicity and identity; and globalisation and contrasts between the general public, state officials and elected representatives. Recent publications include *The Open Economy and its Enemies* (2006) (with J. Duckett); and *Routine Corruption? Citizens and Government in Postcommunist Europe* (2004) (with B. Grodeland and T. Koshechkina).

Martin Myant is Professor at the University of Paisley Business School. He has researched economic and political development in East Central Europe, concentrating on the Czech Republic, Slovakia and Poland. Recent publications include *The Rise and Fall of Czech Capitalism: Economic Development in the Czech Republic since 1989* (2003); and *Varieties of Capitalism in Post-Communist Countries* (2007) (edited jointly with David Lane).

Stuart Paul teaches at the University of Paisley Business School. He has written extensively in the Scottish press on business issues and has published a number of articles on the informal investment market, most recently in the journals *Venture Capital* and *Journal of Small Business and Enterprise Development*.

Ryszard Rapacki is Professor of Economics and Head of the Department of Economics at the Warsaw School of Economics. He has been an expert and consultant to various international organisations (UN Secretariat, UNDP, UNIDO and OECD). His main fields of interest include systemic transformation in Central and Eastern Europe, structural reforms, economic growth and real convergence and public finance. Recent publications include *Poland into the New Millennium* (2001) (edited with George Blazyca); and 'Economic growth accounting in 27 transition economies, 1990–2005', *Ekonomista*, No. 6, 2006 (with M. Prochniak).

Robert Romanowski is a lecturer in the Trade and Marketing Department, University of Economics, Poznań. He specialises in place marketing in multifunctional rural areas and territorial innovative production systems and has been a consultant on rural development issues.

Ewa Sidorenko is currently Senior Lecturer in Sociology at Greenwich University. Since completing her Ph.D. thesis (1998), on 'Neo-liberalism after communism: constructing a sociological account of the political space of post-1989 Poland', she has presented a number of papers at academic conferences. Her research interests include post-communist Polish society; the public sphere, social trust and political culture; the sociology of education; and the sociology of childhood.

Marzenna Anna Weresa is Professor at, and Director of, the World Economy Research Institute at the Warsaw School of Economics. Her research focuses on issues related to technology transfer and innovation in the context of economic transition in Central Europe, and on the effects of foreign direct investment and foreign trade on innovation performance and economic development. Recent publications include *Achieving Competitiveness through Innovation* (2007) (edited with W. Leal Filho); and 'EU eastern enlargement and foreign direct investment flows', in P. Jaworski and T. Mickiewicz (eds), *Polish EU Accession in Comparative Perspective: Macroeconomics, Finance and the Government* (2006).

Geoff Whittam is Reader in Entrepreneurship in the University of Paisley Business School. He has published widely on entrepreneurship and regional economic development, focusing recently on the informal investment market, minority ethnic businesses, women entrepreneurs, and alternative local tax systems.

Preface

The themes explored in this book reflect the main themes in the work of the late George Blazyca (1952–2005), to whom this book is intended as a memorial. The volume developed out of a conference held in November 2006, at the University of Paisley, in memory of, and to continue the work of, George Blazyca. The selected contributions include the best papers presented at the conference and are intended to fit into the thematic areas outlined in the Introduction. These reflect the breadth and coherence of George's academic work and wider political interests. While George was trained as an economist, his interests extended also to the history, politics and culture of Poland and to its changing place in Europe. After completing a Ph.D. on the Polish economy at the University of Sussex, George Blazyca lectured at the University of East Anglia, Coventry Polytechnic and Thames Polytechnic, before moving in 1992 to a Professorship at the University of Paisley, where he served as Director of the Centre of Contemporary European Studies.

His early writing developed the argument that the problems of the Polish economy under communist rule had to be understood in terms of the complexities of Poland as much as the problems of the centrally planned economy. In his book *Planning Is Good for You: The Case for Popular Control* (1983) he argued for the possibility of forms of economic planning that would not produce the negative consequences of those developed in Eastern Europe, and warned against the idea that free-market economics would provide a solution to Poland's problems.

After the end of communist rule in 1989 he edited a series of volumes, *Poland into the 1990s* (with Ryszard Rapacki), *Monitoring Economic Transition: The Polish Case* (with Janusz Dabrowski) and *Poland into the New Millennium: Economies and Societies in Transition* (again with Ryszard Rapacki), which helped bring the work of Polish economists and social scientists to a wider international readership. Interest in comparisons between Scotland and old industrial regions in Poland led to a further edited volume, *Restructuring Regional and Local Economies: Towards a Comparative Study of Scotland and Upper Silesia*. A lasting interest in the implications of EU enlargement in general and in Poland's accession in particular prompted the organisation of a major international conference at the University of Paisley in 2004, entitled 'What does EU enlargement really mean for Scotland?', bringing together academics, politicians, journalists and business leaders from Scotland and all the new accession countries of Eastern, Central and Southern Europe.

As a democratic socialist George argued against the growing dominance of free-market criteria and for the pursuit of social justice in the formulation of economic policy. At the same time, as a committed European, he sought the solution to such problems through a closer engagement with Europe, both for Poland and East Central Europe, and for Scotland and the UK.

Abbreviations

A-PY	All-Poland Youth (*Młodzież Wszechpolska*)
AWS	*Akcja Wyborcza Solidarność* (Solidarity Electoral [or Election] Action)
BAN	Business Angel Network
CBOS	*Centrum Badania Opinii Społecznej* (Centre for Public Opinion Research)
CEE	Central and East European
CEECs	Central and Eastern European countries
CFSP	Common Foreign and Security Policy
CGE	computable general equilibrium
COSAC	Conference of Community and European Affairs Committees of Parliaments of the European Union
DEM	Deutschmark
DfT	Department for Transport
DIH	direct importance hierarchy
EBAN	European Business Angel Network
EIR	economic impact report
ESPON	European Spatial Planning Observation Network
EU	European Union
FDI	foreign direct investment
FIEs	foreign investment enterprises
GDP	Gross Domestic Product
GUS	*Główny Urząd Statystyczny* (Central Statistical Office)
IASON	Integrated Appraisal of Spatial economic and Network effects of transport investments and policies
IFA	Investment Fund Act
IPN	*Instytut Pamięci Narodowej* (Institute of National Memory)
IROP	Integrated Regional Operational Programme
ISD	Institute for Sustainable Development
KERM	*Komitet Europejski Rady Ministrów* (European Committee of the [Polish] Council of Ministers)
KIE	*Komitet Integracji Europejskiej* (Committee for European Integration)

KPH	*Kampania Przeciw Homofobii* (Campaign against Homophobia)
LBA	Lewiatan Business Angels
LiD	*Lewica i Demokraci* (The Left and the Democrats)
LINC	Local Investment Network Company
LPR	*Liga Polskich Rodzin* (League of Polish Families)
MFA	Ministry of Foreign Affairs
MFD	multifunctional development
MPC	Monetary Policy Council
MRD	multifunctional rural development
NBP	*Narodowy Bank Polski* (National Bank of Poland)
ND	National Democracy
NDP	*Narodowy Plan Rozwoju* (National Development Plan)
NEG	New Economic Geography
NIFs	National Investment Funds
NMP	Net Material Product
NPPC	*Narodowy Program Przygotowania do Członkostwa* (National Programme of Preparation for Membership)
OBOP	*Ośrodek Badania Opinii Publicznej* (Centre for Researching Public Opinion)
OER	official exchange rates
PC	*Porozumienie Centrum* (Centre Accord)
PiS	*Prawo i Sprawiedliwość* (Law and Justice)
PO	*Platforma Obywatelska* (Civic Platform)
PPP	Purchasing Power Parity
PPS	*Polska Partia Socjalistyczna* (Polish Socialist Party)
PSL	*Polskie Stronnictwo Ludowe* (Polish Peasants' [or Peasant] Party)
RAPP	relations, arena of presentation, product and participants
RCA	revealed comparative advantage
RLCh	*Ruch Ludowo-Chrześcijański* (People's Christian Movement)
RL-N	*Ruch Ludowo-Narodowy* (National People's Movement)
RM	Radio Maryja
SACTRA	Standing Advisory Committee on Trunk Road Appraisal
SB	*Służba Bezpieczeństwa* (Security Service)
SdPl	*Socjaldemokracja Polska* (Polish Social Democracy)
SdRP	*Socjaldemokracja Rzeczpospolitej Polskiej* (Social Democracy of the Polish Republic)
SH	subtraction hierarchy
SilBAN	Silesian Business Angel Network
SLD	*Sojusz Lewicy Demokratycznej* (Alliance of the Democratic Left)
SMEs	small and medium-sized enterprises
SO	*Samoobrona Rzeczpospolitej Polskiej* (Self-Defence of the Polish Republic)

TEN	Trans-European Network
TINA	Transport Infrastructure Needs Assessment
TSKN	*Towarzystwo Społeczno-Kulturalne Niemców na Śląsku Opolskim* (Social and Cultural Association of the Germans in the Opole Region of Silesia)
UKIE	*Urząd Komitetu Integracji Europejskiej* (Office of the Committee for European Integration)
UOP	*Urząd Ochrony Państwa* (Bureau of State Security)
UP	*Unia Pracy* (Labour Union)
UW	*Unia Wolności* (Freedom Union)
WIH	weighted importance hierarchy
WSI	*Wojskowe Służby Informacyjne* (Military Intelligence Services)
ZChN	*Zjednoczenie Chrześcijańsko-Narodowe* (Christian National Union)
ZPKIE	*Zespół Przygotowawczy KIE* (Preparatory Workgroup of the KIE)

Introduction

Terry Cox and Martin Myant

Poland has experienced many changes and transformations over its history, and it has been reinvented in a range of different political and economic forms. In some periods Poles have been colonised and absorbed into different neighbouring kingdoms and empires, while at other times they have lived under kingdoms or republics bearing the name of Poland. Between 1795 and 1918 Poland ceased to exist as a separate country, its territory divided between the neighbouring powers of Russia, Prussia and Austria. However, during the nineteenth century, as nationalism spread across Europe, Polish patriots struggled for the reinvention of Poland as a nation state in its own right, an aim eventually fulfilled in 1918. Independent Poland disappeared again in 1939 as its territory was occupied by Nazi Germany and the Soviet Union, and after the Second World War it experienced a further reinvention, with a significant redrawing of its territorial boundaries, to become part of the Soviet bloc, a people's republic with a centrally managed economy.

Under communist rule the theme of reinvention continued as successive leaderships explored distinctive Polish variants to the Soviet model, culminating in the 1980s with the confrontation with Solidarity, the imposition of martial rule and, in 1989, the election of the first non-communist government since the 1940s. Since 1989 Poles have continued to be preoccupied with the form their country should take, and there have been intensive discussions over the character of the transformation of the Polish economy, politics and society. In the course of these debates Poland has sought to reinvent itself as a modern European state with a market economy and a liberal democratic political system and as a member state of the European Union (EU). In this context, major divisions have developed over the most appropriate strategies of economic transition, problems of regional development, questions of sustaining and asserting Polish national identity and, most divisively, increasingly bitter ideological debates about the future direction of Poland.

Different political actors have sought inspiration from a variety of possible sources. Some could look to lasting national or religious identities, often pointing to strong condemnation of the communist past and to reluctance to welcome outside influences on Poland's internal development. Others sought continuation of various socialist, or left, traditions as expressed less in the communist past than in trends within the Solidarity movement of 1980–81. In economic thinking the dominant influence was from orthodox, free-market economic theory as developed in the USA and Western Europe. With this came an emphasis on liberalisation, privatisation and opening to the world economy. These in turn could clash with national sentiments, with concerns over social stability and fairness and with hopes that there might be something positive worth keeping from socialist or left traditions. Poland's international reorientation – towards the West, NATO and, above all, the EU – also brought scope for alternative interpretations. 'Europeanisation', if understood in the strongest sense as the direct impact of EU institutions on internal development, was important, and widely welcomed, in relatively few policy areas. Incorporation into the wider European entity aroused suspicion and opposition from political trends that saw greater openness to the outside world as a threat to values derived from Poland's own, apparently specific, past.

These more recent, post-1989, conceptions for a reinvention of Poland provide the background for this book, and the individual chapters are intended to contribute towards an assessment of the post-1989 transformation in Poland. They provide contrasting assessments across different thematic areas of economic transformation, the heritage of the past and the question of national identity, the implications of EU accession for political development and questions of regional and local development. In each important policy area there was an input from various possible versions of Poland's post-1989 reinvention, but their respective weightings varied. In some policy areas, advocates of one or more possible versions of development were indifferent and provided no significant input. In some cases there was more obvious conflict and in other cases there was agreement between advocates of different possible directions of development. The overall outcome therefore appears as a complex combination of different conceptions of Poland's reinvention.

The chapters in Part I cover Poland's economic reinvention after 1989, pointing to differing assessments of the economic reform strategy adopted after 1989 and of some key macroeconomic policy initiatives. Tadeusz Kowalik focuses on his personal contacts with George Blazyca and on the latter's writing on the Polish transformation. The chapter illustrates the dilemmas faced by those on the left during an economic transformation towards capitalism. Kowalik is identified with the 'Solidarity left' trend in Polish politics, and he was highly critical of the 'shock therapy' of 1990, which he considered excessively restrictive and a cause of unnecessary social costs. He remained critical of claims of an unqualified economic success in the following years. Blazyca, despite undeniable socialist sympathies and close agreement with Kowalik on many other political issues, seemed to 'suspend' his socialist beliefs when dealing with post-1989 Poland. His lasting hope was that engagement in the EU would bring a reorientation in Poland's politics. Initial signs were not promising as Poland appeared to move further from any left traditions either from its own past or from elsewhere in Europe.

Ryszard Rapacki provides a comparative overview of Poland's economic performance, as measured by growth in per capita GDP. The 1950–89 period saw Poland lose ground relative to other countries, including, particularly in the 1980s, other East European economies. However, rapid growth after 1989 moved Poland up the hierarchy of transition economies and restored the country to broadly the same relative position as in 1980, with per capita GDP of about 46 per cent of the EU average. Rapacki takes this as an indication of benefits from the 'shock therapy' of the early 1990s. However, the period after 2002 saw a slowing down of growth rates and, at the end of the period he studied, Poland remained a middle-income country. Extrapolating past growth trends points to Poland fully reinventing itself as a modern economy by reaching the EU average level somewhere between 2035 (if the successes of the 1990s can be repeated) and 2071 (if growth continues at the rate of the years from 2000 onwards).

Marzenna Anna Weresa analyses the importance of foreign direct investment for Poland's post-1989 economic growth. Thanks to the post-1989 liberalisation, multinational companies were able to invest in Poland either by buying Polish enterprises or by establishing their own plants on greenfield sites. This is frequently seen as a basis for improved international competitiveness, and Weresa analyses this with indicators of productivity and of trade performance, both applied to branches of manufacturing industry over the period 1995–2004. The available data enable her to distinguish between the contributions of firms under foreign and under Polish control, and she demonstrates a generally positive impact of inward direct investment. This is clearest in the motor vehicle branch, which came to be dominated by foreign firms and saw a rapid improvement in both productivity and trade performance. In some other sectors the relationship is more complex, with cases of greater improvements for Polish than for foreign firms.

Marian Górski follows the nature of fiscal and monetary policies from 1993 to 2005. He uses the IS-LM framework which, owing he suggests to its Keynesian origins, was unpopular among much of the Polish economic community and was ignored by the monetary authorities. Górski uses this to show differences in policy approach between central bank governors and governments of different political complexions. Monetary policy was almost always expansionary, despite claims that it was generally restrictive. Fiscal policy was more varied, being neutral or restrictive under a predominantly Social Democrat government and expansionary under a Solidarity government. This conflicts with the received wisdom that fiscal policy was typically expansionary. An extension of the analysis to incorporate international influences and a matching of fiscal and monetary policies to past economic performance enables the author to suggest that the most favourable policy mix for growth appears to be an expansionary monetary policy with a restrictive fiscal policy.

The chapters in Part II explore aspects of current Polish politics in the context of Poland's development as a liberal democracy and its accession to the EU. In particular they deal with different attempts to invent and reinvent effective institutional frameworks to enable the emergence of a stable party system and to achieve effective coordination of Poland's domestic policy making with that of the EU. On the question of the party system, as Frances Millard notes, stable political parties form the 'building blocks' of democracy. However, in Poland their development has been rather volatile and this has contributed to a continuing problem of unstable governments and the alienation of the Polish public. Since 1989 governmental power has swung between the two main political blocs that derive from the Solidarity movement on the one hand and the Social Democrats on the other. The division between these two broad movements reflects a deep cleavage in Polish politics between the inheritors of the Solidarity dissident movement and those of the reform wing of the former ruling communists. However, this pattern was broken by the 2005 election when, in the context of a serious defeat for the Social Democrats, the Solidarity-based winning party, Law and Justice (PiS), failed to agree on a coalition with the next largest party, Civic Platform (PO), which also derived from Solidarity. Instead, PiS made an agreement with non-Solidarity nationalist and populist forces from Self Defence (SO) and the League of Polish Families (LPR). This in turn has created new sources of uncertainty by providing support for arguments for even more fundamental political reinventions, centring on the project of a new Fourth Republic, aiming finally to eradicate what are seen in this perspective as the remaining legacies of the communist period.

Different patterns of institutional reinvention have also been evident in the executive and legislative branches of the Polish political system as it has sought to adjust, first, to meeting the requirements for EU accession and, then, to coordinating national and EU policy making as a member country. As Jowanka Jakubek notes, joining the EU involved a difficult struggle for successive governments to meet the criteria for EU membership by implementing the *acquis*, but since securing membership they have faced even more challenges. As Polish policy makers have grappled with the change from the implementation of EU standards to full participation in EU-level decision making, the role and influence of the executive have increased, centred especially on the office of the prime minister. Jakubek shows how institutions developed at one stage of the process have proved to be less effective at later stages and how a constant process of innovation has taken place. In the current period, with Poland as a full EU member country, Polish governments are again faced with finding more efficient ways to coordinate their European actions, especially in policy-making areas.

The chapters in Part III link issues of the character of Polish politics with Poland's longer-term history and national identity. Ewa Sidorenko explores the roots of the widespread discourse of populism and nationalism that underlies the Fourth Republic project described by Millard. For Sidorenko there is an unresolved contradiction between the new-found stability of Poland's new democracy in the context of membership of NATO and the EU and a recurrent theme of crisis and threats to Poland's integrity in much of contemporary public discourse in Poland. This discourse focuses on patriotic values and the promotion of moral education based on Catholic values in a way that presents negative images of foreign influences, cosmopolitan values and cultural diversity, and sees these as challenges to traditional aspects of 'the Polish way of life'. Sidorenko locates these developments in the context of processes of rapid social change and the fragmenting of identities. Further, however, she argues that the current stress on populism, patriotism and traditionalism should be understood as an attempt to resist social change in a way that is path dependent, drawing on a legacy of ideas that emerged as part of the resistance to communism. In place of the way dissident ideas utilised the imagery of Polish national identity as distinct from the interests of the communist state, similar images are now used to resist the cultural changes that Poland is experiencing as part of its current political transformation and integration into Europe.

The themes of nationalism and Catholicism are also a central focus of the chapter by Clare McManus-Czubińska and William Miller. Drawing on public opinion data from questions they placed in the 2005 Polish National Election Study, the authors confirm the widespread belief and commitment to Roman Catholicism of the Polish population and their respect for the Church above most other social institutions. They also show a close link between Catholicism, Polish patriotism and opposition to foreign immigration. However, contrary to what might be assumed from these data, the authors then show that a majority of Poles draw a clear distinction between their religious beliefs and practices and their views on the relation between Church and state and on a wide range of other political opinions. Their survey results show Poles are opposed to the Church attempting to exert an influence on voting choices or policy issues. A large majority also supports Poland's continuing membership of the secular, 'post-Christian' EU, and do not see this as incompatible with preserving a distinctive Polish culture. Moreover, on the question of what other countries would be acceptable future EU members, Poles were happier to accept 'Muslim' Turkey than 'Christian' Russia, and to see a poor human rights record as a bigger barrier to membership than a non-Christian tradition.

As Ewa Kokoszycka shows in her chapter, secular and cosmopolitan themes, of the kind revealed by the contemporary data of McManus-Czubińska and Miller, have in fact been a long-standing feature of Polish culture. Focusing specifically on the history of vegetarianism in Poland, Kokoszycka traces its development around the turn of the twentieth century, during the period of the partition when Poland did not exist as a nation state. Exploring the forms taken by Polish vegetarianism and the networks between people who became vegetarian, she shows how its growth can be understood as part of wider trends of the revival of Polish society. She suggests that

Polish vegetarianism, as well as demonstrating a concern for health and well-being, was also concerned with the health of the Polish nation. Thus, alongside its international links and cosmopolitan outlook, Polish vegetarianism was part of the revival of a national culture. Through its networks and publications, vegetarianism helped bring Poles together despite the national or imperial boundaries that divided them at the time. Polish vegetarianism can therefore be seen as closely connected with both the rise of modernity and the revival of Polish patriotism.

Krystian Heffner's contribution further demonstrates the flexible nature of identity in the context of European integration. He follows the national and regional identity of the population of the Opole region in southern Poland. The German population was largely expelled at the end of the Second World War, although the boundaries between Germans and Poles were never precise in a region with elements of its own identity. New Polish migrants came from territory incorporated into the Soviet Union, and official policy was to assert a clear Polish identity. After 1989 a combination of internal circumstances, including the reaction of part of the population against the cultural and political repression of the communist period, and external opportunities – Germany's policies towards 'Germans' living in other countries – led many citizens to seek joint Polish–German citizenship. Their identity remained flexible and pragmatic. German citizenship provided access to employment in Western Europe. This was also built from networks of family and other contacts, traceable back to previous migrations. As a result, part of the population of the Opole region could take advantage of the free movement of people even before EU accession.

The chapters in Part IV cover regional and local development. Eamonn Judge provides a comparison of the role of transport policy in economic development in Poland and the UK. Taking the example of motorway development in each country, Judge explores both the different paths taken by the academic and policy debates in each country and the linkages between them. A particular contrast is in the degree to which theoretical and policy debates became politicised in each country. While the relation between transport and economic development was not a politically contentious issue in the UK, in Poland it became embroiled in the cleavages of national politics (thus providing a further illustration of the contentious nature of Polish politics discussed in the chapters of Millard and Sidorenko). A further contrast was that the Polish debate revolved around national economic priorities to a greater extent than in the UK. In Poland there was a relative lack of a specific regional focus in the debate, so that questions of which regions would gain or lose from the development of a new motorway system were scarcely discussed. Finally, there has been a significant difference in the extent to which research on these issues has developed in Poland compared to the UK, while at the same time there has been more progress in Poland in applying recently developed theoretical models than has been the case in the UK.

The direct influence of EU membership is particularly important for policy making on regional development, bringing access to support from Structural Funds and Cohesion Funds. The hope from Brussels was that, apart from contributing directly to economic development, this help, and the conditions attached to it, would contribute to the development of methods of good governance, foster cooperation between partners and encourage a systematic approach to regional development. Adam Drobniak follows the experience of Structural Funds in the Silesia region in southern Poland up to 2006. The detailed study shows the uptake across the region. The sums involved were small in relation to the problems faced. However, some municipalities were able to benefit enormously while some others failed to exploit the new funding opportunities. There was also some mismatch between the priorities for funding set out by the central government and the structure of applications from municipalities. Most applications were for basic infrastructure projects. There was less interest in support for areas such as education and innovation strategies. Also, although partnership and cooperation were seen as central to the conception of the Structural Funds, there was so little coordination of projects between municipalities that road improvement projects could stop at municipal boundaries.

Issues of local and regional development are taken further by Robert Romanowski, who looks at multifunctional rural development in a part of central Poland. This refers to diversification beyond production of basic agricultural products, and the aim of the chapter is to identify the priority policy areas for encouraging such a process. Romanowski develops a methodology by adapting ideas from standard marketing theory. Analysis of opinions of a variety of actors enables him to conclude that the most consistent gap was in the weak development of partnership relations between local authorities and other local actors. Dissatisfaction over participation in the local planning process was spread across all types of municipality. Beyond that, there were substantial differences in perception between different actors and between different kinds of municipality. In the least developed the greatest need seemed to be for improving the technical infrastructure, while in the most developed participation was the biggest source of dissatisfaction.

Mike Danson, Ewa Helinska-Hughes, Stuart Paul, Geoff Whittam and Michael Hughes take forward the comparison between UK and Polish experience, looking at the support for small and medium-sized enterprises from business angels, private individuals who supply venture capital to firms in exchange for an equity stake. Evidence from Scotland suggests that they play an important role for start-up companies. It is not surprising that their role has been small in Poland, but networks have appeared and there are remarkably strong similarities between the kinds of people who become business angels in the two countries and in their modes of operation. The analysis leads to policy recommendations that could help the development of business angel activity in Poland.

Part I

Economic transformation and recent economic developments

1　George Blazyca on shock therapy and the third way

Tadeusz Kowalik

Socialist academic

The aim in this chapter is to look at the works on Poland of George Blazyca as a historian of economic and social ideas. That means that I shall pay attention to his ideas rather than to economic tools or even theories. In a way George Blazyca and Ryszard Rapacki prescribed this role for me, nominating me as 'a self-confessed socialist (in tradition of the Solidarity Left rather than the Communist party)' (Blazyca and Rapacki 2001: 2). George was post-humously described in a similar way by David Hearst in his obituary entitled 'Socialist academic with a profound grasp of the Polish economy' (*Guardian*, 31 March 2005). I happen to belong among those Polish colleagues or friends of George who believed that he was a convinced socialist, although after the collapse of communism both of us had profoundly to redefine the very notion of socialism.

My knowledge of George's work is limited to three books he co-edited and to two essays (Blazyca and Rapacki 1991, 2001; Blazyca and Dąbrowski 1995; Blazyca 2000, 2006). I met him many times and discussed a lot of fundamental problems of the contemporary world and particularly of capitalism and the systemic transformation in the region of Central Europe. I can therefore look at his publications in the light of my own personal recollections.

However, I am sure that, for many Polish readers of Blazyca's publications on the Polish economy, such a presentation of him would be a great surprise. Indeed, in his writings and publications, he not only carefully avoided any socialist or even social-democratic rhetoric, but also brought to English-speaking readers' attention many contributions written by neo-liberal economists.

How can this puzzle be explained? It is not easy to find an answer. We can start with a look at the main books and essays co-edited, co-authored and written by him.

Balcerowicz's shock therapy

The book *Poland into the 1990s: Economy and Society in Transition* (Blazyca and Rapacki 1991) brought together thirteen essays by Polish scholars on different aspects of the economy and society. George co-edited this book and co-authored an introduction, both with Ryszard Rapacki. The book was written in July 1990, with the perspective of half a year of implementation of Leszek Balcerowicz's famous 'shock therapy', sometimes also called the 'Big Bang', and the two authors of the introduction clearly noted the 'immense cost' of this surgery. They wrote: 'real incomes were cut by around 36% in the first half of 1990 (compared to the same 1989 period), output fell by 30% and unemployment accelerated sharply upwards' (Blazyca and Rapacki 1991: 2). They also noticed that the plan was too severe on domestic demand, likening it to 'shooting a sparrow with too many cannon'. But 'none of this', they continue, should be taken to suggest that this plan was unsuccessful. 'Inflation was brought down, firms came up against hard budget constraints ... black market was eliminated and ... universal shortage disappeared' (Blazyca and Rapacki 1991: 3).

We can notice that they did not suggest that the authorities should relax and slow down the implementation of their programme. On the contrary, they wrote that 'the next steps ... are more fundamental and may be more trying. Poland will need to overcome the legacy of forty years of generally misconceived economic policy' (Blazyca and Rapacki 1991: 3). Thus, the above-listed sacrifices were only the first step, and the authorities should continue along the same path.

As far as the future was concerned, they were afraid not of the type of social order emerging but of a failure to continue with the chosen strategy. They wrote:

> Undoubtedly, difficult times lie ahead as Poland moves into the 1990s and there is a residual danger that, if the going gets too tough, the unemployment too high and for too long, and the degree of Western assistance is too parsimonious, the country could slip backwards towards a strong-arm internal politics of an almost pre-war vintage. It would be a tragedy if the democratization that has been the Solidarity emblem since 1980 were to be swamped by a misplaced romanticism for a bygone age.
>
> (Blazyca and Rapacki 1991: 3)

One has to acknowledge that some of these forecasts sound prophetic. The economic policy was too tough, unemployment became the highest in the EU over a long period of time, and Western assistance was negligible and rather misplaced. Moreover, never before had there been such popularity in a Polish debate on internal politics for a bitter metaphor from the editor of the Paris-based monthly *Kultura*, Jerzy Giedroic, that contemporary Poland was being ruled by two coffins, that of the pre-war authoritarian Marshal Józef

Piłsudski and that of Roman Dmowski, a leader of a pre-war extreme nationalist and anti-Semitic party. The Solidarity emblem of the 1980s had been swamped, not by misplaced romanticism but by a policy motivated by a conviction that Poland had to pass through a period of primitive accumulation of capital.

And yet, I feel uneasy with the above conclusion. The two authors seemed to have fully accepted a chosen path of transformation, 'shock therapy', not seeing any alternative within a very general framework of 'Western-style capitalism'.

As seen by the neo-liberals

The second important book on the Polish economic transformation, *Monitoring Economic Transition: The Polish Case*, was published four years later (Blazyca and Dąbrowski 1995). With the exception of Chapter 2, authored by George, it was written by ten researchers, all from the Gdańsk Institute for Market Economics. This institute is a well-known think tank of the Gdańsk conservative liberals, founded by their leaders. Dąbrowski himself was one of the institute's directors. Friedrich von Hayek, Milton Friedman and Reaganomics are, or at least were, their ideological trademarks. The topics of the chapters in this most coherent volume covered state firms and privatisation, firms' performance, the financial and banking systems, forecasting, and the place of the Polish economy in Europe.

It would be unfair to say that George uncritically accepted the manifestly neo-liberal views of these authors. He supplied many critical comments. In a section within his chapter covering social and regional differentiation (Blazyca 1995: 25–6), he added some crucial information about the social consequences of shock therapy, above all about high unemployment. This was over 16 per cent on average, but in some regions close to, or even above, 30 per cent! Moreover, his conclusion was a drastic warning:

> A firm timetable for EU membership looks likely to be one of the single most important issues for the future and the failure to agree on one is likely to have immense consequences both political and economic. But most important, and perhaps potentially most dangerous, will be the damage that might be done to any successful transformation by social and regional disparities that grow in unrestrained manner.
>
> (Blazyca 1995: 35)

What is striking, however, is that he simply limits himself to informing about these real and potential facts, not pointing out that the authorities did not have any convincing programme for dealing with these pathological phenomena. In several remarks he rather defended the government's economic policy, in which there was much more continuity of the Balcerowicz policy than change. This continuity was at that time noticed by many Polish and foreign observers. For George, his collaborators seemed to be too pessimistic with regard to the government's policy. It is also striking that, even when writing on a five-year experience, he still limited his wording to 'transformation to Western style economy'. Such notions as capitalism, systemic choice and alternatives and neo-liberalism do not even appear.

Ambiguous success

Now I can make some remarks on my personal experience with the last book, *Poland into the New Millennium* (Blazyca and Rapacki 2001). Here I have to rely on my memory. Initially, when George asked me to contribute to it, I refused. I was just working on a longer study entitled 'Why the social democratic option failed: Poland's experience of systemic change' (Kowalik 2001b), for a book edited by Andrew Glyn. I was convinced that, knowing tough British copyrights and habits, it would be difficult to write something similar without areas of glaring overlap. I recommended, instead, Włodzimierz Pańków, who contributed an essay on Poland's industrial relations.

After a while, however, George came back to this issue, urging me to write a general evaluation of the Polish transformation. If I remember correctly, this was after having received a text from the former prime minister Marek Belka, who was quite happy with the results of the newly emerged Polish socio-economic order. George said that he badly needed an alternative point of view and added something like: 'You can write things that I cannot write'. This surprised me, and I reminded him that he had written such a polemical text, which only needed to be updated. He had contributed to a book which I had co-edited. This was published in Polish. It was an essay evaluating negatively the Polish systemic changes as an outcome of neo-liberal policy and recommending a sort of 'third way'. I describe this remarkable essay below. As a reaction to this, he reminded me of what I had told him in either late 1989 or early 1990. This was a story of a team of American leftists, with Tom Weisskopf (1992), who had wanted to work for the Polish government, advising a very moderate form of market socialism *à la* John E. Roemer. This proposal was flatly rejected by Polish officialdom. The well-known Polish émigré Włodzimierz Brus had a similarly bitter experience. During his first visit to Warsaw since his departure from Poland in 1972, in the autumn of 1989 he argued for following some ideas from the Swedish model (Brus 1992). George stressed that he had understood these stories as advice. If he wanted somehow to be accepted by an academic milieu, he had to collaborate with people from the dominant currents of thought.

This was not that convincing an argument for me, because the atmosphere had radically changed from that at the beginning of the 1990s. A leftist criticism of shock therapy and of the neo-liberal recipe was already part of a public debate. Then, his final argument was that this time he wanted not so much to monitor changes in the economy and society but to present a spectrum of views on systemic changes in Poland. Indeed, in their introductory chapter, George and Ryszard Rapacki wrote that 'the collection should be viewed as a contribution to on-going debate', hoping that it would encourage 'a wider discussion across social science perspectives' (Blazyca and Rapacki 2001: 1). This is how I was convinced to write my chapter, entitled 'The ugly face of Polish success' (Kowalik 2001a), giving a totally different picture of systemic changes in Poland to that given by Marek Belka, although in the title I gave an unnecessary gift to the then prevailing opinion that there had been a success. If, seventeen years after the creation of a new system, we had retained over a long time period the highest rate of unemployment in the EU, if unemployment allowances had been almost abolished and if the quite high rate of growth of GDP was accompanied by rapidly growing numbers in absolute poverty, then it is impossible to describe this as a success, albeit one with an ugly face.

The third way for Poland?

At the beginning of the 1990s I, with Jerzy Hausner, the leftist economist who was a professor at the Economic University in Kraków, initiated a series of public lectures by Polish economists from abroad. These were to be lectures on freely chosen topics, but in such a way that they would show to the Polish audience the main lines of the lecturer's life's work and scientific interests. We managed to publish these lectures in a book, *Polscy ekonomiści w świecie* (Kowalik 2000). Although George was not an émigré, and only 'half' of Polish origin, we included him because of his strong ties with Poland and the Polish economists' milieu. George's lecture was presented, in my absence from Poland, at the end of 1995 or the beginning of 1996. His remarks on the Polish changes, entitled 'Observations on the Polish transformation: are there really no "third ways"?' (Blazyca 1996, 2000), amounted to the most radical essay of his that I know, not only on the Polish transformation but also on American and British capitalism.

Trying to answer the question of why neo-liberalism was attractive in Poland in 1989, Blazyca enumerated three factors. He reminds us: that it was at that time the climax of the popularity of the Reaganite and Thatcherite free-market ideology and a manifestation of a belief in Fukuyama's (1992) 'end of history'; that there was strong pressure for financial orthodoxy from the international financial institutions; and that both of these factors gained additional strength from the presence of self-assured, neo-liberal economists and technocrats dominating political power.

In a separate section, entitled 'A critique of "late capitalism" in the UK and US', Blazyca repeated the arguments of John K. Galbraith (1993) and Will Hutton (1995) against the Anglo-Saxon model of capitalism. George pointed out the following characteristics of this model: persistently high unemployment while some worked excessively; the division of society into working and non-working families; the privatisation of social life; the existence of a near-permanent underclass with no prospects; and 'short-termism' pervading business thinking.

In the concluding remarks of his lecture, entitled 'What future for Poland – is there a third way?', George was rather trying to encourage Poles to search for an adequate systemic policy, mainly exploiting the experience of the East Asian countries in their industrial and regional policies. He also pointed out that even Fukuyama had passed on from glorifying the end of history to studying the role of trust in sustainable development. The following words of George, written more then ten years ago, still sound valid:

> The communist/anti-communist divide that seemed so powerful in Poland [on an earlier visit] is not much help in trying to build a vision for the future. Much more important is activity designed to build social institutions, involving trade unions, employers and educators. Building what is becoming fashionably known as 'trust relationships' is critical. It also very importantly helps in reducing the costs of doing business – transaction costs.

In fact, the sharp division between post- and anti-communists became even deeper after 1995. However, there was something new, namely the nationalist right-wing winners of the 2005 parliamentary elections negated liberal economic policy in the name of a 'Poland of Solidarity' and a 'social economy'. However, the winners had not articulated, by the end of 2006, any alternative vision.

My subjective account of George Blazyca's intellectual endeavours in Poland, as embodied in books and essays, can be confronted with David Hearst's opinion (*Guardian*, 31 March 2005):

> A lifelong socialist, Blazyca did not abandon his core beliefs, as many of his generation did. Nor did he succumb to neo-liberalism, as communism collapsed in Poland in 1989 . . . Poland provided Blazyca with a case study of the potential for, and the constraints implied by, socialist politics. He tempered his view of privatisation and the creation of a free market in Poland with his forensic knowledge of the realities of the Polish economy, or, as he often said himself, economies – such were the yawning gaps of income and wealth within one country. But he never wavered in his belief that Poland's re-engagement with Europe was the ultimate guarantor of its political freedom.

I would agree with Hearst that Blazyca 'did not abandon his core beliefs' but, for a while and when writing on Poland's economy, he suspended them. His writings and book projects were, by and large, devoid not only of socialist rhetoric but also of socialist content. Even in his most radical text, the one on the third way, his thinking remained either within such models of capitalism as the German social-market economy or the so-called East Asian tigers or, at the level of theory, within the social-liberal concepts of John K. Galbraith or Will Hutton's stakeholder capitalism.

Why was that? Was it only a matter of the protective colours we sometimes use in order to be present in a public debate? I do not think so. I believe that there was something deeper in it, though I do not have a clear answer to this puzzle. In this respect I see a clear analogy with Jacek Kuroń, a legendary leftist, emblem of a Polish democratic opposition, who in the years 1989–93 manifestly suspended his leftist attitude, declaring that in order to be a leftist you have to build beforehand the foundations of a market economy. Only after the defeat of his political formation did Kuroń understand that, as he wrote, when you build a house and start with constructing its foundations, you have to know what sort of house you want to have. Moreover, both seemed to be not that far from the belief that Poland had to go through a period of primitive accumulation of capital. Thus, in a backward country, it was too early for socialist values to be implemented. That is why Blazyca attached great importance to Poland's membership of the EU, hoping that it would facilitate the transformation of the Polish economy into a modern industrial one.

Poland his love, Poland his pain

George started his involvement with Polish affairs not only because of his Polish roots and not only out of purely professional interest. He was hoping that, despite everything, 'really existing socialism' was an interesting experience of shaping a better social order and society. Even in the 1970s Poland, termed at that time as 'the warmest barracks in the Soviet Camp', was more interesting than any other Central European country. Poland had a tradition of the most eminent, renowned economists, such as Michał Kalecki and Oskar Lange, and was the most open to the West. At the beginning of the 1980s, the outburst of the Solidarity mass movement, which ended with martial law, made Polish events front-page news over a significant period of time. In 1989 Poland came out once again as the first country experiencing a collapse of communism. Many socialists and social democrats hoped that this would open a door to market socialism, at least as a transitory form. Some Poles, Jacek Kuroń amongst them, proudly stressed the pioneering role of our country. All these events had raised the most fundamental systemic issues, making Poland the most attractive object of research from both points of view, as a scene of fundamental choices over values and as an object of study for professional economists analysing the process of reconstruction of an economy. There was also a stream of self-nominated advisers with ready-made recipes for what they believed should be done.

The most active period of George's work coincided with a period of waning international interest in Poland. For many of us, in the last twenty-five years, Poland passed from great and encouraging news, where the impossible became possible, to exotic news and from glory to infamy. One cannot ignore the opinion of Wojciech Sadurski of the Law Faculty of the European University Institute in Florence that including in the government a leader of the League of Polish Families, Roman Giertych, in the capacity of deputy prime minister and minister of education, Poland went further than Austria when Haider's party entered the government (Sadurski 2006). A deputy minister of education publicly said that Charles Darwin's theory was a lie and, despite favouring creationism, was not immediately dismissed. For both of us, however, the most important cause of infamy was the military aggression on Iraq in which our countries took an active part.

It should be noted that my contacts, and afterwards friendship, with George Blazyca were based not so much on cooperation, but rather on a similarity of our views. For example, when he visited us shortly after the US-led coalition's military invasion of Iraq, even in the corridor he shouted: 'So far I have not met even one person against.' It was self-evident for us that the word 'against' related to the aggression on Iraq. And he did not need to ask me, or my wife, what we thought of it. It was also clear for both of us that he was talking not about ordinary people, who, in spite of the well-known, sometimes blind, pro-Americanism of Polish society, were in the great majority either against this aggression or highly reluctant. He was talking about the Polish scholars he had had the opportunity to meet.

It can be said that it is not an accident that the last essay, or at least one of the last essays, he wrote was on Iraq. He undoubtedly regarded the intervention as unjust and the prolonged occupation as a political scandal. However, when he wrote about it, he tried to use professional language. He attempted to understand the motives and was far from simply condemning the aggressors and occupiers.

His contribution to the volume on the 'Bush doctrine' (Blazyca 2006) is mostly about Poland. It so happens that my last conversation with George was about just this issue. He gave me a call just before going to hospital, asking me for comments on his essay, which was mainly, almost exclusively, on the Polish attitude to this war. On this occasion I could have realised the extent of the gap between his emotional attitude and a professional analysis. Even when he wrote that one of the motives, besides prestige and geopolitical security, of the Polish military presence in Iraq was 'good business', the big contracts for post-war reconstruction, he managed to keep ethics as far from economics as possible. He simply noticed that, up to that time, Polish firms had got orders ten times smaller than the initial promises. How he wanted to remain loyal to his beloved country! He was meticulously searching, if not for demonstrations or a change of opinions, then at least for a change of tone. He wanted to testify that 'it may be that we are in the early stages of a major re-orientation of CEEC foreign policy'. He expected that the CEEC (Central and Eastern European countries) region would engage more vigorously with EU developments. Needless to say, the radical shift to the nationalist right tends to point, at least for the time being, in the opposite direction.

References

Blazyca, G. (1995) 'Monitoring economic transformation', in G. Blazyca and J. Dąbrowski (eds), *Monitoring economic transition: the Polish case*, Aldershot: Avebury.

Blazyca, G. (1996) *Observations on the Polish transformation: are there really no 'Third Ways'?*, Economics and Management Working Papers, No. 90, Paisley: University of Paisley.

Blazyca, G. (2000) 'Uwagi na temat polskich przemian – czy naprawdę nie ma "trzeciej drogi"?', in T. Kowalik (ed.), *Polscy ekonomiści w świecie*, Warsaw: PWN.

Blazyca, G. (2006) 'Central Europe and its post-communist foreign policy', in M. Buckley and R. Singh (eds), *The Bush doctrine and the war on terrorism: global reactions, global consequences*, London: Routledge.

Blazyca, G. and Dąbrowski, J. (eds) (1995) *Monitoring economic transition: the Polish case*, Aldershot: Avebury.

Blazyca, G. and Rapacki, R. (eds) (1991) *Poland into the 1990s: economy and society in transition*, London: Pinter Publishers.

Blazyca, G. and Rapacki, R. (eds) (2001) *Poland into the new millennium*, Cheltenham: Edward Elgar.

Brus, W. (1992) 'Refleksje o postępującej nieoznaczoności socjalizmu', in A. Jasińska and W. Weselowski (eds), *Demokracja i socjalizm*, Wrocław/Warsaw: Ossolineum.

Fukuyama, F. (1992) *The end of history and the last man*, New York: Free Press.

Galbraith, J. K. (1993) *Culture of contentment*, London: Penguin.

Hutton, W. (1995) *The state we're in*, London: Jonathan Cape.

Kowalik, T. (ed.) (2000) *Polscy ekonomiści w świecie*, Warsaw: PWN.

Kowalik, T. (2001a) 'The ugly face of Polish success: social aspects of transformation', in G. Blazyca and R. Rapacki (eds), *Poland into the New Millennium*, Cheltenham: Edward Elgar.

Kowalik, T. (2001b) 'Why the social democratic option failed: Poland's experience of systemic change', in A. Glyn (ed.), *Social Democracy in Neoliberal Times: The Left and Economic Policy since 1980*, Oxford: Oxford University Press.

Sadurski, W. (2006) 'Giertych – gorszy Haider', *Gazeta Wyborcza*, 18 July.

Weisskopf, T. (1992) 'Toward a socialism for the future, in the wake of the demise of the socialism of the past', *Review of Radical Political Economics*, 24: 1–28.

2 Poland's economic development level in comparative perspective, 1950–2005

Ryszard Rapacki

The aim of this chapter is to show the most aggregate quantitative results of Poland's systemic transformation, showing changes in the country's absolute and relative development levels. The focus is on per capita GDP compared with that of other countries, in particular fellow transition economies and EU members.

The analysis consists of four parts. In the first part, to shed more light on the present comparative position of Poland on the world development ladder, a historical perspective is provided. Between 1950 and 1989, during the period of the command economy, Poland witnessed a trend of real divergence. The development gap widened not only towards Western industrialised economies but also vis-à-vis fellow socialist countries.

In the second part, the rapid catching-up process vis-à-vis both groups of economies between 1990 and 2005 is illustrated with data on economic growth and indices showing relative development levels. During this period Poland was the fastest-growing transition economy while also displaying higher GDP growth rates than the average for the EU-15, the pre-2004 EU members.

The third part shows the comparative position of the Polish economy in the world and in the enlarged European Union, in terms of both economic potential, measured by total GDP, and development level, measured by per capita GDP, in 2005.

The concluding part summarises the findings of the paper and sketches the prospects of the real convergence process of the Polish economy towards the future development level in the EU-15 countries.

The command economy – lagging behind[1]

Throughout its contemporary history Poland has tended to remain on the periphery of the mainstream of economic development taking place in the Centre, meaning mostly in Western Europe, and later in North America, Japan and South-East Asia. As a result, in 1950 the country was still relatively underdeveloped, with per capita GDP representing less than half of the level prevailing in the most advanced, industrialised countries such as the

United Kingdom, France and Germany. However, the figures in Table 2.1, from shortly after the Second World War, show Poland ahead of the less developed economies in Southern Europe, such as Spain, Portugal and Greece, and achieving a development level comparable to that of Italy and Hungary.

The period of 'real socialism', or the command economy, witnessed a dramatic widening of the development gap relative to industrialised Western European economies. By 1989, at the outset of the systemic transformation, Polish per capita GDP amounted to only slightly more than one-third of the latter. Poland also experienced a real divergence of its growth pattern vis-à-vis the less developed countries of Southern Europe. As data in Table 2.1 clearly demonstrate, by 1989 Greece, Portugal and Spain had successfully caught up with and, by a significant margin, overtaken Poland on the economic development ladder. Moreover, Poland had also lost ground relative to most fellow socialist countries.

Table 2.1 Selected countries' per capita GDP at Purchasing Power Parity as a percentage of that of Poland

	1950	1980	1989
Western Europe			
Germany	167	237	279
Italy	106	226	274
France	204	234	268
United Kingdom	243	201	256
Spain	57	159	199
Ireland	134	164	195
Greece	80	174	178
Portugal	69	122	159
EU-15 average	–	215	262
		(46.5)*	(38)*
Central Europe			
Czech Republic	141	160	197
Estonia	–	113	142
Hungary	101	122	146
Latvia	–	108	137
Lithuania	–	116	145
Slovakia	141	131	155
Slovenia	–	193	194
Bulgaria	–	90	122
Romania	–	81	89
Russia	–	104	132
Ukraine	–	97	124

Sources: Orłowski (1996); IMF (2005).

Note: * Poland's development level as a percentage of the EU-15 average.

The process of real divergence was particularly pronounced in the 1980s. The reasons behind this are quite straightforward: between 1979 and 1982 Poland suffered, alone among socialist countries, a deep contraction of output, or more precisely of Net Material Product or NMP, amounting to a combined 25 per cent. The fall of output was a clear symptom of mounting inefficiencies of the centrally planned economy, compounded by martial law, introduced in December 1981, and by the ensuing sanctions imposed on Poland by most Western countries. As a result of the foregoing trends, not only did the development gap between Poland and the relatively more advanced socialist countries increase, for example vis-à-vis the Czech Republic from 60 per cent to almost 100 per cent, but Poland was also over-taken by some of the less developed command economies, in particular Bulgaria and Ukraine.

As a result, Poland's comparative economic position within the group of 'transition economies' deteriorated. By 1989, in terms of per capita GDP measured by Purchasing Power Parity (PPP), Poland was ranked fourteenth among twenty-seven countries of East Central Europe and Central Asia, compared to eleventh place in 1980.

To conclude the foregoing discussion, it should be noted that, owing to the adverse economic trends experienced at the turn of the 1970s and 1980s and its poor economic performance throughout the 1980s, Poland suffered a loss of its international comparative position. It thereby entered the road from plan to market in 1990 lagging behind not only all Western economies but also half of the entire group of former socialist countries.

Catching up after 1989

The 1990s and the beginning of the new century witnessed a rapid real convergence trend, or catching-up process, of the Polish economy vis-à-vis both the EU countries and all the transition economies.

As shown by data in Table 2.2, at the outset of systemic transformation in 1989, Poland's per capita GDP in PPP amounted to 38 per cent of the EU-15 average. Put the other way round, the average development level recorded in the fifteen EU member countries represented 262 per cent of that of Poland. Moreover, the development level of all the other former socialist countries shown in Table 2.2, with the exception of Romania, exceeded that of Poland by between 20 per cent and almost 100 per cent.

By 2005 this development gap had substantially narrowed both towards the EU-15 countries and towards the transition economies, the only exceptions being Ireland and, to a certain extent, Spain. With regard to the former group, Poland's per capita GDP in PPP amounted to 46 per cent of the EU-15 average or, viewed from the opposite perspective, the EU-15 average represented 216 per cent of Poland's development level. This is equivalent to a catching up by 8 percentage points between 1989 and 2005. The process of real convergence was particularly pronounced with regard to major EU

Table 2.2 Relative development levels in Poland, the EU countries and selected transition economies, 1989–2005 (per capita GDP at PPP, Poland = 100)

	1989	1992	2000	2001	2002	2003	2004	2005
Germany	279	350	239	239	234	232	222	217
France	268	320	243	248	242	238	224	218
Italy	274	327	248	237	231	225	210	203
UK	256	291	240	246	250	249	239	232
Spain	199	244	197	202	205	208	200	196
Ireland	195	252	269	280	287	287	282	276
Portugal	159	212	172	173	171	155	147	142
Greece	178	210	152	157	165	172	167	166
EU-15 average	262	316	234	237	235	232	222	216
	(38)	(32)	(43)	(42)	(43)	(43)	(45)	(46)
Czech Republic	197	194	136	141	143	145	145	145
Estonia	142	114	88	92	97	102	104	110
Hungary	146	140	113	121	125	128	122	124
Latvia	137	93	75	80	83	87	88	93
Lithuania	145	128	81	87	90	96	98	102
Slovakia	155	137	101	104	109	111	106	108
Slovenia	194	176	156	161	161	162	162	162
Bulgaria	122	108	57	61	61	64	61	64
Romania	89	79	53	57	61	62	63	65
Russia	132	127	72	74	77	80	82	83
Ukraine	124	110	41	44	46	49	53	53

Sources: IMF (2005); Eurostat (2000–05).

Note: Data in parentheses show Poland's development level as a percentage of the EU-15 average.

countries, such as Germany, France and Italy. It is worth stressing in this context that Poland was the only transition economy, except for the very special case of Bosnia and Herzegovina, that had by 2005 succeeded in narrowing the development gap towards the 'core', pre-2004, European Union. This is shown in Table 2.3.

Poland also succeeded in narrowing the development gap towards all former socialist countries, including those not shown in Table 2.2. The process of catching up was especially fast vis-à-vis the Czech Republic, Slovakia, Bulgaria, Russia and Ukraine. As a result, by 2005 in terms of per capita GDP in PPP, Poland was ranked seventh in the entire group of twenty-seven transition economies, compared to its fourteenth place in 1989.

Although the comparative economic performance of the Polish economy was remarkable during the 1990–2005 period, one should not lose sight of the broader historical perspective discussed in the preceding section. Seen from this angle, Poland's relative development level did not essentially improve between 1980 and 2005. Comparing relevant indices in Tables 2.1 and 2.2, one can easily notice that per capita GDP in 2005 relative to the EU-15 average was roughly at the same level as that recorded in 1980, 46.0 compared

Table 2.3 The development gap between transition economies and the EU-15, 1989–2005 (per capita GDP in PPP, EU-15 = 100)

	1989	2005
Poland	38	46
Czech Republic	75	67
Estonia	54	53
Hungary	56	56
Latvia	52	43
Lithuania	52	48
Slovakia	59	51
Slovenia	74	74
Bulgaria	46	30
Romania	34	32
Russia	50	38
Ukraine	47	25

Sources: Calculated from IMF (2005); Eurostat (2005).

to 46.5 per cent, although some caution is in order, as the GDP estimates for the command economies prior to 1990 might be seriously biased.

However, parallel to that general development, Poland experienced diverging trends with regard to individual EU member countries and the transition economies. On the one hand, it succeeded in narrowing the development gap towards the major EU economies, including Germany, France and Italy. On the other hand, between 1980 and 2005 its comparative economic position deteriorated vis-à-vis some other, mostly less advanced, EU members, such as Ireland, Spain and the UK. At the same time Poland's relative development level increased compared to that of all transition economies, both the more and the less economically advanced.

The improvement in Poland's relative development level by 2005 was in part due to the fastest economic growth in the whole group of twenty-seven transition economies. The relevant data are shown in Table 2.4. The average annual growth rate of Polish GDP in real terms during 1989–2005 reached 2.7 per cent, including the episode of a 17.8 per cent contraction of output in 1990–91, owing to the effects of the 'transformation recession'. It should be stressed, however, that in a comparative perspective the transformation recession in Poland was both the shallowest[2] and the shortest – lasting only two years – in the whole group of transition economies. This outcome may be interpreted as a pay-off for Poland's 'shock therapy', or the implementation of the so-called Balcerowicz Plan from the end of 1989.

Between 1992 and 2000 the real average growth of GDP in Poland amounted to 5 per cent annually, and the country was then dubbed a 'soaring eagle' of East Central Europe (De Broeck and Koen 2001). Thus, as a result of both the shallowest GDP decline in the early stage of systemic

Table 2.4 GDP growth in transition economies and the EU-15, 1990–2005

| | Real GDP growth rate | | | | Real GDP index in 2005 | |
| | Average annual % growth | Annual % growth | | | | |
	1990–2005	2003	2004	2005	1989=100	2000=100
Poland	2.7	3.8	5.4	3.2	153	115
Czech Republic	1.2	3.2	4.7	6.0	121	119
Estonia	1.1	6.7	7.8	9.8	119	144
Hungary	1.4	3.4	4.6	4.1	125	122
Latvia	0.0	7.2	8.5	10.2	99	147
Lithuania	−0.1	10.5	7.0	7.5	96	144
Slovakia	1.6	4.5	5.5	6.0	128	127
Slovenia	1.7	2.7	4.2	3.9	131	118
Bulgaria	−0.2	4.5	5.6	6.0	93	128
Romania	0.1	5.2	8.4	4.1	103	132
Russia	−0.8	7.3	7.2	6.4	87	135
Ukraine	−2.3	9.6	12.1	2.4	58	146
EU-15	2.1	1.0	2.3	1.4	139	108

Sources: Calculated from EBRD (2005); Eurostat (2005); World Bank (2005).

transformation and the fastest economic growth during the 1990s, Poland's GDP in 2005 represented 153 per cent of the level recorded in 1989, at the outset of the systemic transformation. This compares favourably with similar indices for all other former socialist countries and also exceeds the relevant indicator for the EU-15. As far as the former group is concerned, however, one important point should be noted. In the years after 2000 Poland lost its leading position as the fastest-growing economy of the region. It was outpaced by all transition economies shown in Table 2.4. The average annual growth rate of the Polish economy during 2001–05 was 2.8 per cent, while similar indices for the Baltic countries exceeded 7.5 per cent.

As we pointed out earlier, the process of systemic transformation in Poland was accompanied by the real convergence of its development level towards the EU countries. As indicated in Table 2.3, the development gap vis-à-vis the EU-15 average narrowed by some 8 percentage points between 1989 and 2005. This effect, however, can only partly be explained by economic growth rate differentials. Throughout the entire period, including the contraction of output in 1990–91, the GDP growth rate in Poland was only slightly higher than the average for the EU-15 countries (2.7 per cent compared to 2.1 per cent). The differences in growth dynamic were much more pronounced after 1991: during 1992–2000 the 5.0 per cent achieved in Poland can be compared with 2.3 per cent for the EU-15 average. In 2001–05 the comparable figures were 2.8 per cent and 1.6 per cent respectively.

The most plausible explanation for the process of Poland's catching up with the target development level in the European Union can be found in diverging demographic trends. Whereas the population in Poland between 1989 and 2005 remained practically unchanged, increasing from 38,118,000 to 38,157,000, the EU-15 countries' population increased by some 4.5 per cent, from 369 million to nearly 386 million. These diverging demographic trends translate into larger GDP growth rate differentials in per capita terms. While for Poland the relevant rate amounted to 2.8 per cent annually, the EU-15 countries recorded an average per capita GDP growth of 1.7 per cent per annum.

One more factor that may explain some disparities between the pace of Poland's real convergence with the EU-15 countries and GDP growth rate differentials was the upward revisions of the historical GDP levels in Poland made by the Central Statistical Office in November 2005 and September 2006. These related to the GDP values recorded in domestic currency for the 2000–05 period and, compared to previous official data, increased the GDP levels in the range of 1–4 per cent for particular years. This translates into a faster catching up than in the absence of such statistical revisions.

The Polish economy in 2005 in comparative perspective

As demonstrated in the preceding section, the sixteen years of systemic transformation in Poland after 1989 should be seen as a success story in terms of the narrowing of the historical development gap towards more advanced countries both in Western and in East Central Europe. One of the most spectacular dimensions of the successful transition from the centrally planned to the market economy was the fastest economic growth among all transition economies between 1989 and 2005. One may legitimately ask where the Polish economy, capitalising on these past achievements, stood in 2005 in terms of its relative development level and what its prospects were for further catching up in the following years. To address the first question we present a concise picture of Poland's economic potential and development level in a broad comparative perspective, against the background of the world economy as well as its rank within the enlarged European Union, meaning the EU-25 plus three prospective members, Bulgaria, Romania and Turkey, of which the first two became full members in 2007. The second issue will be dealt with in the concluding section.

Figure 2.1, based on statistics from the World Development Indicators database, presents the ranking of the largest economies in the world, using GDP in official exchange rates (OER) and in Purchasing Power Parity (PPP) as criteria. According to these data, by 2004 Poland was ranked twenty-sixth (OER) and twenty-second (PPP) in the world in terms of its economic potential, or the size of the economy. It was also ranked sixty-fourth and seventy-second in the world in terms of its development level, using per capita GDP in OER and PPP respectively.

Data from Eurostat (2007) show that by 2005 Poland was the seventh-

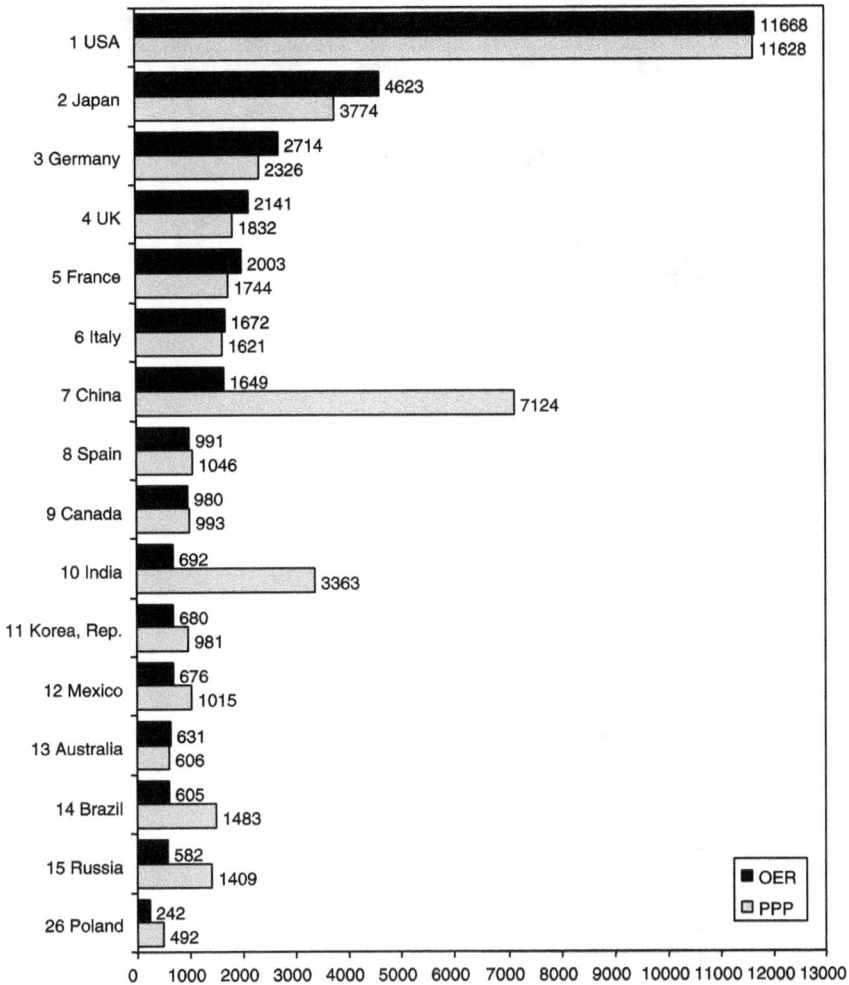

Figure 2.1 Poland and the largest economies in the world, 2004 (GDP, USD billion).

Source: World Bank (2006).

largest economy in the EU-25, using GDP in PPP. Based on official exchange rate conversions, it was ranked tenth in the enlarged European Union and eleventh, after Turkey, if the three candidate countries are also included. The relevant data are shown in Figure 2.2.

Finally, in terms of its per capita GDP (PPP) Poland belonged to the group of the least developed member countries of the enlarged European Union. In 2005 it was ranked twenty-fourth, second to last in the EU-25, signifying some deterioration relative to 2000 when it was twenty-second. Its development level was above only that of Latvia plus all three candidate countries, Bulgaria, Romania and Turkey. Figure 2.3 presents the full picture.

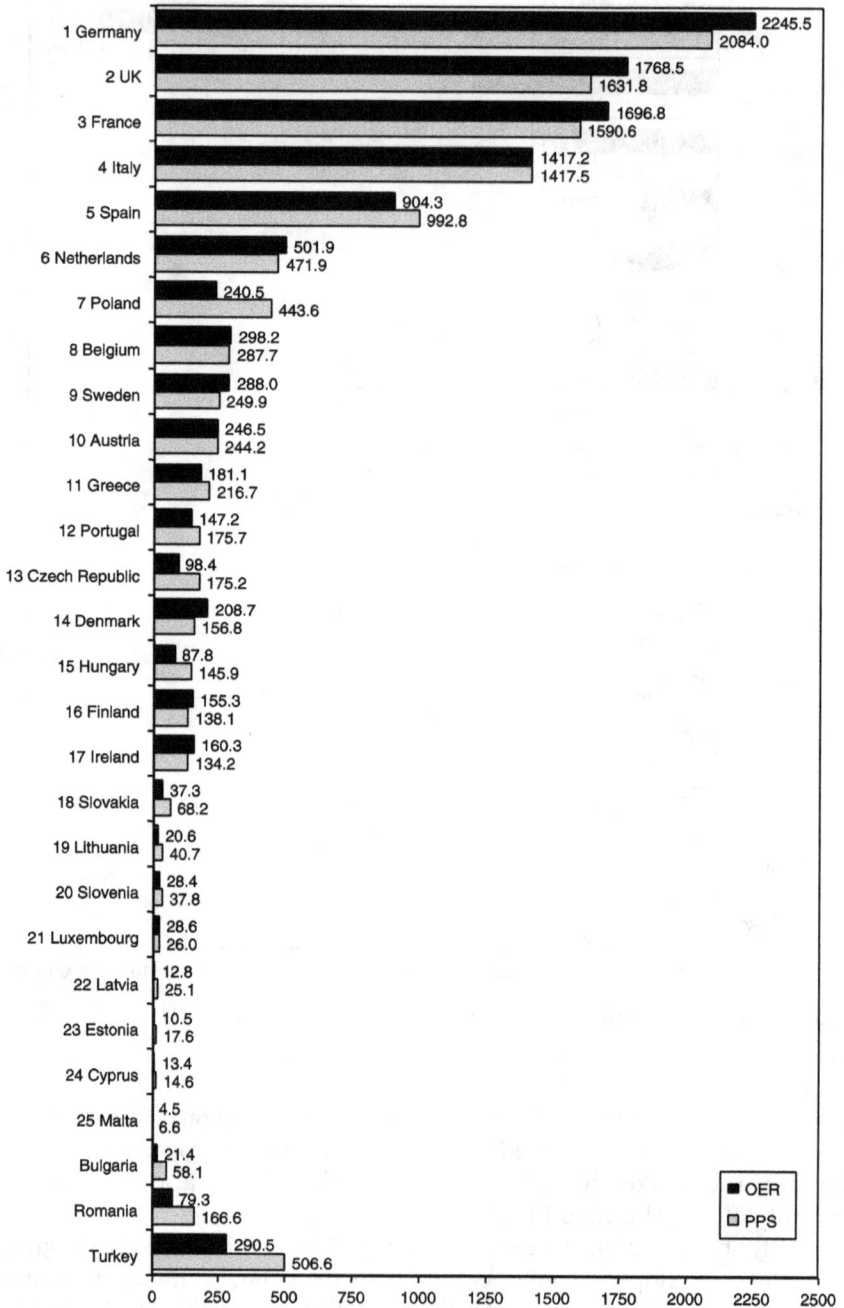

Figure 2.2 The EU economies by size, 2005 (GDP, euro billion).

Source: Eurostat (2005).

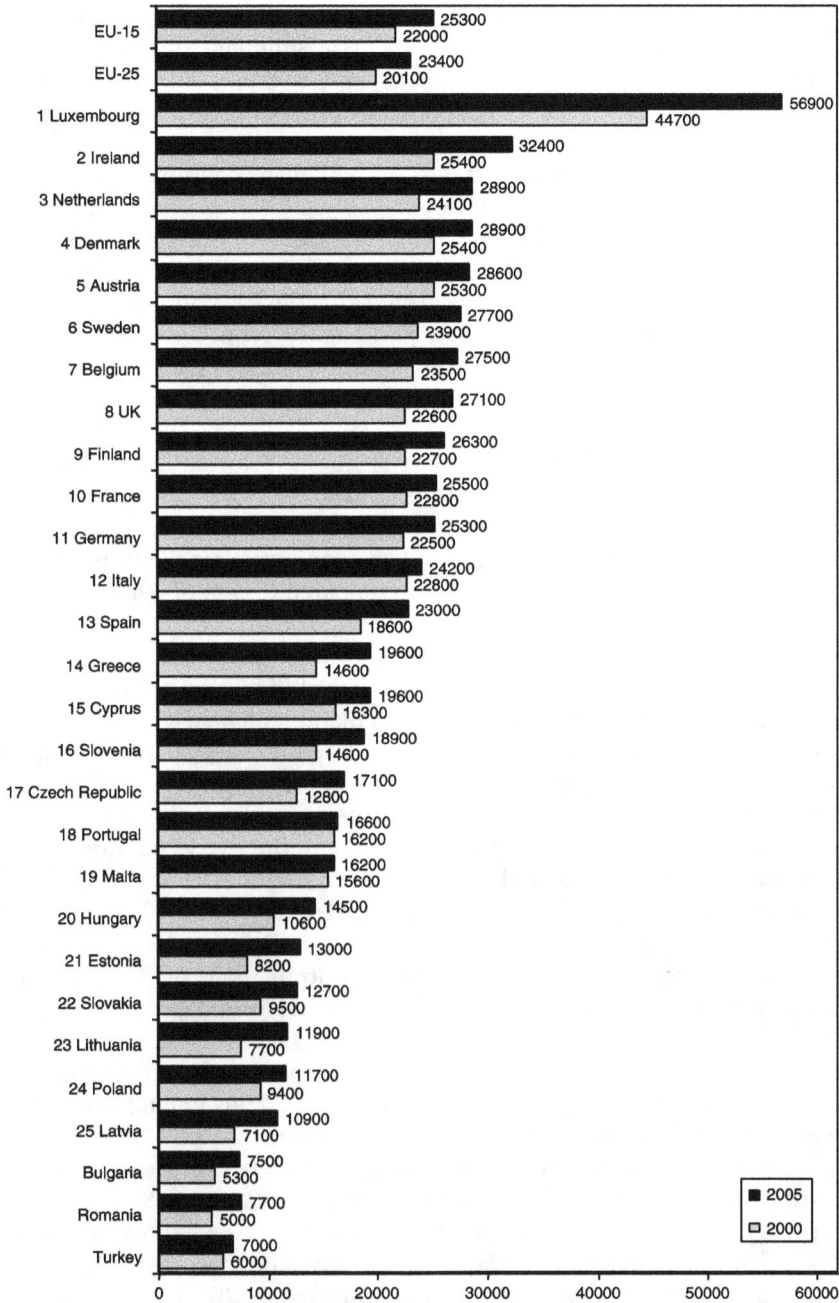

Figure 2.3 EU countries by development level, 2000–05 (per capita GDP in PPS, euro).

Source: Eurostat (2005).

Conclusion

The concluding part of the chapter presents a summary of major findings stemming from the foregoing discussion. We will also attempt to sketch the prospects of Poland's catching up with the future development level in the EU-15.

The most salient development trends of the Polish economy between 1950 and 2005 may be summarised as follows:

1   The period 1950–89 (the command economy) witnessed a widening development gap or real divergence towards the EU countries.
2   The real divergence process was particularly pronounced in 1980–89, both with regard to the EU and vis-à-vis most of the socialist countries.
3   Poland recorded the fastest economic growth in the entire group of transition economies between 1990 and 2005.
4   As a result, during the period of systemic transformation Poland succeeded in substantially catching up both towards the EU countries and towards the most advanced transition economies.
5   Despite some slowdown of the Polish economy after 2000, its present relative development level improved compared to that of 1989.

Notwithstanding the fact that the Polish systemic transformation, seen from the angle that is most relevant to the present chapter, turned out to be mostly a success story, one should not forget that Poland remained a middle-income country and was still far from achieving its strategic goal of closing the historical development gap, and ultimately fully catching up, with the EU-15.

What are the prospects of continuing the process of real convergence in economic development levels between Poland and the EU-15 countries in the years to come? The two most likely scenarios of future catching up are based on extrapolating the past growth trends recorded in 1992–2000 and 2001–05 respectively. Under the first, optimistic, scenario Poland would sustain its growth rate close to an estimated potential output trend of 5 per cent per annum. On the other hand, the EU-15 countries would grow on average along the path experienced in 1992–2000, that is 2.6 per cent annually. If this were the case and the growth rate differential amounted to 2.4 percentage points, the full catching up would take thirty years. Thus Poland would have completely closed the development gap towards the EU-15 by 2035.

Under the second, more pessimistic, scenario both the Polish economy and the EU-15 would stick to their growth patterns of 2000–05, meaning 2.8 and 1.6 per cent real GDP growth per annum respectively, or half of the growth rates differential compared to the first scenario. Then the real convergence process would last sixty-six years and be completed in 2071.

To conclude, it is worth emphasising that both scenarios are consistent with the general proposition of *conditional convergence* put forward by Robert Barro (1991) as well as with the findings of recent empirical studies on real convergence in the EU accession countries from Central Europe, carried out by the team headed by the present author (Matkowski and Próchniak 2006; Rapacki and Próchniak 2006).

However, the question as to which of the two – and there could of course be more, including a range of intermediate cases – scenarios will come true is subject to many uncertainties embedded, *inter alia*, in the future course of changes in the institutional environment of economic growth in Poland. Among the most crucial determinants of these changes is the issue raised by George Blazyca (2000) as to the kind of capitalism that is most appropriate for, and likely eventually to emerge in, Poland, a point taken further in discussions of the importance of EU membership for the development of different models of capitalism (Hanson 2007).

Notes

1 This and the subsequent section of the paper draw from Rapacki 2006a and 2006b.
2 A similar scale of output contraction was experienced only in the Czech Republic. Moreover, according to revised official data by GUS, the combined decline in GDP in Poland in 1990–91 amounted to only 14.7 per cent.

References

Barro, R. (1991) 'Economic growth in a cross section of countries', *Quarterly Journal of Economics*, 106: 407–43.

Blazyca, G. (2000) 'Uwagi na temat polskich przemian – czy naprawdę nie ma "trzeciej drogi"?', in T. Kowalik (ed.), *Polscy ekonomiści w świecie*, Warsaw: PWN.

De Broeck, M. and Koen, V. (2001) 'The "soaring eagle": anatomy of the Polish take-off in the 1990s', *Comparative Economic Studies*, 42: 1–33.

EBRD (2005) *Transition Report Update*, London: European Bank for Reconstruction and Development.

Eurostat (2000–07) Database, http://epp.eurostat.cec.eu.int (last accessed 12 March 2007).

Hanson, P. (2007) 'The European Union's influence on the development of capitalism in Central Europe', in D. Lane (ed.), *Transformation of state socialism: system change, capitalism, or something else?*, Basingstoke: Palgrave.

IMF (2005) *World Economic Outlook Database*, Washington, DC: International Monetary Fund, www.imf.org./external/pubs/ft/weo/2005/02/data/index.htm (last accessed 12 March 2007).

Matkowski, Z. and Próchniak, M. (2006) 'Convergence of the economic growth of the accession countries in relation to the European Union', in D. Rosati (ed.), *New Europe: report on transformation*, Warsaw: Foundation Institute for Eastern Studies, pp. 169–80.

Orłowski, W. M. (1996) *Droga do Europy: makroekonomia wstępowania do Unii Europejskiej*, Warsaw: Zakład Badań Satystyczno-Ekonomicznych GUS and PAN, Zeszyt 34.

Rapacki, R. (2006a) 'Mimo sukcesów do czołówki nam daleko', *Rzeczpospolita*, 6 September.

Rapacki, R. (2006b) 'Comparative economic performance', in M. Weresa (ed.), *Poland: competitiveness report 2006*, Warsaw: Warsaw School of Economics, pp. 17–28.

Rapacki, R. and Próchniak, M. (2006) 'Charakterystyka wzrostu gospodarczego w krajach postsocjalistycznych w latach 1990–2003', *Ekonomista*, 6: 715–44.

World Bank (2005) *World Development Indicators 2005*, Washington, DC: World Bank.

World Bank (2006) *World Development Indicators 2006*, Washington, DC: World Bank.

3 Foreign direct investment and the competitiveness of Polish manufacturing

Marzenna Anna Weresa

There has been substantial discussion in the economic literature of the impact of foreign direct investment (FDI) on a country's competitiveness, reflected in its ability to compete in an international environment. In the case of the manufacturing sector, the concept of international competitiveness can be narrowed to the competitiveness of goods produced by enterprises operating in this sector. Thus, international competitiveness of the manufacturing sector can be defined as an ability of different national economies to sell various goods on international markets and consequently increase citizens' welfare. This is the so-called ability-to-sell concept (Sachverständigenrat 2004: 352; Misala 2006: 251–3). For the present chapter this is followed in relation to the foreign trade performance of the manufacturing sector only, with an examination of the impact of FDI on the competitiveness of Polish products on international markets. The analysis starts with a review of some theoretical approaches, going on to assess the empirical evidence on the competitiveness of different branches of manufacturing.

FDI and trade competitiveness

FDI leads to international production and it can be seen as an alternative to exporting as a way to deliver goods and services to foreign markets (Buckley and Mucchielli 1997: 34–7). This means that there should be some interrelationship between FDI and trade. There are at least two aspects of this interrelationship. One is the influence of FDI on the volume and value of trade, and the other is connected with qualitative parameters of trade reflected in the competitiveness of tradable goods. In other words, FDI impacts on a country's foreign trade performance both directly and indirectly. The direct impact can be seen either in the substitution of trade by international production or in their complementary expansion. These two possibilities, substitution or complementarity, are explained by different FDI and trade theories, and conclusions are different for individual models. Another aspect of the FDI–trade interrelationship is the indirect impact of foreign production on the competitiveness of exports.

Foreign trade always has been the most important vehicle linking national and regional economies. The success of a country's products on international markets is a test of its competitiveness. A country's pattern of foreign trade is a result of both external and internal factors. During the transition process in Central and Eastern Europe both production and foreign trade have been restructured as a result of the introduction of the rules of a market economy. In the case of Poland the first step towards the restructuring of foreign trade was made at the end of 1988 by the abolition of the state's foreign trade monopoly and the liberalisation of FDI inflows. The launch of the transition process in 1990 and gradual progress in economic performance brought an improvement in the investment climate for foreign firms and individuals in terms both of legal conditions and of the business environment. The rules of doing business became the same for all enterprises, including firms with foreign capital involvement.

The opening of the Polish economy was aimed at improving efficiency through increased specialisation. The opening of Poland's economy to international trade and investment was a step towards exploiting gains from trade and FDI. The gains from free trade have been widely discussed, starting from the classical Ricardian model, based on comparative advantage. The determinants of comparative advantage were explained more broadly by neo-classical theories, which considered the prices of goods and factors of production, such as in the Heckscher-Ohlin factor endowment model, and were further developed by introducing technology variables (Posner 1961: 323–41). New theories of trade have incorporated new elements, such as increasing returns to scale, imperfect competition and product differentiation (Helpman and Krugman 1985).

The opening of Poland's economy to FDI brought additional tangible benefits in the form of financial assets, capital goods and intermediate inputs. It also improved the country's competitiveness through the transfer and diffusion of technology and the upgrading of its technological and innovative potential. All studies on FDI and competitiveness demonstrate that foreign investment enterprises always bring some positive externalities to the host market, which can provide positive feedback to sustain growth and improve competitiveness in the long run (see for instance Dunning 1988: 57–8). These externalities are an effect of technology transfer and technology spillovers. They can also be created indirectly through subcontracting, strategic alliances, licensing agreements or the import of capital goods.

The liberalisation of trade and investment flows to Poland was a step towards exploiting these gains from trade and FDI. It increased competition in the internal market, although some barriers to free trade remained for the few first years of transition. These included licences for permission to trade, export and import quotas and a requirement for approval for trade in some specific commodities. These restrictions were eliminated during the early 1990s. However, one of the most important, if not the most important, of the obstacles to free trade was financial. In the late 1980s exporters were obliged to sell a part of their export earnings to the central bank at an exchange rate far below the free market rate. Importers were divided into two categories. The first group could buy convertible currencies at a low rate, while the latter had to pay the higher, market rate. An important change was making the Polish currency convertible, so that domestic enterprises could convert złotys to other currencies in order to import and get their export earnings in convertible currencies (Berg and Sachs 1992: 117–18). This goal was also gradually achieved during the 1990s.

The transition policies and liberalisation of FDI flows made it possible for the private sector to grow rapidly, and its position in production, exports and imports strengthened. Improving competitiveness of Polish manufacturing and the improvement in foreign trade performance was a result of the expansion of new private businesses, including greenfield FDI and the privatisation of existing public enterprises.

There are several ways in which foreign capital inflows could impact on the competitiveness of exports. Theoretically, rising competitiveness could be expected, assuming that foreign investors possess ownership advantages, although these advantages are sooner or later acquired by domestic firms. Ownership advantages include a variety of features (Dunning 1992: 81), such as technological know-how, patents, trading expertise, trademarks or other intangible assets. As long as FDI causes the diffusion of these advantages in the host country's economy, it affects indirectly the structural competitiveness of domestic enterprises and their products. Moreover, the presence of foreign investors increases competition and forces domestic firms to modernise their production processes and products. These indirect effects are stronger in the case of investment in technologically advanced goods. FDI into these sectors causes an increase in productivity of capital invested in the country and stimulates innovation activity. The upgrading of technology and the transfer of technical know-how may alter the pattern of competitiveness. There are several pieces of econometric evidence, as well as case studies for some countries, proving that technological externalities of FDI, such as knowledge spillovers or demonstration effects, influence the factor productivity of local firms and their propensity to export (for example Aitken *et al.* 1994: 25; Markusen and Venables 1997: 15–16). More efficient production processes and the introduction of new goods and services, which are expected to have an impact on export performance, should be reflected in a country's revealed comparative advantage (RCA), as explained below. Furthermore, the pattern of inter- and intra-industry trade might be affected. Theoretical models show that FDI might create or displace intra-industry trade (Markusen and Venables 1996: 22–3). There is empirical evidence that in some sectors at least the growth of intra-industry trade can be associated with the inflow of foreign capital (Hoekman and Djankov 1996: 24).

Determining the impact of FDI on competitiveness depends on measuring the latter at the level of industrial branches, and several methods are available for this. Two will be used here. One is to compare the productivity of individual industries. The other is to use the revealed comparative advantage index.

Productivity clearly links to competitiveness. An improvement in the latter means higher efficiency, which should be reflected in labour productivity changes. Furthermore, it has been proven that a competitive position depends on innovativeness (Dunning 1988: 141–2; Porter 2001: 202). Efficiency gains in industry branches are the result of quality improvements, modernisation of products and processes and the introduction of new technologies. Industry can only gain a competitive advantage through innovative activity, which can be seen in productivity changes (Porter 2001: 198).

However, when defining competitiveness as the capacity to produce high-value products and services that meet the test of world markets, the appropriate method for measurement is to focus on the international dimension and hence on foreign trade performance. Therefore, to evaluate international competitive position, the revealed comparative advantage index can be used. It is defined as follows:

$$RCA_i = \ln (X_{ij}/M_{ij}):(X_j/M_j)$$

where X_{ij} is the export of commodity i by country j,

M_{ij} is the import of commodity i by country j,

X_j is total exports of country j,

M_j is total imports of country j,

RCA_i values range from $-\infty$ to $+\infty$. An RCA_i above zero points to a revealed comparative advantage; the reverse is true of values below zero.

Changes in labour productivity of individual industries

Using the first of these methods, the changes in productivity, the starting point is the growth rate of labour productivity measured as gross value added per employee, as shown in Figure 3.1.

In 1994–99, the fastest average annual growth of labour productivity was in the production of the following items: office machinery and computers (47 per cent annually); radio, TV and communication equipment (27 per cent); medical instruments (24 per cent); pulp and paper (15 per cent); rubber and plastic products (14 per cent); machinery and equipment (13 per cent); motor vehicles (12 per cent); and electronic devices (12 per cent). During the next five-year period (2000–04), the leading branches in terms of labour productivity growth were: non-metallic products (growth rate at 38 per cent annually); motor vehicles (38 per cent); metal products (15 per cent); office machinery and computers (14 per cent); machinery and equipment (14 per cent); electronic devices (13 per cent); and radio, TV and communication equipment (11 per cent).

These were also the leading branches in terms of FDI flows into Poland. The analysis of the branch pattern of direct foreign investments in recent years

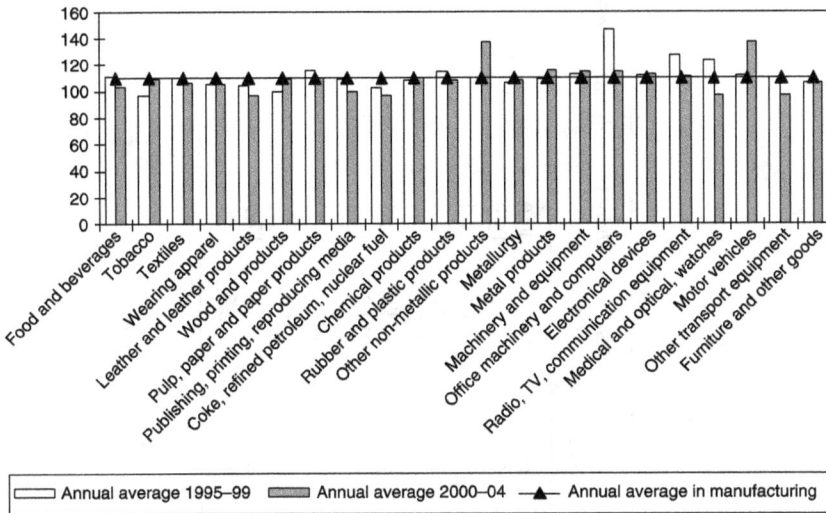

Figure 3.1 Growth of labour productivity in individual branches of Polish manufacturing, 1995–2004 (constant prices, previous year = 100).

Source: Calculated from GUS (1996a, 1998, 2000, 2002, 2005b).

shows that the largest share of the direct investment in Poland has been made in the manufacturing sector. At the end of 2004 the value of investment in manufacturing amounted to $36,071 million, which was 38 per cent of the total FDI stock in Poland (NBP 2005: 120). The subsections of manufacturing attracting the largest foreign capital flows were: production of motor vehicles, food processing, production of wood, publishing and printing, production of chemicals and manufacturing of metal products, as shown in Table 3.1.

All these branches, except for food processing, experienced the highest productivity growth over the 1995–2004 period. Furthermore, as shown in Figure 3.2, the highest growth rate of FDI stock in this period was in the production of motor vehicles and other transport equipment; the production of radio, TV and communication equipment; the production of office machinery and computers; and metal products. These branches belonged to the most dynamic in terms of labour productivity growth in 1995–2004, which could indicate that FDI inflow was accompanied by positive changes in productivity, leading to improvements in competitiveness.

FDI and competitiveness of Poland's foreign trade

Poland's international competitive position, reflected in the country's overall business relations, improved in the 1995–2005 period, with both exports and imports growing strongly, as shown in Figure 3.3. Poland's share in world exports doubled in 1995–2005, albeit still remaining relatively low. In

Table 3.1 FDI stock in the Polish manufacturing sector by industry branches, 1995–2004

NACE		1995 $million	Share in total %	2002 $million	Share in total %	2004 $million	Share in total %	Average annual growth rate in %
3995	*Manufacturing*	3,830.9	100.0	17,152.7	100.0	23,750.1	100.0	62
1605	Food products	1,007.4	26.3	3,746.7	21.8	3,778.0	15.9	38
1805	Textiles and wearing apparel	146.9	3.8	242.0	1.4	334.4	1.4	23
2205	Wood, paper, publishing and printing	645.8	16.9	1,994.8	11.6	2,847.2	12.0	44
2400	Chemical products	448.7	11.7	2,120.8	12.4	2,455.0	10.3	55
2500	Rubber and plastic products	306.5	8.0	1,119.7	6.5	1,473.9	6.2	48
2805	Metal products	255.2	6.7	916.1	5.3	2,014.2	8.5	79
2900	Mechanical products	121.3	3.2	519.2	3.0	901.1	3.8	74
3000	Office machinery and computers	20.6	0.5	64.4	0.4	163.4	0.7	79
3200	Radio, TV and communication equipment	63.5	1.7	500.1	2.9	641.0	2.7	101
3400	Motor vehicles	124.9	3.3	2,213.9	12.9	4,248.9	17.9	340
3500	Other transport equipment	21.6	0.6	174.2	1.0	216.2	0.9	100

Sources: Calculated from NBP (1998, 2003, 2005).

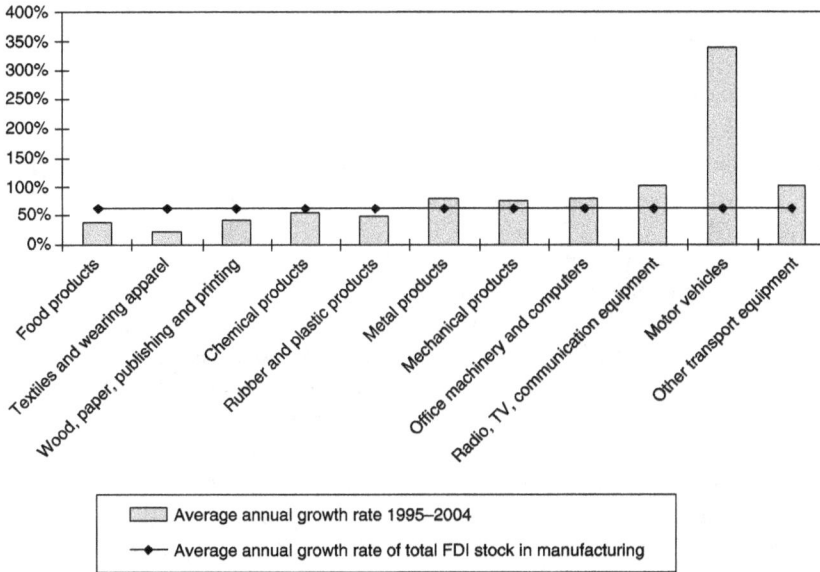

Figure 3.2 Annual percentage growth rate of FDI stock in branches of Polish manufacturing, 1994–2004.

Source: Calculated from NBP (1998, 2003, 2005).

2005 the value of Poland's exports constituted only 0.8 per cent of total world exports. After 1999 the growth rate of Poland's exports surpassed that of imports and, as a result, the export/import ratio improved by nearly 20 percentage points and the trade deficit decreased.

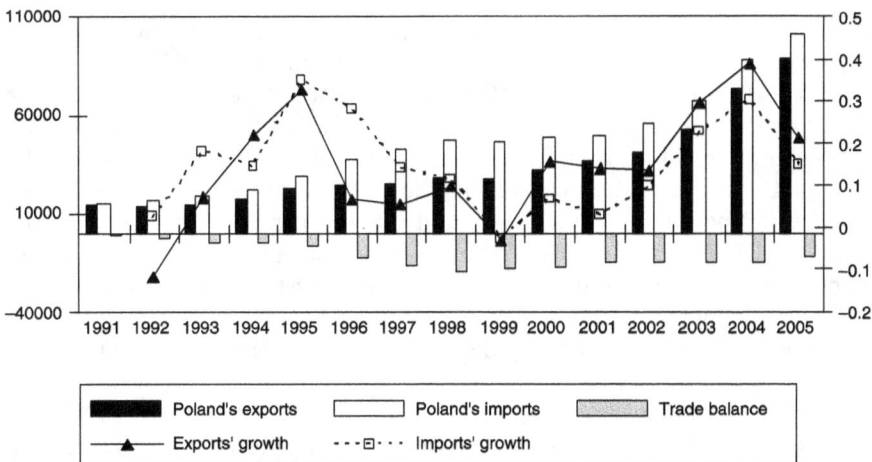

Figure 3.3 Poland's foreign trade in 1991–2005 (USD million and percentage changes).

Source: Calculated from GUS (1996b, 2005a, 2005b).

The commodity structure of Poland's trade changed significantly over the period from 1995 to 2005. In 2005 the main export items were: motor vehicles and transport equipment (16.0 per cent of total exports); chemicals (11.5 per cent); food and beverages (10.8 per cent); machinery and equipment (9.6 per cent); and furniture and other products (9.2 per cent). In 1995 the ranking order was: metal products (12.1 per cent); leather and leather products (11.3 per cent); motor vehicles and transport equipment (9.7 per cent); food and beverages (9.5 per cent); and furniture and other products (9.3 per cent). These changes are reflected in the RCA index.

The change in foreign trade branch structure can be measured by the correlation between RCAs (Hoekman and Djankov 1996: 13). The correlation coefficient between the RCAs in 1995 and 2005 is positive, but relatively low (0.33), which means that there were significant changes in the commodity composition of Poland's foreign trade over that period. These positive shifts in the commodity structure of trade can be seen in the growing share of medium-high-tech goods (in particular, motor vehicles and electrical machinery and equipment) in exports, and in particular in export to the EU countries. However, labour-intensive goods still constituted nearly one-third of Polish exports in 2005, although its share was diminishing, being crowded out by commodities that are technology intensive and difficult to imitate.

The impact of FDI on foreign trade is followed by comparing firms with significant foreign ownership with firms under exclusive, or almost exclusive, Polish ownership. The distinction is made here on the basis of the OECD definition of FDI. Foreign investment enterprises (henceforth FIEs) are understood here as firms located in Poland in which foreign investors own more than 10 per cent of shares, while Polish firms are defined here as enterprises of which 90 per cent of the shares are domestically owned.

The influence of FIEs on the volume of Poland's total exports is relatively large. After 1995, both the exports and the imports of FIEs increased at a higher pace than that of Poland's total exports and imports. Their share in foreign trade therefore grew. In 1995 FIEs exported $7,876 million, creating 34.4 per cent of Poland's exports, while in 2004 their exports reached $41,849 million, which is 56.7 per cent of the total. The highest share of FIEs in Poland's exports was observed in the following product groups: motor vehicles (89 per cent in 2004); fats and oils (82 per cent); pulp and paper products (81 per cent); optical and measuring instruments (78 per cent); and machinery and equipment (76 per cent). The lowest shares of FIEs were in exports of mineral products (10 per cent); livestock and animal products (29 per cent in 2004); footwear and headgear (36 per cent); and crop products (37 per cent).

Imports of FIEs developed even more rapidly than exports. In 1995 FIEs imported $12,224 million worth of goods (42.1 per cent of Poland's imports), while in 2004 their imports increased to $53,464 million, constituting 60.6 per cent of total imports. The most important role was played by FIEs in creating imports to Poland of the following goods: food products (73 per cent of the total imports of this category in 2004); machinery and equipment (72 per cent); pulp, paper and paperboard products (66 per cent); and plastics and products thereof (64 per cent). The lowest share of FIEs was observed in Polish imports of arms and ammunition (0.6 per cent); works of art (10 per cent); and livestock and animal products (25 per cent).

Apart from the influence of FDI on the volume of exports and imports, the inflow of foreign capital has also shaped the qualitative parameters of Poland's foreign trade. This is reflected in an improvement in competitiveness of goods as measured by the RCA indices. After 1995 Poland maintained or gained a comparative advantage in trade in the groups of goods presented in Table 3.2. In some cases FIEs possessed a comparative advantage in trade, while Polish firms did not. For example, motor vehicles did not belong to Poland's trade specialisation in 1995, as indicated by the negative value of the RCA index (−0.0463). In 2004 the RCA index for vehicles was positive (0.2278) and Poland was relatively specialised in this group of products. The reason for this shift in specialisation is the inflow of FDI into this sector, as confirmed by the positive RCA index calculated for FIEs and the negative index calculated for Polish firms, as shown in Table 3.2. Other examples are: soap, lubricating and dental preparations; cocoa; articles of stone, cement and mica; paper and paperboard products; and books and products of the printing industry. Trade in these goods suggested a relative disadvantage in 1995, but becoming a relative advantage in 2004. The comparison of RCAs for foreign enterprises and Polish firms shows that this positive change in RCAs can be attributed only to trade of FIEs, as the RCA index for Polish firms remained negative.

Another pattern in RCA changes can be observed for goods such as: meat; sugars and confectionery; miscellaneous edible preparations; essential oils, perfumery and cosmetics; tobacco; ceramic products; and glass and glassware. In 1995–2004 there was an improvement in RCA indices for these groups, thanks to both FIEs and Polish firms.

The opposite tendency for FIEs and Polish-owned firms can be observed as regards comparative advantages in trade of the following items: preparations of cereals, flour and milk; preparations of vegetables and fruit; rubber and articles made of rubber; and other textile articles. Although these goods belonged to Poland's trade specialisation in 1995 as well as in 2004, it should be pointed out that during the analysed period RCA indices deteriorated for Polish firms and improved for firms with foreign capital involvement. It might indicate that foreign investors either overtook Polish competitors or crowded them out of the market.

In summary, FDI into industries where Poland had a comparative advantage in foreign trade in some cases improved this advantage and strengthened existing local firms (for example production of meat, glass), but in other branches Polish competitors started to lose their advantages in trade (for example processing of vegetables and fruit, dairy or cereals).

It is also worth analysing the trade in goods which did not belong to Poland's trade specialisation, meaning that RCA indices remained negative,

Table 3.2 Poland's trade specialisation related to FDI (showing products where RCA > 0 in 2004 and improved after 1995)

CN code	Group	RCA Poland		RCA FIEs		RCA Polish firms	
		1995	2004	1995	2004	1995	2004
2	Meat and edible meat offal	0.5338	1.1447	0.7080	1.2291	0.4380	1.0461
17	Sugars and confectionery	0.0483	1.2244	0.2487	0.8381	-0.0748	1.7056
18	Cocoa	-0.2681	0.2481	-0.8608	0.3758	1.3087	-0.0619
19	Preparations of cereals, flour and milk	0.6045	0.9249	0.5283	0.9340	1.2508	1.0474
20	Preparations of vegetables and fruit	1.1079	1.1306	1.0175	1.4144	1.2499	0.7477
21	Miscellaneous edible preparations	-0.5284	0.1287	-0.8346	0.0965	0.0028	0.2521
24	Tobacco	-1.5624	0.1052	-1.3384	0.1629	-1.9939	0.3852
33	Essential oils, perfumery, cosmetic or toilet preparations	-0.8307	0.2616	-1.1727	0.3581	-0.4472	0.0293
34	Soap, lubricating and dental preparations	-0.5243	0.2288	0.0132	0.3602	-0.9336	-0.0650
40	Rubber and articles made of rubber	0.0185	0.2929	-0.3902	0.4193	0.1493	0.0124
48	Paper and paperboard	-0.4908	0.0130	0.0979	0.3241	-1.1232	-0.8197
49	Books, newspapers and products of the printing industry	-1.4611	0.3603	-1.5491	0.7240	-1.1884	-0.2616
63	Other textile articles	0.8895	0.9923	0.6947	1.1069	1.1902	0.8367
68	Articles of stone, cement and mica	-0.4100	0.4387	-0.2860	0.8293	-0.4644	-0.2176
69	Ceramic products	-0.3996	0.2534	0.0844	0.3895	-0.5900	0.1205
70	Glass and glassware	0.2493	0.3555	0.0067	0.2061	0.3992	0.6209
87	Vehicles	-0.0463	0.2278	0.2131	0.4149	-0.3607	-0.5326

Sources: Calculated from GUS (1996b, 2005b); IKCHZ (1996, 2005).

Note: The CN code is the Combined Nomenclature, the tariff and statistical nomenclature of the EU's customs union.

but were improving after 1995. This group of goods can be divided into three sub-groups:

1   commodities with improved RCA indices for foreign and Polish firms;
2   products for which RCA indices deteriorated for FIEs and improved for Polish enterprises;
3   commodities for which RCA indices improved for FIEs and decreased for Polish enterprises.

The first group, as shown in Table 3.3, includes: certain items of the food industry (coffee, tea and spices; vegetable extracts); selected products of the chemical industry (tanning or dyeing extracts; paints and varnishes; putty; inks; miscellaneous chemical products); plastics; corks; nickel and articles thereof; nuclear reactors; boilers; machinery and mechanical appliances; electrical machinery and equipment and parts; sound reproducers, television image and sound recorders, as well as electrical machinery and equipment and parts. Improving competitiveness in this group is a result of foreign investment as well as of the gradual upgrading of local production. FDI transferred technology to these sectors and also speeded up the process of technology imitation and diffusion in the local environment. Both competition and demonstration effects played a significant role in building comparative advantages.

The second of the above mentioned groups consists of the following products: cereals; products of the milling industry; photographic goods; aluminium and articles thereof; toys, games and sports articles. In this case, competitiveness of Polish exports increased as a result of the activity of Polish firms, while FIEs were losing their competitive position. This means that they negatively affected the overall competitiveness of these industry branches.

The third group of goods for which Poland's competitiveness also improved during 1995–2004 includes certain textiles (wool; man-made filaments; man-made staple fibres; special woven fabrics). Positive changes of RCA indices for FIEs and negative shifts for Polish firms indicate that in the case of this group of goods the foreign capital inflow improved their international competitiveness.

Conclusions

Theory suggests that foreign direct investment is an important stimulus to the international competitiveness of host economies. In the case of Poland, the positive impact of FDI on the competitiveness of the manufacturing sector is confirmed by relatively higher productivity growth rates in branches where the inflow was the most dynamic. Increases in labour productivity led to improvements in foreign-trade competitiveness, reflected in shifts in RCA indices. Comparison of the RCA indices for Polish firms and FIEs, calculated using two-digit data on Poland's foreign trade in the period 1995–2004, shows that the impact of FDI on Polish manufacturing varies for individual

Table 3.3 Products for which Poland did not have a comparative advantage but for which RCAs improved

CN code	Group	RCA Poland		RCA FIEs		RCA Polish firms	
		1995	2004	1995	2004	1995	2004
9	Coffee, tea and spices	-2.7034	-1.0049	-3.6142	-1.0144	-1.7771	-0.9701
10	Cereals	-2.4135	-1.4225	-1.5374	-2.3610	-3.6299	-0.9282
11	Products of milling industry	-0.9246	-0.3064	-0.4059	-0.4839	-1.2464	0.1955
13	Lac; resins; vegetable extracts	-4.0491	-1.9014	-3.4317	-1.4062	-4.4943	-2.8117
32	Tanning or dyeing extracts; paints and varnishes; putty; inks	-1.5604	-1.1970	-3.0841	-1.6723	-1.2617	-0.7850
37	Photographic goods	-3.0302	-2.1953	-3.9692	-4.1164	-2.1630	-1.6000
38	Miscellaneous chemical products	-2.0342	-1.5331	-2.5701	-1.5089	-1.7983	-1.5728
39	Plastics and products	-1.0348	-0.6463	-1.0810	-0.7272	-0.9917	-0.5414
45	Cork and products	-2.4817	-0.8028	-2.5309	-1.2073	-2.0836	-0.4692
51	Wool; animal hair	-1.0189	-0.6891	-0.3132	-0.0122	-1.5634	-2.1392
54	Man-made filaments	-1.8053	-1.2138	-2.4259	-0.7826	-1.6110	-1.8777
55	Man-made staple fibres	-1.6718	-1.4371	-2.4970	-1.4445	-1.4810	-1.4944
58	Special woven fabrics	-1.9666	-1.8602	-1.3673	-1.7264	-2.4807	-2.0193
75	Nickel and articles made of nickel	-3.3065	-2.2858	-3.7501	-2.3814	-3.2116	-2.2412
76	Aluminium and articles made of aluminium	-0.2686	-0.1661	-0.0055	-0.2890	-0.4313	0.0117
84	Nuclear reactors; boilers; machinery and mechanical appliances; parts thereof	-1.0559	-0.2397	-1.2599	-0.0820	-0.9408	-0.5743
85	Electrical machinery and equipment and parts; sound reproducers, television image and sound recorders, parts and accessories of such articles	-0.2992	-0.0109	-0.0120	0.0925	-0.5431	-0.2254
90	Optical, photographic, measuring instruments	-1.5874	-0.6775	-1.0858	-0.2826	-1.8542	-1.5271
91	Clocks and watches	-2.1768	-0.8336	-3.3447	-0.2037	-2.1820	-1.5783
92	Musical instruments	-0.7741	-0.4351	-1.0074	0.6049	-0.8665	-0.7983
95	Toys, games and sports articles	-0.4337	-0.3930	0.0135	-0.4474	-0.6266	-0.4176

Sources: Calculated from GUS (1996b, 2005b); IKCHZ (1996, 2005).

industry branches. Changes in trade specialisation were associated with the activity of foreign-owned firms, which contributed to improving competitiveness in motor vehicles, paper and paperboard products, products of the printing industry, perfumery and cosmetics, tobacco, ceramic products, and glass and glassware, as well as selected items of textiles. In the case of goods such as cereals, products of the milling industry, photographic goods, aluminium and articles made of aluminium, and toys, games and sports articles, the competitiveness of Polish exports increased as a result of the activity of Polish firms, while firms with foreign involvement had a negative impact. The importance of FDI in shaping the pattern of competitiveness of Polish products on international markets grew as the share of FIEs in Poland's foreign trade increased.

References

Aitken, B., Hanson, G. and Harrison, A. (1994) *Spillovers, foreign investment, and export behavior*, NBER Working Paper, 4967, Cambridge, MA: National Bureau of Economic Research.

Berg, A. and Sachs, J. (1992) 'Structural adjustment and international trade in Eastern Europe: the case of Poland', *Economic Policy*, 14: 117–73.

Buckley, P. J. and Mucchielli, J. L. (eds) (1997) *Multinational firms and international relocation*, Cheltenham: Edward Elgar.

Dunning, J. (1988) *Multinationals, technology and competitiveness*, London: Unwin Hyman.

Dunning, J. (1992) *Multinational enterprise and the global economy*, Wokingham: Addison-Wesley.

GUS (1996a) *Rocznik Statystyczny Przemysłu*, Warsaw: Główny Urząd Statystyczny.

GUS (1996b) *Rocznik Statystyczny Handlu Zagranicznego*, Warsaw: Główny Urząd Statystyczny.

GUS (1998) *Rocznik Statystyczny Przemysłu*, Warsaw: Główny Urząd Statystyczny.

GUS (2000) *Rocznik Statystyczny Przemysłu*, Warsaw: Główny Urząd Statystyczny.

GUS (2002) *Rocznik Statystyczny Przemysłu*, Warsaw: Główny Urząd Statystyczny.

GUS (2005a) *Rocznik Statystyczny Przemysłu*, Warsaw: Główny Urząd Statystyczny.

GUS (2005b) *Rocznik Statystyczny Handlu Zagranicznego*, Warsaw: Główny Urząd Statystyczny.

Helpman, E. and Krugman, P. (1985) *Market structure and international trade*, Cambridge, MA: MIT Press.

Hoekman, B. and Djankov, S. (1996) *Intra-industry trade, foreign direct investment and reorientation of East European exports*, CEPR Discussion Paper, 1377, London: Centre for Economic Policy Research.

IKCHZ (1996) *Inwestycje zagraniczne w Polsce*, Warsaw: Instytut Koniunktur i Cen Handlu Zagranicznego.

IKCHZ (2005) *Inwestycje zagraniczne w Polsce*, Warsaw: Instytut Koniunktur i Cen Handlu Zagranicznego.

Markusen, J. R. and Venables, A. J. (1996) *The theory of endowment, intra-industry, and multinational trade*, NBER Working Paper, 5529, Cambridge, MA: National Bureau of Economic Research.

Markusen, J. R. and Venables, A. J. (1997) *Foreign direct investment as a catalyst for industrial development*, NBER Working Paper, 6241, Cambridge, MA: National Bureau of Economic Research.

Misala, J. (2006) 'Comparing national competitiveness: basic measurement problems', in M. A .Weresa (ed.), *Poland: competitiveness report 2006: the role of innovation*, Warsaw: Warsaw School of Economics.

NBP (1998) *Zagraniczne inwestycje bezpośrednie w Polsce*, Warsaw: Narodowy Bank Polski.

NBP (2003) *Zagraniczne inwestycje bezpośrednie w Polsce*, Warsaw: Narodowy Bank Polski.

NBP (2005) *Zagraniczne inwestycje bezpośrednie w Polsce*, Warsaw: Narodowy Bank Polski.

Porter, M. (2001) *Porter o konkurencji*, Warsaw: Polskie Wydawnictwo Ekonomiczne.

Posner, M. (1961) 'International trade and technical change', *Oxford Economic Papers*, 13: 323–41.

Sachverständigenrat (2004) *Erfolge im Ausland – Herausforderungen im Inland*, Wiesbaden: Fachverlage.

4   The macroeconomic effects of fiscal and monetary policy in Poland, 1993–2005

Marian Górski

This chapter presents an application of Mundell and Fleming's version of John Hicks's model for a small open economy to Polish conditions in the years 1993–2005. The model views macroeconomic equilibrium in terms of a combination of a real interest rate level and Gross Domestic Product (GDP) consistent with equilibrium on the money market, on the commodity and services market and in foreign trade and external financial flows. This provides a basis for assessing the monetary policy pursued by the National Bank of Poland, identifying periods of more or less expansionary and restrictive policies. Similarly, increases and decreases in the budget deficit in real terms in particular years are used to show the degree to which fiscal policy was restrictive or expansionary. Periods can be identified and set against the fiscal policies pursued by different government coalitions. This makes it possible to challenge the commonly held view that, in the process of transforming the Polish economy, governments pursued quite an expansionary fiscal policy, while the central bank pursued a restrictive monetary policy (Wasilewska-Trenkner 2005). In the last part of the chapter the changes in the real risk-free rate of return of domestic investors are set against the real interest rates confronting foreign investors, which are affected by nominal domestic rates of return and by changes in the exchange rate of the Polish złoty.

Applying the IS-LM model

The macroeconomic effects of the financial policy of a state are reflected in the rate of economic growth, the inflation rate, the unemployment rate, interest rates and fluctuations in currency rates. To interpret the impact of fiscal and monetary policies on economic growth in Poland in the years 1993–2005, I shall apply the IS-LM equilibrium model for a small open economy, taking further previous work using the model for a closed economy as applied to Poland in an early stage of its transformation (Górski and Jaszczyński 1991), in the version presented by Mundell and Fleming (Burda and Wyplosz 1997). That model assumes a point of overall equilibrium in the economy, that point being a determinant of the GDP and the interest rate (i) corresponding to the equilibrium on the markets for goods and services and on the financial markets. Obviously, that model can be of crucial importance for the interpretation of the macroeconomic effects of fiscal and monetary policies, despite the fact that the monetary authorities did not take it into account in the period under investigation in their decision-making process, seemingly owing to its Keynesian origin, its original author being John Richard Hicks (1904–89), an English economist and a representative of the Keynesian current in the so-called neo-classical synthesis. The model is displayed graphically in Figure 4.1.

It is worthwhile recalling that in a small open economy, meaning one with insignificant impact on global prices and currency rates, the economic equilibrium oscillates around the intersection of the curves which represent, respectively, monetary equilibrium (the LM curve), the equilibrium on the market of goods and services (the IS curve) and the equilibrium of the foreign movement of goods and capital (the curve of international financial integration). The latter determines interest rates (i*), taking into account the currency-exchange risk for foreign investors. If overall economic equilibrium

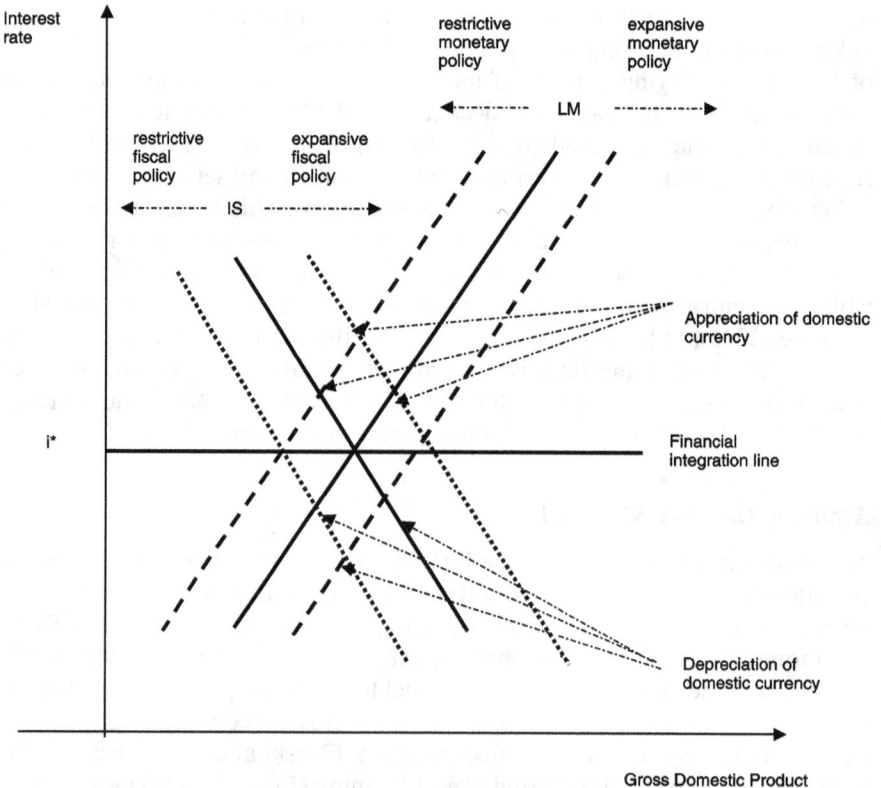

Figure 4.1 The IS-LM model in a small open economy according to Mundell and Fleming.

Source: Burda and Wyplosz (1997: 406).

occurs at an interest rate higher than the rate of financial integration (i > i*), the domestic currency appreciates: in the opposing case (i < i*), the domestic currency depreciates against foreign currencies. The shifts of the curves of partial equilibriums are interpreted as a sign of either an expansionary or a restrictive financial policy of the state. A shift of the IS curve to the right reflects an expansionary fiscal policy, and a movement of that curve to the left indicates a restrictive fiscal policy. A shift of the LM curve to the right represents an expansionary monetary policy, while a shift to the left shows the restrictive character of that policy. If the point of equilibrium is above the line of financial integration, the combination of fiscal and monetary policies being applied at the time should lead to an appreciating domestic currency.

Here the researcher's methodological problem is that in the IS-LM model we are dealing with IS and LM curves that are purely theoretical constructs, developed chiefly for educational purposes, that cannot be estimated empirically. Nevertheless, it may be possible to find the points of overall economic equilibrium using this model, the outcome variables being the level of GDP and the interest rate. These are known for a particular economy in a particular period. However, it remains an open question whether or not they are the result of an overall economic equilibrium.

Two doubts arise at this point. The first relates to the relevance of the IS-LM model for describing the problems of the 'real' economy and the second to the question of whether the Polish economy was and remains inclined to balance out, so that its condition can be interpreted using a model of overall equilibrium. The statistical data utilised in the empirical verification of the IS-LM model in the conditions of the Polish economy in the years 1993–2005 are provided in Table 4.1.

In the empirical version of the model, the GDP variable is replaced with the rate of growth of GDP in fixed prices. The abstract term 'interest rate' is exemplified by the actual expected average annual Lombard rate of the National Bank of Poland (NBP). The Lombard rate is the rate at which the NBP is willing to grant short-term loans to commercial banks against pledged securities. This situation was extremely rare in the circumstances of over-liquidity of the banking sector in Poland, since the NBP mostly applied reverse repos, selling its money bills (NBP bills) to commercial banks as per the reference rate (the reverse repo rate). In the conditions of the Polish economy, the Lombard rate is not the best equivalent of a risk-free interest rate, but it is the only interest rate of the NBP available for the whole period of the study. Moreover, as indicated in Figure 4.2, it moves in line with other important interest rates and can therefore be taken as representative. It should be pointed out that in the IS-LM model the trends in changes in interest rates (i.e. either an increase or a decrease) are of greater importance than interest rate levels. In this case, too, the Lombard rate is in line with the others.

Figure 4.3 shows the combination of the economic growth rates and the expected real Lombard rate in the years 1993–2005. Sub-periods can be distinguished in that period:

Table 4.1 The macroeconomic statistical data for the Polish economy, 1992–2005

	1992	1993	1994	1995	1996	1997	1998	1999	2000	2001	2002	2003	2004	2005
GDP real growth rate, %	2.6	3.8	5.2	7.0	6.1	6.8	4.8	4.1	4.0	1.0	1.4	3.8	5.4	3.5
GDP, 1992 = 100	100.0	103.8	109.2	116.8	124.0	133.4	138.8	144.4	150.2	151.7	153.8	159.7	168.3	174.2
Year-on-year inflation rate, %	43.0	35.3	32.2	27.8	19.9	14.9	11.8	7.3	10.1	5.5	1.9	0.8	3.5	2.1
Price level, 1992 = 100		135.3	178.9	228.6	274.1	314.9	352.1	377.8	415.9	438.8	447.2	450.7	466.5	476.3
Unemployment rate in %, year end	14.3	16.4	16.0	14.9	13.2	10.3	10.4	13.1	15.1	19.4	20.0	20.0	19.1	17.6
Nominal Lombard rate %, year end	36.00	33.00	31.00	28.00	25.00	27.00	20.00	20.50	23.00	15.50	8.75	6.75	8.00	6.00
Real Lombard rate %, year end	−4.90	−1.69	−0.90	0.16	4.25	10.53	7.33	12.3	11.72	9.48	6.72	5.90	4.35	3.82
Real expected Lombard rate %, year end		−0.60	−0.02	1.30	5.50	9.70	10.50	12.07	10.35	13.03	10.06	6.72	3.74	4.68

Source: Calculated from NBP, www.nbp.pl/Statystyka/Instrumenty banku centralnego 1993–2006; Central Statistical Office, www.stat.gov.pl/Informacje staty-styczne – podstawowe dane (both accessed 11 April 2007).

Notes: In 1992 the NBP applied only rediscount and refinancing rates. The estimated Lombard rate for this year is 3 percentage points above the discount rate.

The real expected Lombard rate is calculated by the formula: $RELR = \dfrac{1 + (NLR_{t-1} + NLR_t)/2}{\pi_t}$

where: NLR_{t-1} is the nominal Lombard rate at year (t–1) end, NLR_t is the nominal Lombard rate at the year (t) end, and π_t is the inflation rate in the year t.

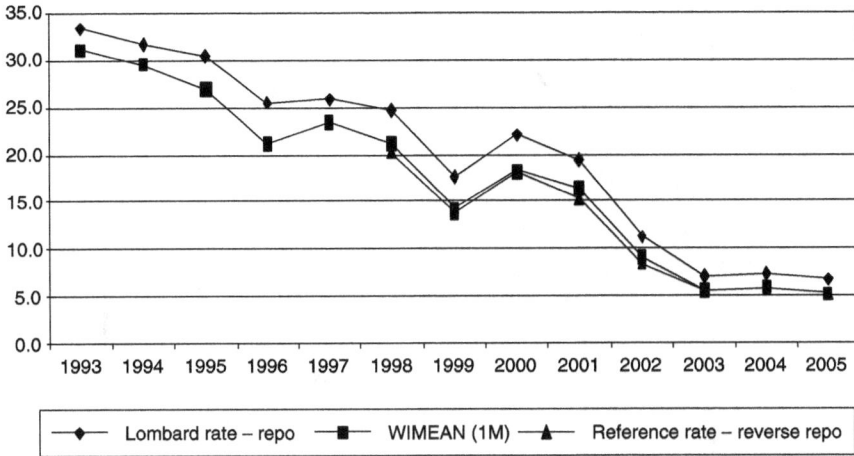

Figure 4.2 Lombard rate, WIMEAN (1M) and reference rate, 1993–2005 (average annual rates).

Source: NBP, www.nbp.pl/Statystyka/Instrumenty banku centralnego 1993–2006 (accessed 11 April 2007).

Notes: WIBID (1M) – Warsaw Interbank Bid Rate (1 month); WIBOR (1M) – Warsaw Interbank Borrowed Offer Rate (1 month); WIMEAN (1M) is calculated by the formula:

$$\text{WIMEAN (1M)} = \frac{\text{WIBID (1M)} + \text{WIBOR (1M)}}{2}.$$

- 1993–1997: a period of economic growth, at high rates from 1995 (from 3.8 per cent to 7.0 per cent), parallel to the high rise in the real interest rate which started the period below zero (from −0.6 per cent to 9.7 per cent).
- 1998–2001: a decrease in the rate of economic growth (from 6.8 per cent to 1.4 per cent), with high and still rising interest rates (from 10.5 per cent to 13 per cent).
- 2002–05: a rise in the rate of economic growth (from 1.4 per cent to 5.4 per cent) alongside a decline in the real interest rate (from 10.0 per cent to 3.7 per cent). There was some deviation from that trend in 2005, but it resumed in 2006, with GDP growth of over 5 per cent and a real Lombard rate falling to around 3 per cent.

The relationship between the rate of economic growth and interest rates from 1998 confirms the classic negative correlation between the two. In the period between 1998 and 2001, also known as the period of cooling down of the economy, the high and rising level of real interest rates, generally attributed to the restrictive policy of the central bank, was accompanied by an evident decrease in the rate of economic growth. Also, this phenomenon is often linked with the emergence of the 'crowding-out effect', whereby an

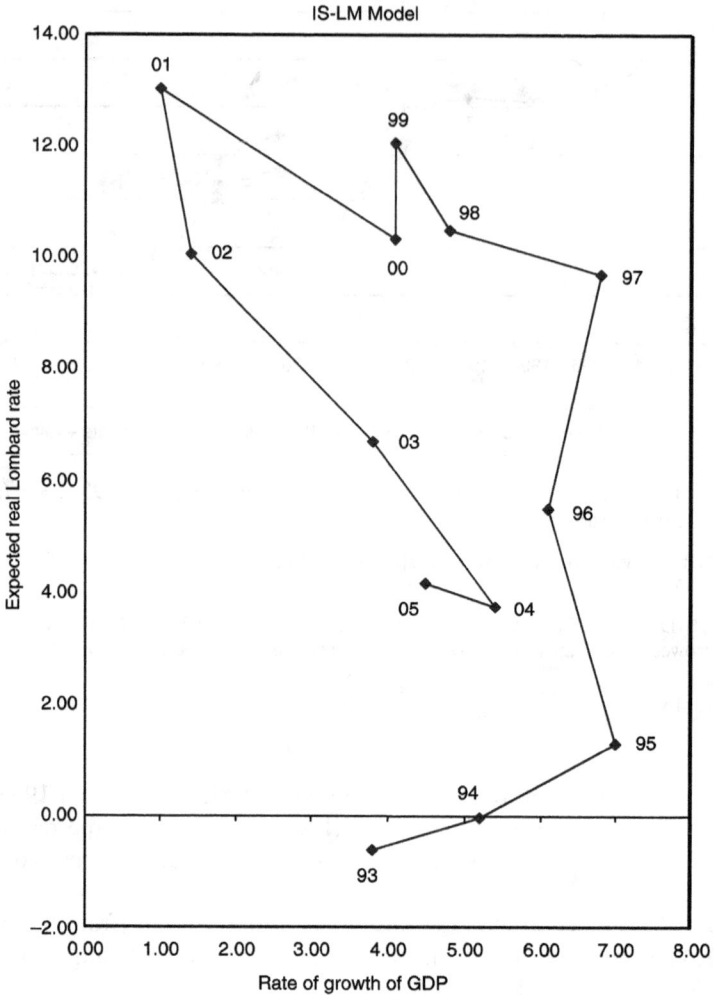

Figure 4.3 The rate of economic growth and real interest rates in Poland, 1993–2005.

Sources: National Bank of Poland, www.nbp.pl/Statystyka/Instrumenty banku centralnego 1993–2006; Main Statistical Office, www.stat.gov.pl/Informacje (accessed 29 March 2007).

increase in interest rates was mainly due to the growing financial needs of the budget and in turn crowded entrepreneurs out of the credit markets.

Slackening of monetary policy in the period from 2002 to 2005 led to a decrease in real interest rates, which in turn led to higher economic growth, though not as high as in the years 1995–97.

The period between 1993 and 1997 was interesting, since it did not confirm the classic interdependency between the two discussed variables. There was an increase in both economic growth and real interest rates, widely inter-preted as an indication of restrictive policy from the NBP. This view was, for example, presented by Professor W. Koziński, the First Deputy Governor of the NBP at the time. The apparent paradox could be due to the fact that economic growth was primarily driven by structural factors. After a period of deep recession and significant structural changes, concerning ownership, the nature of the system and the structure of production, the economy reacted by increased growth regardless of, if not in opposition to, unfavourable financial conditions. We can speak of an eclectic approach applied in monetary policy, which was not highly restrictive in the early part of the period, meaning between 1993 and 1995. The situation began to change in 1996, but there was still no significant reduction in economic growth rates.

In the terms set by the IS-LM model, economic growth is achievable when restrictive monetary policy is applied, provided there is an expansionary fiscal policy. The relationship between monetary policy and the rate of economic growth therefore cannot be established without taking into account the character of fiscal policy in the same period. Below I shall provide an assessment of the degree to which monetary and fiscal policies were expansionary or restrictive.

Monetary policy

Table 4.2 presents the correlation between the rate of growth of GDP and the rate of growth of the supply of real money in the years 1993–2005. The average annual rate of growth in the above period was 4.34 per cent, with an average annual increase in money supply of 6.37 per cent, which exceeded the rate of economic growth by about 2 percentage points.

> Basically, up to 1998 the strategy of monetary policy in Poland concentrated on having an indirect effect on the level of prices by influencing the money supply, while after 1999 the policy was based on the strategy of direct inflation targeting.
>
> (Przybylska-Kapuściska 2006: 18)

However, it must be borne in mind that, even in the period of direct inflation targeting, altering the money supply was one of the effects of monetary policy. Even when the decisions made by the central bank and the Monetary Policy Council (henceforth MPC, a body chaired by the NBP Governor which was given responsibility for monetary policy from 1998) were based directly on monitoring the changes in the inflation rate, the effect of money supply could, and would, have an impact on inflation, if not immediately then in future periods, since the rate of money supply growth in a given year influences the volume of future monetary resources.

As shown in Table 4.2, monetary policy in that period was carried out according to two different regimes. The first regime, covering the years from 1993 to 1997, was the period when the sole responsibility lay with the Governor of the NBP; the other was the period from 1998 to 2005, when that

Table 4.2 **Key data on monetary policy and monetary authorities, 1993–2005**

	1993	1994	1995	1996	1997	1998	1999	2000	2001	2002	2003	2004	2005
GDP real growth rate (r) %	3.8	5.2	7.0	6.1	6.8	4.8	4.1	4.0	1.0	1.4	3.8	5.4	3.5
Average annual	r = 4.34												
Changes in money supply (M2) in nominal terms, %	36.0	38.3	34.9	29.2	30.9	25.2	19.3	14.0	9.2	–2.4	6.4	7.5	18.4
Changes in money supply (M2) in real terms, % (μ)	0.5	4.6	5.6	7.8	13.9	12.0	11.2	3.5	3.5	–4.2	5.6	3.9	16.8
Average annual	μ = 6.37												
Nature of monetary policy	N	E	E	E	EE	EE	EE	N	N	R	E	N	EE
Authority in charge of the monetary policy	NBP Governor r = 5.77% μ = 5.12%			Monetary Policy Council r = 3.45% μ = 6.36% 1st term of office r = 3.17% μ = 4.90%						2nd term of office r = 4.29% μ = 10.15%			
NBP Governor	Hanna Gronkiewicz-Waltz r = 5.77% μ = 7.29%						Leszek Balcerowicz r = 2.95% μ = 6.38%						

Sources: Calculated from NBP data, www.nbp.pl/Statystyka/podażM pieniadza 1993–2006; Central Statistical Office data, www.stat.gov.pl/Informacje statystyczne – podstawowe dane (accessed 11 April 2007).

Note: The nature of monetary policy is explained in the text.

responsibility lay with the MPC. Hanna Gronkiewicz-Waltz, the Governor of the NBP in the years 1993–2000, managed the central bank subject to both regimes, and the subsequent Governor, Leszek Balcerowicz (2001–06) cooperated with the MPC during its first (1998–2003) and second (2004–09) terms of office.

The degree to which monetary policy was expansionary or restrictive can be shown by grouping into the following categories, used in Table 4.2:

- Restrictive policy (R) – a decrease in the real money supply is observed.
- Neutral policy (N) – the money supply increases, but at a rate below the average annual rate of economic growth in the whole period (4.34 per cent).
- Expansionary policy (E) – an increase in money supply exceeds the annual average rate of economic growth but remains below 10 per cent.
- Highly expansionary policy (EE) – the real money supply increases above the 10 per cent rate.

The first point to note is the relatively high stability of the growth of money supply in the particular sub-periods. The average annual increase in the real money supply was 6.37 per cent over the whole 1993–2005 period, with figures of 5.77 per cent in the period of sole responsibility of the Governor of the NBP and 6.36 per cent in the period when the responsibility was also shifted to the MPC. The extent of variation in all periods and under all governors was rather small.

Exceptions from that rule were 2002, when the money supply decreased even in nominal terms (–2.4 per cent), and 2005, when the real money supply increased by nearly 17 per cent. The decrease in the money supply in 2002 was a result of the introduction of a tax on personal income from interest, commonly referred to as the 'Belka tax', from the name of the minister of finance who introduced it. There is no doubt that this was also the reason for a minor increase in the money supply in the two successive years. A sudden rise in the money supply in 2005 may have been a reaction to its decrease in 2002.

Considering the criteria adopted for assessing the orientation of monetary policy, based on the changing money supply, it appears that:

- For the majority of years (eight) the NBP pursued an expansionary approach. This was particularly the character of monetary policy in the years 1994–99 and 2005. The orientation of the NBP in the other years can be described as neutral, except for 2002, when it was clearly restrictive.
- An acceleration of the rate of economic growth in the years 1993–97 covered a period of neutral monetary policy in 1993, expansionary monetary policy in 1994–96 and highly expansionary monetary policy in 1997.

- A decrease in the rate of economic growth in 1998–2002 was accompanied by high monetary expansion in 1998–99, neutral policy in 2000–01 and restrictive policy in 2002.
- An acceleration of the rate of economic growth after 2003 was achieved with a neutral orientation of monetary policy in 2003–04 and its high expansion in 2005.

The facts given above do not conform to the generally accepted assessment of the orientation of monetary policy in the three periods defined in exemplifying the IS-LM model for the Polish economy. This refers in particular to a different assessment of monetary policy in the years 1994–2001. Differing assessments can be related to interpretations of the propensity to hold money which can be explained around the familiar model for interpreting the impact of monetary policy on economic growth and inflation which is based on the assumption of a constant value.

This is based on the following formula:

$$\mu = \pi + r$$

where:

μ is the money supply growth rate,

π is the inflation rate,

r is the rate of growth of GDP in fixed prices.

This formula is derived from converting the equation of overall equilibrium:

$$M = 1/k \times GDP$$

and it applies under the assumption of a constant propensity for economic entities to hold money, meaning that k is a constant. This propensity, or the economy monetisation rate, is expressed as a ratio of money supply to Gross Domestic Product ($k = M/GDP$). That ratio for the Polish economy in the period from 1993 to 2005 is shown in Figure 4.4.

In Poland, the condition of a constant propensity to hold money was not fulfilled. The monetisation rate grew continually until 2001, when it reached 42.1 per cent. The 'Belka tax', introduced in 2002, led to essential changes in the monetary aggregates. The global supply of money, measured as M2, first decreased and then grew, with an increase in the share of cash. This situation lasted until 2004. A considerable change took place in 2005, when the large increase in the money supply translated into a significant rise in the monetisation rate (45.4 per cent) and not into inflation. The rate of monetisation of the Polish economy was growing, and it can be expected to continue to grow until it reaches the level of other countries in the European Union.

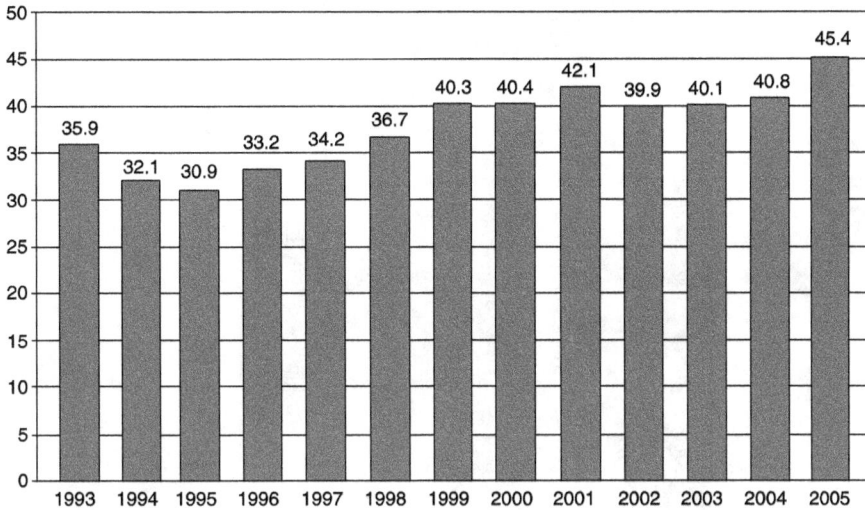

Figure 4.4 Monetisation ratio in the Polish economy, 1993–2005.

Sources: Calculated from NBP data, www.nbp.pl/Statystyka/podaż pieniadza 1993–2006; Central Statistical Office data, www.stat.gov.pl/Informacje statystyczne – podstawowe dane (accessed 11 April 2007).

Note: The monetisation ratio indicates the propensity to hold money and is calculated as M2/GDP as a percentage. M2 is currency in circulation plus current and term deposits.

Fiscal policy

The effects of targeting monetary policy to economic growth are observable, along with the effects of the approach applied in fiscal policy at that time. The data provided in Table 4.3 allow for an assessment of the restrictiveness or degree of expansionary pressure from fiscal policy in successive years in the period from 1993 to 2005. We shall measure this phenomenon by the percentage change in the state-budget deficit from a real perspective, as shown in Table 4.3.

Assessments of fiscal policy, analogous to those for monetary policy and referring to annual changes, are as follows:

- Highly restrictive policy (RR) – a decrease in the real budget deficit by more than 20 per cent.
- Restrictive policy (R) – a decrease in the real budget deficit by more than 5 per cent and less than 20 per cent.
- Neutral policy (N) – a decrease or an increase in the real budget deficit within the range from −5 per cent to +5 per cent.
- Expansionary policy (E) – an increase in the real budget deficit by more than 5 per cent and less than 20 per cent.

Table 4.3 Basic data on fiscal policy and governing coalitions in Poland, 1993–2005

Variables	1993	1994	1995	1996	1997	1998	1999	2000	2001	2002	2003	2004	2005
GDP real growth rate (r), % Average annual	3.8 $r = 4.34$	5.2	7.0	6.1	6.8	4.8	4.1	4.0	1.0	1.4	3.8	5.4	3.2
Changes in the budget deficit in nominal terms, %	−37.2	32.2	29.8	23.1	−35.6	123.5	−5.4	23.1	110.2	21.8	−6.0	11.8	−31.2
Changes in the budget deficit in real terms, %	−53.6	0.0	1.6	2.7	−44.0	99.9	−11.8	11.8	99.2	19.5	−6.7	8.0	−32.6
Nature of fiscal policy	RR	N	N	N	RR	EE	R	E	EE	E	R	E	RR
Governing coalitions		SLD–PSL				AWS–UW				SLD–UP			
Average annual GDP growth rate, %		6.27				3.47				3.44			
Change in budget deficit, %		−31.1				+292.6				−6.8			
Minister of finance		Grzegorz Kołodko Marek Belka (1997)				Leszek Balcerowicz			Jarosław Bauc	M. Belka G. Kołodko		A. Raczko M. Gronicki	

Source: Calculated from data from the Ministry of Finance, www.mf.gov.pl/deficyt budżetowy; Central Statistical Office data, www.stat.gov.pl/Informacje statystyczne – podstawowe dane (accessed 11 April 2007).

Note: The nature of fiscal policy is explained in the text.

- Highly expansionary policy (EE) – an increase in the budget deficit by more than 20 per cent.

A problem arises when assessing the responsibility for budget deficits in the first year of governments' terms of office. Polish elections were held in the autumns of 1993, 1997, 2001 and 2005. The budget for the first year of a new term of office was therefore developed by the former government. Over this period, Poland was governed by the following coalitions:

- 1994–97: a coalition of the Alliance of the Democratic Left (SLD) and the Polish Peasants' Party (PSL);
- 1998–2001: a coalition of Solidarity Electoral Action (AWS) and the Freedom Union (UW);
- 2002–05: a coalition of the Alliance of the Democratic Left (SLD) and the Labour Union (UP).

As clearly shown in Table 4.3, fiscal policy was much less stable than monetary policy. The most significant effects for the condition of the state budget originated in 1998 and 2001, when the real budget deficit doubled. During the whole period when power was in the hands of the coalition between Solidarity Electoral Action and the Freedom Union, the budget deficit almost tripled.

The fiscal policy of the coalition between the Alliance of the Democratic Left and the Polish Peasants' Party appeared to be highly restrictive, since during that coalition's term of office the state budget deficit fell by more than 30 per cent. There was a neutral fiscal policy in the first three years of that term, but the deficit was reduced by 44 per cent in the last year.

The fiscal policy of the coalition between the Alliance of the Democratic Left and the Labour Union can be considered overall to be restrictive. The deficit decreased by nearly 7 per cent. That, however, was mainly due to a 32 per cent reduction in 2005. In the first year of the term (2002) the deficit grew by nearly 20 per cent.

The interdependency between fiscal policy and economic growth is shaped under the influence of changes in the propensity to save, defined as the ratio of accumulation to Gross Domestic Product: (GDP – consumption)/GDP. That correlation in individual years in the period from 1993 to 2005 is shown in Figure 4.5. Evidently, this variable is somewhat more stable than the propensity to hold money. In the years 1993–99 it ranged from 19 per cent to 21 per cent, and in the years 2001–05 it was at a lower rate of 15–17 per cent. The propensity of wealthy households to save was increasing. However, their savings were consumed by a rise in public debt, leading to higher consumer expenditure of households, which was financed from the state budget.

In the light of the above facts, a claim that financial policy in Poland involved expansionary fiscal policy alongside restrictive monetary policy was a myth, although it was asserted both in specialist literature and in statements

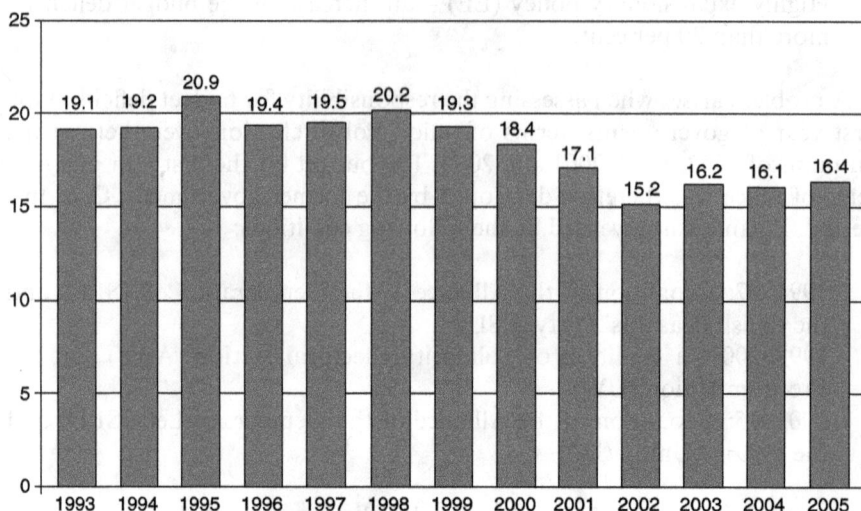

Figure 4.5 Propensity to save in the Polish economy, 1993–2005.

Source: Calculated from Central Statistical Office data, www.stat.gov.pl/Informacje statystyczne – podstawowe dane (accessed 11 April 2007).

Note: Propensity to save is (GDP – consumption)/GDP as a percentage.

by representatives of the monetary authorities. They often maintained that their policy would have been much less restrictive if it were not for the highly expansionary fiscal policy.

To sum up, considering the course of the curve in Figure 4.2, the assessment of the orientation of monetary policy provided in Table 4.2 and the assessment of the orientation of fiscal policy provided in Table 4.3, we can conclude the following:

- The accelerated economic growth in the years 1993–94 and its high level in the years 1995–97 was achieved in conditions of expansionary monetary policy and neutral (or sometimes restrictive) fiscal policy. The growing level of interest rates may suggest a rigid, if not positive, elasticity of money demand against interest rates. This contrasts with the theoretical prediction of a negative elasticity of demand for money.
- A decrease in the rate of economic growth in the years 1998–2002 took place under conditions of highly expansionary fiscal policy and expansionary monetary policy, although this was neutral towards the end of the period. Therefore, the major reason for the reduction in the growth rate was budget expansion leading to the 'crowding-out effect', despite expansionary and neutral approaches in monetary policy.
- An acceleration of economic growth in the years 2003–05 came in conditions of restrictive fiscal policy, alongside neutral, and eventually expansionary, monetary policy.

- Overall, in the whole period up to 2006, the high rate of economic growth was achieved in conditions of expansionary monetary policy and restrictive fiscal policy.

Incorporating international influences

The interpretation of the IS-LM model for a small open economy means that fiscal policies that influence the level of interest rates, if the exchange rate is flexible, should lead to changes in that exchange rate. This can be followed over the post-1991 period, during which different rules of exchange rate policy were applied (Ryć 2003):

- October 1991–May 1995: the system of creeping devaluation. The central exchange rate of the Polish złoty was devalued on a daily basis in relation to a currency basket based mainly on the US dollar and Deutschmark, and in line with the rate of domestic inflation. The system formally allowed for fluctuations of the market exchange rate within a range of ±2 per cent.
- May 1995–April 2000: the system of creeping ranges of fluctuations of exchange rates. The rate of monthly devaluation of the złoty was reduced, and the allowable range of fluctuations of the market exchange rates was increased around a central exchange rate (rising up to ±7 per cent, to ±12.5 per cent, and then to ±15 per cent).
- April 2000: the system of a floating exchange rate. The exchange rate was based on the supply and demand for foreign currencies. The central bank could influence exchange rates by active participation in the market, but chose not to do so.

Although a floating currency exchange rate was fully applied only in 2000, and despite the wide range of fluctuations in the earlier periods, the NBP did not intervene on the currency markets. It can therefore be assumed that the exchange rate was developing according to market rules, at least from 1997. Figure 4.6 shows changing exchange rates against the US dollar, euro and the currency basket, giving a 50 per cent weight to each of those currencies. The points below the X-axis indicate nominal appreciation of the złoty, while points above that axis indicate currency depreciation. Attention should be drawn to the very varied rates of change in exchange rates in particular years, obviously an indicator of a relatively high currency risk for foreign investors. However, the considerable diversity of exchange rates in the successive years (such as an appreciation of the złoty by more than 20 per cent against the US dollar in 2004 and its depreciation by 9 per cent in the following year) can also indicate a large share of foreign speculative capital, with its inflows and outflows influencing currency exchange rates in a small open economy such as the one that we undoubtedly have in Poland.

Figure 4.7 shows the ratio of nominal depreciation of the złoty in the years

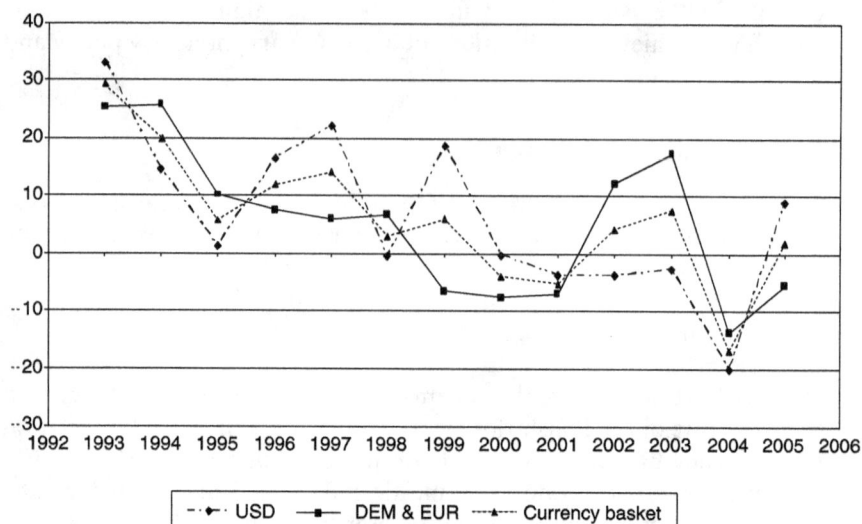

Figure 4.6 PLN appreciation (−) and depreciation (+), 1993–2005, against US dollar, euro and basket of 50 per cent of each currency, percentage change on previous year.

Source: Calculated from data from NBP, www.nbp.pl/Statystyka/kursy walut NBP (accessed 11 April 2007).

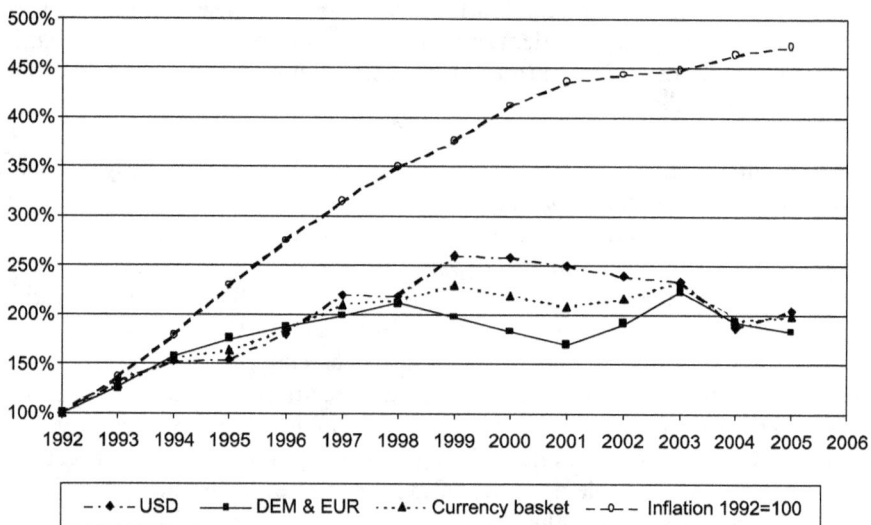

Figure 4.7 Inflation, PLN exchange rate to the US dollar, euro and basket of 50 per cent of each currency, 1993–2005, as percentage of 1992 level.

Sources: Calculated from data from NBP, www.nbp.pl/Statystyka/kursy walut NBP; Central Statistical Office, www.stat.gov.pl/Informacje statystyczne – podstawowe dane (accessed 11 April 2007).

1993–2005 compared to the exchange rates at the end of 1992 and the inflation index in the same period. In nominal terms, the złoty depreciated by over 100 per cent against the US dollar and by over 80 per cent against the euro. However, considering that the inflation rate in Poland in that period exceeded 475 per cent, the real value of the złoty must have been subject to strong appreciation. This had a significant impact in differentiating the rates of return on investments made in Poland by domestic and foreign investors.

The rate of return on financial investment is a function of the price of money (the risk-free interest rate) and the level of risk related to a particular investment (investment-specific risk). We will continue comparing real rates of return on risk-free investment for domestic and foreign investors. Investment-specific risks should be the same for domestic and foreign investors. It can therefore be assumed that the differences in the real rate of return for domestic and foreign investors reflect the differences in the rates of return for the two groups of investors in all the financial investments undertaken in Poland.

Let us assume that the real risk-free rate of return for domestic investors is represented by the nominal Lombard rate, as shown in Figure 4.2, deflated by the rate of increase in the prices of consumer goods and services, as shown in Table 4.1. The real level of the rates of return for foreign investors also depends on changes in the exchange rate and the inflation rate in the country of origin. For present purposes, and in the interests of simplicity, that element can be left out. The real rate of return for foreign investors, as a percentage, can then be calculated with the following formula:

$$\mathrm{RRRFI} = \frac{\mathrm{ER}_{t-1}\,(1 + \mathrm{NLR}_t) - \mathrm{ER}_t}{\mathrm{CER}_{t-1}} \times 100$$

where:

RRRFI is the real rate of return for foreign investors,

ER_{t-1} is the exchange rate at the end of year t–1,

ER_t is the exchange rate at the end of year t,

NLR_t is the nominal Lombard rate in the country where the investment is undertaken.

The real risk-free (except for the currency and political risks) annual rates of return for foreign investors in Poland who made investments in US dollars or euros and according to the currency basket (50 per cent US dollar and 50 per cent euro) in the years 1993–2005 are presented in Table 4.4 and Figure 4.8.

The average annual risk-free rate of return for domestic investors in the whole period was 5.59 per cent, while the average annual rate of return on investments was 15.0 per cent on the investments in US dollars, 13.22 per cent

Table 4.4 PLN appreciation (−) and depreciation (+), 1993–2005, percentage change on previous year, against US dollar, euro and currency basket of 50 per cent US dollar and 50 per cent euro, and the real rate of return on domestic and foreign risk-free investments

	1993	1994	1995	1996	1997	1998	1999	2000	2001	2002	2003	2004	2005	Average annual
USD rate in PLN	2.13	2.44	2.47	2.88	3.52	3.5	4.15	4.14	3.99	3.84	3.74	2.99	3.26	
USD Depreciation +/ Appreciation − in nominal terms, %	33.1	14.6	1.2	16.6	22.2	−0.6	18.6	−0.2	−3.6	−3.8	−2.6	−20.1	9.0	**5.63**
Rate of return on investments in USD, %	33.1	16.4	26.8	8.4	4.8	20.6	1.9	23.2	19.1	12.5	9.4	28.1	−3.0	**15.00**
EUR rate in PLN DEM before 1999	1.24	1.56	1.72	1.85	1.96	2.09	4.17	3.85	3.58	4.02	4.72	4.08	3.86	
EUR Depreciation +/ Appreciation − in nominal terms, %	25.3	25.8	10.3	7.6	5.9	6.6	−6.4	−7.7	−7.0	12.3	17.4	−13.6	−5.4	**4.76**
Rate of return on investments in EUR, %	6.1	5.2	17.7	17.4	21.1	13.4	26.9	30.7	22.5	−3.5	−10.7	21.6	11.4	**13.22**
Depreciation +/ Appreciation − currency basket, in nominal terms, %	29.2	20.2	5.7	12.1	14.1	3.0	6.1	−4.0	−5.3	4.3	7.4	−16.8	1.8	
Rate of return on investments, currency basket, %	19.6	10.8	22.3	12.9	12.9	17.0	14.4	27.0	20.8	4.5	−0.7	24.8	4.2	**14.37**
Real Lombard rate, %, at year end	−1.7	−0.9	0.2	4.2	10.5	7.3	12.3	11.7	9.5	6.7	5.9	4.4	3.8	**5.59**
Foreign–domestic rate of return, in percentage points	4.8	11.7	22.1	8.7	2.4	9.7	2.1	15.3	11.3	−2.2	−6.6	20.4	0.4	**7.39**

Source: Calculated from data from NBP, www.nbp.pl/Statystyka/kursy walut NBP (accessed 11 April 2007).

Note: On 1 January 1999, 1 EUR = 1.95583 DEM.

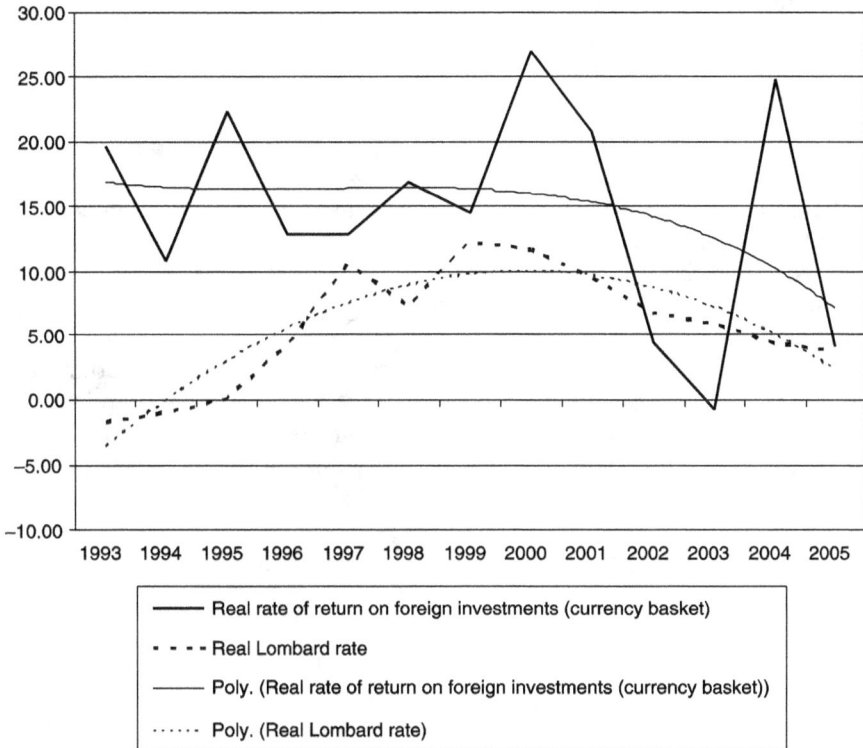

Figure 4.8 Real rates of return on domestic and foreign risk-free investments, 1993–2005.

Sources: Calculated from data from NBP, www.nbp.pl/Statystyka/Instrumenty banku central-nego 1993–2006; Central Statistical Office, www.stat.gov.pl/Informacje statystyczne – podsta-wowe dane (accessed 11 April 2007).

Note: Poly. = Polynomial.

on the investments in euros, and 14.36 per cent on the currency basket investments. The rates of return for foreign investors were treble the rates for domestic investors. This was an effect of the strong appreciation of the złoty. Higher rates of return for foreign investors were a bonus for the currency and political risks they incurred. However, it remains an open question whether the high rates of return realised by this group of investors in Poland were enough to compensate for the risks they incurred.

The level and changeability of the domestic and foreign rates of return are shown in Figure 4.8. With an average annual rate of return at 5.6 per cent, domestic investors realised the highest rates of return (10 to 12 per cent) in the years 1997–2001, and the lowest (ranging from −2 per cent to 0 per cent) in the years 1993–95, plus about 4 per cent between 2004 and 2005. Such changeability in the rates of return is estimated remarkably well ($R^2 = 0.8293$) by a polynomial of degree three:

$$RLR = -0.0013t^3 - 0.2618t^2 + 4.3873t - 7.7350$$

where:

RLR is the real Lombard rate,

t shows successive years (1 to 13) from the start of the period.

A far greater diversity is observable in the rates of return for foreign investors. The highest rates of return from the currency basket were obtained in the years 1995 (22.3 per cent), 2000 (27.0 per cent) and 2004 (24.8 per cent). The lowest rates of return were realised by foreign investors in 2003 (0.7 per cent) and 2002 and 2005 (approximately 4 per cent). The highest rates of return were realised during the periods of strong currency appreciation, and the loss in 2003 was mainly due to strong depreciation of the złoty relative to the euro. The changeability of the rates of return on foreign investments can be estimated by a polynomial of degree three, but the R^2 of 0.1248 points to the statistical insignificance of this relationship:

$$RRRFI = -0.0175t^3 + 0.2472t^2 - 1.0832t + 17,7820$$

where:

RRRFI is the real rate of return on foreign investments,

t shows successive years from 1 to 13.

The study shows greater diversity and irregularity in the changeability of the rates of return on foreign investments in Poland. This may indicate a high currency risk, rewarded with an adequate bonus. It could also be evidence of a considerable share of foreign speculative capital in Poland. Parallel to the successful process of the transformation of the Polish economy, crowned by Poland's accession to the European Union in 2004, the political risk of foreign investors in Poland decreased, which should have been reflected in a levelling of rates of return for domestic and foreign investors. This, however, is not confirmed by the data provided in this chapter, and in particular by the highly changeable rate of return on foreign investments in the years 2003–04.

Concluding remarks

It is commonly maintained that Polish governments pursued expansionary fiscal policies, while the central bank pursued restrictive monetary policies. This has been not confirmed. The analysis here indicates that, in the period 1993–2005, the governments in power applied a highly diversified fiscal policy. It was often neutral and restrictive when the Social Democrat–Peasant coalition was in power and strongly expansionary under the Solidarity (Akcja Wyborcza Solidarność) government. This expansion was necessitated by reforms, primarily in the pension and health-care systems. At that time, albeit with a few exceptions, the National Bank of Poland pursued an expansionary monetary policy. The most favourable policy mix for economic growth in the Polish economy policy mix seems to be expansionary monetary policy with restrictive fiscal policy.

The high real rates of return on foreign investments realised in Poland have constituted a significant determinant of comparative advantage of the Polish economy, demonstrated by the inflow of foreign capital. In the circumstances of relatively low interest rates in Poland, and their increase in the USA and the euro zone, this advantage can continue only if the appreciation of the złoty continues. However, such an appreciation is unfavourable for further economic development. The stability of exchange rates may be ensured if Poland declares its will to enter the euro zone and access ERM II as soon as possible. Further inflow of capital, especially in the form of direct invest-ment, can be ensured by means of other comparative advantages of the economy, such as the qualified and relatively inexpensive workforce, a favour-able climate and an extensive domestic market for goods and services, all of these being preconditions for maintaining high rates of economic growth. Economic growth, in turn, as shown by evidence in earlier parts of this chapter, can be most rapid in the conditions of a restrictive fiscal policy which will also not lead to increased demand for foreign capital to finance a growing public debt.

References

Burda, M. C. and Wyplosz, C. (1997) *Macroeconomics: a European text*, Oxford: Oxford University Press.

Górski, M. and Jaszczyński, D. (1991) 'Makroekonomiczne uwarunkowania i skutki polityki stabilizacyjnej w Polsce', in G. Kołodko (ed.), *Polityka finansowa, stabi-lizacja, transformacja*, Warsaw: Instytut Finansów.

Przybylska-Kapuściska, W. (2006) 'Strategia bezpośredniego celu inflacyjnego w nowych krajach członkowskich Unii Europejskiej', *Bank i Kredyt*, No. 4, Appen-dix: Bankowość centralna od A do Z.

Ryć, K. (2003) *Tendencje kursu złotego a sytuacja polskiej gospodarki*, Working Paper, Warsaw: Wydział Zarządzania Uniwersytetu Warszawskiego.

Wasilewska-Trenkner, H. (2005) 'Koordynacja polityki fiskalnej i monetarnej przed przystąpieniem do strefy euro', *Master of Business Administration*, No. 4, Warsaw: Wpisz, pp. 9–12.

Part II
EU accession and Polish politics

5 Party politics in Poland after the 2005 elections

Frances Millard

Poland's politics were reinvented and reinvented again in the period from 1989 to 2007, but not always in ways expected or anticipated. Poland created a new democracy and a capitalist economy: it transformed a one-party state into a system based on the constitutional separation of powers, with routine elections and unfettered political competition. This represented a clear success, shared with the other countries of the old 'Soviet bloc'. Accession to the European Union in 2004 was both a symbol and a manifestation of the profound changes that had occurred. However, the development of stable political parties – the building blocks of democracy and its key socio-political institution – proved more difficult to achieve. Poland was not the only country with volatile parties. Slovakia offered another obvious example. However, in Poland the state of the parties – their ideologies, their internal and inter-party relations, their organisation, and their relations with society – constituted a major reason for prolonged government instability and political alienation.

Notwithstanding a broad government–opposition consensus on the fundamental tasks of transformation, including the crucial foreign policy reorientation westward to the European Union and NATO, Polish elite political culture after 1990 remained highly adversarial, with adverse consequences for the development of a stable party system. In the first freely elected parliament (1991–93) the communist party's successor, Social Democracy of the Polish Republic (SdRP), was treated in parliament as a pariah party. Despite an 'exit from communism' marked by negotiated settlement between the communist regime and the Solidarity opposition at the Round Table in 1989, the main political divide until 2005 remained that between former communists and their allies in the broad Alliance of the Democratic Left (*Sojusz Lewicy Demokratycznej*, SLD) and parties of Solidarity provenance.

Although this divide remained crucial for coalition formation, the social democrats increasingly gained support from the electorate by successfully reinventing themselves as a European social democratic party. The pinnacle of their success came with 41 per cent of the vote in 2001, after which the now-unified party (still the SLD) foundered on the rocks of corruption and incompetence, went into rapid decline, and split. Meanwhile, the mass opposition movement based around the Solidarity trade union needed to recast itself for democratic political competition. Solidarity splintered into many small right-wing groupings. After failing to meet the demands of new electoral thresholds, most did not enter parliament in 1993. By 1997 a major element of the movement had come together again to win the election as Solidarity Election Action (AWS), anchored by the trade union movement. However, in the course of that parliament it divided once again and mutated into another successive incarnation of Solidarity parties. Governmental power oscillated with successive elections: it was held by Solidarity in 1991–93; by SLD with the Polish Peasant Party (*Polskie Stronnictwo Ludowe*, PSL) in 1993–97; by Solidarity in 1997–2001; and by SLD (briefly with the PSL) in 2001–05.

The September 2005 election broke this pattern of oscillation between the two opposed camps. The party of the Kaczyński twins, Law and Justice (*Prawo i Sprawiedliwość*, PiS), a party that had its roots in the Solidarity movement, emerged as the largest parliamentary party, with 27 per cent of the vote; after much discussion, it finally reached a formal coalition agreement with two non-Solidarity parties, Self-Defence (*Samoobrona RP*, SO) and the League of Polish Families (*Liga Polskich Rodzin*, LPR). Previously, these parties had not been regarded as potential coalition partners. However, as events unfolded, the solidification of the party system, expected (or even identified) by many scholars as an element of the process of democratic consolidation, appeared no closer after the 2005 elections (Sartori 1976: 21–2; Hofferbert 1998: 1; Bakke and Sitter 2005). Indeed, 2006 was widely regarded as a year of constant political crisis. For some, even democracy itself was at stake. This chapter explores the nature of the political turbulence that followed the 2005 election and analyses its implications for party development.

The 2005 election and its aftermath

The outcome of the 2005 elections was that two parties that claimed their origins in Solidarity emerged as the two largest parties in parliament. The second party in terms of numbers in parliament was Civic Platform (*Platforma Obywatelska*, PO), with 24 per cent of votes. However, despite their shared roots in Solidarity, the two parties failed to achieve a coalition agreement following the victory in the concurrent presidential election of Lech Kaczyński, the PiS candidate, over PO candidate Donald Tusk (Millard 2006). To begin with, PiS bargained for support for its minority government; then it achieved a stabilisation pact and finally, in May 2006, the coalition. This period continued until October 2007 when PO defeated PiS in premature elections. (Neither the League of Polish Families nor Self-Defence crossed the electoral threshold in 2007 and thus were excluded from the new parliament.)

The eventual partners of PiS in government, SO and (key elements of) the LPR could not be regarded as Solidarity heirs. SO was the creation of its leader, Andrzej Lepper, whose political career had begun with the mobilisation of discontented and often debt-ridden peasants. In January 1992 SO registered as a trade union and in June as a party, but the two were never clearly distinguishable. Lepper's party was notorious for its style of confrontational direct action and radical rhetoric in defence of the 'poor and the disadvantaged'. It maintained a demonstrable anti-establishment record, targeting the 'losers' of transition with an ambiguous 'programme' offering simple solutions to complex problems. Its disruptive tactics and anti-democratic discourse drew extensive media attention as well as that of the new Bureau of State Security (*Urząd Ochrony Państwa*, UOP) in 1992. Its parliamentary breakthrough in 2001 was a surprise. SO did not register in the opinion polls until August 2001, and only at the end of the campaign did polls suggest that it would cross the electoral threshold. Lepper's image consultant proved highly effective, and he became a convincing and persuasive spokesman for the disaffected. SO attracted 10.2 per cent of the vote, succeeding where the PSL had failed, namely in attracting voters from towns as well as the countryside. In 2005 SO positioned itself to benefit from the failure of the social democrats by reinventing itself as 'the new party of the left', hoping to scoop up former SLD voters. Its vote increased only slightly (11.4 per cent), but the changes in the relative strengths of other political parties gave it a new strategic significance.

LPR was a more recent creation: it had only registered a few months before the September 2001 elections. It was the first anti-EU parliamentary party, opposing accession as an affront to national sovereignty and a threat to national identity. The LPR drew together ten or so nationalist and clerical formations, along with some well-known individuals associated with the Solidarity movement, such as Antoni Macierewicz, who had belonged to (and created) a succession of small parties; Jan Łopuszański, originally associated with the Christian National Union (ZChN); and Zygmunt Wrzodak, a former Solidarity trade union activist known for his radicalism and his anti-Semitic outbursts. The LPR also gained from the patronage of Radio Maryja, the powerful voice of Catholic fundamentalism. In 2001 it won 7.9 per cent of the vote from the traditionalist national-religious constituency. In the course of the 2001–05 Sejm the LPR suffered the defection of half its deputies, who were reduced in number from thirty-eight to nineteen. During this period the League was essentially colonised by elements of the small Nationalist Party under the leadership of Roman Giertych, whose father and grandfather were associated with the right-wing National Democrats (Endeks) of the inter-war period. The loss of Radio Maryja's exclusive patronage in the elections of 2005 was a bitter but not immediately fatal blow to the LPR: though it lost voters, its share of the vote held at 8 per cent.

The decision of PiS to draw into government these two parties, previously regarded as extremist and hence 'uncoalitionable', surprised many observers for two reasons. The first stemmed from the widespread assumption – based on their own long-standing commitment – that PO and PiS would form a coalition government after the elections. Beyond their appeal to a Solidarity lineage, both parties had much in common, not least their social conservatism. This included a commitment to lustration and, for PO, the full publication of all files from the communist period. Traditional values centred on family and religion and decommunisation were common currency for both parties. PO was expected to win the election and with it the premiership, already designated for Jan Rokita. Not only had PO performed consistently well in the polls since the end of 2003, but, with one exception,[1] most final polls also gave PO the lead. Even after the parliamentary election, but before the second-round presidential victory of Kaczyński over Tusk, the expected outcome was, if not a PO–PiS coalition, then certainly a PiS–PO one. This was the case despite the fact that both parliamentary and presidential elections centred on the increasingly bitter confrontation of these two Solidarity parties.

Though as the largest party PiS claimed the task of government formation, its leader, Jarosław Kaczyński, chose Kazimierz Marcinkiewicz as premier-designate. Jarosław wished to strengthen his brother Lech's bid for the presidency by countering potential voter unease at the prospect of twin Kaczyńskis occupying the highest offices of state. Within PiS Marcinkiewicz was viewed as a relative liberal (more sympathetic to the laissez-faire economic approach of PO), and he immediately initiated coalition negotiations with PO; but the parties made no progress in resolving their programmatic disputes, nor in matters of portfolio allocation. Government formation was essentially put on hold until the balance of power was clarified by the presidential result. PiS, however, gave early witness that it held the stronger hand. When the new parliament assembled on 19 October, PiS refused to support PO's candidate for the post of marshal (speaker). Then Lech Kaczyński's victory handed PiS all the trumps. The outward forms of negotiation continued, but PO rejected the subordinate role offered by PiS, particularly the latter's domination of all the 'power ministries'. When negotiations failed on the eve of the constitutional deadline for the Sejm's instauration of a new government, President Kwaśniewski accepted Marcinkiewicz's minority PiS government, which won support from SO and LPR.

The second reason why 2005 generated such unexpected outcomes stemmed from PiS's own election manifesto and its ideological underpinnings. The overarching theme of PiS's approach was its rejection of the chosen path of post-communist transformation and the need for a new constitutional settlement based on moral revolution and patriotic renewal of Solidarity's core ideals and values. This was the project for a new 'Fourth Republic' to replace the corrupt, degenerate system of the Third (from 1991). The inauguration of the Fourth Republic would entail moral cleansing through deep lustration, anti-corruption measures and reaffirmation of Catholic values; its new Constitution would repair the state; it would heal society with a social contract, including fundamental changes in social and economic policy. This new dawn would mean the end of the enduring negative legacy of the Round Table negotiated in 1989 between the regime and Solidarity.

It was the Round Table 'contract' that lay at the heart of Jarosław

Kaczyński's analysis of the situation. By pursuing the 'erroneous path' of continuity, the Round Table had generated the conditions for the emergence of a system of control and exploitation (the *układ*) based on a web of interlocking informal networks of powerful interest groups, lobbies and personal coteries allied with state security services and organised crime, pursuing wealth and power through crime, corruption and cronyism (Kaczyński 2005). Rooting out the *układ* meant dismantling the structures and removing the personnel that made it possible: hence the need for new institutions such as a Truth and Justice Commission and an Anti-Corruption Bureau and a greater role for the Institute of National Memory (IPN). Given its moral emphasis, PiS's collaboration with extremist parties seemed unthinkable. Jarosław Kaczyński had repeatedly stressed that his party would not cooperate with parties with criminal elements or a communist past, both of which were certainly grounds for refusing to treat with SO.

The new political alliance

The breakdown of discussions with PO and the emergence of a political alliance between PiS and both SO and LPR developed in a period of escalating political uncertainty, in part manufactured by PiS itself. The first stage rested on political agreement and the second on a 'stabilisation pact' among the three parties. The third stage was the constitution of a formal coalition in May 2006, albeit followed by the replacement of the prime minister by Jarosław Kaczyński in July, the collapse of the coalition in September, and its re-emergence in October.

Gaining support for the vote of confidence in Marcinkiewicz's government did not prove difficult, as PiS made programmatic and personnel concessions to SO and LPR. PiS endorsed Lepper's nomination as deputy marshal of the Sejm immediately following the election. Marcinkiewicz, said Giertych, had made 'clear gestures in our direction' with promises of a new-baby bonus (*becikowe*), pro-family tax policies and longer maternity leave, while offering SO a 'good programme for agriculture' (Majda 2005). In the vote of confidence on 10 November, support for Marcinkiewicz's minority government came from PiS, SO, LPR and also the PSL.

Once the vote of confidence had taken place, the survival of PiS's minority government was not in doubt. That the other parties could agree an alternative candidate for prime minister (the constructive vote of no confidence) was improbable in the extreme, nor would the new president exercise his (limited) powers of dissolution without PiS's consent. There was a clear measure of programmatic agreement across the Sejm, including with PO, though not with the now-small SLD. Marcinkiewicz had also quickly proved a popular choice. So Jarosław Kaczyński's desperate search for a majority and his manoeuvring over the coming months remained somewhat puzzling, despite his palpable ambition, missionary zeal, winner-take-all approach to democracy, and record of aversion to compromise.

PiS did not have things all its own way however. In December 2005 it saw defeats on the government's version of the new-baby bonus and the timing of elections to replace Lech Kaczyński as Warsaw's president. To bring SO and LPR into line, Jarosław Kaczyński reactivated the threat of early elections. If the Sejm failed to pass the budget, the president could dissolve parliament. The matter proved complex because of technical constitutional issues centring on whether all legislation fell with the preceding Sejm or whether the budget constituted an exception. If the budget also fell, the final date for the president's signature would be later. But the threat of elections was effective, and the situation settled, if only briefly. On 1 February PiS, SO and LPR signed a 'stabilisation pact', reported by Radio Maryja and its television station Trwam with all other media excluded.

However, the announcement of the pact brought little respite. The agreement had listed 144 laws which all would support, and the parties voted together in the Sejm, but SO and LPR did not refrain from criticism of the government. LPR's Roman Giertych in particular proved a thorn in the government's side. Election excitement rose again in mid-March, with PiS demanding that the Sejm dissolve itself to permit early elections. The reasons remain obscure, though Jarosław Kaczyński continued to give the impression that he stood in the defence of a besieged fortress. In a speech to the Sejm on 17 February he noted the mobilisation of the *układ* for a counter-offensive: 'the mendacious elites [*łże-elita*] of the Third Republic have fallen into line [but] . . . We will fight the *układ*. We aim to destroy it . . . We will show it. We will also show its current defenders' (Kaczyński 2006a). In March Kaczyński told Radio Maryja that 'we have to deal the *układ* its final blow – electoral defeat'.[2] Instead, PiS's Political Council rescinded its decision of 2002 prohibiting a coalition with Lepper, and talks commenced between the two parties. On 27 April PiS signed a formal coalition agreement with SO and with a small splinter group from the League. The LPR then joined the coalition, giving the government a parliamentary majority. Lepper became a deputy prime minister and minister of agriculture; Giertych became deputy premier and minister of education. The new government was confirmed on 5 May.

Given its stress on cleansing the system, it was unsurprising that many saw PiS's alliance with SO (in particular) and LPR as a loss of the moral high ground, confirmed with the formal constitution of the coalition government. Both the stabilisation pact of February 2006 and the coalition agreement specified that convicted criminals should not serve in government. The coalition agreement stated that: 'Only honest and competent persons may hold public office. Those convicted of a criminal offence . . . or suspected of corruption or links with the criminal world will be excluded' (Koalicyjna 2006).

However, Lepper had a long history of confrontation with the law. He had been variously accused of planned assassination, assault, lies, extortion, tax evasion, public order offences and bribe taking; the procuracy had undertaken some hundred investigations of his past or current activities by the time of the 2001 election. He had a string of convictions, all with suspended sentences and fines, for slander, assault and violations of public order. During the course of the 2005 campaign Lepper was convicted of slandering fellow politicians from the tribune of the Sejm in 2001 (again, his prison sentence was suspended), and he was threatened with further charges by both PO and PiS for allegations made in a campaign cassette prepared for SO's candidates.[3] This latest conviction for slander was confirmed by the appellate court shortly after Lepper entered government. It made no difference. The new line was essentially that Lepper had been subjected to persecution for his political views. A number of SO deputies had also been found guilty of offences ranging from the falsification of election signatures to extortion and theft. Lepper had himself belonged to the communist party, and a number of former SLD deputies now belonged to SO, including its chief of staff, Janusz Maksymiuk. Only Grzegorz Tudorek, Lepper's candidate for minister of transport, proved too much for Kaczyński: not only did Tudorek have an SLD past but he was currently on trial for economic offences.[4]

The new allies did not make comfortable bedfellows. Yet Kaczyński's decision to ally with SO and LPR was explicable on grounds not just of political expediency but also of the programmatic consensus alluded to above. Jarosław Kaczyński had always taken an instrumental view of his own shifting political alliances. He was open about the new coalition: he did not want it, but the parliamentary arithmetic dictated it. President Lech Kaczyński obliged, noting that 'While Self-Defence was for many years regarded as a populist party, it evolved to become a suitable partner in government.'[5] The desire for power and the similarity of programmes made agreement relatively straightforward, though this did not rule out intra-governmental conflict.

PiS's election programme identified the main problems as poor privatisation decisions, high unemployment, shamefully high levels of deprivation, threatening demographic catastrophe, and a crisis of Polishness and patriotism. Lepper could have endorsed every word. There was little love of Poland's role in the European Union in PiS's manifesto. It claimed that the EU represented a national threat, both by encouraging outward migration and in its plans for a European super-state and a pan-European identity 'at the expense of national states and national identities' (PiS 2005). This was music to the ears of the nationalist LPR, which had similarly propagated the slogan of a Fourth Republic but was committed to withdrawal from the EU. The coalition agreement merely aimed to 'strengthen Poland's image in the international arena, especially in cooperation with the European Union', and to ensure the securing of EU funds.

The coalition required numerous personnel changes to satisfy the demands of the new partners, and Marcinkiewicz's position was clearly weakened. Foreign minister Stefan Meller was not a PiS man but he was appointed largely to reassure the international community (Paradowska 2006). However, he resigned after Lepper joined the government, to be replaced by the less reassuring Anna Fotyga, a long-standing friend of President Kaczyński with little obvious competence. Both junior parties exerted pressure for allocation of more posts. Lepper attempted to remove PiS nominees from the agricultural agencies; he also demanded a role in the 'power ministries', Interior and Defence, as well as a greater role in the provinces (*województwa*), positions in the media and more jobs in Treasury-controlled state enterprises (*spółki*) in order to 'protect the workers'.[6]

The appointment of Giertych as education minister was particularly controversial and led to fierce demonstrations by both teachers and pupils against his alleged incompetence and his specific proposals. Among Giertych's planned initiatives were the introduction of 'patriotic education', school uniforms, and a reduction in the number of authorised textbooks. He also dismissed the respected director of the Centre for Promoting Teaching Excellence (which Giertych wished to abolish) for allegedly authorising a textbook that 'fostered homosexuality'. The book in question had been promoted by the Council of Europe, and the director's dismissal prompted protests from the Helsinki Committee and the Secretary-General of the Council of Europe. Even PiS's own minister of internal affairs described Giertych as 'a difficult and risky partner' (Żakowski 2006).

Prime Minister Marcinkiewicz was clearly uncomfortable with his new colleagues. The budget was a particular bone of contention, with the minor parties presenting a huge shopping list of new expenditures. In government, PiS had become aware that the EU retained some leverage; this meant that the government needed to take the budget deficit seriously. The coalition partners were not the only source of strain, however. In June Minister of Finance Zyta Gilowska, formerly of PO but (like Meller) triumphantly recruited to the government as a calling card for the outside world, threatened to resign over differences with the president on proposed tax changes. Instead, on 23 June Marcinkiewicz dismissed Gilowska over allegations (later rejected by the Lustration Court) that she had cooperated with the communist-era security services. This was Marcinkiewicz's 'greatest crisis' (Gauden *et al.* 2006), and Jarosław Kaczyński criticised the dismissal as over-hasty. Trouble with the Kaczyńskis had been brewing for some time. Marcinkiewicz had no independent political base and he was not a member of PiS's inner circle. He was personally popular, but support for his government had been ebbing. He had made a number of appointments without consulting Jarosław Kaczyński – including Gilowska's replacement at Finance. Kaczyński was also reportedly furious about an alleged meeting between Marcinkiewicz and PO leader Donald Tusk. Rumours began to circulate about his departure and, indeed, on 7 July PiS's Political Council unanimously recommended Jarosław Kaczyński as the new prime minister. Kaczyński received a vote of confidence on 19 July.

Kaczyński's new government proved short-lived, however, and again called into question the wisdom of a coalition with capricious partners. Major legislation for the establishment of the Anti-Corruption Bureau and the abolition of the Military Intelligence Services (WSI) would have passed anyway (all save the SLD voted in favour). Persistent intra-coalition disputes were highly visible, and Lepper constantly threatened to withdraw from the government. Both junior partners wanted a fundamental revamping of the proposed 2007 budget, including vastly increased social expenditure and higher pay for health workers and teachers. LPR was angry at the appointment of Antoni Macierewicz as the 'liquidator' of the Military Intelligence Services. Macierewicz himself caused a political storm by asserting (but later withdrawing the claim) that most Polish foreign ministers since 1989 had been agents of the Soviet security services.[7] SO demanded a parliamentary debate on the Polish presence in Afghanistan and Iraq. In September, Lepper was still dragging his feet over the proposal for his party to join the other coalition partners in combining their votes so that they counted together in the apportionment of seats. This was now enabled by the new system of *apparentement*[8] introduced by the three parties in a new electoral law for local government elections in November.

Kaczyński's government lasted only two months. On 21 September 2006 Kaczyński restored Gilowska to the government and ejected Lepper. The government, he said, could no longer tolerate Lepper's dissension and loutish behaviour. Elections looked a distinct possibility – indeed Lepper had begun discussions with Tusk on the prospects of PO's proposed vote to dissolve the Sejm (Subotić and Śmiłowicz 2006). On 24 September the government announced a vote of confidence; if not forthcoming, it would support a motion for the Sejm to dissolve itself. PiS, said Kaczyński, was not afraid of November elections. It was 'no accident' that opposition was mounting just as decisive decisions were being taken for the Fourth Republic. 'Poland', responded Tusk, 'cannot afford another twelve months of quarrels, conflicts, aggression, price rises, and the compromising of our authorities at home and abroad.'[9] Even church hierarchs gave voice to their unease. The Metropolitan of Kraków said, 'the Nation does not deserve such treatment ... The Nation wants to respect its parliament and its parliamentarians, its politicians and its government.' The Bishop of Tarnów said, 'After the elections citizens got chaos and conflict instead of stability. Politicians, that is not the way!'[10]

In fact, Kaczyński may have miscalculated, believing that he could win a vote of confidence without Lepper, but with the support of disaffected SO deputies[11] and perhaps with the PSL. Certainly PiS began an intensive trawl for support, and it is likely, as Lepper claimed, that various inducements were proffered to change sides (Murawski 2006). PO also accused Kaczyński of 'buying votes' wherever he could – from PO as well as SO.[12] That there was truth to the allegations was confirmed with the revelation by the private television station TVN of the 'Beger tapes', secretly filmed conversations of SO's Renata Beger with representatives of PiS.[13] The emissaries made encouraging noises in response to Beger's conditions for joining PiS, including a job in the Ministry of Agriculture, first place on the party list, and help in resolving her legal problems, associated with the suspended sentence she had received for falsifying signatures for the 2001 election.

The tapes evoked a strong reaction and an equally strong counter-offensive from PiS. Prime Minister Kaczyński spoke on evening television, stating that:

> 2006 is the best year of the last seventeen. We have reason to be proud . . . But these changes create anxiety for those who . . . form the 'gray network' of formal and informal circles that hitherto . . . have decided Polish affairs. These people, these circles, are losing . . . Today they are on the counter-attack.
>
> Law and Justice is conducting discussions with deputies . . . concerning support for our government; support for change. And one of these conversations was exploited as a provocation. It was conducted in a normal way, concerning matters that are commonly discussed in the course of such negotiations. Calling these discussions corruption is a lie. It is hypocrisy. Those who say this know perfectly well that they are not speaking the truth. They want to cause a political crisis. They want to restore to Poland the authority of the *układ*. We will not permit it.
>
> (Kaczyński 2006b)

Kaczyński implicated PO directly in the 'defence of the *układ*'. He suggested that the unpublished report on the Military Intelligence Services would show why 'for that alone it was worth forming the coalition'. Moreover, when the National Bank got its new chair he suggested, 'everything will come out in the open' (Subotić and Lisicki 2006). Speaking to a PiS demonstration at the Gdańsk shipyard a few days later he accused his opponents of standing 'where ZOMO stood' in 1980.[14]

The tapes put Jarosław Kaczyński in a difficult position. PO was leading in the opinion polls, and in some polls the margin of its lead over PiS was increasing.[15] Hopes of treating with dissident SO deputies faded as the exodus from Self-Defence halted, while the PSL ceased its own formal negotiations. But events moved quickly. On 6 October Lepper and Giertych mooted the reconstitution of the coalition. When the Sejm met on 12 October, the speaker postponed the session and with it the vote on dissolution. Lepper returned to government as deputy prime minister and minister of agriculture on 16 October. The three parties alone did not have a majority, but the government retained the support (with some jobs) of the dissident fraction, the National People's Movement (RL-N, *Ruch Ludowo-Narodowy*, later the RLCh, People's Christian Movement), former LPR deputies and now also some from SO. This new–old coalition successfully defeated the proposal to dissolve the Sejm. A new–old coalition agreement added mechanisms to smooth the process of relations within the government; it did not differ much from that agreed in May – the idea of an 'economical [*tanie*] state' had disappeared. The parties also agreed to 'block' their votes for the local government elections on 12 November. If the *apparentement* system worked effectively, success would add local strongholds to PiS's already substantial control of the levers of power.

Despite the extraordinary confusion of the situation in parliament after October 2005, PiS took over virtually all key levers of power, with some sops to its junior partners. Within a few months it had secured the speakership of the Sejm, the ombudsman, and the head of the IPN. From March 2007 the IPN was responsible for confirming the veracity of thousands of new lustration affidavits. PiS also increased the size of central government itself by at least seventy-five new jobs (Gnacikowska 2006). It effectively secured the National Broadcasting Council and increased its supporters in the National Judicial Council. Its appointees moved into provincial government, the management boards of state enterprises and state radio and television, and new or reconstituted government agencies. It destroyed the Military Intelligence Services (WSI) and began the construction of a new intelligence system. LPR and SO exacted a high price – a greater presence in the broadcasting media and budgetary concessions – for their support of PiS's nominee as the new chair of the Polish National Bank. How far the politicians could influence the Constitutional Tribunal remained an open question, but they openly toyed with altering its composition after an unfavourable judgment in March 2007. The new chair of the Constitutional Tribunal had once been associated with PiS. PiS, SO and LPR also nominated members of the Tribunal; SO's and LPR's nominees were not well received by the legal establishment.

Implications for party development

The turbulence of political developments after the 2005 elections signalled a significant change in inter-party relations but augured no better for the development of a stable configuration of political parties. In the new post-2005 context described above, even the lines of competition were blurred. The main division was that between PiS and PO. The government–opposition divide separated PiS, SO and the LPR – along with disaffected elements of the latter two parties in the small RL-N (later RLCh) – from PO, the SLD and the PSL. Clearly neither fault line represented the clear left–right division of 'standard' West European politics. PiS, LPR and PO were self-styled parties of the 'right'. The SLD was striving to rejuvenate its identity as a party of the 'left'. PO, like other 'Solidarity' parties before it, was fearful of any alliance with the SLD. SO had also described itself as a left-wing party in the election campaign of 2005, though observers more often regarded it as 'populist'. The PSL remained essentially a class party of the peasantry, challenged in its rural heartland by the electoral success of SO. It was programmatically closer to the government in many respects, but it was too small to replace SO as a coalition partner, and too vulnerable to join a government in which SO 'owned' the ministry of agriculture.

PiS, as befitted its governing status, was the axis around which all others spun. PiS's own strategy was three-pronged: first, to maximise its parliamentary support by bargaining with any party except the SLD to secure itself key posts; second, to undermine and possibly engender a split in PO, its chief competitor; and third, to engulf and ingest the LPR and possibly SO too. We have seen above the success of the first arm of the strategy. The second failed (at least to spring 2007), and the third saw at least some short-term success.

The conflict between PO and PiS poisoned the political atmosphere. Tensions between PO and PiS had surfaced from time to time in the pre-election period, but they had become bitter in the course of the 2005 election campaign. The near-destruction of the once powerful SLD provided fertile conditions for a new 'war at the top' between PiS and PO. The decline of the SLD from 2003 onward had not been unprecedented; governments traditionally lost power with successive elections. But Leszek Miller's arrogance and myopia as the SLD descended into a quagmire of perceived corruption and incompetence, which destroyed public confidence and split the party, provided an opening which PiS readily acknowledged.

The withdrawal of the left-wing candidate Włodzimierz Cimoszewicz in the 2005 presidential election campaign had left the way open for a battle between PO's candidate Donald Tusk and PiS's Lech Kaczyński. With the left no longer a credible threat (Marek Borowski and the new Polish Social Democracy party SdPl lacked support and had few resources), PiS reoriented its campaign to attract the left-wing vote, stressing state intervention in the economy, greater welfare spending, and focusing on the problem of unemployment. PiS presented a stark choice between PO's 'liberal Poland', serving the rich with its flat-tax proposals, and its own 'social' or 'solidary' Poland. Lech Kaczyński condemned PO's advocacy of a 'liberal experiment' that would cause the 'hierarchisation and oligarchisation' of society and aid the emergence of 'conservative and populist dictatorship'. He argued that Cimoszewicz's resignation now made disputes over the legacy of communism 'of lesser currency' (*mniej aktualnej*).[16] Personal attacks increased, and tension escalated when a PiS spokesman claimed (falsely) that Tusk's grandfather had volunteered for the Wehrmacht in the Second World War.

Tusk came first in the first round of the presidential ballot, but he had few sources of additional votes for the second round against Lech Kaczyński. SO and the PSL endorsed Kaczyński, who continued his strong attacks on the evils of liberalism. Tusk in turn stressed the 'socialism' of his opponent. Kaczyński won by a clear margin, and PiS gained the prize it had most coveted. PiS had the upper hand in coalition negotiations with PO, but it did not play its cards well. Jarosław Kaczyński's approach was winner-takes-all, and he made no concessions to PO's sense of shock and betrayal as he denied them the speakership of the Sejm and took a firm grip on the power ministries. Personal animosities also played a role, with a lack of mutual trust and PO's anxiety that the Kaczyńskis would not hesitate to use them as a whipping boy for economic failure. Despite a rhetorical commitment to seeking a coalition, Kaczyński had room for manoeuvre, with SO, LPR and the PSL securing Marcinkiewicz's vote of confidence.

The manner in which PiS used government patronage to buttress its own position and to secure support from SO and LPR further undermined any residual hopes of a coalition with PO, which effectively died at the end of January 2006. Kaczyński appeared for a time to woo Jan Rokita, and Rokita's failure to maintain party discipline caused the leadership some headaches; yet there seemed little immediate likelihood that PO would split. It led solidly in the opinion polls and did well in local government elections, with a surprisingly successful 'blocking' arrangement with the PSL and a sound performance in the large cities, especially Warsaw. However, rumours persisted that Rokita would depart and try to set up a new political party of the centre-right, and there were evident tensions between PO's more 'liberal' and more 'traditionalist' elements.

Jarosław Kaczyński's response to criticism of the new alliance was to take the offensive, and he introduced a new variation on his major theme: PO could not be trusted, for it was sympathetic to, or even itself part of, the *układ*. Giving Jan Rokita the Ministry of the Interior, for example, would be 'essentially granting absolution for all political offences in recent times' (Paradowska 2005). For the Kaczyńskis it was also clear that coalition failure was the fault solely of PO, and this was the general party line. PO took rather longer to mobilise itself for the offensive, yet over the course of the year the politics of naked animosity came to dominate. For PO, PiS was a threat to democracy and the 'guarantees of freedom secured by the independent institutions built with such difficulty' (Tusk 2006). For PiS, PO was an agent of the *układ*.

PiS's attacks on PO continued after the (temporary) break-up of the coalition in September 2006 with selective leaking of documents from 'Colonel Lesiak's cupboard' (Cieśla and Wójcik 2006; Marszałek 2006a, 2006b, 2006c), purporting to suggest that as head of the Prime Minister's Office in 1992–93 Jan Rokita (and others) had been complicit in the 'surveillance of the right'. Kaczyński was a master of the diversionary tactic, although he had long maintained that the security services had plotted to destabilise the right wing after the fall of the Olszewski government in 1992. The matter was revived in 1997 when the then head of the UOP acknowledged that 'interesting documents' had been found in the office of Lesiak, a functionary of the UOP and before that of the former communist security services, the SB (*Służba Bezpieczeństwa*). These were alleged to confirm that in 1993 a plan had operated to divide and compromise activists of a number of small right-wing parties (and the left-wing Polish Socialist Party, PPS), including Kaczyński's first political party, the *Porozumienie Centrum* (Centre Accord, PC), through surveillance and the infiltration of secret agents. On 10 October Jarosław Kaczyński demanded that Rokita 'leave politics now and forever' for grave crimes against democracy.[17] Tusk spent seven minutes at the Presidential Palace, with 'consultations' cut short, he said, because of the president's 'highly emotional state'.[18] Colonel Lesiak was not convicted, and the evidence of a plot to undermine the right was as thin as before. In similar vein, Kaczyński's promises of startling revelations from the WSI report and the secrets of the National Bank failed to confirm the existence of the all-powerful *układ*.

It is tempting to resort to psychological explanations of this furious confrontation, likened to 'stags with their horns locked together, preferring to fall rather than yield in the struggle', whose battle risked the demolition of the state itself (Ziemkiewicz 2006). Certainly a number of sociologists noted the profound differences in the perceptions of reality proffered by PiS on the one hand and PO on the other (Wnuk-Lipiński 2006; Wódz 2006). Jarosław Kaczyński's views of post-communist developments had not altered greatly over the years, no matter how little evidence sustained the notion of an all-embracing *układ* (Kaczyński 1991: 87–8; Torańska 1994: 90–169). Kaczyński was always prone to conspiracy theories and to hyperbolic rhetoric. Colonel Lesiak's cupboard contained no surprises. Kaczyński's dark insinuations about the Military Intelligence Services promised a bombshell, but the report's revelations of treachery and criminality were tendentious and poorly evidenced. Nor could one have imagined from the report that the Kaczyński twins were high-ranking officials in Lech Wałęsa's presidential chancellery when the WSI was first created. However, as noted above, this was also a political battle over much shared common ideological and programmatic ground. Indeed, analysts of the weekly *Polityka* characterised PO as frightened to develop its own defence of past achievements and a clear vision of the future of Poland and Europe; in sum PO offered little more than being 'not-PiS' (Janicki and Władyka 2006).

The stakes were indeed high. Jarosław Kaczyński made no secret of his ambition to colonise the entire right wing of the political spectrum. In the early 1990s he had aspired to emulate the German Christian Democrats. More recently his model had become Fidesz, which had gradually embraced the whole of the Hungarian centre-right to become a key actor in an (essentially) two-party system. PiS moved first to increase its hold on the conservative Christian electorate. In the break-up of AWS, which had formed the core of the government from 1997 to 2001, PiS had already attracted major elements of the Christian National Union (ZChN). Its initial election strategy in 2005 concentrated on its commitment to traditional Christian values, as well as its patriotism and moral renewal through decommunisation and 'deep lustration'. The fundamentalist Catholic Radio Maryja (RM), with a huge following extending beyond the 'mohair berets' of its elderly devotees, favoured PiS, and following the election PiS politicians advertised their close links to RM's patron, Father Rydzyk.

The LPR was the first to feel the bandwagon effects of PiS's electoral victory. PiS began to attract members from the LPR, including local councillors. Internal ructions also contributed to the LPR's decline. Roman Giertych's authoritarian style and perceived electoral failure provoked defections early in the new parliament, followed by divisions within the small group of LPR MEPs. Giertych's initial reluctance to consider a coalition with PiS further divided the party, as did the subsequent adherence to the stabilisation pact. In

March 2006 several deputies appealed to the forthcoming party congress to resign from the pact: 'The government has showed itself to be the continuation of previous cabinets emerging from the Round Table elites . . . continuing our support can lead only to marginalisation.'[19]

By the spring the RM media had begun openly to attack Giertych and the LPR, and from April 2006 LPR was consistently registering no more than 2 or 3 per cent in the polls and had lost six of its thirty-four deputies. Giertych's move from 'zero radicalism' to renewed radicalism – including a proposed constitutional amendment to embrace the right to life 'from conception', gathering signatures for the restoration of capital punishment, strong attacks on 'gay propaganda' in schools, and a new programme of 'patriotic education' – did little to stem the tide. After January 2007, however, the LPR regained some credibility with Radio Maryja in supporting the cause of the conservative Archbishop Wielgus, forced to resign as Metropolitan of Warsaw after lying to the Church authorities about his record of collaboration with the communist security services. The Kaczyńskis had taken the unprecedented step of intervening with the Vatican to prevent Wielgus's promotion. In March RM bitterly attacked the president's wife, Maria Kaczyńska, for signing a petition against changing the constitutional wording of the right to life.

SO's electorate was more attuned to economic issues than that of LPR. However, as with other parties, compared with 2001 their support was highly volatile (Markowski 2006: 829–30). PiS's social welfare emphasis and its penchant for conspiracy theories seemed well suited to attract SO voters, who were the least educated of all, if also rather secular (Markowski 2006: 824, 828). Indeed, PiS also made special efforts to attract the rural electorate. SO's support fell after the election, already indicating voters' willingness to move elsewhere. Moreover, as with LPR, there were some signs within the party structures that SO members preferred to move to a more successful party. This is one reason why Lepper was so eager to enter government. Lepper certainly expressed his anger over PiS's poaching of his activists, as well as the willingness of his dissidents to negotiate separately with Kaczyński. But SO had always been marked by conflict. In the 2001 Sejm it had lost 40 per cent of its deputies. In the first year of the 2005 Sejm it lost nine deputies (16 per cent). Lepper appeared strengthened after his return to government in October 2006, but he could easily overplay his hand. SO looked more secure than the LPR, but its survival could not be guaranteed.

Finally, we need to comment briefly on the SLD. The SLD won 11.3 per cent of the vote in 2005, just behind SO, with fifty-five seats. Its role in the new parliament verged on irrelevance, and it received little media attention. Although the SLD was PiS's most consistent parliamentary opponent, PO proved reluctant to fuel PiS's attacks by making common cause with the ex-communists. Despite the wounds generated by its split, the SLD recognised the folly of a divided left and made approaches to Borowski's splinter, Polish Social Democracy (*Socjaldemokracja Polska*, SdPl), which had won 3.9 per cent of the vote in 2005. A united front, embracing SLD and SdPl along with the Labour Union (in electoral alliance with the SLD in 2001 and the SdPl in 2005) and remnants of the Democratic Union, now the Democrats (*Demokraci.pl*), stood as 'the Left and the Democrats' (*Lewica i Demokraci*, LiD) in the local elections in November. They came a creditable third. However, in the short term their prospects were not good. PO was mopping up the anti-PiS vote, maintaining levels of some 30 per cent in the first months of 2007 (CBOS 2007a, 2007b, 2007c). PiS failed to offer convincing evidence of the *układ*, and PO gained from PiS's unholy coalition alliance. In the longer term one must be more sanguine about the reconstitution of a centre-left force. Religious issues came to the fore once again with issues of lustration in the Church, the right to life, and attacks on homosexuals. In parliament only the SLD spoke for secular voters. At the same time most Polish voters remained 'left' on economic policy matters, including welfare. If many left voters moved to PiS, there remained ample scope for disillusionment and a move away again. However, the excellent economic results, due in no small measure to membership of the European Union, also offered a cushion against public reaction. The peculiar nature of Polish politics meant the disappearance of the centre from the menu of political offerings. But it is hard to see the centrist voter as having disappeared.

Conclusion

Political developments in Poland after the 2005 elections were turbulent. Though politics had been contentious after 1989, with frequent changes of government and highly inflammatory rhetoric, the period after 2005 was an exceptional period, dominated by confrontation between PiS and PO. Both parties claimed their origins in the Solidarity movement of the 1980s, and both regarded themselves as parties of the right. History had maintained a strong grip on Polish politics after 1989, when Solidarity parties and former communists alternated in power. This was also the plan for the dominant parties after 2005: a new Solidarity coalition of *Platforma* and PiS against the remnants of SLD. Instead, the consequences of the 2005 election led to a breaking of the mould, with PiS reaching accommodation with non-Solidarity nationalist and populist forces in order to secure its project of a new Fourth Republic. PO constituted the major force of opposition, despite a clear overlap of programme and perspective with PiS. However, the role of history in shaping Polish politics did not disappear, as history became the instrument of political struggle.

The battle between PO and PiS represented a new 'war at the top' within the Solidarity movement. We have not reviewed the historical roots of this dispute, nor the nature of Solidarity's first 'war at the top', but in many respects this war was not new at all but a continuation of earlier battles, notably in 1990–93. This was the period when Jarosław Kaczyński first articulated his view of the system or *układ* of ex-communists and liberals dominating the transformation process with the aid of the still-communist security services. According to this view, the history of post-communist Poland was the history of the *układ*. The *układ* caused and explained the dysfunctions of Poland's political, social and economic development. Kaczyński's discourse saw PO transmogrified from a worthy partner in government to the embodiment of the *układ* itself.

The contest between PO and PiS arose from the failure of the SLD governments of 2001–05 and the resulting reconfiguration of political parties. SLD weakness removed any serious threat from the left and enabled PiS to concentrate its attention on its major rival, PO. The remaining parties in parliament, SO, the LPR and the PSL, were eager for power and vulnerable to PiS's periodic threats of premature parliamentary elections. PiS, SO and LPR concluded their stability pact and then a formal coalition. PSL remained outside, mainly owing to its own political conflicts with SO. However, relations within the new PiS–SO–LPR government were troubled. Kaczyński assumed the premiership in July, but as he pursued a strategy of colonising the smaller parties he failed to stem the conflicts and later to rejig the coalition. The LPR and PSL looked threatened with political extinction from the national stage. Although PiS and PO dominated, there seemed no long-term prospects for a stabilisation of the party system around the two giants of the right. Both parties retained clear internal divisions stemming from their origins. In the case of PiS this was reflected in the continuing central role played by early activists of Kaczyński's first party, the PC, after 1990 and the subordinate role of the Christian National/Right Alliance wings. In the case of PO, in its baldest form it represented tensions between Tusk's liberals and Rokita's conservatives.

How far can we go beyond the particular features of a country to explain its politics? Political turmoil in the period under discussion was not limited exclusively to Poland. Following EU accession there were changes of government in the Czech Republic and Hungary. Subsequent elections saw political paralysis in the Czech Republic and the emergence of a left–populist –nationalist coalition in Slovakia not dissimilar to that in Poland. In Hungary the explosion of protest and violence in the autumn of 2006, following revelations that the prime minister had consistently lied about the economy, was unprecedented. Sobell has linked these developments as 'a letting out of long-repressed steam, held back by the need to comply with the demands of EU accession' (Sobell 2006: 2). Now, at last, elites could be disobedient to the demands and norms of EU behaviour. They could also complete their unfinished 'transition business' of addressing inequalities, redressing social imbalances and completing structural reform.

However, the idea of an 'anti-EU malaise' is not altogether convincing. The European Union played little role in Central European elections (save perhaps in Slovakia in 1998). Poland, Slovakia and the Czech Republic all reaped immediate economic benefits from the inflow of funds that followed accession. In April 2006 a CBOS poll found that 80 per cent of Poles were supporters of the European Union (CBOS 2006). It may well be that, for elites, meeting the convergence criteria seemed less pressing than had the requirements for accession itself. A number of parties, including Fidesz in Hungary, the Civic Democrats in the Czech Republic and also PiS, never hesitated to wheel out a Euro-sceptic stance when it seemed opportune; but one does not gain preferred policies in the EU by being obstructive or difficult. Even Jarosław Kaczyński felt forced to reprimand Roman Giertych for advocating the aim of a European-wide 'right to life from conception' in a European forum (though neither appeared to realise that abortion was not a matter for the EU).

The problem of 'transition' is a persuasive theme, though it is not a new one. Voters in Central Europe have long given their votes to parties promising to ease the pain of transition. One problem in Hungary was the competitive upward bidding in the auction of election promises by both Fidesz and the Socialist Party, whose socio-economic programmes became harder and harder to distinguish. In Poland in 2005 PiS most successfully appropriated the welfare mantle of the discredited social democrats. The fundamental dilemmas of politics and the parties did not change in the fifteen years following transition: how could politicians serve both the demands of capitalist development and the needs of their citizens? How could the winners be encouraged and the losers protected?

Notes

1 The exception was OBOP in *Gazeta Wyborcza*, 22 September 2005. The Centre for Researching Public Opinion (OBOP) and GfK Polonia polls were regularly reported in *Rzeczpospolita*. For a summary table of the Centre for Public Opinion Research (CBOS) surveys of party preferences in 2004–05 see 'Preferencje partyjne na tydzień przed wyborami', *Komunikat z badań* BS/150/2005, September 2005, Warsaw: CBOS.
2 *Rzeczpospolita*, 17 March 2006.
3 *Rzeczpospolita*, 23 July 2005.
4 *Rzeczpospolita*, 26 April 2006.
5 *Rzeczpospolita*, 2 May 2005.
6 *Rzeczpospolita*, 22 June 2006.
7 *Rzeczpospolita*, 23 August 2006.
8 This is an arrangement permitting two or more party lists to be joined (in Poland 'blocked'). The parties appear on the ballot as separate entities, but votes given for each are combined in the allocation of seats.
9 *Rzeczpospolita*, 25 September 2006.
10 *Rzeczpospolita*, 25 September 2006.
11 See *Rzeczpospolita*, 23–24 September 2006.
12 *Rzeczpospolita*, 25 September 2006.
13 Extracts from the taped conversations were broadcast on the programme *Teraz My* on TVN, 28 September 2006. They were also made available on the internet through the *Gazeta Wyborcza* website.
14 *Rzeczpospolita*, 2 October 2006. ZOMO was the motorised division of the communist police (*Milicja Obywatelska*) and a potent symbol of communist repression.
15 GfK Polonia on 29 September found 36 per cent supporting PO and 20 per cent

supporting PiS. Fifty-nine per cent of respondents favoured early elections following the *Teraz My* tapes; *Rzeczpospolita*, 2 October 2006.
16 *Gazeta Wyborcza*, 20 September 2005.
17 *Rzeczpospolita*, 10 October 2006; see also Lisecki and Magierowski (2006).
18 *Rzeczpospolita*, 11 October 2006.
19 *Rzeczpospolita*, 8 March 2006.

References

Bakke, E. and Sitter, N. (2005) 'Patterns of stability: party competition and strategy in Central Europe since 1989', *Party Politics* 11(2): 243–63.
CBOS (2006) 'Bilans dwóch lat członkostwa w Unii Europejskiej', *Komunikat z badań* BS/76/2006, April, Warsaw: CBOS.
CBOS (2007a) 'Preferencje partyjne w styczniu', *Komunikat z Badań* BS/6/2007, January, Warsaw: CBOS.
CBOS (2007b), 'Preferencje partyjne w lutym', *Komunikat z Badań* BS/23/2007, February, Warsaw: CBOS.
CBOS (2007c), 'Preferencje partyjne w marcu', *Komunikat z Badań* BS/42/2007, March, Warsaw: CBOS.
Cieśla, W. and Wójcik, K. (2006) 'Inwigilacja prawicy: Czy na odnalezionym dokumencie widnieje podpis b. szefa kontrwywiadu?', *Rzeczpospolita*, 18 October.
Gauden, G., Subotić, M. and Śmiłowicz, P. (2006) 'To był największy kryzys', Interview with Kazimierz Marcinkiewicz, *Rzeczpospolita*, 26 June.
Gnacikowska, W. (2006) 'Tanie pastwo PiS'u: 75 nowych etatów w rządzie', *Gazeta Wyborcza*, 3 March.
Hofferbert, R. (1998) 'Introduction: party structure and party performance in new and old democracies', in R. Hofferbert (ed.), *Parties and democracy: party structure and party performance in old and new democracies*, Oxford: Blackwell, pp. 1–9.
Janicki, M. and Władyka, W. (2006) 'Partia Nie-Pis', *Polityka*, no. 43, 28 October.
Kaczyński, J. (1991) *Odwrotna strona medalu*, Warsaw: Most.
Kaczyński, J. (2005) 'Wstęp', in PiS, *Program 2005: IV Rzeczpospolita – Sprawiedliwość dla Wszystkich*, Warsaw: PiS, pp. 7–13.
Kaczyński, J. (2006a) Speech to the Sejm, from the live transmission of the Sejm's proceedings, 5th session, 10th sitting, 17 February, http://www.sejm.gov.pl (accessed 29 September 2006).
Kaczyński, J. (2006b) 'Orędzie premiera Jarosława Kaczyńskiego', 28 September, http://www.rzeczpospolita.pl/gazeta/wydanie_060928/kraj/kraj_a_16.html (accessed 29 September 2006).
Koalicyjna (2006) *Koalicyjna Deklaracja Programowa 'Solidarne Państwo'*, http://www.kprm.gov.pl (accessed 27 May 2006).
Lisecki, P. and Magierowski, M. (2006) 'Zbrodnia na polskiej demokracji', Interview with Lech Kaczyński, *Rzeczpospolita*, 13 October.
Majda, A. (2005) 'Powiedzieli "Rz": Roman Giertych, przewodniczący klubu parlamentarnego LPR', Interview with Roman Giertych, *Rzeczpospolita*, 9 November.
Markowski, R. (2006) 'The Polish elections of 2005: pure chaos or a restructuring of the party system?', *West European Politics*, 29(4): 814–32.
Marszałek, A. (2006a) 'Inwigilacja prawicy', *Rzeczpospolita*, 9 October.
Marszałek, A. (2006b) 'Dokumenty PAP', *Rzeczpospolita*, 9 October.

Marszałek, A. (2006c) 'Kto zlecał tajne operacje pułkownikowi Lesiakowi?', *Rzeczpospolita*, 13 October.

Millard, F. (2006) 'Poland's politics and the travails of transition after 2001: The 2005 elections', *Europe–Asia Studies*, 58(7): 1007–31.

Murawski, J. (2006) 'Usuną nas wszystkich', Interview with Andrzej Lepper, *Rzeczpospolita*, 23–24 September.

Paradowska, J. (2005) 'Sam PiS czy SAMPiS?', *Polityka*, no. 44, 5 November.

Paradowska, J. (2006) 'Moze być pięknie', Interview with Jarosław Kaczyński, *Polityka*, no. 2, 14 January.

PiS (2005) *Program 2005: IV Rzeczpospolita – Sprawiedliwość dla Wszystkich*, Warsaw: PiS.

Sartori, G. (1976) *Parties and party systems: a framework for analysis*, Cambridge: Cambridge University Press.

Sobell, V. (2006) *Central Europe unhinged*, 2 October, Hong Kong: Daiwa Institute of Research.

Subotić, M. and Lisicki, P. (2006) 'Możemy podjąć taką decyzję, żeby władzy nie stracić', Interview with Jarosław Kaczyński, *Rzeczpospolita*, 29 September.

Subotić, M. and Śmiłowicz, P. (2006) 'Premier Kaczyński wyrzuca Andrzeja Leppera z rządu', *Rzeczpospolita*, 22 September.

Torańska, T. (1994), *My*, Warsaw: Most.

Tusk, D. (2006) Speech to the Sejm, 5th session, 13th sitting, 14 March, http://www.sejm.gov.pl (accessed 18 March 2006).

Wnuk-Lipiński, E. (2006) 'W sieci układu', *Rzeczpospolita*, 22–23 April.

Wódz, J. (2006) 'Otwarta droga dla mocnego człowieka', *Rzeczpospolita*, 25 July.

Żakowski, J. (2006) 'Pies przewodnik', Interview with Ludwik Dorn', *Polityka*, no. 20, 20 May.

Ziemkiewicz, R. (2006) 'Bijatyka, która demoluje państwo', *Rzeczpospolita*, 10 October.

6   Polish experiences with European policy coordination 1991–2006

Jowanka Jakubek

The problems of European policy coordination are familiar to all member states of the European Union (EU), but states differ in the extent to which policy coordination influences their role in EU institutions and their participation in European policy making. The difficulties for new member states such as Poland are particularly challenging but seem to confirm in general that the capacity of a member state to coordinate European policy also affects its influence on EU policy making. Adapting the Polish political system to the EU framework has given the Polish authorities a considerable number of problems, and institutional developments have contributed to a constant process of reinvention in Polish politics, both in terms of coordinating European activities in the pre-accession period and also later in dealing with the struggle to implement the *acquis communautaire* and become an EU member. The expectations from the European Union's side did not end with accession, and the amount of work required from the Polish government seems to be increasing. The authorities are therefore facing new challenges of engaging in the European decision-making processes and becoming an effective player in the now twenty-seven-member team.

The different quality and magnitude of European challenges in the unprecedented enlargement of 2004 have shaped a distinctive pattern of integration and Europeanisation. The building of relations with the EU was based on a strong conditionality, with a clear incentive structure and an extended period of step-by-step gradual adaptation. After the formulation of the Copenhagen criteria,[1] the candidate countries were also monitored on the extent to which they were coping with the EU's expectations. This visible power asymmetry, with the incentives present on one side and requirements posed on the other, contributed to the emergence of a relatively strong and centralised core executive, responsible for the coordination of European affairs in the pre-accession period. Owing to the necessary speed of the adaptation process and the wish on the EU side to negotiate with only a few empowered actors, it seemed necessary to impose a hierarchical, centralised and top-down dynamic to the accession process. With the strictly limited scope of bargaining, 'impositional Europeanisation' and the pressure to adopt all the *acquis* before entry, the attention of domestic actors was concentrated on the capacity to implement EU law and practice. After the accession, there was a qualitative change in relations with the EU, and new challenges emerged – of effective participation in decision making and of exercising influence in the new partnership framework. After Poland became a member of the EU the main task shifted from the administrative field to the political space. Different possibilities for action increased the role of ministers and expert officials, and also the role of parliament. Thus, the mechanisms of European policy coordination can be perceived as elements of a power game in which different actors try to dominate in different ways.

For Poland, EU membership has been clearly positive in economic terms, and it is difficult to find any area that has been harmed by entering the EU. In the catalogue of areas affected by membership there are many that are important to the government, including: policy making; legislation; the application of EU law by the domestic courts and administration; the direct application and enforcement of EU regulations by inspections and control-ling bodies; and technical support for participation by providing experts, translators and interpreters. This chapter aims to provide an overview of the Polish institutional setting of European policy coordination in the pre-accession and post-accession periods and to evaluate the latest developments and reform proposals. It examines the problems of European policy coordin-ation and the main institutional actors and their roles, first in the pre-accession process and then in the post-accession period. In the final part an attempt is made to evaluate the activities of the Polish government in the EU and to draw some conclusions on the possible directions for policy development.

Pre-accession problems with European policy coordination

The development of mechanisms of European policy coordination in Poland began in the early 1990s as early post-communist governments adopted the target of joining the European Union. In the pre-accession period the issue of compliance with EU requirements was of paramount importance. The authorities were under pressure from both European and domestic institu-tions to fulfil the requirements, resulting both from a strong willingness in Poland to join the EU and from the intrusive character of EU requirements themselves. The types of EU influence were diverse, including gate-keeping (in relation to access to negotiations and the establishment of successive stages of negotiations); benchmarking and monitoring; the imposition of legislative and institutional templates; and aid and technical assistance and advice (Grabbe 2003a, 2003b). The logic of conditionality was to provide strong external incentives for the government to comply with EU require-ments in two different aspects: democratic conditionality (criteria concerning democratisation) and *acquis* conditionality (criteria concerning adoption of EU law and practice) (Schimmelfennig and Sedelmeier 2004). The external pressures coming from the EU were accompanied by constraints at the national level and the existing constellation of actors and their networks. Not only the legal aspects of the preparation for membership but also a whole range of behavioural and sociological factors contributed to the setting up of the procedures for coordination of Poland's adaptation to EU requirements. The impact of changes in the core executive on the degree of compliance was visible from the early stages. Subsequently, the patterns of adjustment developed at different rates: at a relatively low rate in 1997–99, with an upward shift in 2000; then at a lower rate in 2001 and back to a high level in 2002 (Zubek 2005).

In the pre-accession period the government experienced many difficulties in adapting to EU requirements, the weak position of the European affairs minister being one of them. Another problem was the rather belated introduction of a system of rewards and sanctions for the ministers, as well as insufficient supervision and monitoring of progress, especially in the beginning of the process.[2] However, once the supervision process had been established, that resulted in ministers paying more attention to more urgent and pressing tasks, such as the four major domestic reforms that were implemented in the late 1990s: the reforms of the health system, education, administration and pensions. Officials complained about inadequate guidance in terms of the specification of the problems to be addressed by Polish legislation, as well as the confidential classification of some of the documents provided by the core executive agencies, and insufficient communication between the decision makers and officials responsible for preparing draft legislation. Some of the problems were dealt with by headhunting well-qualified officials, working closely with the prime minister to facilitate cooperation between the chief negotiator and ministries (Zubek 2005: 606). From then on, it was easier to identify the responsible officials, and the deadlines were given more precisely.

With those instruments in place, the process moved at a faster pace from 2000. After introducing a system of sanctions and rewards, the core executive was also able to pursue stricter legislative priorities for the ministries. The transfer of planning functions from the level of ministry to the centre enabled better coordination of policy making with the negotiation process. Frequent monitoring also helped to shift ministers' attention to EU-related legislation, ensuring that it was given priority over other kinds of draft legislation. Another important factor contributing to a greater degree of compliance was the provision of sanctions and incentives by the EU. Apart from the conditionality mechanisms mentioned above, the EU provided for sanctions and rewards in the technical assistance programmes, personal interventions by EU officials, pressure against delaying the closure of negotiation chapters, and annual progress reports by the European Commission. Governments based on their respective parties could also provide pressure through party links for ministers to fulfil their tasks.

Main actors and pre-accession institutional setting

The preparation and passing of legislation to meet EU targets required important contributions from both parliament and government. Within government this required the establishment of new institutional actors. The first such institutional step was the setting up in 1991 of the Bureau for European Integration (*Biuro do Spraw Integracji Europejskiej*) and the Bureau for Foreign Assistance (*Biuro do Spraw Pomocy Zagranicznej*) within the Council of Ministers' Office of the Polish government.[3] These offices were established even before the signing of the Europe Agreement in June 1993 and submission of a formal application in April 1994. Their task was to support the work of the Government Plenipotentiary for European Integration and Foreign Assistance. However, once the negotiation process had speeded up, this framework no longer proved effective, and it was abolished and replaced by a new ministry – the Committee for European Integration (KIE) – with its own permanent secretariat. Within the framework of the KIE two further groupings were set up to provide it with further support: the Office of the Committee for European Integration (UKIE) and, at a later stage, a Preparatory Workgroup of the KIE (*Zespół Przygotowawczy KIE*, ZPKIE).

The Committee for European Integration (KIE)

The Committee for European Integration (KIE) was established by the Law of 8 August 1996. Its main task was to coordinate the functions of all the ministries and other institutions directly engaged in the process of integration with the EU and as such it was responsible for the strategic decisions on Polish integration with the EU, both before accession and after Poland became a member of the EU. The role of the chair of the KIE in 1996 was performed by the prime minister, but shortly afterwards it was delegated to another minister, with the title of Secretary of the Committee. The other members of the committee were the ministers responsible for public finance, economy, labour, agriculture, the Treasury, environment, transport, interior, foreign affairs, health and justice.[4] Although the committee remained under the formal chairmanship of the prime minister, who was the main decision-making figure in the pre-accession period, the main business of the committee was handled by the secretary, who was responsible for its functioning and for the handling of European affairs within the government machinery. This shift influenced the effectiveness of supervision, as the regular minister did not have the comparable institutional influence of the prime minister. The KIE at that time operated on the basis of monthly meetings for junior ministers and civil servants, serving as a debating forum. It did not have agenda-setting powers and possessed only limited authority, focusing on commenting on draft legislation. Institutional coercion could only be exercised then in crisis situations by interventions of the KIE chair supported by the prime minister, which cannot be thought of as an effective tool, given the minister's weak position.

As preparations for accession progressed and more detailed work was required, the KIE drew on the work of a wider range of people. In the late 1990s an extended list of ministers, directors and experts was invited to KIE meetings, and in 2001 some of its functions were delegated to the ZPKIE, chaired by an under-secretary of state. This provided a framework for closer cooperation to process the details of EU-related legislation while the main KIE decided on the most important and strategic documents, including those concerning the negotiation strategy. Greater effectiveness was now achieved by the regularity with which the ZPKIE was able to scrutinise the transposition progress as well as by the presence of ministry lawyers at inter-ministerial meetings where problems were addressed.

The Office of the Committee for European Integration (UKIE)

The Office of the Committee for European Integration (UKIE) was established a few months after the KIE itself, in October 1996. It was created on the basis of a Regulation of the Chairman of the Council of Ministers of 2 October 1996 to provide organisational support for the KIE.[5] The UKIE formally continued the work previously conducted by the Bureau for European Integration (*Biuro do Spraw Integracji Europejskiej*) and the Bureau for Foreign Assistance (*Biuro do Spraw Pomocy Zagranicznej*). Its main task was to coordinate the work of all ministries and institutions directly engaged in the process of Poland's integration with the European Union.

Before Poland joined the European Union, the efforts of UKIE were to a large extent focused on speeding up the process of harmonisation of Polish law with the *acquis communautaire*. The work of both the government and parliament needed to be conducted more quickly and efficiently in relation to European legislative proposals, and the UKIE tried to achieve this by preparing a special coordinating instrument for this work – the National Programme of Preparation for Membership (*Narodowy Program Przygotowania do Członkostwa*, NPPC) – and establishing a special procedure of conduct for European legislative proposals. UKIE also provided opinions on the best way to match proposals for new Polish laws with those of the EU, as well as monitoring the adaptation of existing laws and general processes of adjustment to EU membership. In order to ensure Poland met all the requirements for accession, the government made a decision in 2001 that all work linked to the adoption of European Acts should be completed by deadlines that were agreed by all the ministries and central offices. Formally, the role of the UKIE was to help strengthen coordination between line ministries in the making of legislative changes as well as other harmonisation processes. However, since the UKIE was not in a higher institutional position than the line ministries, it had no means of applying sanctions over them. Therefore, while in theory meeting the government's targets should have been achieved by the UKIE playing a coordinating role, with the execution of decisions being carried out by the ministries, in practice the UKIE often had to carry out the tasks instead of the ministries.

Parliament

Alongside the government institutions, a major role in the accession process was played by the Polish parliament in the passing of legislation necessary for implementing the *acquis communautaire*. Before accession, both chambers of the parliament, the Sejm and the Senate, experienced serious problems in dealing with a considerable backlog in complying with the *acquis*, especially since some branches of law needed to be changed significantly or even created *ab initio*. The reconciliation of Polish and European laws therefore became the parliament's priority, overshadowing the bulk of legislative activities in the domestic sphere. Other problems included inadequate political guidance and ineffective scrutiny procedures over the work of parliament (Lazowski 2007). In 2000, in order to speed up the process of reconciliation of laws, parliament amended its standing orders and created a special parliamentary European Legislation Committee. The lower chamber, the Sejm, also tried to put pressure on the government by adopting a resolution urging the executive to give priority to the work of reconciling Polish and EU legislation.[6]

At that time there was no formal possibility for the Polish parliament to influence European Union decision making. Its role was therefore limited to the implementation of the *acquis* and the harmonisation of its legal order with the European Union framework. The Sejm tried to exercise some control in the domestic arena by scrutinising the government's handling of the negotiations for EU entry. The voice of the parliament was strongly heard in the debate on the revision of the Treaty of Nice and it also advocated tough negotiations on financial issues and CAP subsidies (Lazowski 2007). A less critical stance was taken by the Sejm in 2003 in its resolution on the Treaty establishing a Constitution for Europe.[7] In the course of preparation for EU membership, members of parliament also had the opportunity to participate in closer cooperation with the European Parliament, for example with observer status, and in the work of the European Convention on the Future of Europe. In the longer perspective all these efforts were to prove useful in the development of a system for the coordination of European affairs.

Post-accession problems with European policy coordination

Since accession the character of relations between Poland and the EU has changed, as Poland has become a member country, and this in turn has produced new problems. These have occurred, on the one hand, in the policies Polish governments have pursued as an EU member and in relation to the EU and other member states and, on the other hand, in the functioning, roles and composition of the institutions dealing with European policy coordination.

The European policy of the Polish government

Poland, as a new member state, has been given a substantial credit of trust and understanding, especially while having a minority government and difficulties in domestic politics. During the first year of Polish membership of the EU there was a Democratic Left Alliance (*Sojusz Lewicy Demokratycznej*) government under Prime Minister Leszek Miller but, between the time when he left office in May 2004 and the elections in September 2006, there was a minority 'expert' government under Prime Minister Marek Belka. In 2005 the soft-eurosceptic Law and Justice (*Prawo i Sprawiedliwość*) party won the election and a year later formed a coalition with the populist Self-Defence (*Samoobrona*) party and the League of Polish Families (*Liga Polskich Rodzin*). Since then, the situation on the Polish political scene has been watched more carefully by the other member states, which have had concerns based on an election campaign that was widely perceived to be populist and eurosceptic (Atkins *et al.* 2006).

The new government's first months sent mixed signals. Prime Minister Kazimierz Marcinkiewicz claimed success in the budgetary negotiations during the December 2005 European Union summit in Brussels. The Polish government participated in several initiatives at EU level, such as the letter of six countries asking for liberalisation of the services market[8] and Poland's initiative to deepen EU integration in the field of energy policies. An important step for the government was the enlargement of the G5 Group of Interior Ministers in Heiligendamm in March 2006. Hopes were also expressed that Poland could play a role in a number of policy areas, such as the Constitutional Treaty, agriculture reform, liberalisation of the services market, and the eastern dimension of the Common Foreign and Security Policy (CFSP) (as a potential bridge to further enlargement to Ukraine), and also might provide the old EU with some fresh thinking and new ideas.

At the same time, however, there were some problematic situations, such as the actions of the agriculture minister, Krzysztof Jurgiel, during the debate on sugar reform, which raised questions about the predictability and reliability of the Polish government.[9] The Polish government threatened to use a veto to block agreement over VAT rates, as well as disagreeing with the Commission over the merger of the Italian banking group UniCredit.[10] In 2006, Poland vetoed the launching of negotiations on a new EU–Russia treaty, claiming that the Russian meat import ban was an attempt to bring disunity between old and new EU states and to punish Warsaw for supporting the 2004 Orange Revolution in Ukraine. Another controversial stance of the Polish government was on the Constitutional Treaty, where it tried to reopen negotiations on the voting system agreed by the preceding government and threatened to use its veto if negotiations were not reopened

(Rettman 2007a, 2007b). There were also many missed opportunities in which the government could have proposed new policy directions as well as participated more effectively in the decision-making processes.

In its dealings with Europe the Polish government tried to prove that it was fighting for Poland's national interests, arguing that its predecessors had been submissive. However, the inference that can be drawn from its actions is that the government seemed to prefer methods of confrontation instead of those of compromise and consensual agreement. In Brussels and other EU capitals there was a feeling that the Polish government placed less value on effectiveness than on toughness and the demonstration of it in order to woo its national electorate. Poland started to be perceived as an awkward partner, prejudiced and mistrustful. The government's stance on European issues has often been criticised as multiplying the confrontations and weakening the position of Poland in the EU, particularly in view of future negotiation possibilities. The large number of votes given to Poland in the Nice Treaty is said to be of no help if the government cannot build coalitions and persuade other member states of its policy views (Smolar 2006).

It is too early, however, to draw far-reaching conclusions based on the first three years of Polish membership of the EU. An important factor in explaining its behaviour may be the timing, as well as other contingency factors, which shaped the agenda of the first governments after EU accession. Europeanisation, on the contrary, stresses the permanent processes that influence the institutions, actors, government priorities, political discourse and many other areas.

Main actors in the post-accession institutional setting

The Committee for European Integration (KIE)

Since accession the minister of foreign affairs has replaced the prime minister in chairing the committee, while the prime minister has retained the power to appoint up to three members of the committee with experience or functions relevant to the tasks of the KIE. In the current institutional setting, the KIE is therefore composed of the minister of foreign affairs, appointed as the chairman of the committee, the secretary of the KIE (with the rank of a secretary of state) and the various minister members. Although it remains a political body, and has been assigned new tasks relating to active participation in EU decision-making activities, it now has a rather less specific scope of activities and takes a rather passive role in policy-making debates. Now, after accession and the qualitative change in the relationship with EU institutions that has resulted, the KIE has come to be perceived as ineffective in its dealing with European affairs. Its framework is thought to be unclear, too complicated and not efficient enough, and a further reform is under discussion, with the involvement of the offices of the minister of foreign affairs and the prime minister.

The Office of the Committee for European Integration (UKIE)

Since accession, the priorities of the UKIE have also changed, owing to the new character of Poland's relationship with the EU, but it still retains a more proactive role. The most important current tasks of the UKIE have been to participate in creating and ensuring the effective implementation of European law as well as the coordination of European issues throughout the government machine, making sure that current policy is consistent with EU membership commitments. The UKIE was made responsible for coordinating the preparation of Poland's official positions for presentation in EU institutions and bodies, such as the Council of the European Union, Coreper I and Coreper II,[11] and monitoring the work of EU committees and working groups. It is also supposed to supervise the training of the employees of ministries and central offices to service EU membership commitments, to monitor the representation of Polish nationals in EU institutions and to supervise further professional training of public administration officials. The realisation of these tasks, however, seems to have become more difficult since the dissolution of the Department for European Training. There is now a rather unclear strategy for informal lobbying in favour of Polish civil servants, as well as there being no equivalent of the Civil Service College in the UK that would prepare Polish officials to work in EU institutions.

A further range of UKIE tasks concerns the representation of Poland before the European Court of Justice (preparing representatives of the government to participate in proceedings against Poland brought before Community courts) and managing the membership funds. It prepares analytical studies of new strategies and tendencies in European integration, as well as more significant policy proposals. These tasks are of critical importance for the purposes of formulating Poland's European policy, but without proper guidance from political bodies they are at risk of being just paper assessments. When it comes to the coordination of European policy in the wider political arena, UKIE has acted since accession as an intermediary in the cooperation between the government and parliament (Act of 11 March 2004).[12] In this respect, its efforts are supposed to result in consensus between the two institutions on Polish participation in EU law making.

At present, the UKIE remains the main administrative body – ministry *sui generis* – responsible for European policy coordination, as it was in the pre-accession period. The strength of the UKIE is the very well-prepared personnel of educated technocrats and headhunted officials. The government's recruitment policy in the pre-accession period was concentrated on finding the best possible candidates to prepare the country for integration, and it was willing to provide much better salary conditions than in other sectors of the rather poorly paid government administration.

The European Committee of the Council of Ministers (KERM)

Perhaps the biggest change in government institutions in the post-accession period has been the establishment in March 2004, just on the eve of EU accession, of a new European Committee of the (Polish) Council of Ministers (*Komitet Europejski Rady Ministrów*, KERM). A large part of the tasks of the old ZPKIE was transferred to the KERM, with a view to setting up a forum for the discussion and adoption of the official positions of the Polish government on European issues and for the discussion of other issues of relevance to European integration. Its purpose was to ensure that the Polish authorities acted in a proper and coherent manner in the European arena. The composition of KERM is diverse, bringing together top-ranking officials from all the main governmental bodies.[13] KERM is tasked with reconciling differences of views and resolving inter-ministerial conflicts that may arise during the preparation of the Polish government's positions for the EU Council and Coreper meetings. If the ministries fail to agree a common position, KERM forwards the draft document to the full Council of Ministers, which makes the final decision. More generally KERM deals with a wide range of matters, including the drafting and timetabling of legislation relating to the transposition of EU law into the Polish legal system, as well as information on the state of implementation of EU law and a wide range of other issues.[14]

Thus, in the present institutional setting, KERM has quite significant powers, and also acts as the final point of assessing technical measures related to EU policies. It not only acts as the Council's auxiliary body, but is also supposed to put European policies on the government's daily agenda and coordinate the activities of ministers in the EU Council. Nevertheless, the activities of KERM remain to a large extent secondary and linked to Coreper meetings in respect of coordination of ministerial positions. It does not have any policy-making powers and therefore participates in EU policy only in current, administrative terms. Nevertheless, it has been argued that the coordination system based on KERM is the optimal one, as it allows the horizontal assessment of issues under debate and the limitation of post-accession misunderstandings and difficulties (Jasinski and Skoczek 2007).

Parliament

After Poland gained EU membership, the involvement of the Polish parliament increased in both quantitative and qualitative terms. The operational mode of the relations between the government and parliament has also changed regarding European affairs. Shortly before accession, the Polish parliament adopted the Act governing cooperation between the Council of Ministers and parliament on issues relating to the European Union. Since then, according to article 2 of the Act, the Council of Ministers has not only had a legal obligation to cooperate with the Sejm and the Senate on European issues, but also has been obliged to follow rules for the referral of all relevant documents to parliament.[15] The activities of the Polish parliament in the European field therefore now include scrutiny of proposals for EU legislation and the transposition of EU law, as well as putting pressure on the government by using soft instruments such as parliamentary resolutions and debates. Debates and resolutions are meant to have a significant impact on the government's activities. In general the parliament holds a relatively strong position in the Polish political system, and this has been further strengthened by the series of weak coalition and minority governments that Poland has experienced in recent years. The parliament is also involved in bilateral and multilateral cooperation with the parliaments of other EU member states.[16]

In the field of legislative action, however, relations between parliament and government have not changed substantially. Since accession, EU law is supposed to have been respected in areas where it is unconditionally binding, but in practice EU influence seems to be rather weak. Overall, EU accession has meant for parliament not only a move from fast transposition to more effective implementation of laws and participation in European law making by discussing legislative proposals, but also a whole range of political challenges in national politics and in balancing the powers of other domestic actors. There is also a problem for the efficiency of parliamentary mechanisms in the limited expertise and understanding of EU-related matters by members of parliament.[17] Even so, parliament's role has undoubtedly increased; being freed from the previous pressures to concentrate on the fast implementation of the *acquis*, it has been able to participate in a wider range of activities in the coordination of EU affairs.

Proposed reform

The coordination of European policy in Poland has gone through many changes and improvements, both on the way to Poland joining the European Union and after it became a member in 2004. From the imposed concentration of powers in the hands of the core executive in the pre-accession period, it has moved on to the wider ground, including more institutional actors and providing a possibility of deepened participation in European decision making. Surprisingly however, three years after EU accession, Poland still uses the old framework of EU policy coordination, even though the nature of its relation with the EU has changed substantially. The institutional framework of KIE, UKIE and KERM is not addressing the requirements of membership and therefore proves to be ineffective. The role of parliament seems to be more of a success story. Therefore, certain failures to participate effectively in EU activities could be explained by the inefficient mechanisms of European decision making in the Polish government, as well as the absence of a government body dedicated to elaborating policy proposals and then trying to influence EU decision making. The lack of transparency and effective supervision by the prime minister, and inadequate use of the often overly complicated mechanisms in the government machine to coordinate the positions of the ministries, as well as weak control over the ministers' actions in the European arena, seem to be the main factors contributing to the sometimes awkward impression the government makes in that field.

In February 2006, recognising that some changes were required to the existing legal framework of European policy coordination, the government introduced a legislative proposal to amend existing legislation governing the KIE and UKIE.[18] In the proposal, the KIE was to be given new coordinating functions regarding European policy integration. In comparison with the existing legal framework, the proposed provisions meant a qualitative change in EU policy coordination, strengthening the position of the Ministry of Foreign Affairs as ultimately responsible for Poland's role in EU institutions, and adjusting the coordinating function of KIE to the challenges of EU membership. Also (in article 1, point 8 of the proposal) the position of the prime minister was to be strengthened; he was granted the power to call a meeting of the committee at any time and to preside over it. The legislative proposal would dissolve the UKIE as the office responsible for the operation of the KIE (article 3, point 1) and transfer its organisational structure and employees to the Ministry of Foreign Affairs. This meant that the ministry was to become responsible for providing administrative assistance to the KIE, and UKIE employees were to be provided with the same conditions of work and salary as they had before.[19]

After their publication the proposals soon came under criticism. In passing its opinion on the proposed legislation, the Legislative Council[20] particularly criticised its hybrid character – keeping the KIE but with administrative structure provided by the Ministry of Foreign Affairs (Wronkowska-Jaskiewicz 2006). They also raised the question of why the prime minister was given the power to call and preside over KIE meetings, especially since this placed the minister of foreign affairs in a contradictory position in a formal chain of command that ran from the prime minister to the KIE and then to the foreign minister (in the role of providing administrative support for the KIE). The dissolution of the UKIE was therefore predicted to have a negative impact on the administration of European affairs, and the Legislative Council called for the provision of a detailed plan for the transition period. In their opinion, the proposal dealt only with the 'external' aspect of EU membership and did not provide for necessary changes to the 'internal' issues of ensuring the effective enforcement of EU law within Poland. In this regard it was particularly critical of the confusion created concerning the relation between the KIE and the Government Legislative Centre, which retained its general responsibility for the coordination of the legislative activities of the cabinet, prime minister and other governmental bodies.

Conclusions

For the Polish government, joining the EU was the reward for a difficult struggle to meet the conditions for membership; but membership now poses even more challenges. The most significant change brought about by joining the EU has been the shift from implementation and policy downloading to proper participation in EU decision making. These developments have increased the role of the executive (the roles of the prime minister, ministers and some civil servants), but have also given parliament new areas in which to develop its activities. In the field of European policy coordination, Poland still faces many difficulties. Although the objectives of the government have changed, the pre-accession institutional framework is still in place. Arguably, the old mechanisms are now proving to be ineffective, and that influences Polish activities on the EU level, forcing the government to look for a more efficient way to coordinate its European actions, especially in policy-making areas.

From the government's perspective, the quality of European policy coordination is accounted in millions of euro every year – therefore it is desirable to employ a large number of qualified civil servants. Having a good strategy and investing money in training and recruiting experts seem to be cost-effective tools, as they can reward the government with better access and use of the EU funds. Influencing the decision-making process depends after all not only on the size of a country, but rather on putting forward interesting ideas, being able to persuade other member states of them, contributing to formulating future EU policies and making use of the practices of reaching agreements.

However, the planned reform needs to be implemented with careful thought, as the emerging system of coordination of EU policy requires not only substantial improvement but also deep remodelling. Ministers do not yet always seem to understand that participation in the European project means taking positions and exercising influence rather than merely implementing what has already been decided, in contrast with the principle of conditionality before accession. Poland seems still to be in a learning phase and does not yet take the practices of EU decision making for granted. Apart from the threat of being discredited on the international scene, the proper use of the incentives provided by the EU is an important feature, which cannot be ignored by any European government.

Acknowledgements

The author would like to thank Dr Grazyna Kacprowicz, Professor Michal Kulesza, Richard Laming, Dr Adam Lazowski, Professor Carlos Closa Montero, Professor Edward Page and Professor Grzegorz Rydlewski for their useful comments on the earlier drafts of this chapter.

Notes

1 In June 1993, the Copenhagen European Council recognised the right of the countries of Central and Eastern Europe to join the European Union when they

had fulfilled three criteria: political (stable institutions guaranteeing democracy, the rule of law, human rights and respect for minorities), economic (a functioning market economy) and incorporation of the Community *acquis* (adherence to the various political, economic and monetary aims of the European Union).

2 The sanctions included the 'naming and shaming' of non-complying ministers or departments. Support was also provided by means of resolving interdepartmental conflicts more effectively, as well as providing more methodical guidelines for the officials (Zubek 2005).

3 Council of Ministers' Resolution No. 11/91, 26 January 1991, establishing the office of a Government Plenipotentiary for European Integration and Foreign Assistance (in Polish). Uchwała Nr 11/91 Rady Ministrów z dnia 26 stycznia 1991 r. w sprawie ustanowienia Pełnomocnika Rządu do Spraw Integracji Europejskiej oraz Pomocy Zagranicznej (unpublished resolution, available in Polish at http://wigwam.loiv.torun.pl/skrypty/materialy/aaaaaaaabw.urrwp.doc?PHPSESSID=35618b026e1782062a5196a886e3bb29%3EUnia+Europejska%3C%2Fb%3E (accessed 10 June 2007). The Council of Ministers referred to here is the chief executive committee or 'cabinet' in the Polish system of government and should not be confused with the Council of Ministers of the EU, which is referred to in this chapter as the 'European Council of Ministers'.

4 Law of 8 August 1996 on the Committee for European Integration, article 4.4, *Journal of Laws*, 30 August 1996, as amended. An English translation of the Act is available on the UKIE website: http://www1.ukie.gov.pl/HLP/files.nsf/0/79B6DA-B015CB37A9C1256E7B00489328/$file/LawCEI.pdf (accessed 30 April 2007).

5 Rozporządzenie Prezesa Rady Ministrów z dnia 2 października 1996 r. w sprawie nadania statutu urzędowi Komitetu Integracji Europejskiej Journal of Laws (Dziennik Ustaw) No. 116/1996 Item 556, available in Polish at: http://www1.ukie.gov.pl/HLP/files.nsf/0/A0A72AC40708ADF7C1256E7B004922F3/$file/r3.pdf (accessed 10 June 2007).

6 Resolution of the Sejm of the Republic of Poland of 18 February 2000 on Preparations for Membership in the European Union, *Monitor Polski*, No. 6/2000, Item 124.

7 Resolution of the Sejm of the Republic of Poland of 2 October 2003 on the Treaty establishing a Constitution for Europe, *Monitor Polski*, No. 47/2003, Item 694.

8 This was related to the proposed Bolkestein directive.

9 In February 2006, Mr Jurgiel threatened that Poland would invoke the so-called Luxembourg compromise to block the deal.

10 The government tried to block the proposed merger of two local affiliates of UniCredit (Pekao and BPH banks) after the merger with the German HVB. The dispute alarmed the European Commission, as well as Poland's central bank and the banking regulatory commission.

11 The Permanent Representatives Committee or 'Coreper' (article 207 of the Treaty establishing the European Community) is responsible for preparing the work of the Council of the European Union. It consists of the member states' ambassadors to the European Union and is chaired by the member state which holds the Council presidency. Coreper works in two configurations: Coreper I, consisting of the deputy permanent representatives, deals with technical matters; Coreper II, consisting of the ambassadors, deals with political, commercial, economic or institutional matters.

12 Act of 11 March 2004 on cooperation of the Council of Ministers with the Sejm and the Senate on issues related to the Republic of Poland Membership in the European Union, Journal of Laws (Dziennik Ustaw) No. 52/2004. An English translation of the Act is available on the UKIE website: http://www1.ukie.gov.pl/HLP/files.nsf/0/CDD1E39082B254D6C1256EA0003B5EFF/$file/2004ActOnCooperationWithSejmAndSenateOnEUissues.pdf (accessed 30 April 2007).

13 The European Committee of the Council of Ministers is composed of: the minister of foreign affairs as chair; the secretary of state in the Office of the Committee for European Integration as deputy chair; the secretary of KERM; and other members – secretaries and under-secretaries of state in ministries engaged in European integration issues. See Order issued by the Chairman of the Council of Ministers on 23 March 2004 (Zarządzenie Nr 30 Prezesa Rady Ministrów z dnia 23 Marca 2004 r. w sprawie Komitetu Europejskiego Rady Ministrów), *Monitor Polski*, No. 14, Item 223, §2.1; later amended by Order no. 9 issued on 28 January 2005 (Zarządzenie Nr 9 Prezesa Rady Ministrów z dnia 28 stycznia 2005 r.).

14 It also considers draft decisions regarding the allocation of EU appropriations and of other means of foreign assistance; positions for meetings of the EU Council and of Coreper; positions on EU reforms; positions on EU legislative proposals; positions regarding EU documents subject to the consultation procedure with member states, and assessments of these documents made by relevant EU institutions and bodies; positions regarding the timetable of work of the EU Council, the annual legislative plans of the European Commission, and assessments of the annual legislative plans of the European Parliament and of the EU Council; positions regarding draft international agreements to which the European Union, European Communities or their member states will become parties; and positions on drafts of non-binding EU Acts, in particular on guideline proposals in the sphere of economic and monetary union and employment. It considers decisions on matters relating to proceedings before the European Court of Justice, documents concerning the preparation of employees of ministries and other central offices, public information programmes on the impact of accession and reports on their implementation, and information on the state of play of the translation of European law into Polish (Zarządzenie Nr 30 Prezesa Rady Ministrów z dnia 23 Marca 2004 r. w sprawie Komitetu Europejskiego Rady Ministrów), *Monitor Polski*, No. 14, Item 223, §3.2).

15 Act of 11 March 2004 on cooperation of the Council of Ministers with the Sejm and the Senate on issues related to the Republic of Poland Membership in the European Union, *Dziennik Ustaw* [Journal of Laws], No. 52/2004. An English translation of the Act is available on the UKIE website: http://www1.ukie.gov.pl/HLP/files.nsf/0/CDD1E39082B254D6C1256EA0003B5EFF/$file/2004ActOnCooperationWithSejmAndSenateOnEUissues.pdf (accessed on 30 April 2007).

16 For example, within the framework of COSAC (Conference of Community and European Affairs Committees of Parliaments of the European Union), there has been close cooperation with fellow Visegrad countries (the Czech Republic, Slovakia and Hungary) and the Baltic states (Lithuania, Latvia and Estonia).

17 One example was the discussion of the nomination of commissioner Danuta Huebner, where some of the MPs proved their limited understanding of the powers and responsibilities of this post and expected the commissioner effectively to represent Polish national interests.

18 This was part of a proposal to amend existing legislation on the organisation and functioning of central government administration bodies and their subordinate units as well as to make changes to some other Acts introduced on 8 February 2006 (Autopoprawka do rządowego projektu ustawy o zmianach w organizacji i funkcjonowaniu centralnych organów administracji rządowej i jednostek im podporządkowanych oraz o zmianie niektórych ustaw z dnia 30 listopada 2005 sygn. BDG.0131-2897-05/3 – projekt autopoprawki z dnia 8 lutego 2006).

19 UKIE employees are provided with higher wages than MFA employees; the purpose was to recruit the most qualified and experienced expert officials and lawyers in order to facilitate and speed up the preparations for membership.

20 The Legislative Council is an expert advisory body giving opinions to the prime minister and government on law making and the evaluation of legislative proposals.

References

Atkins, R., Cienski, J. and Parker, G. (2006) 'Europe frets as Poland heads down populist path', *Financial Times*, 15 March.

Grabbe, H. (2003a) 'How does Europeanization affect CEE governance? Conditionality, diffusion and diversity', *Journal of European Public Policy*, 8: 1013–31.

Grabbe, H. (2003b) 'Europeanization goes east: power and uncertainty in the EU accession process', in K. Featherstone and C.M. Radaelli (eds), *The Politics of Europeanization*, Oxford: Oxford University Press.

Jasinski, F. and Skoczek, J. (2007) 'Koordynacja polityki integracyjnej w Polsce', in A. Lazowski (ed.), *Unia Europejska: prawo instytucjonalne i gospodarcze*, 3rd edn, Warsaw: Kluwer Wolters Polska.

Lazowski, A. (2007) 'The Polish parliament and EU affairs: a concise actor or an accidental hero?', in J. O'Brennan and T. Raunio (eds), *National parliaments within the European Union: from victims of integration to purposive actors?*, London/ New York: Routledge.

Rettman, A. (2007a) 'Poland to fight for "square root" law in EU treaty', *EU Observer*, 29 March.

Rettman, A. (2007b) 'Poland defends red line on future EU treaty', *EU Observer*, 18 April.

Schimmelfennig, F. and Sedelmeier, U. (2004) 'Governance by conditionality: EU rule transfer to the candidate countries of Central and Eastern Europe', *Journal of European Public Policy*, 11: 661–97.

Smolar, A. (2006) 'Świat i Polska według braci Kaczyńskich', *Gazeta Wyborcza*, 31 March.

Wronkowska-Jaskiewicz, S. (2006) Opinion of the Legislative Council on the amendment to the government legislation proposal on the changes in organisation and functioning of central government administration bodies and their subordinate units as well as on the change of some other Acts from 8 February 2006 [Autopoprawka do rządowego projektu ustawy o zmianach w organizacji i funkcjonowaniu centralnych organów administracji rządowej i jednostek im podporządkowanych oraz o zmianie niektórych ustaw z dnia 30 listopada 2005 sygn. BDG.0131-2897-05/3 – projekt autopoprawki z dnia 8 lutego 2006], unpublished paper.

Zubek, R. (2005), 'Complying with transposition commitments in Poland: collective dilemmas, core executive and legislative outcomes', *West European Politics*, 28: 592–619.

Part III
History and national identity

7   Which way to Poland?

Re-emerging from Romantic unity

Ewa Sidorenko

Poland's status as a nation state has never been more secure. In the years since the collapse of communism, Polish independence has been reinforced by the anchoring of its security within the structures of NATO and by accession to the EU. However, despite these developments, much of public discourse in Poland continues to imply threats and crisis by focusing on patriotism, the need for moral education, and the cultivation of acceptable values. This chapter investigates the character of the public sphere in Poland and links it to the dynamics of processes of rapid social change and the fragmenting of identities. It argues that the current populist recourse to patriotism, deployed as an attempt to resist the character of social change, is not arbitrary. Rather, it is path dependent;[1] it represents a legacy drawing on processes which were originally mobilised for resistance to communism. Whilst inclusive and productive under communism, under contemporary conditions such ideas can be destructive and generate an ecology of social exclusion.

All-Poland Youth

After the 2005 elections much coverage in the Polish media, including internet discussions, has been devoted to a number of connected issues originating from a politically significant section of the political spectrum. These include an ongoing focus on *lustracja* (lustration – the screening of public figures for their possible collaboration with the communist secret service) and controversial initiatives by the minister of education, Roman Giertych, including ideas of moral renewal jointly articulated by the Catholic and right-wing coalition. These generate much discussion around issues of patriotism, moral education, and the cultivating of acceptable values.

One of those conservative voices in the current climate is the youth organisation called *Młodzież Wszechpolska* (All-Poland Youth, A-PY). Originally set up in 1922, it was reactivated in 1989 by Roman Giertych. It aims to promote traditional, Catholic and patriotic values among young people and to train political elites. During the inter-war period, All-Poland Youth was closely linked with the right-wing National Democracy (ND) party, and it was also associated with some of its extreme activities such as violent attacks on Jewish and Ukrainian minorities. In the 1930s, it supported the introduction of the infamous *numerus clausus*, the capping of the number of school and university places available to Jews, leading to enforced separation of Jewish students in state education (Flak 2006). Its proclaimed political aims included Poland becoming a strong state based entirely on the Catholic Church's teaching, and a state 'free from foreign influence'.

Today, All-Poland Youth's logo is supplemented by the slogan: 'Tradition and Modernity'. It has an extensive internet presence, with websites clearly addressing the young. As a youth movement, it operates through a variety of social and political activities, such as discussions, lectures, political meetings, holiday camps, happenings and 'I love Poland' street campaigns. It also disrupts demonstrations in support of tolerance, abortion rights and other issues. Highly eurosceptic, anxious about foreign capital investment in Poland and possible revisionism by Germany towards Poland's western borders, it is against secularisation and the 'onslaught of decadent' influences from the West. In particular, it stands against liberal and cosmopolitan values. It calls into question the political credibility of some Polish anti-communist opposition activists on the grounds of their alleged undercover sympathy towards the previous regime. This, however, is not necessarily part of 'the mainstream' support for *lustracja* but, arguably, a covert form of anti-Semitism.[2] All-Poland Youth is particularly critical of homosexuality, gay movements and feminism. It regards homosexuality as almost synonymous with paedophilia and has recently started campaigning for restoration of the death penalty for 'paedophile murderers'. As education minister, Giertych, who is the honorary chairman of All-Poland Youth, has been critical of, and powerful enough to curtail, activities of organisations promoting tolerance. For instance, in 2006 he was able to cut the funds of Campaign against Homophobia (KPH) and to dismiss the director of the Centre for Teacher Training for allowing a Polish edition of an EU publication concerning promotion of tolerance. Despite its own rhetoric of serving a perfectly benign social cause (promoting patriotism among the young), there is ample evidence that A-PY deploys aggressive language and creates negative images of social groups that it considers to be different. Consequently, All-Poland Youth is regarded by its critics as a right-wing nationalist movement which has not just been closely involved in the legitimate election campaign of *Liga Polskich Rodzin* (the League of Polish Families) but also been engaged in violent clashes with gay activists during equality parades, and in 2006 it was seen to be displaying the Nazi salute (Traynor 2006).

Despite being a minority of activists, All-Poland Youth is highly organised and targets the young. Moreover, the aims of All-Poland Youth are explicitly educational; it provides organisational structures for the shaping of identity among the young and indeed for producing skilled and modern political activists. It has a large network of central and locally managed websites with numerous links to other Catholic and right-wing organisations. One of the explicitly consciousness-raising publications is Roman Giertych's

Kontrrewolucja Młodych [Counter-revolution of the young], which sets out All-Poland Youth's political, social and economic goals. The stated goals are to take over the structures and governance of the state and to rid Polish culture of the residue of communism. According to Giertych, Poland is not sovereign because:

> a true limitation to our freedom comes from KGB agents sold to Western intelligence and people (who became dissidents from the Polish Communist Party in 1968) who, supported financially by Western governments, have involved themselves in Polish politics in the last twenty years.[3]

It is important to realise that for anyone familiar with this discourse 'the 1968 communist dissidents' is a coded reference to 'the Jews'.[4] Thus, despite the recent disappearance of the most explicit racist, anti-Semitic and homophobic texts from the All-Poland Youth websites, the provincial Polish language sites continue to display material which is unambiguous for its target audience yet not easy to decode by non-Polish speakers. The organisation is aimed at people in their late teens and early twenties, a particularly malleable material for identity formation. Thus, the voice of All-Poland Youth, deploying a wide range of images, resources and identities, needs to be taken very seriously.[5]

Thus, precisely because of the representative democratic system of rule, it matters what well-organised groups, even if they are technically minorities, say and do. In fact, as we can see now in real politics, it matters more what All-Poland Youth stands for than what Kraków or Warsaw intellectuals think. As Rafal Pankowski of *Tygodnik Powszechny* has aptly observed: 'The specificity of the Polish case is not so much the scale of the support for nationalist views as the scale of social complicity with them, and the inactivity of the authorities' (Pankowski 2004). Thus, no matter how tempting it is to dismiss the phenomenon of All-Poland Youth as technically a minority or as an example of irrationality which we can explain away, the discourse which it deploys is part of the path dependency of Polish politics; it cannot be dismissed because it is well rooted and shared by others. This discourse deploys a (neo-) Romantic, organic notion of nationhood, a moral unity which evokes an obligatory sense of sacredness and posits a dominant collective identity. The genesis of this imagery is part of Poland's past, but, when deployed under current political conditions, its consequences have to be seriously considered.

Current processes of rapid social change can be compared in their magnitude with those of the nineteenth-century experience of industrialisation and urbanisation. Fragmentation of old patterns of wealth distribution, new forms of power, striking inequality, high unemployment, mass (actual and intended) exodus from Poland and disenchantment with political processes – these are just part of the background to the conservative reactions to change. But to provide numerous factors is not enough; we are not dealing with a closed system but with a dynamic reality. What we need is a qualitative characterisation of the emergent processes and their implications for the character of the emerging public sphere. So the key theme in this chapter is an analysis of the non-linear dynamic between the processes of fragmentation and differentiation, on the one hand, and the conservative resistance to these, which draws on the available collective identities, on the other.[6]

The existential terrain for patriotism?

Complexity and paradox are no strangers to the Polish experience. The battleground for 'patriotism' as understood by All-Poland Youth is a country in crisis in which rapid change is producing much uncertainty. Thus, despite external economic indicators of growth, and despite the security of Poland's international position, the country is politically unstable, with an ongoing turmoil over *lustracja*, corruption and low levels of social trust. According to Millard (1999), the new Polish democracy is emerging with difficulty, amid the reality of material and social insecurity: 'Social dislocation produced an anxious population, worried about the rise of crime and personal security. Tolerance of difference appeared very low, affecting groups such as gypsies, gay people, or those suffering from AIDS' (Millard 1999: 178). Moreover, there was an alarming rate of exodus from Poland after its accession to the EU in May 2004, prompted by material insecurity, unemployment and low wages as compared to those in other countries of the EU.

An insight into the background to the current conservative turn can be found by examining the recent Polish film *Ode to Joy*. Written and directed by three young graduates of the Łódź Film School, the film comprises three short stories which come together in a final scene: unknown to each other, the characters travel on the same coach to London to start new lives. Each of the stories explores events leading up to the decisions of these young people to leave Poland. Set in different parts of the country and diverse social backgrounds, the stories are united in the image of relationships in Poland that they provide. The young people try hard to find a place for themselves and fulfil their quite ordinary dreams but, as they lack financial resources, their attempts are thwarted. Yet these stories cannot be reduced to economic themes; what they show is the isolation of the characters from, and fragmentation of, their own communities. This occurs not because these individuals are maladjusted or wish to be different, but because they themselves and their communities – the family, the workplace, lovers and friends – will not, or more likely cannot, understand and support each other. There is a palpable absence of togetherness, of communication-bonded human solidarity – not an absence of love or a desire of caring, but an absence of the ability to share, to trust, to listen and to understand. These relationships are characterised by mistrust, fear and loneliness. In contrast to the twenty-something main characters, older and mature people are portrayed as lonely and lost or, if successful, then ruthless, brutal, abusive and exploitative. It is tempting to use the word 'individualism' to describe the position in which people now encounter reality. It is also tempting to suggest that at a certain level this experience transcends Polish reality and that Poland, along with other post-communist societies, is evolving towards the familiar existential landscape of late-modern societies: that individualism, isolation and existential loneliness have (finally?) arrived in Eastern Europe.

Despite the similarity with the American imagery of urban isolation, this individualism, fragmentation and loneliness is different; it has a different history. It does not stem from the Protestant background of a reformed Church and its (tight and repressive) communities; it has not lived through the welfare capitalism of the New Deal or the post-war social democracy of Western Europe. It does not share the background of Western socialism which questioned both liberal dangers and hopes, and its later demise from the 1970s. It cannot draw on a residue of institutional attempts to express the idea of a social contract and to deal with social problems by means of non-governmental organisations, lobbies and charitable organisations, and through a discourse of identity and civil rights politics. It is not founded on the desire to break through an unjust social order to further the rights of minority groups. In other words, it is situated in a different social ecology and it has no liberal philosophy behind it.[7] In that sense, both philosophically and importantly sociologically, it is a phenomenon which requires its own analysis. The film *Ode to Joy* is a work of fiction, but the image of the existential landscape it presents is a lived reality for many in Poland, and against that background the conservative response is attractive and persuasive. As the current mass migration is a dynamic consequence of this crisis, the discourse of patriotism of the right tries to appeal to the familiar sources of identity and social gravity: the nation, the Church, the family.

This kind of anomic individualism can be seen as a form of breakdown of social solidarity. This individualism lacks a philosophical underpinning and therefore is not supported by a corresponding sense of trust in social order. What sense of the public sphere can coexist with this anomic individualism? Before examining the problem of this *anomic* individualism, I now attend to the character of the public sphere in Poland. What is of interest here is the possibility of democracy at the level of the public sphere: where numerous issues of a complex social order manifest themselves and become an object of the community's concern. It is the public sphere where societal interests and political options become articulated, ignored or silenced: the historically and culturally specific discursive space in which the possible is delineated. My specific focus here is the domination of the public sphere by a particular form of collective identity and the dynamic processes which shape the public sphere and interact with the anomic individualism.

I therefore draw on the Habermasian (1989) sense of the public sphere as a space for collective will formation: a wider social ecology for the creation of societal self-knowledge. Yet the limitations of space mean I will focus only on one part of the public sphere, unable to engage with its full complexity. Thus, following critiques of Habermas's both normative and historical analysis of the changes within the public sphere, it might be more appropriate to talk about multiple public spheres rather than just one. Indeed, can we exclude the existence of insights of feminist articulations from our description of the public sphere in Poland? Those critics of Habermas who insist that the reality of societal knowledge production must include varieties of spaces, not least those apparently most democratic and made possible by information technology, make a very good point here.[8] Yet to include a multiplicity of publicness might obscure that particular social ecology which generates actual governing.

Equally, despite Habermas's own admission of the complexities of actual governance, what I would like to retain from his earlier preoccupation is the commitment to the principles of reason and openness as the 'ought' for public debates on the assumption that the quality of society depends on its openness and ability to conduct reasoned debates.[9] It is manipulated by the media, the interests of capital and the authoritarian tendencies of some political parties, but the public sphere still matters. I am interested in this space because history has shown us that the character of discourse which permeates the public sphere could destroy democracy itself.

What is argued here is that the contemporary character of the public sphere represents a legacy, or path dependence, of processes which emerged under communism. Drawing on recent work in complexity theory[10] I would argue that the voices (which are not limited to the visible and organised articulations of All-Poland Youth) calling upon the Romantic notion of patriotism as a resource for Poland's uncertainty over its identity are drawing on the productive strategy of survival under communism. However, what was indeed productive and useful as a form of resistance is now detrimental to the viability of the emerging structures of democracy: a plurality of identities and voices. In the next section I would like to sketch the complex and dynamic ecological processes which shaped the public sphere under communism and which elevated tradition and the Romantic notion of patriotism to a special significance in Poland.

The public sphere under communism

What is of interest here is the path dependence of new discursive constructions on the character of the available pre-1989 public sphere.[11] Under communism there was no public sphere in the normative Habermasian sense within either the official or clandestine settings.[12] However, despite the absence of civil society or a 'true' public sphere some form of societal self-knowledge did emerge; it is therefore of interest what knowledge did evolve and how. Owing to the shortage of space, the complex relationship which the communist state had effected with the disempowered society cannot be fully described here. Below, I explore two connected processes: de-structuration and re-traditionalisation.

De-structuration

One of the significant effects of communist domination was a disappearance (or, one could claim, an absence) of the notion of social structure as epistemologically significant. This phenomenon has been dealt with by writers dealing with politics of interest, by claiming that post-communist societies were suffering from a visible lack of interest-conscious social agents. Other writers observe a phenomenon of atomisation, mass society (Arato 1982) or associational wasteland (Offe 1993) under communist conditions. These terms describe the same or a very similar process. In this thesis de-structuration does not aim to describe an absence of classes or social groups, as clearly communist societies are just as stratified as any other.

De-structuration stands for the kind of societal self-knowledge in which social groups and classes, despite their 'real' existence, do not perceive themselves in terms of common interest or a shared social identity. This is a qualitative description of what is often meant by an absence of civil society. Yet a qualitative description demands that we do not leave the blanks on the map – just because West European patterns are absent there, it does not follow that there is nothing to see. Instead, both the official and the clandestine publicness deploy the powerful notion of one overriding collective identity: the nation and its interest.[13] By stating that, I do not proclaim their moral equality; I am merely interested in a dynamic social ecology in which societal self-knowledge was constructed.

Re-traditionalisation

Another aspect of the character of societal self-knowledge construction under communism is the process of re-traditionalisation. This process might be said to have evolved out of complex legitimation needs of the communist system and out of strategic demands of the opposition. Thus, despite its overt commitment to modern ideas of progress, communism unintentionally generated a specific kind of tradition construction in which tradition was elevated to a site of political struggle. On the one hand, the regime endeavoured to secure patriotic legitimation through its recourse to various traditions whist trying to infuse them with socialist ideology.[14] On the other hand, the opposition considered the nation and Polishness to be threatened, and so the narrowly defined private sphere is seen as both an escape from oppression and a site of anti-communist resistance, where tradition becomes a source of ontological security. This complex process constituted tradition as an area of political contestation and also a space of freedom: essential unadulterated national values which refer to a normative idea of the natural order of things. It contains strong nationalist sentiments in which the concept of Poland and the Polish nation are central.

So far, the social ecology of societal self-knowledge construction has been described briefly with the concepts of de-structuration and re-traditionalisation. These are intended as tools to conceive of the complexities in which societal self-knowledge is produced. I want to emphasise the dynamics of such a process; by looking at communist propaganda (official discourses) we could not understand the process of the unofficial knowledge construction circulating in 'private', or even across, spaces. Both de-structuration and re-traditionalisation converge in constituting 'Poland' as a dominant theme and form of collective subjectivity. Three versions of societal self-perception are visible in Poland.

We, the nation . . .

The use of the idea of the nation developed over time and, I would argue, through positive feedback is called upon again today.[15] The idea of the nation constituted through the process of re-traditionalisation refers to an idealised, Romantic 'imagined community'. I refer here to the Romantic conception of Poland as a set of contemporary reconstructions of the complex varieties of both patriotism and the idea of Poland. However, Walicki (2000) identifies not one but three traditions of Polish patriotism, each originating at a different historical juncture and interacting with the existing strands. What is significant for the present is that, despite their particular differences, their overall similarities highlight the path-dependent contemporary construction.

The first, historically speaking, conception of the nation is linked to the pre-partition Polish gentry democracy (Walicki 2000). The Polish nation is there understood as a diverse multicultural and multi-ethnic entity of gentry citizens (10 per cent of the whole population). The system of democratic rule was based on the principle that legitimate decisions needed to be taken unanimously; a single vote could, in the *liberum veto* system, disrupt the entire parliamentary process. For Walicki (2000), this is not evidence of individualism but, quite the contrary, of collectivism. Thus patriotism, under gentry democracy, demanded that the will of the nation comes before the individual interest. It was expected that the acceptance of the will of the majority would not just have a formal character but would affirm the correctness of the majority judgement (Walicki 2000).

In the Polish Romantic tradition as described by Walicki (2000) the concept of the nation is decoupled both from the notion of the political community (as owing to the partitions in the late eighteenth century the Polish state had ceased to exist) and from an actually existing ethno-linguistic community (as a spiritually demeaning reduction). Thus the nineteenth-century Romantic conception constructs Poland neither as a political community nor as a culture but as a spiritual entity. After unsuccessful uprisings in the nineteenth century against the partition empires (1830, 1848, 1863), Poland was seen by its patriots as suffering, its fate full of tragedy. Yet Poland's pain was meaningful in its Christlike salvation role. Betrayed and crucified, it was endowed with a Messianic role for other nations.[16] With this understanding of the nation's ontology, '[t]he object of patriotic feelings ceased to be an ethnic community: patriotism was identified as faithfulness to the "national idea", given to Poles in their traditions, and revealed in a new guise as a universal mission of salvation' (Walicki 2000: 251). Poland then, with its broken body, became a Spirit which was to guide humanity to an ideal, just, republican order amongst nations.

This Romantic conception of the nation creates a strict hierarchy of social values in which individual (life-world) interest is inferior to the national idea. The religious understanding of the homeland makes faithfulness towards the idea of Poland morally and emotionally dominant and demands actions irrespective of their practical consequences. Hence heroic participation in hopeless battles is not seen from the Romantic perspective as politically futile or irresponsible but as morally desirable. Sacrifice of individuals and even whole generations is necessary for the good of the cause. Echoes of this deep-seated conviction were visible in the 1939 campaign following Nazi attack on Poland and, famously, in the Warsaw uprising of 1944 and, as I argue below, in the anti-politics of some of the 1980s opposition. Walicki (2000) traces the cult of national martyrology back to this Romantic construction and sees its legacy present in the post-martial-law Poland. True patriotism, in this conception, does not require action based on rational calculation in the name of practically understood national interest, but it demands an honourable, uncompromising stance, irrespective of individual or even collective costs. This form of patriotism has turned the cult of national tragedy into a virtue (Walicki 2000) and has rendered the needs of ordinary, everyday living as inferior to the needs of the national cause, 'as if life was a treason' (Walicki 2000: 253).

Walicki (2000) identifies a third form of patriotism in Poland, understood as a defence of an objective national interest through a legitimate nationalist egoism and political realism. In this conception, sovereignty of the nation must come before the liberty of its citizens. The nation, in this conception, was understood as an organic product of ethnic differentiation (Walicki 2000), and its boundaries were drawn around common language and culture. This type of patriotism, more readily called nationalism and associated with National Democracy, supported the idea of a strong, expansive state unified in its ethnic and cultural homogeneity and systematically attending to the national interest. Walicki (2000) claims that all of the above conceptions of patriotism have manifested themselves in the last years of communism, within the opposition.

Each of the above forms of patriotism had evolved under different political conditions, with corresponding difference in terms of postulated political and moral goals. Walicki also observes the persistence of these three varieties into the late communist period and uses them to account for some of the differences within oppositional strategy. However, for the purpose of this argument it is interesting to see a certain continuity in all three types of patriotism, particularly as it manifests itself in Poland after the imposition of martial law in late 1981. Thus, irrespective of the differences between the first two and the last notions of patriotism, the nation is conceived of as a community of a certain homogeneity. Even the multi-ethnic gentry democracy postulated the will of the nation to have a dominant moral value. In the latter two conceptions the value of national unity becomes even more explicit: the moral and emotional Romantic version which later, in the early twentieth century, acquires a more modern meaning linking nationality to common ethnicity, language and possibly even race. Significantly, however, for all three, unity remains a powerful *postulate*. Whilst the Romantic tradition postulates moral and spiritual unity, the tradition of National Democracy demands political and ethnic unity. In neither is there space for a legitimate expression of individual or group interests which differ from the national one.

Thus, given that the story of the Polish nation is characterised by struggles for statehood, the postulated national unity acquires a particular significance and tends to overshadow other forms of subjectivity.[17] In the context both of the partitions and of communist domination, the nation's identity developed apart from and against the state.[18] Thus, under Soviet domination, a mobilisation of the idea of national unity was part of the effective resistance to communism (Sidorenko 1998, 2000). Patriotism, the only morally correct position, postulated a faithfulness to the Romantic idea of homeland as an ideal and to its traditions (Walicki 1993).[19] Marginalisation from the communist-dominated public sphere rendered the narrowly understood private sphere and tradition of special importance: the spaces for both free expression and political activity. In the struggle against communism, Poland, its freedom, the truth about its history, and its authenticity became the highest values, and in that context the nation represented the only legitimate collective subject. This Romantic and highly politicised conception of the nation meant that other collective subjects could not emerge.

At the same time, as the discourse of patriotism is mobilised on both sides of the political divide, national ties represented a key base for social solidarity under communism. According to Walicki (1993) the discourse of patriotism was an antidote against atomisation. Therefore, the nation under communism in Poland becomes what under late and arguably post-modernising capitalism is no longer available: a coherent centre, the single collective subject able to articulate its general interest.

Under new post-communist social and cultural conditions, the popular discourse of patriotic unity has arguably conflated both the Romantic notion of unity postulated in ideas of the ideal homeland and the National Democracy tradition of the realistically understood national interest. This was particularly visible in the opposition of the right wing of the political spectrum to Poland's accession to the EU and, to a certain extent, in the ongoing preoccupation with *lustracja*. Interestingly, Millard (1999: 21) considers whether *lustracja* could not be regarded as a periodic 'ritual cleansing'. This seems a very relevant reading given the organic character of the patient's body: the cleansing is necessary to achieve its homogeneous and spiritual purity. Clearly then after 1989 the postulate of unity and the primacy of the national interest has produced some less positive consequences. These could be seen as costs, and they continue to affect the character of the emerging public sphere. As early as 1993 David Ost warned of the dangerous political consequences of de-structuration. When conflicting interests have no institutional underpinning (e.g. in trade unions) and no collective platform for expression, politics could articulate the ambiguity of interests through other criteria, for instance identity and ethnicity, which could divert passions to the non-economic sphere, towards blame (Ost 1993).[20]

The cost of the postulated national unity resulted in suppression of any other forms of difference. The one dominant identity towering over others, national identity understood as a particular set of values and characteristics, rendered other collective identities, be they class interest, gender identity, ethnic minority or indeed any other form of difference, as trivial and divisive. So the deployment of available symbolic resources for moral and political resistance also created, or just reinforced, a path dependency which today hinders a development of a more democratic, diverse and trusted public sphere.

On the surface then we have a paradox: Poland is indeed becoming more and more diverse, with not only old local and ethnic identities being restored (Kashubian, Silesian, German and indeed Jewish identities emerging), but also new immigrant minorities visible and some non-white Polish children. Countless other identities have also surfaced, with well-developed academic and organisational forms of feminism, as well as gay and lesbian groups. Yet, despite the *actual* fragmentation of collective identities, pluralism itself is failing to take root in Poland (Bojar 2002). It is not the shortage of voices which affects the condition of the public sphere today because, as Sergiusz Kowalski observed, 'pluralism is not a *fact* of plurality but its public acceptance' (Bojar 2002: 97).[21]

On the surface this seems a paradox, but these processes are not taking place in an emotional vacuum or societal harmony. The setting includes new forms of inequality, much insecurity, regions of very high unemployment, and a sense of alienation from and disillusion with the political process, frequently marked by evidence of corruption. This new complex cultural ecology creates a fertile ground for populism, evoking shared symbolism to offer reasonably easy solutions to existential anxieties of a society in crisis. The current right wing in Poland reaches for that narrow but deep stock of shared and powerful symbols. It is in that sense that the current reference to national interest and the threats to Polish identity exhibits and reinforces a path dependency.[22]

This path dependency, which exerts a dynamic influence today, involves again a mobilisation of symbolic imagery, the homogenising concept of the dominant national identity and ideas of culturally, economically and politically understood national interest. The nation is once again conceived of in an organic, neo-Romantic sense: it is defined as rooted in a clear, traceable ethnic and religious lineage; it is connected to what is regarded as pre-historic Polish lands; and most importantly it is inextricably linked to Catholicism.[23] It has a static, essential, non-negotiable character in which Catholic values reflect the natural order of things. According to the concerned right, national identity today is under threat, not just from structural connections with global forces but most immediately from the negative Western cultural influences penetrating and degenerating the traditional Polish way of life. Homosexuality, feminism, liberalism and 'excessive' tolerance are the prime targets of their attacks. In a recent article on All-Poland Youth's homophobia, Marcin Starnawski (2006) looks at the anti-Semitic programme and activities of this organisation in 1922–45 and points to an analogy between the way in which Jews were constructed as a dangerous 'other' then and the way in which homosexuals are taking their place today. Starnawski does not claim that as a group homosexuals are actually facing extermination. After all, APY and LPF do not postulate extermination; they *only* want to isolate them. Yet, last November in Poznań the March of Tolerance was disrupted by aggressive chanting: 'We'll do to you what Hitler did to the Jews' (Starnawski 2006).

Here is the most extreme example of this particular path dependency, and it might be difficult to accept the notion that we are in fact dealing with a continuity here. Much of Polish recent scholarship is devoted to the examination of varieties of nationalism and patriotism and to distinguishing between the innocuous and dangerous types. The problem is that, at the level at which nationalism and patriotism operate, at the grass roots, it tends to lose this subtlety of use.[24] It is, however, a reserve of genuine emotion, sentiment and energy, and when members of a community believe their collective identity is under threat it is not difficult to tap into those resources. It might therefore be unsettling to consider that what until recently was a benign method of societal mobilisation today is a force of exclusion and potential harm.

Each as an individual?

Having discussed the current manifestation of the process of re-traditionalisation, I now return to the issue of anomic individualism. It is suggested here that, despite the fact that it had not resulted from a liberal philosophy, individualism emerged as a consequence of the dysfunctional conditions of the communist economy and polity, and indeed it was reinforced by the experience of resistance to the system.[25] Thus the postulate of national unity and the hold of a dominating identity have interesting consequences. On the one hand, under communism, both minority and individual interest were seen as divisive in relation to those of the imagined community, and alien to what Walicki (2000) identifies as a collectivist tradition. On the other hand, in the everyday context without a collective expression (which could be regarded as a threat to national unity), invisible in the public sphere, private interests were acutely real. They were most readily experienced, and dealt with privately and within the private sphere.[26] Thus despite the long history of collectivism in Poland (Walicki 2000) in the actual experience (of material contradictions) of life under socialism this particular individualism was constituted by the inability of the collective interest to be articulated. This individualism, arguably drawing on the anarchist elements in Polish political traditions (Davies 1981), expresses scepticism towards not just a powerful state but also the social contract and at the same time an acceptance of an idea of some traditional, timeless order. It develops in a re-traditionalised culture in which identities are grounded in the discourse of the authenticity of the traditional, natural as opposed to communist order of values: the nation and the family are two primary sources of subjectivities.

The idea that individualism could emerge despite traditional (pre-modern) collectivism, socialist ideology and decades of nationalised economy may seem paradoxical if not untenable. But this notion, without liberal bourgeois roots, emerges under very specific socio-historical conditions, which constitute freedom differently. This individualism is a practical response to both material and political conditions and appears as a radical form of negative freedom, as a postulate that freedom involves a possibility of opting out from the social contract or, in other words, as scepticism towards the social. Individual freedom is understood as a utopian state in which the social contract does not bind. It is this kind of individualism which the experience of communism reinforces.

What is also specific about this individualism is that it is not in opposition to traditional family ties. As the private worlds try to isolate themselves against the 'outside', atomisation – if that is a useful metaphor at all – occurs at a different level. The unit of atomisation is not the Orwellian isolated individual but, rather, the family and close friends. The meaningful and trustworthy social horizon is limited to informal and familial relationships to the extent that it almost makes sense to describe the late communist social environment with Thatcher's infamous reflection that 'there is no such thing as society, only individuals and their families': hence the metaphors used by other authors – amoral familism, or the privatised society (Tempest 1997).

So the specificity of this kind of individualism lies in a feeling that one can only count on oneself and one's family, whilst society at large represents an unfriendly and competitive environment. It does not mark the break-up of traditional relationships or a greater detachment, freedom or mobility of the individual, with the simultaneous emergence of modern strategies of societal trust, such as the rituals of civil indifference. Rather, the key organising principles for identity construction remain traditional: the imagined community of the nation and the family. Thus, unlike the Western kind of individualism which signals the shift of authority from without to within and hence a modern social order, Polish individualism is based on re-traditionalised subjectivity necessarily turned against the system and a doubt whether more rational cooperative social relations are possible. Scepticism towards the system does not represent just a disapproval of communism but a further erosion (or absence) of the mechanisms of trust in the mutuality of social relations. Individualism here represents the only utilitarian position: it is a pragmatic 'lifeboat' and an ecologically viable strategy.

Individualism as a pragmatic strategy contrasts with the existential terrain of modernity in which individualism is a result of pluralisation of knowledge and value systems. Late modernity involves a disappearance of established life trajectories, and the *necessity* for the self to choose an identity. The absence of tradition's guidance through the varieties of options on offer means that the self, like modernity itself, is reflexive; individuals have 'no choice but to choose' (Giddens 1991: 81). The choice is not restricted to the fulfilment of utilitarian needs but, rather, is about lifestyle which defines identity. But under the conditions of communism, individuals have no choice but to be individualist. This individualism is not defined by the primacy of lifestyles (Giddens 1991) – it is a response to specific problems of ontological security generated by communism. The existential anxiety that life under communism opens up relates to both utilitarian and moral questions, which the individual cannot but be faced with. Utilitarian problems concern the fulfilment of needs within the limitations of the shortage economy. Thus it would be absurd to claim that self-identity under communism does not involve a reflective project; the existential terrain of communism also includes choices. The choices however are not so much about lifestyle and, however focused on the fulfilment of utilitarian needs, they can rarely be separated from moral choices. Hence the question about self-identity is often a reference to the overriding values, such as the nation ('Am I a good Pole?'), religion ('Am I a good Catholic?') or the family ('Am I a good daughter?').[27]

Does the very fact of such an existential problematic resemble the psychological condition of late modernity? Unlike under the conditions of late modernity, moral dilemmas – in particular those in relation to communism itself – tend to be settled with a sense of *certainty* understood by the philosopher of the Solidarity movement Jozef Tischner as a Christian right or by the then dissident Václav Havel as 'living in truth'. Both writers find certainty in their (Romantic) solutions. That sense of certainty contrasts strongly with the existential terrain of late modernity, which does not provide such comforts. Moreover, under communism only moral solutions must do. The measure of victory at that time was not so much a pragmatic outcome of the struggle but a moral resistance to what was perceived as evil.[28] Thus whilst anti-communist resistance postulates the Romantic conviction of Right over Might, it does so by appealing to the only possible subject of effective campaign: one's own self. So both utilitarian and moral dimensions of the ontological insecurity of life under communism generate individual and anti-political solutions.

This moral strategy involves an implicit recognition that no collective action can bring about a desired effect. Thus the moralising quality of anti-communist resistance adopts methodological individualism which strongly resembles Weber's proto-postmodern solution to the condition of the iron cage, and the explicitly postmodern Bauman's answer to the problem of moral uncertainties (Bauman 1993). In both cases the individual, and *not* the collectivity, is at once the object and the subject of real change. There is however a fundamental difference: whilst Weber and Bauman realise that the global solution will never be possible, oppositional philosophy speaks with a certainty which claims, 'trickle-down' fashion, practical benefits for the collectivity.[29] Moreover, not only does the moral solution become pragmatic, but it is also about a restoration of the (naturally) moral order of things. Once again, the experience of communism constitutes a particular anti-political individualism which does not generate associability, necessary for a healthy functioning public sphere. What it also does is to evoke the Romantic tradition of positioning the spiritual as superior to the rational and to everyday life.

What the above aimed to show is how contingencies of communism – the impossibility of politics of interest, the dominant national unity, and individualism as a lifeboat strategy both as a practical and a moral response to existing dilemmas – have disabled associability potential. Eighteen years on, we now observe a much more complex picture in which new identities and interests are attempting to be formed. Yet what seems to be just as strong, if not stronger, is the anomic form of individualism which renders societal and interpersonal trust difficult. Compared to communism, the contemporary landscape of alienation now includes fierce competition for good education, work, money, prestige and power. And, as the film *Ode to Joy* shows, the world is seen as a harsh Hobbesian reality in which greed and selfishness are regarded as the irredeemable essence of humanity.

Or we, the citizens?

Against this moral and existential landscape, the populist and nationalist intervention seems logical. A-PY brings hope of solidarity, selflessness, the notion that money is not everything and, fundamentally, a restoration of traditional collective and unifying identity at a time when isolation and fragmentation are becoming the norm. The discourse of national unity, now with its originally separate strands conflated into a neo-Romantic version, is appealing because it responds to an ecological need. New identities have emerged and have unsettled social order, not just in the economic sphere but in many settings and social institutions; certainty and traditional authorities have given way to uncertainty and a reaction to new sources of power and prestige. The discourse of the populist right aims to reverse the process of fragmentation of the dominant collective identity and to restore certainty to the notion of Polishness.[30] But a unification of collective identity was a battleground project; in peacetime, when the enemy has gone, identities become less stable – unless, as the right are doing, we invent a new enemy. This is why the populist reach for the single projection of totality is highly dangerous for democracy. Competing interests under capitalism are a fact of its ecology; different group identities are inevitable in a complex tapestry of contemporary cultures. To deny them or to organise them hierarchically is to deny a condition for democratic and peaceful coexistence. A strong warning comes from Michael Mann (2005), who catalogued many cases of ethnic cleansing. The presence of an organic, as opposed to stratified, idea of who we, the people, are has been an ingredient in all extreme versions of ethnic cleansing. When the *demos* is conflated with *ethnos*, in other words where the people is considered to be defined on ethnic grounds, other ethnic groups within the territory might find themselves discriminated against. The latter constitutes an organic conception of the people which is understood as one and indivisible. The notion of the people then carries an idea of ethnic purity which may be threatened by the 'deviant' minorities.

Which way is Poland going then? How is it reinventing itself? There is still a powerful and potentially destabilising reserve of the organic sense of community identity, which is problematical in itself. Here, it also overlaps with anomic individualism, which projects a harsh image of a social reality in which one is fundamentally alone. But, as Mann's warning (2005) suggests, a more stable society is one in which difference is anticipated and interests shared.

Notes

1 This chapter deploys some key concepts from complexity theory, in which a key assumption is that social processes are highly dynamic and at the same time self-organising (Smith and Jenks 2006).
2 There are a number of such code expressions used by the current right wing. They range from the seemingly legitimate expression of doubt about whether certain well-known Solidarity activists (e.g. Michnik or Kuroń) had ever really acted against the communist regime, to more ambiguous general references to the 'post-Solidarity left wing' or 'ex-KOR activists', as in http:// www.mwjelenia.republika.pl/kontrrewolucja/walkaokontrole.html (accessed 17 April 2007), where these very phrases stand for 'the Jews' (owing to their alleged 'Jewishness'). Others can be more overt, as in the case of Adam Michnik for instance, where this takes the form of more or less explicit forms of anti-Semitism; see for instance an essay posted by the popular daily *Nasz Dziennik*: http:// www.informacje.int.pl/adam_michnik (accessed 17 April 2007).
3 The Polish version of this quotation is: 'prawdziwym ograniczeniem naszej wolności są agenci KGB sprzedani wywiadom zachodnim oraz ludzie (dysydenci z PZPR w roku 1968), którzy za pieniądze rządów zachodnich uprawiają od dwudziestu lat politykę w Polsce', R. Giertych, http://www.mwjelenia.-republika.pl/kontrrewolucja/sojuszzrosja.html (accessed 2 March 2007).
4 In response to a wave of anti-communist student protests in March 1968, the communist party launched an anti-Semitic campaign, alleging that social disturbances had been a Zionist plot. As a result the ruling party, the military, universities and other public offices were purged of people of Jewish origin. Between 1968 and 1971 tens of thousands of people were forced to emigrate.
5 By contrast, the majority is not organised at all, and nor is any other minority representing a measured, calm voice of reason such as *Platforma Obywatelska* (Civic Forum), for example, a liberal democratic opposition party.
6 There was a similar conservative reaction to change immediately in the aftermath of 1989; that 'first-wave' populist conservatism was drawing on class identities as a result of shock-therapy policies, but the current conservatism materialised with the emergence of the SLD-led government in 1993.
7 See also Walicki (2000) on the issue of individualism in which he explains an absence of philosophical individualism by showing that the system of gentry

democracy was anti-authoritarian but not individualist; the individual (or minority) was expected to accept the position of the majority.

8 Indeed independent voices are numerous in Polish online debates.

9 This commitment does not disappear later; he shifts his attention to a more philosophical question of the conditions of the possibility of reason in human communication.

10 See Urry (2005); Smith and Jenks (2006).

11 Elsewhere, I attend to the public sphere in the post-1989 period and characterise it as a political vacuum, which, suffering from a deficit of interests, offered no resistance to a strong neo-liberal ideology. The reforms were justified in relation to *national* interest, which at that time had been a reference to a familiar and highly charged notion to highlight an existing pattern – a recourse to the notion of national interest which implies societal unity (Sidorenko 1998, 2000).

12 The public sphere as a realm of social life in which an unrestricted process of societal reflection upon its condition takes place through open and rational debate.

13 This is a reference to the needs to legitimate power by the former and to mobilise for political activity and support by the latter.

14 Take the example of the harvest festivals which, despite their traditional origin, were, in the name of celebrating the contribution of the working class, hijacked into communist party occasions. At the same time, unofficial celebrations, often taking the form of special Mass offerings commemorating important events from history, were considered anti-state activities. From the oppositional point of view the morally correct position was to boycott the first and support the latter.

15 In complexity theory, positive feedback refers to an amplification rather than a positive judgement.

16 An even earlier origin of the special religious Polish mission and, in particular, its close connection to Catholicism can be traced. Davies points to the 1620 reference to Poland as a guardian of the eastern frontiers of Christianity and, significantly, to the 1656 crowning of the Virgin Mary as the Queen of Poland after a miraculous delivery from the Swedish siege (Davies 2002).

17 Since the collapse of communism this issue has been debated: see for instance Kurczewska (2002), who argues that this conception is already giving way under the pressure of fragmentation; yet she also documents after Nowicka and Nawrocki (1996) that at least in 1996 Polishness still continued to be the key collective identity in Poland.

18 There have been various social consequences stemming from that, not least a difficult relationship with legality in general.

19 For Walicki this is politically significant in itself: the ideal homeland does not require responsibility for it; it therefore affects the idea of citizenship.

20 This point was made by Ost specifically in relation to post-1989 Poland. It is based on the same premises that Mann (2005) uses in his work on the dark side of processes of democratisation; that accepted pluralism is necessary and that its denial (de-structuration) in the form of a projected cultural homogeneity poses threats to minorities.

21 'There is no pluralism in a country where various others: blacks, Jews, communists or Seventh Day Adventists do indeed exist but meet with dislike [*niechec*] and ostracism. There is no pluralism where some political, economic and cultural options, although not forbidden, yet become the object of marginalising practices in the name of . . . moral principles, historical justice or raison d'etre' (Kowalski, in Bojar 2002: 97–8).

22 Only a few years ago, Kurczewska (2002) was quite confident that nationalist populism, although occasionally visible, did not pose a real threat to the emergent democracy. Interestingly, one of the reasons for her optimism was the explicit anti-Semitism of ultra-nationalists, which she considered marginalised them politically.

But, since then, the official publications of say Mlodziez Wszechpolska have removed the more explicit evidence of their anti-Semitism. As an organisation, All-Poland Youth is true to its slogan: *tradycja i nowoczesnosc* (tradition and modernity); it understands the power of the image.

23 Under communism, whilst the Church became an open and inclusive space for oppositional sentiments and activity, the identity of Pole the Catholic had been re-energised.

24 Patterns that are simple and easy to comprehend or comply with tend to be ecologically robust (see the concept of memes in Smith and Jenks 2006).

25 Others document the specific anarchist (as opposed to liberal) sense of individualism in Poland: see for instance Lepkowski (1983); Davies (1981).

26 In fact, an unintended consequence of the communist economic failure is the constitution of the autonomous enterprising subject, which resembles a form of Foucault's liberal governmentality (Sidorenko 1998).

27 At the same time, individual functioning within the shortage economy opens up constant ethical dilemmas involving joining the communist party, participation in the black market economy, corruption, more or less corporate theft, etc.

28 This is not to say that collective dissident activity was condemned but that 'revolution . . . [was] an event in the realm of the spirit . . . A truly great revolution [was] a holiday of the liberation of a human being from the fear of other human beings' (Tischner 1984: 53–4) and 'The best resistance to totalitarianism is simply to drive it out of our souls' (Havel 1986: 154).

29 'Does not the perspective of a better future depend on something like an international community of the shaken which, ignoring state boundaries, political system, and power blocks, standing outside the high game of traditional politics, aspiring to no titles and appointments, will seek to make a real political force out of a phenomenon of human conscience?' (Havel 1986: 157).

30 A very similar process in relation to the rise of Christian fundamentalism in the USA is described by Castells: 'There is . . . something . . . shared by men, women and children. A deep-seated fear of the unknown, particularly frightening when the unknown concerns the basis of everyday, personal life. Unable to live under secular patriarchalism but terrified of solitude and uncertainty in a wildly competitive, individualistic society where family, as a myth and as a reality, represented the only safe haven, many men, women and children pray to God to return them to the state of innocence where they could be content with benevolent patriarchalism under God's rules. And by praying together they become able to live together again' (Castells 2004: 29).

References

Arato, A. (1982) 'Critical sociology and authoritarian state socialism', in J. B. Thompson and D. Held, *Habermas: critical debates*, London: Macmillan.

Bauman, Z. (1993) *Postmodern ethics*, Oxford: Blackwell.

Bojar, K. (2002) 'O zrodlach slabosci etosu demokratycznego w Polsce', in E. Mokrzycki, A. Rychard and A. Zybartowicz, *Utracona Dynamika? O niedojrzalosci polskiej demokracji*, Warsaw: IFiS PAN.

Castells, M. (2004) *The power of identity: the information age – economy, society and culture*, vol. 2, Oxford: Blackwell.

Davies, N. (1981) *God's playground: the history of Poland*, vol. 1, Oxford: Clarendon Press.

Davies, N. (2002) 'Polska mitologia narodowa' [Polish national mythology], in *Smok wawelski nad Tamiza*, Kraków: Znak.

Flak, M. (2006) 'Młodzież silna, nieskazona', Interview with the historian Andrzej Chojnowski, *Tygodnik Powszechny*, 15 May, http://tygodnik.onet.pl/ 1547,1335551,dzial.html (accessed 17 April 2007).

Giddens, A. (1991) *Modernity and self-identity*, Cambridge: Polity Press.

Giertych, R., *Kontrrewolucja Młodych*, http://www.mwjelenia.republika.pl/kontrre-wolucja/sojuszzrosja.html (accessed 2 March 2007).

Habermas, J. (1989) *The structural transformation of the public sphere*, Cambridge: Polity Press.

Havel, V. (1986) *Living in truth*, London: Faber & Faber.

Kurczewska, J. (2002) 'Po co nam patriotyzm?', in E. Mokrzycki, A. Rychard and A. Zybartowicz, *Utracona Dynamika? O niedojrzalosci polskiej demokracji*, Warsaw: IFiS PAN.

Łepkowski, T. (1983) *Myśli o historii Polski i Polakow*, Warsaw: CDN.

Mann, M. (2005) *The dark side of democracy: explaining ethnic cleansing*, Cambridge: Cambridge University Press.

Millard, F. (1999) *Polish politics and society*, London: Routledge.

Nowicka, E. and Nawrocki, J. (eds) (1996) *Inny-obcy-wrog: Swoi i obcy w świadomości młodzieży szkolnej i studenckiej*, Warsaw: Oficyna Naukowa.

Offe, C. (1993) 'The politics of social policy in East European transitions: antecedents, agents and agenda of reform', *Social Research*, 60(4).

Ost, D. (1993) 'The politics of interest in post-communist East Europe', *Theory and Society*, 22.

Pankowski, R. (2004) 'Krajobraz brunatnieje', *Tygodnik Powszechny*, 29 February.

Sidorenko, E. (1998) 'Neo-liberalism after communism: constructing a sociological account of the political space of post-1989 Poland', Ph.D. thesis, Goldsmiths College, University of London.

Sidorenko, E. (2000) 'Feminism? How do you spell it?', Unpublished paper presented at a two-day gender studies seminar, Warsaw, April.

Smith, J. and Jenks, C. (2006) *Qualitative complexity: ecology, cognitive processes and the re-emergence of structures in post-humanist social theory*, London: Routledge.

Starnawski, M. (2006) 'Stare sztuczki w nowych dekoracjach', Article posted on 1 September on lewica.pl – lewicowy portal informacyjny, http://www.lewica.pl/ ?id=11548 (accessed 10 September 2006).

Tempest, C. (1997) 'Myths from Eastern Europe and the legend of the West', in R. Fize and S. Rai, *Civil society, democratic perspectives*, London: Cass.

Tischner, J. (1984) *The spirit of Solidarity*, San Francisco, CA: Harper & Row.

Traynor, I. (2006) 'Nazi claims and sex scandal threaten Polish government', *Guardian*, 9 December, http://www.guardian.co.uk/international/story/ 0,,1968078,00.html#article_continue (accessed 10 December 2006).

Urry, J. (2005) 'The complexity turn and the complexities of the global', *Theory, Culture and Society*, 22(5).

Walicki, A. (1993) *Zniewolony umysł po latach*, Warsaw: Czytelnik.

Walicki, A. (2000) *Polskie zmagania z wolnością*, Kraków: Universitas.

8 European civilisation or European civilisations: the EU as a 'Christian club'?

Public opinion in Poland 2005

Clare McManus-Czubińska and William Miller

For centuries, Europe has been divided between Catholic, Protestant, Orthodox, Muslim and secular traditions, all of which might have some claim to be recognised as territorial-religious 'civilisations', despite their common roots. According to Huntington's much contested thesis, such concepts were to become more prominent towards the end of the twentieth century, as the end of the 1918–89 'clash of ideologies' would be followed by an inevitable 'clash of civilisations', defined primarily by religion (Huntington 1993). Critics have pointed out that most conflicts have been within such 'civilisations' rather than between them, that the great clash of civilisations has not yet occurred – and that mere occurrence would not prove 'inevitability' (Arjomand and Tiryakan, 2004; Fox 2005; Henderson 2005). However, the debate raises the question of the extent to which the public in different countries view the world through civilisational spectacles, and the extent to which these traditions structure the public's attitudes towards political issues. Given the strength of the Catholic tradition in Poland, and its relation to Poland's joining the European Union (EU) with its range of territorial-religious traditions, the character of public opinion in contemporary Poland is of particular significance for the exploration of these questions.

In order to structure our interpretation of public opinion in Poland on civilisational issues it may be useful to outline some clear visions or images of 'Europe', of the EU in particular, and of 'home country' and foreign countries. Borrowing terms from the literature on nationalism (Hussain and Miller 2006), we can distinguish: 1) a civic/constitutional vision; 2) an ethnic/ historical/traditional vision; and 3) a multicultural/diverse vision. The civic/ constitutional vision focuses on laws, treaties, mutual obligations within the community, and the values of liberalism, human rights and democracy – a community of rights and obligations. It is often applied to the EU as a 'union of values', a 'civic community . . . distinct from cultural . . . Europe' (Risse 2004). In sharp contrast, the ethnic/historical/traditional vision focuses upon supposedly common, binding, historical experiences, and on religion or culture – a community of people who have much in common. It is applied especially to 'Europe' rather than the EU, defined as Christendom or a 'Christian club'. The multicultural/diverse vision combines the notion of rights and obligations with a recognition of the diversity of historical experiences, religion and culture that goes beyond liberal toleration – a vision of a community supposedly strengthened rather than weakened by diversity. It depicts diversity as an asset, not a burden. It is frequently applied to the EU and to some states within the EU. In addition, Sjursen's (2002) discussion of 'utility' as a justification for EU enlargement implicitly highlights a fourth, utilitarian vision of the EU, as a zone of peace and plenty, 'a code for jobs, prosperity, freedom to travel and work' (Woollacott 2002), not necessarily a community at all, but simply a good place to live.

These competing visions will be explored in relation to Polish public opinion, using data from questions placed by the authors in the 2005 Polish National Election Study (PNES). We focus on the extent to which the Polish public envisions the EU as a 'Christian club' and how this relates to their attitudes to the possibility of Turkish membership of the EU. From Huntington's civilisational perspective, the Polish public, as the most Catholic in Europe, should react strongly against Turkey's accession, which would bring another 70 million Muslims to add to the 20 million already in the EU. They should have more mixed but nonetheless still negative attitudes towards the admission of Orthodox countries such as Ukraine, Russia or Georgia. And they should even be rather uncomfortable in the existing EU, which, in large measure, does not share the same faith and practice as the Polish public. However, as Dyer (2005) has argued, while 'many' in Europe and 'most' in Turkey are believers, religious belief 'does not swallow up their whole identity'. This may be applied to Poland, which also has a 'national interest' perspective on EU enlargement, as well as a 'civilisational' perspective. And, as we shall show, the Polish public is much more concerned to insist on accession states observing European standards of human rights (a civic/constitutional vision) than to insist on them having a Christian tradition.

Religiosity, secularism and civilisational thinking

Our analysis is structured around a complex model that posits a chain of influence as shown in Figure 8.1.

It would be surprising if religiosity did not have an impact on secularism, but religiosity should not be equated with anti-secularism. Indeed, if Onis (2004) is correct, the link between personal religiosity and political secularism (in the sense of a separation of Church and State) may be notable for the weakness of the (negative) correlation between them, not the strength. In addition, attitudes towards a post-Christian or non-Christian EU should not be equated with the acceptability of specific candidates for accession. Other factors may outweigh the religious/civilisational influence. So the correlation between support for the general principle of a Christian club and the acceptability of specific candidates for accession may also be notable for the weakness of the correlation between them, rather than the strength.

Unusually perhaps, our hypothesis is neither that these key correlations

(i)	(ii)	(iii)	(iv)	(v)
Socio-economic background				
	→ Personal religiosity			
		→ Political secularism		
			→ Attitudes to: a post-Christian or non-Christian EU	
				→ Acceptability of specific candidates for EU accession

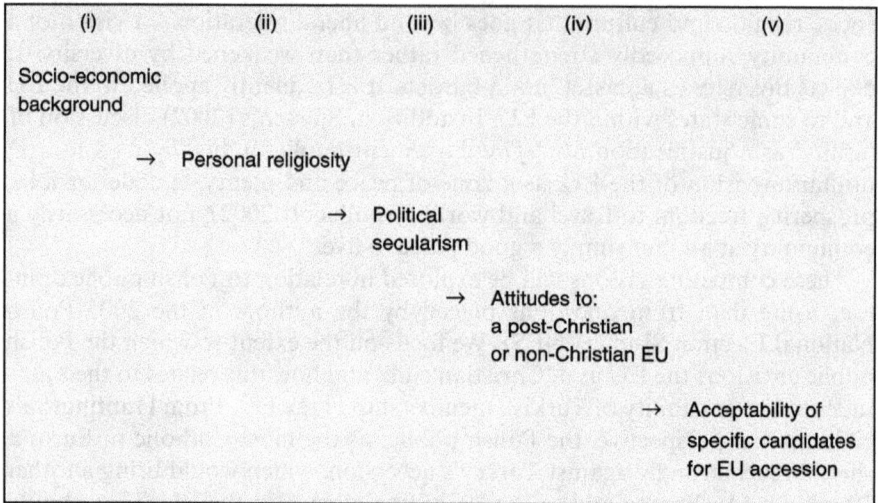

Figure 8.1 Complex influences on Polish attitudes towards the EU.

will be insignificant nor that they will be strong. It would be extremely surprising if these correlations were insignificant. And it would be simplistic to assume that they are strong. Rather, we suggest these correlations should be detectable, even statistically significant, but nonetheless weak. In particular we expect the analysis to show that in Poland the simplistic equations – religiosity = (low) secularism; and still more so religiosity = opposition to Turkey's accession – are more misleading than enlightening.

A Catholic country for a Catholic people?

Poland is widely regarded as the most Christian and Catholic country in Europe. Asked by the PNES2005[1] to place themselves on a scale from 'non-believer' through 'agnostic' and 'believer' to 'devout believer', 88 per cent declared themselves to be believers of some kind (77 per cent simply believers plus another 11 per cent 'devout' believers), only 10 per cent agnostics and a mere 2 per cent non-believers. Moreover these terms have a peculiar meaning in the ultra-religious context of Poland: 86 per cent of the self-designated 'devout' attend services at least once a week – and many of them more frequently; but 50 per cent of the non-devout believers also attend once or more a week. Still more significantly, 69 per cent of agnostics attend at least once a year, and over half of them attend 'several times' a year. Even a quarter of the non-believers say they attend Church at least occasionally. When asked for their religious denomination, 94 per cent of agnostics declare themselves as Roman Catholic and only 3 per cent of them give no denomination. Amongst the very few declared non-believers, one in five declare themselves to be Catholic non-believers. Conceptually, there is a difference between frequent

Table 8.1 Religion and religiosity

	Non-believers %	Agnostics %	Believers %	Devout believers %	Full sample %
Attendance at religious service					
Never	75	22	2	2	5
Less than once a year	10	9	2	0	3
About once a year	0	13	3	1	4
Several times a year	5	29	20	3	19
Once a month	0	8	10	3	9
Two or three times a month	0	10	13	5	12
Once a week or more	10	9	50	86	49
	100%	100%	100%	100%	100%
Denomination					
Roman Catholic	19	94	99	97	96
Other	0	3	1	3	2
Non-believer	81	3	0	0	2
	100%	100%	100%	100%	100%

Note: All percentages quoted in this chapter are calculated after excluding those with no opinion or mixed views.

attendance and claims to be devout. It is the difference between extensive and intensive commitment to the faith. But in practice the two correlate strongly ($r = 0.48$): the non-believers are by far the least frequent attenders; and the devout by far the most frequent attenders.

Measured either by attendance or by a 'devout' self-image, religiosity is highest in the oldest cohorts, and amongst women, the least educated, those employed in farming, and those living in smaller towns and villages and in the region of the former Austrian partition. People in the oldest quartile are 21 per cent more likely than the youngest to attend at least once a week, and over twice as likely to declare themselves devout. Women are 14 per cent more likely than men to attend church at least once a week and almost twice as likely to declare themselves devout. Education correlates more with a devout self-image ($r = 0.12$) than with attendance ($r = 0.05$), while rurality correlates more with attendance ($r = 0.21$) than with a devout self-image ($r = 0.14$). Those with post-secondary education are almost four times as likely as those with only an elementary education to declare themselves agnostics or non-believers, and those who live in villages are 26 per cent more likely to attend at least once a week than those who live in the largest cities.

Church and nation: religiosity and national pride

Not surprisingly, religiosity correlates strongly with high levels of trusting the Church, irrespective of whether religiosity is measured either by attendance ($r = 0.48$) or by a 'devout' self-image ($r = 0.41$). Trusting the Church rises from a mere 29 per cent amongst non-attenders to 88 per cent amongst those who attend at least once a week; and from 36 per cent amongst agnostics and non-believers (taken together) to 96 per cent amongst those who declare themselves devout.

Less obviously, religiosity is also tied into nationalism. It correlates quite strongly with simple pride in Poland (r = 0.15 with attendance; 0.17 with a devout self-image; and 0.24 with trusting the Church). Those who are 'very proud' to be Polish citizens rise from 41 per cent amongst agnostics and non-believers (taken together) to 73 per cent amongst those who claim to be devout. And the numbers who are very proud of being Polish rise from 42 per cent amongst those who distrust the Church 'a lot' to 75 per cent amongst those who trust the Church 'a lot'. National pride correlates far better with trusting the Church than with trusting anything else, so it is difficult to avoid the conclusion that what makes people most proud of Poland is its Church – and perhaps also that to identify with Poland is to identify with its Church. Conversely, the numbers who 'oppose the settlement of foreigners in Poland' rise from 20 per cent amongst agnostics and non-believers (taken together) to 41 per cent amongst those who claim to be devout; and from 33 per cent amongst those who distrust the Church 'a lot' to 53 per cent amongst those who trust the Church 'a lot'.

Thus far at least our findings fit the stereotype of Poland as a country that is exceptionally religious, exceptionally Christian and exceptionally Catholic, where religiosity and trust in the Church are very closely connected with positive national pride and also connected to antagonism towards foreign incomers. However, the stereotype fails as soon as we turn our attention from religiosity to secularism.

Church and state: devout but secular?

Onis (2004) argues that there are many 'devout secularists' in both Turkey and Poland: Muslims or Christians who may be personally observant and devout but are nonetheless committed to a secular state. In this view the image of Poland as a secular state with a 98 per cent Catholic population has been obscured by the election of a Polish Pope and by the role of the Church

Table 8.2 The Church and national pride

	Amongst			
	Agnostics and non-believers %	Believers %	Devout believers %	In the full sample %
Are very proud to be a Polish citizen	41	57	73	57
Oppose the settlement of foreigners	20	41	41	38

in the transition from communism. According to the public opinion evidence, while on the one hand the public trust the Church more than any institution except the Polish Army, the absolute level of trust is low. Only 16 per cent say they trust the Church 'a lot', while 55 per cent say they trust it 'a little'. On an eleven-point scale ranging from 'The Church should be separated from state policies' to 'The Church should exert influence over state policies', 74 per cent of Poles opt for the secularist side, 14 per cent for the Church-intervention side, and 12 per cent for the neutral mid-point. Most remarkably, however, 50 per cent opt for the single most extreme point at the secularist end of the eleven-point scale. Even amongst the self-declared 'devout' believers, a majority of 53 per cent take the secularist side, with 30 per cent taking the extreme secularist position at the end of the eleven-point scale.

As always, these answers have to be interpreted in a Polish context. A battery of questions asked whether respondents are or would be 'affronted' by various intrusions of religion into state activities. Only a few (10 per cent) would be affronted by religious symbols or religious oaths in public institutions, but a fifth would be affronted by priests appearing on public TV or by advice on moral issues; a majority (59 per cent) would be affronted by the Church taking a stand on parliamentary legislation; and Poles would be even more affronted (81 per cent) by priests telling people how to vote. Eighty-seven per cent said they 'never' listened to Radio Maryja, a station that habitually did mix religion and politics.

With the exception of attitudes towards voting advice, public attitudes towards these specific 'affronts' correlate more highly with attendance (typically at around r = 0.33) than with devout self-images (typically at around

Table 8.3 A devout but secular nation

	Amongst			
	Agnostics and non-believers %	Believers %	Devout believers %	In the full sample %
Percentage who are/would be affronted by:				
Crosses in public offices	35	7	5	10
Religious instruction in schools	33	7	3	10
Religious character of military oath	32	7	3	10
Priests appearing on public TV	42	21	8	22
Church instruction in moral issues	41	22	7	22
Church taking stands on legislation		61	25	59
Priests telling people how to vote	91	83	56	81
Listen to Radio Maryja	4	13	37	14
Church should be separated from state (extreme point on eleven-point scale)	66	50	30	50

r = 0.23). The reason is clear from Table 8.3: the percentages who are offended do not vary continuously across the three-category religiosity spectrum. There is relatively little difference between believers and devout believers on the milder forms of Church intrusion, which do not affront either. And there is relatively little difference between believers and agnostics/non-believers on the more extreme forms of Church intrusion, which affront both. Only the agnostics/non-believers are much more offended by the milder forms of intrusion, such as crosses in schools; and only the very self-consciously devout remain less than completely affronted by the more extreme forms of intrusion. But what is remarkable is that, even amongst the few with a devout self-image, a quarter say they are offended by the Church taking a stand on legislation, and over half say they would be offended by priests giving advice on how to vote. Similarly, even amongst those who attend church once or more a week, 44 per cent would be affronted by the Church taking a stand on parliamentary legislation, and 74 per cent would be affronted by priests giving advice on voting.

The EU as a post-Christian club?

The EU before May 2004 has been described as a secular 'post-Christian' club in which Poland would be an exception, and indeed we do find evidence that the most religious Poles are much less likely to identify with 'Europe'. Certainly there is a correlation between religiosity and national-versus-European identity. We use a modified Moreno four-point scale of dual identity, running from feeling 'exclusively Polish, not at all European' to feeling 'equally Polish and European' (a negligible number of native Poles feel more European than Polish!). The numbers who feel 'exclusively Polish, not at all European' rise from 32 per cent amongst those who never attend Church to 45 per cent amongst those who attend once a week or more; they rise from 23 per cent amongst agnostics and non-believers (taken together) to 45 per cent amongst those who claim to be devout; and from 38 per cent amongst those who distrust the Church 'a lot' to 58 per cent amongst those who trust the Church 'a lot'. Feeling exclusively Polish and rejecting any identification with Europe correlates at r = 0.15 with Church attendance; at r = 0.12 with a devout self-image; and at r = 0.11 with trusting the Church.

But despite that lack of identification with Europe, there is not much evidence that highly religious Poles feel out of place in the less religious milieu of the EU. Support for continuing membership of the EU correlates (negatively) at r = 0.13 with Church attendance; at r = 0.12 with a devout self-image; and at r = 0.10 with trusting the Church. But even amongst those with devout self-images 70 per cent would vote for continuing Polish membership of the EU if another referendum were held now – as would 77 per cent of those who attend Church once or more every week. The most religious are very comfortable with Poland's membership of the EU, even if the less religious are still more comfortable with it.

Table 8.4 Even the most religious support EU membership

	Amongst			
	Agnostics and non-believers %	*Believers* %	*Devout believers* %	*In the full sample* %
Percentage who feel:				
Exclusively Polish, not at all European	23	39	45	38
Very much more Polish than European	20	20	16	19
More Polish than European	22	22	23	22
Equally Polish and European	35	19	16	21
	100%	100%	100%	100%
Would vote for EU membership in another referendum now	90	80	70	80

The EU as a non-Christian club?

However, would the Polish public feel less at home in a visibly non-Christian Europe than in an allegedly post-Christian Europe? At street level, the public may be more sensitive to a non-Christian Europe than to a post-Christian Europe. We posed two propositions about excluding applicants for EU membership: 1) Countries that do not share the Christian heritage of Europe are not really European and should not be admitted to membership of the EU; and 2) Countries that do not observe European standards of human rights should not be admitted to membership of the EU. In each case respondents were offered a four-point agree/disagree scale of answers. There was overwhelming agreement (88 per cent) that entrants should meet human rights standards; and 46 per cent agreed 'strongly' with that as a requirement for accession. But only about a third (31 per cent) would require accession states to have a Christian heritage. Fully 69 per cent of Poles disagreed with limiting the EU to countries with a Christian tradition, and 26 per cent disagreed 'strongly'. The Polish public is therefore quite strongly opposed to the concept of the EU as a Christian club, while being even more strongly in favour of the EU as a zone where human rights must be protected.

Answers to the two questions are almost uncorrelated, despite the questions being asked in quick succession. Answers to the human rights question are only very weakly correlated with socio-economic background. Only education seems to have much impact. Those with higher levels of education are the least likely to wish to exclude non-Christian countries ($r = -0.13$) but, at the same time, the most likely to wish to exclude countries with poor human rights records ($r = +0.10$). Compared to those with the lowest levels of education they are 22 per cent more likely to disagree strongly with excluding

Table 8.5 Observance of European standards of human rights is a more important criterion for EU membership than Christianity

	Exclude if non-Christian %	*Exclude if not up to European standards of human rights* %
Agree strongly	7	42
Rather agree	24	46
Rather disagree	43	8
Disagree strongly	26	4
	100%	100%

non-Christian countries but, at the same time, 16 per cent more likely to agree strongly with excluding countries that have poor standards of human rights records. They have a strongly 'civic' rather than 'ethnic' vision of what the EU should be – though even amongst the least educated there is overwhelming insistence on adequate human rights, and a two-thirds majority against excluding non-Christian countries. Apart from the impact of education, however, attitudes towards excluding countries with poor human rights records are fairly uniform and consensual – but not so attitudes towards excluding non-Christian countries.

Support for excluding non-Christian countries correlates modestly with rurality ($r = 0.12$), lower education ($r = 0.13$), higher age ($r = 0.13$) and an exclusively Polish identity ($r = 0.12$). It correlates rather more strongly with religiosity ($r = 0.13$ with devout self-images, $r = 0.16$ with frequency of attendance). But it correlates most strongly with indicators of secularism ($r = 0.16$ with being affronted by priests giving advice on how to vote; $r = 0.17$ with trusting the Church; $r = 0.17$ with whether the Church should be separated from the state; and $r = 0.17$ with listening to Radio Maryja).

Support for excluding non-Christian countries is 18 per cent higher amongst the old than amongst the young; 13 per cent higher amongst those with exclusively Polish identities than amongst those who feel equally European and Polish; 15 per cent higher amongst devout believers than amongst agnostics and non-believers; 21 per cent higher amongst those who attend church at least once a week than amongst those who never attend; 15 per cent higher amongst those who are affronted by priests giving advice on voting; 21 per cent higher amongst those who trust the Church 'a lot' than amongst those who distrust it 'a lot'; 17 per cent higher amongst those who think the Church should be involved in politics than amongst those who think it should not; and 18 per cent higher amongst those who listen to Radio Maryja than amongst those who do not.

However, the absolute numbers are critically important here. In no category in the table does a majority agree with the proposition that non-Christian countries should be excluded. The percentage (of those with a view) who opt

Table 8.6 Impact of education on attitudes towards excluding non-Christian countries and countries with poor human rights records from EU membership

	Amongst those whose education is:				
	Elementary	*Vocational*	*Secondary*	*Post-secondary*	*In the full sample*
	%	%	%	%	%
Countries with no roots in Christian tradition should not be admitted to the EU					
Agree strongly	8	7	8	5	7
Rather agree	29	29	19	22	24
Rather disagree	46	40	46	34	43
Disagree strongly	17	24	27	39	26
	100%	100%	100%	100%	100%
Countries that do not observe European standards of human rights should not be admitted to the EU					
Agree strongly	33	39	47	49	42
Rather agree	54	46	41	45	46
Rather disagree	7	11	8	3	8
Disagree strongly	5	4	4	3	4
	100%	100%	100%	100%	100%

for excluding non-Christian countries reaches only 36 per cent amongst those who attend Church at least once a week; 37 per cent amongst those with a devout self-image; 40 per cent amongst the old; 41 per cent amongst those with the highest level of trust in the Church; 44 per cent amongst those who feel the Church should influence public policy and are not affronted by priests giving advice on how to vote; and 46 per cent amongst the small minority who listen to Radio Maryja. Even in the most religious and least secular categories only a minority feel the EU should be a Christian club.

Unacceptable candidates for accession

When offered a choice of six countries – Ukraine, Belarus, Russia, Georgia, Turkey and Israel – and asked to choose their top candidate for EU accession, 70 per cent of Poles opt for Ukraine. They are more divided on candidates for exclusion however. Their top candidate for exclusion is Russia at 41 per cent, followed by Israel at 25 per cent and Turkey at 18 per cent. Whatever the motivations, this is clearly not a civilisational choice, in terms of either exclusion or inclusion. Poles differentiate sharply between nominally Orthodox Ukraine and Russia; Ukraine is by far the most acceptable,

Table 8.7 Social, national, religious and secular correlates with excluding non-Christian countries from EU membership

Countries that do not share the Christian heritage of Europe are not really European and should not be admitted to membership of the EU

	Percentage who agree (including those who agree strongly)
The social correlates	
Age	
– Youngest quartile	22
– Next youngest	29
– Next oldest	35
– Oldest quartile	40
The nationalist correlates	
Self-identification	
– Equally European and Polish	27
– More Polish than European	24
– Very much more Polish	32
– Exclusively Polish	40
The religiosity correlates	
Devout	
– Agnostics and non-believers	22
– Believers	32
– Devout believers	37
Attend	
Never	15
Once a year or less	25
Several times a year	26
Once a month	31
Several times a month	32
Once a week or more	36
The secularism correlates	
Affronted by priests giving advice on voting	
– Yes	29
– No	44
Trust Church	
Distrust Church a lot	20
Distrust Church a little	24
Trust Church a little	34
Trust Church a lot	41
Attitude to role of Church	
Should be separated from state policies	27
Should exert influence over state policies	44
Listen to Radio Maryja	
No	28
Yes	46

Table 8.8 Acceptable and unacceptable candidates for EU accession

	Top choice for accession	Top choice for exclusion	Difference: accession less exclusion
	%	%	%
Ukraine	70	2	+68
Belarus	9	10	−1
Georgia	2	5	−3
Turkey	11	18	−7
Israel	3	25	−22
Russia	7	41	−34

while Russia is the least. Indeed, Orthodox Russia is far less acceptable than Muslim Turkey. Strongly held views on excluding non-Christian states increase the chances of citing Turkey as the top choice for a country to be excluded from the EU by 24 per cent (and decrease the chances of citing Russia by 30 per cent).

However, a single choice overstates Polish preferences. For example, they could have positive attitudes towards two countries, but if their attitudes towards the one were just a little more favourable than towards the other they might opt overwhelmingly for that slightly more favoured country. So we asked separately for each of Ukraine, Belarus, Turkey and Russia whether Poland should: a) act as advocate, helping that country join the EU; b) help it establish good relations with the EU, but no more than that; c) not take any special interest in it; or d) actively oppose its attempt to join the EU. The result was that the Polish public is equally divided between helping and opposing Russian accession to the EU, but by a margin of 39 per cent they would help rather than oppose Ukraine's accession, and by smaller margins they would help both Belarus and Turkey.

Polish attitudes towards the accession of Belarus and Ukraine are completely uncorrelated with views about excluding countries either because they

Table 8.9 Attitudes towards Ukraine, Belarus, Turkey and Russia

	Ukraine %	Belarus %	Turkey %	Russia %
Poland's attitude to this country should be to:				
Help it join EU	40	26	19	12
Help it establish good relations with EU but not join	34	38	31	29
Not take any special interest in it	24	34	43	48
Oppose its attempt to join EU	1	3	8	12
	100%	100%	100%	100%
Percentage who would help country join *less* percentage opposed	+39	+23	+11	0

lack a Christian tradition or because they do not observe EU standards of human rights. However, support for excluding Belarus or Ukraine does correlate with opposition to the settlement of foreigners in Poland (at r = 0.12 with exclusionary attitudes towards Belarus; and r = 0.11 with exclusionary attitudes towards Ukraine). Attitudes towards the exclusion of Russia do not correlate with opposition to foreign incomers, or with excluding countries on the grounds of their observance of human rights, or with excluding countries on the grounds of their religious tradition.

However, attitudes towards Turkey's accession do correlate significantly – albeit weakly – with views about excluding countries that lack a Christian tradition (r = 0.08) and/or do not reach European standards on human rights (r = 0.10). Using a different question – whether the ultimate goal of EU negotiations with Turkey should be to: a) admit it to full membership; b) develop a closer relationship short of full membership; or c) keep things as they are – produces a higher correlation with views about excluding countries that lack a Christian tradition (r = 0.11) but a lower correlation with views about excluding countries that do not reach EU standards on human rights (a statistically insignificant r = 0.05). Those with less strong views about non-Christian countries do not differ much in their attitudes to the specific question of Turkey's accession. But the few (only 7 per cent) who feel strongly that non-Christian countries should be excluded are distinctive in their wish to 'keep things as they are' or even 'oppose Turkey's attempt to join the EU'. And the much larger number (26 per cent) who feel strongly that countries should not be excluded simply because they lack a Christian heritage are distinctive in their support for Turkey's accession. They differ by 24 per cent on citing Turkey as their top choice for exclusion, by 19 per cent on whether Turkey should be admitted to full membership and by 13 per cent on whether Poland should actively oppose Turkey's accession. But again the absolute numbers matter even more than the correlations. Even amongst the few who say they 'strongly' agree with the principle that only Christian countries should be admitted to the EU, only one-fifth say Poland should actively oppose Turkey's accession and an equal number say Poland should actively help Turkey to join.

An overview model

We can depict the flow of influence from socio-economic background through religiosity, secularism and attitudes towards the EU as a Christian club, in a somewhat simplified version of our original block-recursive regression model, as shown in Table 8.11, in which the only indicators shown (drawn from a wider set, not shown) are those that proved to be important in the sense of having an impact that was not merely statistically significant but also at least moderately powerful (with beta coefficients that exceeded 0.10). The model postulates a five-step sequence of influence running from socio-economic factors, through religiosity, secularism and nationalism, attitudes

Table 8.10 Turkey and EU accession

| | Amongst those whose attitude to excluding countries with no roots in the Christian tradition is: | | | |
	Agree strongly %	Rather agree %	Rather disagree %	Disagree strongly %
Top choice for exclusion				
Russia	17	38	44	47
Turkey	38	19	17	14
Poland should:				
Help Turkey join the EU	20	16	17	25
Help Turkey establish good relations with the EU but not join	20	36	31	29
Take no special interest in Turkey	41	40	45	39
Oppose Turkey's attempt to join the EU	20	8	7	7
	100%	100%	100%	100%
In EU–Turkey negotiations the goal should be to:				
Admit Turkey to full membership	17	21	25	36
Improve the relationship but not admit Turkey to membership	35	45	41	31
Keep things as they are	48	34	35	33

| | Amongst those whose attitude to excluding countries which do not observe European standards of human rights is: | | | |
	Agree strongly %	Rather agree %	Rather disagree %	Disagree strongly %
Poland should:				
Help Turkey join the EU	18	19	23	26
Help Turkey establish good relations with the EU but not join	28	33	36	32
Take no special interest in Turkey	43	43	34	36
Oppose Turkey's attempt to join the EU	11	5	6	7
	100%	100%	100%	100%
In EU–Turkey negotiations the goal should be to:				
Admit Turkey to full membership	23	26	29	33
Improve the relationship but not admit Turkey to membership	39	42	40	20
Keep things as they are	38	31	31	46

Table 8.11 Detailed influences on Polish attitudes towards the EU

Socio-economic background	Religiosity		Secularism and nationalism	Attitudes towards the existing EU	Guiding principles of EU enlargement	Attitudes towards Turkish accession	
(i)	*(ii)*	*(iii)*	*(iv)*	*(v)*	*(vi)*	*(vii)*	*(viii)*
Rurality	Church attendance	Listen to Radio Maryja	Secular response to religious symbols	Feel EU affects Polish culture and independence	Trust EU	Exclude non-Christian countries	Help or oppose Turkey's accession
Gender		Trust the Church	Proud to be Polish			Exclude countries that do not meet human rights standards	Admit Turkey to full membership or keep things as they are
Age							
Education							Turkey is top choice for exclusion or inclusion
Class							

to the existing EU and general attitudes towards EU enlargement, to the acceptability of various potential accession states.

Five socio-economic factors proved to have an important influence upon at least some of the subsequent variables: rurality, gender, age, education and occupational class. Three key indicators of religiosity proved to have some influence: frequency of church attendance, regular tuning in to Radio Maryja, and trusting the Church. But these do not seem to be at quite the same point in the sequence of cause and effect. It seems more reasonable to treat frequency of church attendance as a more basic indicator of religiosity (and one that correlates very well with self-descriptions of devoutness) and treat both regular listening to Radio Maryja and trusting the Church as two consequences of that basic religiosity – albeit partially alternative consequences, and consequences that in turn have their own distinct impacts on more political attitudes.

Next we have indicators of nationalism and secularism: pride in being Polish, and a constructed four-point scale of secularism based on reactions to the mixing of politics with religion. There were several alternative possibilities for an index of secularism, but the one we found most useful reflected the respondents' tendency to be 'offended' by various examples of the intrusion of religion into state activities. If none of these offended the respondent we coded them zero on secularism; if Church advice about either voting or legislation offended them, we coded them as 1 on secularism; if priests on TV or Church advice on morals offended them we coded them as 2 on secularism; and if the religious character of the military oath, religious instruction in schools or crosses displayed in public offices offended them we coded them as 3 on secularism. This coding scheme reflects the quasi-Guttman scale pattern of responses to the individual questions.

Then we have two indicators of Polish attitudes towards the existing EU: whether respondents felt the EU 'affects Polish culture and independence' and whether they trusted the EU. As with indicators of religiosity, we do not regard these two indicators as being at quite the same point in the sequence of cause and effect. It seems more reasonable to treat perceptions of the impact of the EU on Polish culture and independence as one of the factors influencing trust in the EU (for good or ill). In turn, some or all of these factors might influence attitudes towards the guiding principles of EU enlargement: whether, first, countries that do not meet EU standards of human rights and, second, countries that do not have a Christian tradition should be excluded from the EU. Finally there are attitudes towards the specific issue of Turkish accession. We measure those in three ways: first, by whether Poland should 'help or oppose' Turkish accession; second, by whether the goal of negotiations should be to 'admit Turkey to full membership, or keep things as they are'; and, third, by whether respondents cited Turkey as their top choice for inclusion or their top choice for exclusion.

The first steps in the model outline the chain of influences from socio-economic background through religiosity to secularism and nationalism.

Table 8.12 Influences on religiosity

Important influences	beta	Dependent variable
(More rural) location	+20 →	Frequent attendance
Female	+15 →	
Frequent attendance	+48 →	Trust the Church
(Older) age	+14 →	
(Older) age	+21 →	Regular listening to Radio Maryja
Frequent attendance	+17 →	

Frequency of church attendance is strongly influenced by rural/urban location and by gender. It is higher amongst women and those who live in less urban locations. Beyond that, however, no other social factors are important. In particular, education, class and – more surprisingly – age are not important. In turn, trusting the Church depends overwhelmingly on frequency of attendance, though (older) age also has a relatively small supplementary impact. Tuning in to Radio Maryja depends slightly more on (older) age than upon frequency of church attendance however.

Both frequent attendance and, even more, trusting the Church sharply reduce secular responses to religious symbols, while distrusting the Church sharply increases secular responses to the intrusion of religion into public life. To a somewhat lesser degree, low attendance also increases secularism sharply. Beyond that, higher education has a smaller but still powerful influence towards secularism. What is less obvious is the powerful impact of trusting the Church on national pride in Poland. Age also increases national pride, though to a much lesser extent than trust in the Church.

The next steps in the model outline the chain of influences from socio-economic background through religiosity, secularism and nationalism to public attitudes towards the existing EU. Analysis shows that socio-economic factors have no impact except through intermediate variables. Moreover, nationalism and secularism – and even trust in the Church – have no independent impact once we take account of a chain of influence that runs from listening to Radio Maryja, through perceptions that membership of the EU is strongly affecting Polish culture and independence, and on to distrusting the EU. These influences are only moderately large, but our analysis shows

Table 8.13 Influences on secularism and nationalism

Important influences	beta	Dependent variable
Trust the Church	−32 →	Secular response to religious symbols, etc.
Frequent attendance	−26 →	
(Higher) education	+13 →	
Trust the Church	+22 →	Proud to be Polish
(Older) age	+10 →	

Table 8.14 Influences on attitudes towards the existing EU

Important influences	beta	Dependent variable
Radio Maryja listener	+13 →	EU affects Polish culture and independence
Radio Maryja listener	+11 →	Distrust EU
EU affects Polish culture and independence	+11 →	

that concern about the EU affecting Polish culture and independence (for better or worse) depends exclusively on the amount of time respondents spend listening to Radio Maryja. Listening to Radio Maryja increases distrust in the EU both directly and through an enhanced concern about the EU's impact upon Polish culture and independence. Significantly, it is only the time spent listening to Radio Maryja, and not the level of trust in the Church, that increases distrust of the EU. So it is only one peculiar aspect of religiosity that increases distrust of the EU.

Then, as shown in Table 8.11, we looked at two guiding principles for EU enlargement: that it should not extend to countries that fail to meet EU standards of human rights and/or do not have a Christian tradition. Public insistence on accession states meeting EU standards of human rights was very widespread, close to universal. The only factor that influenced adherence to that guiding principle was education, with the highly educated contriving to put even more weight upon it than did the rest of the public. However, three factors influenced public support for the principle of the EU as a Christian club. Not surprisingly, those with more secular attitudes were less willing to restrict accession only to Christian states. But fears for the impact of the EU (even the existing EU) on Polish culture and independence had even more influence (in the opposite direction). Beyond those two factors, secularism and cultural fright, the only other direct influence was age: the old were somewhat more favourable to an exclusively Christian club than the young. Listening to Radio Maryja had no independent influence but it was, of course, the only powerful factor behind cultural fright and thus exerted an indirect influence.

Table 8.15 Influences on guiding principles for EU enlargement

Important influences	beta	Dependent variable
High education	+11 →	Exclude countries that do not observe EU standards on human rights
EU affects Polish culture and independence	+19 →	Exclude non-Christian countries
Secular response to religious symbols, etc.	−16 →	
(Older) age	+11 →	

Guiding principles are far from being determining factors however. As the final step in our model we look at the influence of all factors – from the socio-economic to guiding principles – on the specific issue of Turkish accession. We have four questions that address that specific issue: first, two questions about the respondent's top choice for exclusion and inclusion (which we combine into a single indicator of attitudes towards Turkish accession); then one question about admitting Turkey to 'full membership' and another about whether Poland should 'help' or 'oppose' Turkish accession. Only one factor has an important influence upon citing Turkey as the top choice for exclusion rather than inclusion: the principle of a Christian club. But the influences on replies to the other two questions reveal a more complex – and at first sight more puzzling – pattern. In both cases, as before, subscribing to the principle of the EU as a Christian club has a moderately large, though not overwhelming, influence on wishing to exclude Turkey. In one case, the principle of the EU as a zone of human rights has a slightly greater influence. But, in both cases, distrusting the existing EU has as great an influence as or greater influence than any other influence upon wishing to exclude Turkey. We should recall that distrusting the existing EU was itself influenced most of all by listening to Radio Maryja and fearing that the EU had a large impact on Poland's culture and independence. Those who feared the impact of the existing, largely post-Christian, EU on Poland's culture and independence might well be particularly sensitive about the enlargement of the EU to include 70 million Muslims. So those Poles who feared that the existing EU was threatening their culture would fear even more for Poland in an enlarged, and even less Christian, EU.

However, there is one much more surprising finding, although it emerges only when we look at the issue of whether the aim of the accession negotiations should be to admit Turkey to full membership. From that analysis, it seems that, the more respondents trusted the Church, the more favourable they were towards Turkish accession. This is certainly not the pattern we would expect to find between attitudes towards Turkish accession and listening to Radio Maryja, for example. It seems to hint that the influence of religiosity on attitudes towards Turkish accession points in opposite directions, according to which indicator of religiosity we use. So it is either a statistical quirk or a deeper insight into the connection between religiosity and attitudes towards Turkish accession. On the issue of Turkish accession, Radio Maryja represents only one strand of Polish religiosity, while Pope John Paul II, who adopted a neutral stance on Turkish accession, represented another. John Paul's neutrality certainly seemed to be a benevolent neutrality. So if our finding is not merely a statistical quirk then it may reflect the contrast between religion as local/ethnic identification on the one hand and religion as identification with Church/faith/leadership on the other.

If we restrict our attention to just three indicators – trusting the Church, excluding non-Christian countries in principle, and admitting Turkey in particular – then we find a plausible negative correlation between admitting

Table 8.16 Influences on attitudes towards Turkish accession

Important influences	beta	Dependent variable
Exclude non-Christian countries	+16 →	Turkey top choice for *exclusion* (vs top for inclusion)
Distrust EU	+16 →	Do *not* admit Turkey to full membership
Exclude if non-Christian	+16 →	
Trust Church (note sign!)	−14 →	
Working-class occupation	+11 →	
Distrust EU	+21 →	*Oppose* Turkish accession
Exclude if country does not meet EU standards on human rights	+18 →	
Exclude if non-Christian	+16 →	

Turkey and excluding non-Christian countries (r = −0.11). But we also find two apparently contradictory correlations between trusting the Church on the one hand and both including Turkey (r = +0.09) and excluding non-Christian countries (r = +0.17) on the other. Those who trust the Church are 13 per cent more inclined to exclude non-Christian countries on principle, yet at the same time 14 per cent less inclined to exclude Turkey in particular.

A tabulation of attitudes towards Turkish accession by combinations of trust in the Church and a preference for the principle of a Christian club reveals that the most willing to accept Turkey are those who both trust the Church and have no objection in principle to non-Christians joining the EU. And conversely, though less strikingly, the most unwilling to accept Turkey are those who not only oppose the entry of non-Christian countries on principle but also distrust the Church.

Conclusions

We have found, as expected, that the Polish public are very Catholic, very observant and by international standards very devout. They trust the Church more than anything else except the Army. And their Catholicism is linked to

Table 8.17 Influence of trusting the Church on the principle and practice of a Christian club

	Amongst those who trust the Church %	Amongst those who distrust the Church %
Exclude non-Christian countries on principle	35	22
Exclude Turkey	53	67

Table 8.18 Combined influence of trusting the Church and preferring a Christian club

	Exclude Turkey (rather than admit)	
	Amongst those who trust the Church %	Amongst those who distrust the Church %
Amongst those who would admit non-Christian countries	48	64
Amongst those who would exclude non-Christian countries	64	68

national pride, to identification with Poland at the expense of identification with Europe, and to opposition to foreign incomers. Church and Nation are closely connected.

So the first shock is to find that they are intensely secular at the same time – not in the sense of being irreligious but in the sense of being strongly committed to the separation of Church and State in important matters. They do not react against a proliferation of religious symbols in state institutions, but they do react against the Church taking positions on legislation and still more against priests giving advice on how to cast their votes. Even the most religious are overwhelmingly in favour of staying in the secular, increasingly non-observant and irreligious post-Christian EU, and they do not regard this as a threat to their own distinctive culture. On balance, even the most religious accept the concept of a non-Christian EU and reject the proposition that EU accession be limited to countries with a Christian heritage. The Polish public as a whole massively endorse the proposition that EU accession be limited to states that meet European standards of human rights but also massively reject the proposition that EU accession be limited to states with a Christian tradition.

Those who most trust the Church are instinctively more inclined than others to exclude non-Christian accession states on principle, but even amongst them there is no majority for such exclusion. And the second surprise is that, when they focus specifically on Turkey, those who most trust the Church are the most inclusive. In particular, amongst the majority who would not exclude non-Christian countries on principle, there is a moderately strong and positive correlation between trusting the Church and being willing to accept Turkish accession.

At the same time the Polish public draw the sharpest distinction between the acceptability of Ukraine and the unacceptability of Russia – two countries that are drawn from very much the same Orthodox 'civilisational' tradition as each other. We do not have enough evidence in this survey to determine whether the Polish public endorse the positive 'multicultural/

diverse' vision, but we have ample evidence to suggest that they massively reject the crude 'ethnic/historical/traditional' vision of the EU, associated as it is with Huntington's 'civilisational' perspective, and that they massively endorse the 'civic/constitutional' vision.

Note

1 Our data come from the two waves of the 2005 Polish National Election Study. We have restricted the sample to the 1,201 respondents who were interviewed after both the parliamentary and the presidential elections, since some relevant questions were asked in the first wave and some in the second. That ensures comparability, since all our statistics are calculated across the same set of respondents. They have been weighted to be fully representative of the adult population. Most of the attitudinal questions used in this paper (though not the basic religiosity questions) were designed by the authors, with funding provided by the University of Glasgow.

References

Arjomand, S. and Tiryakan, E. A. (2004) *Rethinking civilisational analysis*, London: Sage.

Dyer, G. (2005) 'Turkey, Europe and the clash of civilisations', *Arab News*, 11 October 2005, accessed at www.aljazeerah.info.

Fox, J. (2005) 'Huntington's unfulfilled clash of civilisations prediction', *International Politics*, 42: 428–57.

Henderson, E. A. (2005) 'Not letting evidence get in the way of assumptions', *International Politics*, 42: 458–69.

Huntington, S. (1993) 'The clash of civilisations', *Foreign Affairs*, 72: 22–49.

Hussain, A. and Miller, W. (2006) *Multicultural nationalism: Islamophobia, Anglophobia and devolution*, Oxford: Oxford University Press.

Onis, Z. (2004) 'Diverse but converging paths to EU membership: Poland and Turkey in comparative perspective', *East European politics and societies*, 18: 481–512.

Risse, T. (2004) 'European institutions and identity change', in R. K. Hermann, T. Risse and M. B. Brewer (eds), *Transnational identities*, Lanham, MD: Rowman & Littlefield.

Sjursen, H. (2002) 'Why expand?', *Journal of Common Market Studies*, 40: 491–513.

Woollacott, M. (2002) 'Is it in Turkey's interests to join this Christian club?', *Guardian*, 13 December, p. 22.

9 Patriotic consumption

The origins and development of Polish vegetarianism

Ewa Kokoszycka

'In the country in which the bourgeoisie systematically gorge themselves and working classes dream of doing the same . . . a vegetarian is regarded as a harmless lunatic', wrote Józef Hempel (1908: 1625). In this passage Hempel, a prominent Polish socialist and a vegetarian, condemned the consumption patterns of the upper and working classes and upheld vegetarianism as a sign of a contemporaneous turn towards nature and as a means of moral and spiritual regeneration (Hempel 1910: XIIIf.). What forms did vegetarianism take then, and who chose to be vegetarian? And why and how did vegetarianism develop in Poland around the turn of the twentieth century as part of wider trends towards the revival of Polish society? These are the issues that the present chapter seeks to examine, placing them in the wider context of Polish history in the nineteenth century.

The development of vegetarianism in Poland took place in partitioned Poland in the period covering the last quarter of the nineteenth century and the early twentieth century until the First World War. In this period there was no Polish state, and Poles were nominal citizens of Austria-Hungary, the German Empire and Russia: the countries that had partitioned the Republic of Poland-Lithuania in the late eighteenth century. Under these circumstances vegetarian Poles were not only vegetarians, but also Polish patriots striving to maintain their national identity. Many of them viewed vegetarianism as a way to improve the condition of the Polish nation, and in this way vegetarianism was seen as patriotic. This feature of Polish vegetarianism is the more interesting if we take into account its close relationship with the transnational vegetarian movement: Polish vegetarianism originated as a result of a process of cultural transfer and was adjusted to the special needs of the Polish population as a result of the political circumstances in which they found themselves after the partitions of Poland.[1]

Vegetarianism is typically located in the context of the alternative movements of the period in question; and the development of these movements is commonly regarded both as a corollary of modernisation processes and a protest against modernisation, an expression of the contradictions and tensions of modernity (Krabbe 1974; Sprondel 1986; Hau 2003). Moreover, vegetarianism is usually discussed in histories of taste, as well as the history of food, including food adulteration, nutrition and diets and attitudes towards health (Mennel 1985; Baumgartner 1992; Carpenter 1994; Merta 2003; Heyll 2006). The works in question provide the background for the research of vegetarian consumption, which has been – to my knowledge – studied only to a very limited extent (Baumgartner 1992; Buchholz *et al.* 2001; Gregory 2002).

Importantly, consumption is understood here not only as the acquisition of commodities in order to make use of them, but also as the expenditure on services which were also bought (Wyrwa 1997; Haupt 2003). Analysis of the patterns of consumption of Polish vegetarians should thus concern both daily vegetarian practices and the 'vegetarian infrastructure', including shops, restaurants and health resorts, along with the vegetarian book market. Among the variety of Polish primary sources, the most useful with regard to consumption as defined here are the vegetarian press, books and cookbooks. A particularly informative, and almost omnipresent, source of information is advertisements, which provide information not only on commodities for vegetarians (including vegetarian food products) and vegetarian restaurants, bars and sanatoria, but also on services specifically for vegetarians.

Socio-political background

In situating Polish vegetarianism in terms of time and space, we need to ask what country was the point of reference for Hempel in the above mentioned introductory passage. Where did the process described take place? Could this have been Poland? Poland served as a point of reference for Poles, even though the Polish state at the time was non-existent. The Republic of Poland-Lithuania had been partitioned by Austria, Prussia and Russia in the late eighteenth century, and therefore Poles were nominal citizens of the three states in question. Hempel, for example, was born in 1877 in a Polish family, but was a nominal citizen of the Russian Empire; yet, when he died in 1937, Poland was independent and had been since 1918.

The initial quotation was in all likelihood written in France, to which Hempel moved in the spring of 1908 (Tych 1960–61: 380–2). He was working in the Polish Library in Paris, which became the cultural and political centre for Poles after the unsuccessful uprising of 1831 in Russian Poland. From Paris, Hempel sent his articles to progressive Polish magazines. The text in question was intended for readers of a Polish journal, *Myśl Niepodległa*, which was published three times a month between 1906 and 1931 in Warsaw. Warsaw was also the capital of the former Kingdom of Poland (*Królestwo Polskie*), unofficially called Congress Poland (*Kongresówka*), as established at the Congress of Vienna in 1815. Thus, what Hempel probably referred to in his writing in 1908 might well have been Congress Poland (*Królestwo Kongresowe*), Russian Poland, or Poland before the partitions.

Importantly, both the text by Hempel, which was in fact a review, and the reviewed publication itself (Hornowski 1908) were published in Russian

Poland in 1908 – the former in Warsaw, the latter in Vilnius – while Hempel himself was staying in Paris. This means that the transfer of books, and circulation of information among and between Poles in different parts of Europe, must have been very good indeed, even though they were widely dispersed around Europe and the rest of the world. Moreover, it should be noted that the nineteenth-century development of rail transport greatly enhanced not only human mobility but also the consumption of culture, including vegetarian publications, despite the limitations on cultural freedom imposed by the partitioning powers. As P. Wandycz (1974: 260f.) pointed out:

> institutionally Polish culture was linked with each of the partitioning powers which determined the character and the scope of education, controlled the organisation of scholarly life, traced the limits for the use of the native language, and supervised cultural activities . . . Policies of the partitioning governments created the framework of Polish culture, but even through russification and germanisation measures the governments could not easily replace that culture with their own. Polish culture and the Polish way of life continued to develop and transcend the political boundaries that divided the old commonwealth.

In this context, Polish vegetarianism was developing in all three parts of the former Polish state and beyond, and Polish vegetarians were operating across national boundaries. The fact that they were widely dispersed and yet stayed in touch with one another testifies to their great mobility and flexibility. The relative freedom of movement and choice of domicile allowed Poles living in the Russian, Austrian and German territories to interact with each other; moreover, many migrated as a result of difficult material conditions or the political situation. The political restrictions with which vegetarian Poles had to cope were especially severe in the Russian part of Poland, which was under an almost permanent system of emergency rule. This is why Polish vegetarian Władysław Miłkowski (1847–1928), a journalist and editor, left Warsaw in 1870, tired of the frequent disagreements with the Russian censorship, going to Florence to study philosophy and finally settling down in Kraków (Pieczątkowski 1976: 262f.).[2]

However, unlike Miłkowski and many other Poles who chose to emigrate, others sought to adapt in different ways to the conditions in the occupied territories. For example, a prominent Polish vegetarian, Czarnowski (1861–1935), decided to follow a different career when he faced discrimination in German Poland. Initially he had taught in primary schools in German Poland and in Berlin, but he was dismissed because he gave private lessons in Polish. He subsequently turned to dentistry, in which he completed his studies, and became a famous dentist (Mańkowski 1938: 235).[3] After moving to Berlin for good in October 1888, he also began to teach Polish, but made his living principally as a dentist and – later on – as an editor.[4] He was also a committed vegetarian supporter and a great Polish patriot, even though he was not Polish, but a Kashub (a member of an ethnic group living in northern Poland, at the time closely involved in preserving Polish culture).

The examples given show that, in terms of a social group, Polish vegetarians were representatives of the Polish intelligentsia, while the example of Czarnowski shows also a lack of homogeneity in the ethnic composition of Polish vegetarians, as well as the fact that vegetarian Poles lived and worked beyond the boundaries of the former Poland. Some also dwelled in countries further away than the partitioning states: for instance, Dr Józefa Jotejko (1866–1928), a prominent Polish scientist and vegetarian, who worked for many years in Brussels and Paris (Konarski 1964: 297–300).

Infrastructure of vegetarian consumption

The unusual dispersion of Polish vegetarians conditioned their *modus operandi* and played a part in preventing them from creating an organised movement of which societies were the constitutive elements, as happened in the German or British cases. Instead, it seems, Polish vegetarians operated largely in networks. However, they did manage to build some organisational structures, occasionally even setting up societies. The societies in question were those founded in Warsaw (then under Russia) in 1903, the *Warszawskie Towarzystwo Jaroszów* (*Lekarz-Homeopata* 1902, 1903a, 1903b, 1903c), and in Kraków (under Austria-Hungary) in 1913, the *Współdzielczy Związek Jaroszów.*[5] Moreover, the societies that were founded in Lvov in 1909, then in Austria-Hungary (Jastrzębowski 1910: XLI–XLIV), and a year later in Vilnius, then in Russia (*Ruch* 1910b, 1911; Brang 2002: 220), also maintained a Polish identity, at least to some extent. These locations were also the places in which Polish vegetarianism was developing in general, as it was – in the Polish case, just as in the German or British cases – an urban phenomenon. Vegetarian settings such as societies promoted vegetarianism by means of lectures, the distribution of vegetarian publications and the promotion of vegetarian establishments. In 1912, in Russian Poland there were at least four vegetarian restaurants – three in Warsaw, one in Lodz; in Austrian Poland there were five – two in Kraków and three in Łódź; and in the former Lithuanian part of the Polish-Lithuanian Commonwealth, then in Russia, there were four – three in Kiev and one in Minsk.[6] Moreover, another type of vegetarian establishment, vegetarian health resorts, had been set up outside the cities.

In general, vegetarian settings are important from the point of view of vegetarian consumption, as they constitute concentrations of supply and demand for vegetarian infrastructures, including the vegetarian food market and book and press retailing. It seems that in the Polish case, however, supply and demand were not necessarily determined by place. This can be concluded from the analysis of a Polish vegetarian network centred around the above-mentioned Augustyn Czarnowski, who ran a Polish vegetarian journal and publishing house in Berlin between around 1895 and 1914. Here I will describe the enterprises set up by Czarnowski, as well as some of the vegetarian settings in which he was involved. His example shows how important the role of leaders was in the creating and developing of vegetarian settings. The vegetarian leaders were usually outstanding personalities who acted as the entrepreneurs of vegetarian commodities, as well as of ideas about vegetarianism. Importantly, in many cases, advocating vegetarianism went hand in hand with Polish patriotism – and this was the case with Czarnowski.

Czarnowski was the creator and editor of a journal, *Przewodnik Zdrowia* (the *Health Guide*). It was a monthly publication that was released in the period between 1895 and 1929. The journal was initially printed in Berlin and then in German Poland (Toruń), as were most of the publications by Czarnowski. The periodical was distributed in the German Empire, Russia, Austria-Hungary and the US. Up to 1905 more than forty reprints of articles from the journal were released as separate booklets (Mańkowski 1938). Thus it can be assumed that it was quite successful, even though in the *Health Guide* itself there is no indication of the number of copies in which it was printed (except for a stamp in the November issue from 1895 which informs us that the journal was published in 1,000 copies) (*Przewodnik Zdrowia* 1895).[7] The title of the journal is indicative of its contents, with articles on hygiene, diet, nature cure, marriage and sexual reform. In the journal, diet was considered as a marker of the condition not only of the individual but also of the nation, and thus vegetarianism, considered as a point of departure for broader social changes, was regarded as especially important for the Polish people and its future (*Przewodnik Zdrowia* 1897, 1898). Poles, it was argued, should live according to the principles of nature, i.e. vegetarianism, so as not to degenerate and turn out less worthy than other Slavonic nations or the Germans (*Przewodnik Zdrowia* 1896).

It was possible to buy the *Health Guide* from Czarnowski in Berlin, or from his representatives, usually the publishers or owners of bookshops in which the journal was sold. The fact that the *Health Guide* was read by Poles in Berlin is corroborated by the advertising placed in it, directed specifically towards Poles. Undoubtedly, the rapidly growing Polish population in Berlin provided an attractive market. Whilst in 1870 between 4,000 and 5,000 Poles lived in the city and in its outskirts, by 1910 the number of Polish inhabitants of Berlin had reached 81,000 (Molik 1989: 187).[8] Moreover, already in 1903 the journal had representatives in Austrian Poland (Lvov), German Poland (Poznań) and Russian Poland (Warsaw). In the United States, the periodical could be bought 'in virtually all the offices of Polish journals' (*Przewodnik Zdrowia* 1903).

On the basis of the popularity of the *Health Guide*, Czarnowski was able to start up other related enterprises. Apart from the Health Guide publishing house, he founded the Hygieia Institute, selling homoeopathic medicines and other health products; the Hygieia publishing house and mail-order company; and a further firm, also called Hygieia (Czarnowski & Co.), selling health products and household devices. These firms all advertised their services in the same issue of the *Health Guide*,[9] which shows us that they were all in business at the same time and possibly complemented each other. What is interesting, though, is that under the Hygieia label it was possible to make links to German consumers as well. The Hygieia publishing house was in fact the German equivalent of the Health Guide publishing house. Such links could not have been achieved by means of a Polish label, whereas the word 'Hygieia' was understandable for Polish and Germans alike. Furthermore, the emblem of Hygieia and the Health Guide, representing the Greek goddess Hygieia, with a river and trees in the background, was featured on the cover of the *Health Guide*, as well as that of the Hygeia Institute. It was also their registered trademark and therefore under legal protection (Czarnowski 1909). Moreover, the headquarters of all these firms were the places in Berlin in which Czarnowski was living, as a comparison of Berlin address books and the advertisements of the firms in the *Health Guide* shows.[10]

Between 1906 and 1913 Czarnowski's home was situated in Weissen-burgerstraße 27, now Kollwitzstraße (Mende 1998: 340; Lais and Mende 2004: 341). The house, a two-storey building, was built in 1887; Czarnowski moved in with his wife nine years later. In the building there was a laboratory where the homoeopathic medicines and cosmetics of the Hygieia Institute were prepared.[11] The products – homoeopathic medicines, cosmetics and household devices – could be either ordered by mail or else bought directly in the Hygieia Institute in Weissenburgerstraße 27. Moreover, the house served as a bookshop in which not only were the Polish publications of the Hygieia and the Health Guide publishing houses sold, but also books and brochures in German and translations into German from other languages such as English (Czarnowski 1909). Furthermore, Czarnowski as a dentist and editor saw his patients and clients there, as did his wife, Maria, a nature curer specialising in vegetarianism and other non-surgical methods of heal-ing. This whole establishment resembled a warehouse to some extent, in which commodities and services were sold, as well as a workshop in which they were produced.

Importantly, Czarnowski was actively engaged in activities of the Polish diaspora in Berlin and was as a result quite influential and well known. He was the head of Polish cultural and educational institutions in Berlin, such as *Oświata* (the Enlightenment Society), and represented the interests of the Polish group in relations with the German authorities.[12] From at least 1894 he was head of the Polish school committee, and he organised and took care of Polish schools in the region. He also co-organised cultural and patriotic meet-ings of Poles.[13] In a report of the Berlin police in 1896, he was labelled as 'one of the best-known Polish national instigators'.[14] In general he shaped the life of the Polish diaspora in Berlin with his activities and his publications. The fact that he was, on the one hand, so prominent in the Polish milieu, as well as true to his patriotic ideals, and, on the other, so flexible (changing his profession) and highly effective in the – anti-Polish – Berlin reality partly explains his success as a publisher of writings in both Polish and German and as a businessman with both a Polish and a German clientele. He was the unquestionable leader in the Polish progressive milieu and a publicist, even a propagandist, as well as an entrepreneur of both commodities and ideas. His example highlights the importance of vegetarian leaders who shaped Polish vegetarianism in its early stages.

Another vegetarian leader working with Czarnowski was Dr J. Drzewiecki (1842–1907). Drzewiecki visited Czarnowski in Berlin, and translated publications from English, afterwards printed by the Health Guide publishing house. Drzewiecki was head of the Warsaw Vegetarian Society (*Warszawskie Towarzystwo Jaroszow*), founded in Warsaw at the turn of 1902 and 1903 with thirty-five members (*Lekarz-Homeopata* 1902, 1903a, 1903b, 1903c; *Otchet* 1903–04: 14), and the Warsaw Society of Supporters of Homoeopathy (*Warszawskie Towarzystwo Zwolenników Homeopatii*), founded in Warsaw in 1892 (*Gazeta Lekarska*, 1892). He was also the editor of the monthly journal of the two societies, *Lekarz-Homeopata: Organ Warszawskiego Towarzystwa Zwolenników Homeopatii, poświęcony medycynie homeopatycznej i higienie* (*Doctor-Homoeopath: Organ of Warsaw Society of Supporters of Homeopathy, Dedicated to Homoeopathic Medicine and Hygiene*). This was published between 1902 and 1906, and was later revived between 1932 and 1939 in Warsaw. Drzewiecki was one of the pioneers of homoeopathy and vegetarianism among the Poles (*Lekarz-Homeopata* 1902). A doctor and a homoeopath himself, a patriot and an activist of the national democrats, he was shot (possibly assassinated) in 1907. National democrats were against uprisings as a method of regaining Polish independence and were in favour of achieving it as a result of economic development as well as education of the masses. These ideas should be interpreted in the context of what was then called 'organic work' (*praca organiczna*), a concept that meant strengthening Polish society at its grass roots by means of economic, social and cultural development. The notion had originated in the eighteenth century but was developed by the Polish positivists in the nineteenth century. Even though the idea of 'organic work' was not actually referred to by either Drzewiecki or Czarnowski in their vegetarian writings, their thinking about vegetarianism was very much in line with it.

Another important urban vegetarian setting was centred in Kraków around a Catholic priest, Wincenty Pixa. Pixa was also in touch with Czarnowski (Pixa 1909: 1), and Miłkowski also belonged to this circle. In his vegetarian brochure, Pixa approvingly referred to Janisław Jastrzębowski, a fanatically anticlerical Polish socialist and vegetarian, also active in Austrian Poland, who was also in touch with Czarnowski (Jastrzębowski 1912). Despite the clear differences in their worldviews, all three men had in common not only vegetarianism, very much influenced by the German vegetarian literature, but also Polish patriotism.

The most important Polish health resort run according to vegetarian principles was established by Apolinary and Romualda Tarnawski in 1893 in Kosowo (in Austrian Poland, in the Carpathian Mountains, nowadays in Ukraine). It evolved into a meeting place for Polish vegetarians and Polish patriotic reformers of the period (Tarnawski 1966: 36; Demel 2000: 174f.). Dr Apolinary Tarnawski (1851–1943), himself a sworn vegetarian, applied diet, air and sunbathing, gymnastics and hydropathy as a cure (Tarnawski 1966: 27). Furthermore he:

> wanted to regenerate, both physically and mentally, the whole society just as he restored patients in his resort to health. For him, the sanatorium was a means with which he pursued his chief goal, his mission in life: regeneration of the nation.
>
> (Tarnawski 1966: 20)

Tarnawski was an ardent Polish patriot and supporter of the national democrats, despite his socialist inclinations in early youth (Tarnawski 1966: 58). And even though the sanatorium hosted members of all Polish political factions, it was, above all, the centre of the national democrats, with Roman Dmowski (1864–1939), the main ideologue of Polish nationalism and the co-founder of the National Democratic Party, and its other leaders as patients (Tarnawski 1966: 58f.; Demel 2000: 174f.). The sanatorium was regarded as fashionable (Demel 2000: 174f.) and was highly recommended in, among others, the *Health Guide* (*Przewodnik Zdrowia* 1911). It was so well known that the author of a Polish vegetarian cookbook advertised himself as a cook there (Czarnota 1910). Whether this recommendation had the desired effect or not, the cookbook sold in five editions and was reprinted several times in only twenty-one years between 1909 and 1931. Up to the First World War at least 35,000 copies were sold, including a translation into Russian in 1911 (*Ruch* 1910a; Dobrzyńska 2002: 51).

Importantly, cookery books 'made possible the much more rapid accumulation and wider diffusion of a record of *successful* culinary practice and experience', as S. Mennel (1985: 67) aptly put it. Therefore the popularity of the vegetarian cookbook by Czarnota can be viewed as a corollary of the fact that vegetarianism won broader support among Poles in the first decade of the twentieth century. What is more, the anonymous reviewer of the cookbook attributed its success to the fact that the supply of vegetarian literature in Polish was lower than the demand for it (*Ruch* 1910a). This discrepancy between supply and demand for vegetarian cookbooks among Poles is quite significant, if we consider that Czarnota's work was by no means the only Polish vegetarian cookbook in this period. Further, vegetarian journals or books on vegetarian theory also included recipes as supplements. Interestingly, there were also *non-vegetarian* cookbooks (Norkowska 1903) and advice books on housekeeping (Albinowska 1907) containing vegetarian recipes. The publication of vegetarian cookbooks and the inclusion of vegetarian recipes, not only in vegetarian but also in non-vegetarian books, can be seen as indicative of the fact that vegetarian dishes were gaining wider recognition in the culinary practice of the Poles.[15] The discrepancy between supply and demand for vegetarian cookbooks in Polish only reinforces the thesis of the growing popularity of vegetarianism among Poles in the period in question; it also shows that the market was not prepared for this change in consumer preferences.

Vegetarian consumption as patriotic consumption

Like the British or German vegetarian movements at the turn of the nineteenth and twentieth centuries, Polish vegetarianism was also part of a broader reformist environment, which aimed at hygiene and dietary reforms, natural cures, animal welfare, sexual reforms and an anti-alcoholism campaign. Enacting these changes meant attempting to thoroughly change consumption habits. Nineteenth-century vegetarianism in Britain, Germany, Russia and partitioned Poland meant eschewing not only meat and alcohol, but also hot spices, drugs and tobacco, and sometimes also sugar and honey, along with other animal products. Instead, vegetarians supported alternative medicines and reforms in the way they dressed; they enjoyed sun- and air-bathing, nudism and physical exercises.

Vegetarians commonly believed that, in the words of K. Thomas (1983: 295):

> not only did the slaughter of animals have a brutalizing effect upon the human character, but the consumption of meat was bad for health; it was physiologically unnatural; it made men cruel and ferocious; and it inflicted untold suffering upon man's fellow creatures.

These arguments were in circulation already by the beginning of the eighteenth century, and by the end of the century they 'had been supplemented by an economic one: it was believed that stock-breeding was a wasteful form of agriculture compared with arable farming, which produced far more food per acre' (Thomas 1983: 295). These most basic vegetarian tenets also permeated Polish vegetarian writings in the period in question. However, some ideas developed in the Polish vegetarian literature refer explicitly to the specifically Polish historical experience.

In the Polish case, meat eating signified the decline not only of culture and civilisation but also of the nation. Some argued that ancient Poles were vegetarians. According to Morzycki, an early-nineteenth-century conservative historian and agriculturalist, the Poles became used to eating meat because of contact with the Germans, whereas 'ancient Polish ethics have always been vegetarian!' (Jastrzębowski 1910: XVI). Many authors regarded vegetarianism as a native Polish concept, even though they interpreted its origins in different, sometimes contradictory, ways. For example, while Jankowski (1912) saw Polish vegetarianism as a renewal of the true Polish and Catholic traditions, Jastrzębowski (1910: XVII) maintained that the Poles had been vegetarians even before Christianisation and that the entirely Polish idea of vegetarianism was afterwards corrupted by Jewish–Christian civilisation.

Hempel, in turn, claimed that ancient Poles, despite their Aryan origins, could not have been true vegetarians because the area of land they had inhabited was not rich enough in plants. However, he insisted that the contemporaneous cultural development gave the Poles a chance to recreate the link with their Aryan matrix, the cradle of the whole humankind, through vegetarianism. Thus, for Hempel, vegetarianism was to give Poles a sense of belonging and rootedness in the past of humankind, as well as a starting point for the bright and glowing future (Jastrzębowski 1910: XIV). However, despite differences and contradictions between these invented traditions of Polish vegetarianism, stressing both the specificity and the universality of Polish historical experience, Polish vegetarians agreed that adopting vegetarianism would provide a step towards the spiritual rebirth of the Polish people, a means by which the rebirth of the nation could be secured.

Furthermore, according to Jastrzębowski (1910), not only would vegetarianism enable the Poles to free themselves from foreign oppression but, by adopting vegetarianism, they would acquire a certain amount of independence in life. Such a view had been proposed earlier by Moes-Oskragiełło (1888), who argued that vegetarians were independent, at least from cooks and kitchens; in particular he advocated a diet of unprocessed and raw plant food. The freedom vegetarianism was said to give was seen as especially important for Poles in view of their political situation. As Jastrzębowski (1910: 320) put it: 'for us, Poles, the question of vegetarianism is of special importance. [This is because] none of the governments of the partitioning countries can forbid us to live in a vegetarian way, that is without meat, beer, vodka, tobacco.' In this view, the question of vegetarianism was a political issue, and it was necessary to consider vegetarianism as a manifestation of independence from the system of political oppression exercised by the partitioning countries. Polish vegetarianism can thus be compared to the doctrine of passive resistance developed by Mahatma Gandhi.

Moreover, since meat was regarded as expensive and poisonous, vegetarianism was advocated as beneficial also for the Polish national economy (Jastrzębowski 1910). According to Moes-Oskragiełło (1888), the money saved by adopting a frugal vegetarian lifestyle could be spent on education and other things that were important for the well-being of the nation. Furthermore, not only political and economic but also social arguments in favour of vegetarianism were proposed. Many Polish vegetarians believed that by means of vegetarianism Polish national faults could be overcome. For example, the adoption of vegetarianism would cure the Poles of alcoholism and smoking; the old Polish tradition of obsessive eating would also disappear (Moes-Oskragiełło 1888: 34). This understanding of vegetarianism should thus be viewed in the context of the contemporaneous discourse on 'Polishness' (*polskość*).

In practice, patriotic vegetarian consumption involved the acquisition of commodities produced by Poles; this was also visible in the advertisements for commodities in which the Polishness of the products was stressed, such as those that could be found in the *Health Guide*. In this and other publications by Czarnowski, advertisements of commodities of Polish origin contrasted with the advertisements in German of services and objects of German producers. However, although they were strongly patriotic, Polish vegetarians were receptive to both foreign commodities and ideas. Examples of the latter are the translations into Polish from German (Bircher-Benner 1908), but also from English (Kingsford 1904) and Russian (Tolstoy 1907). Translations from German were the most prevalent; it even happened that Poles read English texts in the German translation, as can be seen from the bibliography in Panek (1906). The Polish debate on vegetarianism had started with the publication in 1884 of a translation from German (Seefeld 1884).[16] This shows that Polish vegetarianism originated in a process of cultural transfer and that its further development was thereafter stimulated by contact with foreign ideas, of which numerous examples can be found in the texts of Polish vegetarians.

Conclusion

Vegetarianism played an important role in bringing together Poles who were scattered over more than three states, even though it was a fringe phenomenon in the period. Despite differences in their political and religious worldviews, many Polish vegetarians had in common not only vegetarianism but also Polish patriotism. They believed that the adoption of a vegetarian lifestyle created an area of personal freedom, which was especially dear to Poles in view of the political oppression they faced under the rule of the partitioning countries. Despite the unfavourable socio-political conditions in which Poles found themselves in the nineteenth century, they took up Western vegetarianism and adjusted it to their particular needs. This instance of cultural transfer is, in my view, a sign of cultural innovativeness and flexibility, *eo ipso* development, rather than of impotence or deficiency. In this manner, the Poles participated in the cultural life of contemporary Europe. On no account is the interrelationship between cultural receptiveness and the focus on preserving national identity specifically Polish. Nevertheless, if we look closely at the Polish vegetarian literature in the period in question, although it was always grounded in contemporary vegetarian thought we discover that, being strongly rooted in the historical context in which it developed, it also gave voice to the wider Polish experience of the time.

Notes

1 The points of reference here are defined almost a priori by the secondary literature, which covers, as regards Europe in the period in question, the leading British (Twigg 1981; Gregory 2002) and German (Krabbe 1974; Barlösius 1997; Buchholz *et al.* 2001) vegetarian movements. To my knowledge, no historical study of Polish vegetarianism has been published yet. Therefore, this paper is based on primary sources relating to Polish vegetarianism, although the most recent and most complete study of the Russian movement also refers to Polish vegetarianism (Brang

2002). The disparity in the secondary literature on the Polish and Western movements is visible also on the level of primary sources. For example, the Polish primary sources on vegetarianism do not include any address books of the members of vegetarian societies, whereas in the British minute books not only is the number, name and sex recorded, but also the age and profession of members of a particular British vegetarian society, just as in the German case. This deficiency in sources prevents, or seriously impedes, a description of the profile of the Polish vegetarians, which can thus be drawn only on the basis of individual biographies. This suggests a qualitative analysis of the sources, since a quantitative analysis would not seem to be possible.

2 Kraków was at the time in Austrian Poland in which the Poles had enjoyed a certain degree of self-government since 1867, and Polish was kept as the official language.

3 See also Landesarchiv Berlin, Berlin: A Pr. Br. Rep. 030 Nr. 12168, *Acta des Königlichen Polizei-Präsidiums zu Berlin, 1895–1897*: 61.

4 See Brandenburgisches Landeshauptarchiv, Potsdam: Rep. 1 Nr. 1077, *Die Agitation der polnischen Bevölkerung, 1880–1901*: 36–7; *Berliner Adressbuch*, 1880–1919; Landesarchiv Berlin, Berlin: A Pr. Br. Rep. 030 Nr. 15356, *Acta des Königlichen Polizei-Präsidiums zu Berlin betreffend der polnischen Schulbewegung, 1891–1898*: 104–6.

5 Archiwum Państwowe, Kraków: Krakowskie Starostwo Grodzkie 256, *Rejestr stowarzyszeń i związków zawodowych, 1919–1931*: 462.

6 This information is derived from advertisements inside the September–October 1912 issue of *Jarskie Życie*.

7 Except for two issues from 1895 and one from 1929, the only surviving copies were published between 1896 and 1914 in Berlin by a publishing house with the same name, i.e. the Health Guide, also run by Czarnowski in Berlin. A police record from 1897 (Landesarchiv Berlin, Berlin: A Pr. Br. Rep. 030 Nr. 12169, *Acta des Königlichen Polizei-Präsidiums zu Berlin, 1897–1898*: 141) informs us it was published monthly in 800 copies as a supplement to another Polish journal in Berlin, *Dziennik Berliński (Berliner Daily)*. However, this is unlikely because there is no evidence of this fact in any Polish source, let alone the *Health Guide*.

8 According to a German scholar, O. Steinert, such a high number of Berlin Poles resulted from adding together the number of Poles living in Berlin and those in the suburbs of Berlin such as Charlottenburg and Spandau, which are now districts of Berlin but at the time were part of Potsdam. According to the census of 1910, there were no more than 37,655 Polish speakers in Berlin (Steinert 2003: 80–1).

9 *Przewodnik Zdrowia* 1910, no. 10, back cover.

10 See entry on 'Czarnowski, A. von', in *Berliner Adressbuch*, Berlin: August Scherl, Deutsche Adressbuch Gesellschaft, between 1889 and 1919.

11 Landesarchiv Berlin, Berlin: A Rep. 010–02, Nr. 10516, Städtisches Vermessungsamt, *Acta örtlichen Strassenbau-Polizei Verwaltung, Abt. 1 zu Berlin, betreffend das Grundstück Weissenburgerstr. No. 27*: 2–4; A Pr. Br. Rep. 030 Nr. 12180, *Acta des Königlichen Polizei-Präsidiums zu Berlin, 1904–1906*: 63–4.

12 Brandenburgisches Landeshauptarchiv (BLHA), Potsdam: Rep. 34 Nr. 3656, *Acten Provinzialschulkollegium zu Berlin betreffend polnischen Unterricht 1893–1908*: 34, 181f.

13 Landesarchiv Berlin, Berlin: A Pr. Br. Rep. 030 Nr. 15356, *Acta des Königlichen Polizei-Präsidiums zu Berlin betreffend der polnischen Schulbewegung, 1891–1898*: 83–4; A Pr. Br. Rep. 030 Nr. 12168, *Acta des Königlichen Polizei-Präsidiums zu Berlin, 1895–1897*: 279–86.

14 Landesarchiv Berlin, Berlin: A Pr. Br. Rep. 030 Nr. 12168, *Acta des Königlichen Polizei-Präsidiums zu Berlin, 1895–1897*: 126.

15 It is not my intention here to quote vegetarian menus, since these would not be representative, given the development of vegetarian cookbooks as a specific genre of vegetarian literature and their subsequent specialisation.
16 For the contemporary reactions to the book see Omikron (1884: 1–2); Kramsztyk (1885); and Moes-Oskragiełło (1885).

References

Albinowska, J. (1907) *Dom oszczędny*, Lwów: Drukarnia Pillera, Neumanna i Spółki.
Barlösius, E. (1997) *Naturgemässe Lebensführung: Zur Geschichte der Lebensreform um die Jahrhundertwende*, Frankfurt am Main/New York: Campus Verlag.
Baumgartner, J. (1992) *Ernährungsreform: Antwort auf Industrialisierung und Ernährungswandel. Ernährungsreform als Teil der Lebensreformbewegung am Beispiel der Siedlung Eden seit 1893*, Frankfurt am Main/Berlin/Bern/New York/Paris/Wien: Peter Lang.
Bircher-Benner, M. (1908) *Podstawy żywienia leczniczego, na zasadach energetyki*, trans. J. Łuczyński, Warsaw: Towarzystwo Zwolenników Przyrodolecznictwa.
Brang, P. (2002) *Ein unbekanntes Russland: Kulturgeschichte vegetarischer Lebensweisen von den Anfängern bis zur Gegenwart*, Cologne: Böhlau Verlag.
Buchholz, K., Latocha, R., Peckmann, H. and Wolbert, K. (eds) (2001) *Die Lebensreform: Entwürfe zur Neugestaltung von Leben und Kunst um 1900*, 2 vols, Darmstadt: Verlag Häusser.
Carpenter, K. J. (1994) *Protein and energy: a study of changing ideas on nutrition*, Cambridge: Cambridge University Press.
Czarnota z Kosowa, J. K. (1910), *Kuchnia jarska na podstawie długoletniej praktyki*, 2nd enlarged edn, Lwów: Księgarnia Polska B. Połonieckiego, Warsaw: E. Wende i Spółka.
Czarnowski, A. von (1909) *Der kleine Kräuterarzt*, 3rd enlarged edn, Berlin: Hygieia.
Demel, M. (2000), *Z dziejów promocji zdrowia w Polsce*, vols 1–2, Kraków: Akademia Wychowania Fizycznego im. Bronisława Czecha w Krakowie.
Dobrzyńska, B. (ed.) (2002) *Bibliografia polska 1901–1939*, vol. 5, Warsaw: Biblioteka Narodowa.
Gazeta Lekarska (1892) 23: 535.
Gregory, J. (2002) 'The vegetarian movement in Britain, *c.* 1840–1901: a study of its development, personnel and wider connections', Unpublished thesis, University of Southampton.
Hau, M. (2003) *The cult of health and beauty in Germany: a social history, 1890–1930*, Chicago, IL/London: University of Chicago Press.
Haupt, H.-G. (2003) *Konsum und Handel: Europa im 19. und 20. Jahrhundert*, Göttingen: Vandenhoeck & Ruprecht.
Hempel, J. (1908) 'Książki', *Myśl Niepodległa*, 82: 1624–5.
Hempel, J. (1910) 'Od autora "Kazań polskich polskich" ', in J. Jastrzębowski, *Precz z mięsożerstwem! Praktyczne wskazówki dla naszych postępowców do wyzyskania drożyzny mięsa w celu duchowego odrodzenia narodu polskiego*, 2nd enlarged edn, Kraków: published by the author.
Heyll, U. (2006) *Wasser, Fasten, Luft und Licht: Die Geschichte der Naturheilkunde in Deutschland*, Frankfurt am Main: Campus Verlag.
Hornowski, W. (1908) *Podstawy szczęścia i rozwoju człowieka*, Wilno: J. Zawadzki.

Jankowski, R. (1912) 'W obronie zakonu Bożego', Warsaw, printed by the author.
Jarskie Życie (1912) 9–10.
Jastrzębowski, J. (1910) *Precz z mięsożerstwem! Praktyczne wskazówki dla naszych postępowców do wyzyskania drożyzny mięsa w celu duchowego odrodzenia narodu polskiego*, 2nd enlarged edn, Kraków: published by the author.
Jastrzębowski, J. (1912) *Historia ruchu wegetariańskiego w Polsce*, Berlin: Hygieia.
Kingsford, A. (1904) *Naukowe podstawy diety roślinnej (jarstwa)*, transl. Ludwik Leszczyński, Warsaw: Drukarnia J. Sikorskiego.
Konarski, S. (1964) 'Jotejkówna Józefa Franciszka', in *Polski Słownik Biograficzny*, vol. 11, Wrocław/Warsaw/Kraków: Wydawnictwo Polskiej Akademii Nauk.
Krabbe, W. R. (1974) *Gesellschaftsveränderung durch Lebensreform: Strukturmerkmale einer sozialreformerischen Bewegung im Deutschland der Industrialiesierungsperiode*, Göttingen: Vandenhoeck & Ruprecht.
Kramsztyk, S. (1885) 'Raz jeszcze o jaroszach', *Kurier Warszawski*, 1: 11–12.
Lais, S. and Mende, H.-J. (eds) (2004) *Lexikon Berliner Strassennamen*, Berlin: Haude Et Spencer.
Lekarz-Homeopata (1902) 1: 42.
Lekarz-Homeopata (1903a) 9: 224–6.
Lekarz-Homeopata (1903b) 10: 242–6.
Lekarz-Homeopata (1903c) 12: 285–8.
Mańkowski, A. (1938) 'Czarnowski Augustyn', in *Polski Słownik Biograficzny*, vol. 4, Wrocław/Warsaw/Kraków: Wydawnictwo Polskiej Akademii Nauk.
Mende, H.-J. (ed.) (1998) *Lexikon: Alle Berliner Strassen und Plätze. Von der Gründung bis zur Gegenwart*, 4 vols, Berlin: Verlag Neues Leben.
Mennel, S. (1985) *All manners of food: eating and taste in England and France from the Middle Ages to the Present*, Oxford/New York: Blackwell.
Merta, S. (2003) *Wege und Irrwege zum modernen Schlankheitskult: Diätkost und Körperkultur als Suche nach neuen Lebenstilsformen 1880–1930*, Stuttgart: Franz Steiner Verlag.
Moes-Oskragiełło, K. (1885) *Odpowiedź na omowy jarstwa, czyli wegetarianizmu panów Omikrona, St. Kramsztyka i A. Mg. z 'Kraju' zakończone uwagami nad godnością dziennikarską 'Kuriera Warszawskiego'*, Warsaw: Księgarnia G. Sennewalda.
Moes-Oskragiełło, K. (1888) *Przyrodzone pokarmy człowieka i wpływ ich na dolę ludzką*, Warsaw: Tłocznia Braci Jeżyńskich.
Molik, W. (1989) 'Berlin in der Sicht polnischer Besucher in der Zeit des Kaiserreiches', in G. Brunn and J. Reulecke (eds), *Berlin: Blicke auf die deutsche Metropole*, Essen: Reimar Hobbing.
Norkowska, M. (1903) *Najnowsza kuchnia wytworna i gospodarska zawierająca 1032 przepisy gospodarskie, z uwzględnieniem kuchni jarskiej*, 2nd edn, Warsaw: Gebethner i Wolff.
Omikron (1884) 'Z postem czy z mięsem', *Kurier Warszawski*, 160b: 1–2.
Otchet (1903–04) *Otchet Sankt: Peterburg-Vegetarianskoe Obshchestvo 1903*, St Petersburg.
Panek, K. (1906) *Jarstwo a higiena żywienia*, Warsaw: E. Wende i Spółka.
Pieczątkowski, F. (1976) 'Miłkowski Władysław', *Polski Słownik Biograficzny*, vol. 21, Wrocław/Warsaw/Kraków: Wydawnictwo Polskiej Akademii Nauk.
Pixa, W. (1909) *Nie jedz mięsa – zostań jaroszem! Napisał jarosz*, Berlin: Hygieia.
Przewodnik Zdrowia (1895) 5: 33.
Przewodnik Zdrowia (1896) 1: 1–2.

Przewodnik Zdrowia (1897) 12: 92–4.
Przewodnik Zdrowia (1898) 4: 28–9.
Przewodnik Zdrowia (1903) 12: 96.
Przewodnik Zdrowia (1911) 6: 156.
Ruch (1910a) 6: 72.
Ruch (1910b) 23: 263.
Ruch (1911) 21: 229.
Seefeld, A. von (1884) *Jarosz i jarstwo: przyczynki do nauki o pożywieniu wyłącznie roślinnym, jako jedynym środku wyzwolenia się od chorób fizycznych, moralnych i społecznych, słowem odrodzenia się rodzaju ludzkiego*, trans. K. Moes-Oskragiełło, Warsaw: Tłocznia Józefa Ungra.
Sprondel, W. M. (1986) 'Kulturelle Modernisierung durch anti-modernistischen Protest: Der lebensreformerische Vegetarismus', *Kölner Zeitschrift für Soziologie and Sozialpsychologie*, 27: 314–30.
Steinert, O. (2003) *'Berlin – Polnischer Bahnhof!': Die Berliner Polen; eine Untersuchung zum Verhältnis von nationaler Selbstbehauptung und sozialen Integrationsbedürfnis einer fremdsprachigen Minderheit in der Hauptstadt des Deutschen Reiches (1871–1918)*, Hamburg: Verlag Dr. Kovač.
Tarnawski, W. (1966), *Mój ojciec*, London: Polska Fundacja Kulturalna.
Thomas, K. (1983) *Man and the natural world*, London: Allen Lane, Penguin Books.
Tolstoy, L. (1907) *Pierwszy stopień, czyli wstrzemięźliwość jako pracnota oraz podstawa ludzkiej doskonałości*, Berlin: Przewodnik Zdrowia and S. Byszczyński.
Twigg, J. (1981) 'The vegetarian movement in England, 1847–1981: with particular reference to its ideology', Unpublished thesis, London School of Economics.
Tych, F. (1960–61) 'Józef Hempel', *Polski Słownik Biograficzny*, vol. 9, Wrocław/Warsaw/Kraków: Wydawnictwo Polskiej Akademii Nauk.
Wandycz, P. (1974) *The lands of partitioned Poland, 1795–1918*, Seattle, WA/London: University of Washington Press.
Wyrwa, U. (1997) 'Consumption, Konsum, Konsumgessellschaft: Ein Beitrag zur Begriffsgeschichte', in H. Siegrist, H. Kaelble and J. Kocka (eds), *Europäische Konsumgeschichte: Zur Gesellschafts- und Kulturgeschichte des Konsums (18. bis 20. Jahrhundert)*, Frankfurt am Main/New York: Campus Verlag.

10 Regional identity and citizenship in Silesia

Krystian Heffner

This chapter follows the problem of national and regional identity of the population of the Opole region of Silesia in South-West Poland. A specific historical background created a population with uncertain, ambiguous and flexible national identity. Pressures for forced assimilation of those not expelled after the Second World War did not destroy the distinct regional identity. It was rather driven underground, to be revived after 1989 when assertion of a German identity became advantageous for much of the local population. The twists and turns of post-war history led to a diversified population structure in Silesia with two different groups. One settled after 1945, many coming from territory further east that was incorporated into the Soviet Union. The other was the indigenous population. The two groups were partly integrated within one socio-economic whole, but partly differentiated by choice of national allegiance.

Specificities of the German and Polish legal frameworks created scope for dual citizenship. The German framework allowed people of ethnic German origin to apply for German citizenship, while the Polish framework allowed them to retain their Polish citizenship. Those who could trace their origin to the pre-war population of the area could therefore gain the benefits of German citizenship. They took this opportunity in such large numbers as to create the largest consolidated group of Germans living outside Germany and also the largest group of EU citizens living outside the EU prior to Poland's accession in 2004.

German citizenship is used mainly for taking jobs in EU countries, mitigating the problem of unemployment and helping the regional economy with transfers of incomes, stimulating consumer demand. Dual citizenship may thus be considered a specific form of individual capital, enabling its owners to function on a foreign labour market. Economic migration is a rational utilisation of the opportunities provided by German legislation to part of the population in this part of Poland.

Specific features of the Silesian identity

National minorities and minority ethnic groups are concentrated primarily, but not exclusively, in 'cultural borderland' regions, generally regions peripheral to capital cities, or in geographical border regions. There is a clear awareness of social distinctness in these regions, and cultural patterns are the result of long years of infusion of numerous cultures and traditions of diverse origin (Szczepański 1999: 19). Cultural borderland regions have undergone changes in their state and administrative affiliations through the centuries, finding themselves under the influence of different political, administrative and economic systems. As a result, populations may lack uniform national identities. Such a diversity of options still manifests itself in the Opole region within Silesia (Heffner 1994).

It has been estimated that Silesians make up about 30 per cent of the population of the Opole region at present. That would mean about 300,000–330,000 people, against 450,000 in 1950. They live mainly in rural areas in the central and eastern parts of the region. Out of the total of 300,000 people of native origin, nearly 200,000 (60 per cent) live in rural areas. The Silesian population is a majority in thirty-four municipalities (*gmina*) and eleven towns, with 60–90 per cent of the population in those cases (Rauziński 1996: 15).

A definitive choice of national identity is less common among the Silesian population, which has functioned for centuries in a social and cultural borderland, than among inhabitants of nationally homogeneous regions. Multidimensional identity or mixed identity is the typical attitude where the choice of different national options appears as something natural and rarely definitive and where its importance is secondary to that of regional links based on a common history and on emotional ties to the territory (Berlińska 1991: 29).

The Silesian population has links to the Polish, German and Czech nations. The most important influences on the cultural pattern of Silesia have been Polish and German. Inhabitants of Silesia are different from the people from both of these nations but, as they have always lived within the territory of one of them, an ambivalent or indifferent approach to nationality is a typical feature. Not being from an independent nation, Silesians have links with each of these nations, albeit with different features (Szmeja 1997: 107–8). Thus, as a result of the clash of Polish and German influences, new values emerged, creating a separate culture. This created the distinctive features of the Silesian borderland population. Sources of this feeling of separateness are seen in the specific history of this group and in the cultural features that emerged from it, as well as in a strong attachment to the territory. This came before allegiance to either a Polish or a German state (Berlińska and Madajczyk 1998: 84).

Although Silesians in the late 1980s and early 1990s enthusiastically identified with Germany, this had very diverse meanings. There were fervent German Silesians who could not accept life in the Polish People's Republic and among Poles and wanted to become 'Germans among Germans'. There were also those who had somehow adapted to life in Poland, but who disliked the system of 'real socialism': they sought some distance from Poles and greater closeness to Germans. There were finally those who had integrated with Poles to a certain extent, but who saw their chance, and the chance for their children, in Germany, while still feeling some distance from Germans (Berlińska 1999: 257).

The majority of Silesians had remained beyond the influence of Polish culture not because they did not accept it, but because they belonged to the social group that does not usually participate in cultural life to any great extent. They were united by a weaker or a stronger feeling of being underprivileged and discriminated against and of not having equal rights. A revived movement of the German minority enabled not only those who saw themselves as clearly German but also the whole community of Silesians, irrespective of their national attitudes, as having to overcome the feeling of being underprivileged in the Polish state.

A number of factors of a historical, cultural and social character shaped the consciousness of the German minority in Poland. These included the wartime experiences and events of 1945, subsequent unfortunate decisions by the Polish state and local administrative authorities, the cultural distance from the incoming population, critical attitudes towards socio-economic developments, and ceaseless comparisons of their situation both to the German reality from before 1939 and to the subsequent reality in the Federal Republic of Germany. These factors were decisive for the German identification of the native Silesian population which constitutes the social base for the German minority in contemporary Poland. Ethnic Germans, and people who continued to declare their German nationality at all times after 1945, constitute only a small percentage of the population identifying themselves with the German minority (Kurcz 1997: 98).

The post-war period led to changes in this social group. The pressures for 'polonisation' and the experiences of discrimination deepened the isolation of Silesians from the Poles and strengthened the feeling of closeness to Germans. These processes encouraged those with unclear or unstable feelings of national identity to identify with Germany. Such people either emigrated in large numbers to the Federal Republic of Germany throughout the whole post-war period or proclaimed themselves members of the German minority in the Opole region of Silesia after the change of system in 1989.

A national verification process, in which the population of local origin was required to prove their Polish origin, strongly influenced changes in the local population's consciousness. This action was concluded in 1949 with Polish citizenship granted to all who did not leave for Germany. An unwillingness to leave was considered at the time to be proof of Polish descent. However, this whole process was humiliating for the Silesian population and, alongside experiences of unjustified expulsions and of the social divisions related to antagonisms between the local and incoming populations, encouraged decisions to emigrate to Germany in later periods.

The repolonisation, or rather polonisation, of culture damaged essential elements of the Silesian cultural identity. Only a part of the cultural heritage of the group could be retained, while much was questioned. Anything that could testify to the regional distinctiveness of Silesians was eliminated. The Silesian dialect was ridiculed and it was forbidden to teach German in schools until 1988. German language services in churches were reintroduced only in 1989. It was strictly prohibited to use the German language not only in public, but also at home, with punishments in different periods including being sent to a labour camp, a fine or removal from a job. Names of streets and localities were changed from German into Polish, which was natural and obvious at that time, but the authorities went a step further and changed historical Slavonic names into literary Polish ones. Slavonic family names were changed to the Polish spelling and German family names were changed into Polish. An obligatory list of Polish first names was introduced. German inscriptions were removed from buildings, churches, chapels and tombstones. German monuments were destroyed. Special commissions raided homes, requisitioning German books and maps and destroying household equipment that bore German inscriptions.

At the same time, the Silesian population was alienated by more general features of social development. The socialist state ideology, dominant after the war, conflicted with deep religious feelings and with a role for the Church in the society. Criteria of work evaluation and the accompanying ideology, such as evaluation according to political affiliation and not the quality of work, similarly meant that what was offered by the Polish state clashed with the aspirations of Silesians (Szmeja 1997: 113). The sluggish socialist economy seemed to confirm the old German saying about the *polnische Wirtschaft*, meaning Polish economy or business practice, and a common German term for a shambles. Many artisan workshops were closed, and farmers suffered the absurdities of the command economy. Generalised collective ownership was seen as conflicting with the sacred right of Silesians to the heritage that they had fought for and robbed many of them of the last argument for staying in Opole Silesia. Thus the cultural base of Silesians was undermined by repolonisation and the attempt to subsume all within one national standard. Cultural differences between the new settlers and Silesians, as well as cultural alienation within the Polish nation, created an unattractive or even unacceptable image of Poland for Silesians (Lis 1991).

Ethnic differences were combined with social differences. Relative to the Polish population, Silesians had lower education, occupied lower positions in the social structure and participated in power only to a small extent, and the impact of their culture on the national culture was negligible. The dominant role in the region was played by newcomers in practically all fields of social life (Berlińska 1991: 30). Thus, although Silesians remained on their own territory, they exerted no influence on its post-war cultural character. Polish culture dominated.

The cultural distinctiveness of Silesians could be manifested only at the level of local communities. Certain elements of Silesian folklore were even presented as proof of a Polish connection. However, Silesians adopted a defence mechanism against their perceived marginalisation, which amounted to isolationism and a reluctance to become involved outside their closed community. Institutional contacts were kept to the necessary minimum. There were few mixed marriages and educational aspirations remained low.

Germans proved to be better allies in the confrontation with this forced polonisation and discrimination. They treated the Silesian population as members of their national community throughout all the post-war years and offered support and assistance. The gap in the material conditions of life and between Poland and Germany was another important factor influencing national identity. Increasing freedom enabled contacts with friends and relatives living in the Federal Republic. Thanks to the exchange of information, people could develop opinions about living standards in the two countries. Initially, the information was confirmed by letters and photographs and later by discussions with relatives during their visits to Poland. Still later, the image of Germany was shaped by presents received from guests and parcels sent to Poland. Although the value of these presents was of a rather symbolic nature when set in terms of conditions in Germany, it was much higher for the recipients in Poland. Moreover, these items were often beyond what was available in Poland. All this shaped the image of a better 'German world'. Finally, with the relaxation of restrictions on foreign travel, it became possible to experience directly the living standard in the Federal Republic of Germany. Germans living in Poland left for the Federal Republic for good or to work for a time. Some resettled in Germany, and those who went there only to work brought back evidence of a higher standard of living achieved by 'becoming Germans' or being 'close to Germans and the Federal Republic'.

Emigration of Silesians to Germany

Those from Opole Silesia who declared German origin or nationality could gain German citizenship (*deutsche Staatsangehörigheit*) and were treated in a privileged way by the government of the Federal Republic of Germany. They were granted the status of 'displaced people' (*Aussiedler*) or, for those arriving after 1980, late displaced people (*Spätaussiedler*). The basic legal position for qualifying for these categories can be found in Article 116 of the German constitution, which defines as a German 'anyone who possesses German nationality or who was a refugee or expelled person of German nationality, or his spouse and descendants, from the territory of the German Reich as of 31 December 1937' (Grundgesetz 2006).

The term *Aussiedler* appeared immediately after the end of the Second World War and was applied to German nationals forcibly removed from Poland, Czechoslovakia and Hungary to Germany following the decisions of the Potsdam Conference at the end of the Second World War. Polish literature uses the translation of the word *Aussiedler* as 'displaced person' (instead of a more adequate 'expelled person'). This does not fully reflect the German notion, as the exact translation of the term 'displaced person' would be *Über-siedler*. This word, however, was used in the Federal Republic of Germany to describe a person who arrived from the German Democratic Republic. The notion of 'late displaced person' appeared in writings to describe people arriving from Poland following the Protocol of 9 October 1975 (Trzcielińska-Polus 1997: 8).

This legal position meant that the notion of a German, and the right to German citizenship, embraced the native population living in territories incorporated into Poland after the war. This population has, therefore, the right to German citizenship even if included in the 'collective' granting of Polish citizenship under the law of 8 January 1951. This had specified that Polish citizenship could be granted at the request of the person concerned or by the administrative authorities even without any such request. The latter procedure was applied to the native population. However, under German law, acceptance of citizenship of another country does not mean loss of German citizenship: that can only be lost when voluntarily renounced (Johannes 1996: 70–6). It was therefore possible for people to gain German citizenship, or rather to have its continuity confirmed, if they could prove that they had never lost it in terms of German law (cf. Łodziński 1997).

This meant that the native Silesian population, living in closed communities in the central and eastern part of the voivodship, was strongly represented in migration to Germany. The term 'migration monoculture' in Opole Silesia was used by some researchers to describe this one-way movement of people (Jaźwińska *et al.* 1997: 60), in which the Opole region was particularly prominent. About 200,000 people undertook permanent emigration from the early 1950s. The rate varied over time, increasing when passport regulations and migration policies were liberalised.

There was negligible emigration from some municipalities, but in some cases more than 20 per cent of inhabitants emigrated in the course of the ten-year period 1979–1988. This reflected the diversity of the region's population, with the native Silesians shaping the 'emigration picture'. This had a negative impact on the demographic situation of the local population, with declining numbers of births, an ageing population, the break-up of families and the weakening of social bonds. The most important unfavourable aspect was the fact that more people emigrated in the 1951–95 period than were born to the native population. The resulting unfavourable age structure and qualification level of the population hindered economic development. Economically active and educated people dominated among both permanent and subsequently temporary emigrants. Permanent and temporary emigration reached between 10 and 20 per cent of the labour force in areas of intense economic emigration during the 1980s and 1990s (Heffner and Solga 2001).

The possibility of 'obtaining' German citizenship, or having it confirmed in terms of German law, by people emigrating from territories belonging to

Germany before the Second World War, including Silesia, led to a differentiation in the prospects for starting a new life in a foreign country. The status of 'expelled people of German origin' meant that state authorities were obliged to provide the right to individual security and the right to participate in all state structures. Migrants were also granted all possible assistance by the German state during the initial period of adaptation, including economic and social assistance and special language courses. They received the same as people granted asylum in terms of assistance with food, housing, rent, child maintenance and training. They also received rights to unemployment benefits, invalidity and old-age pensions and forms of help aimed specifically at the 'expelled' population to aid integration, including compensation for abandoned assets and recognition for past training, years of work and military service in the country of origin in the calculation of pension and unemployment benefits. However, in the 1980s, changed regulations led to some reduction in economic and social assistance (Łempiński 1988; Bartz 1995b: 25; Trzcielińska-Polus 1997: 62–4).

The long list of forms of assistance led inhabitants of the Federal Republic of Germany to view incomers as a privileged group in comparison with the local population. German society frequently criticised the mass inflow of 'expelled people' and the assistance granted to them. Manifestations of dislike for foreigners, including 'expelled people', were undoubtedly one of the reasons for policy changes, although the 'expelled people' contributed to economic growth by providing more people of working age, easing pressures on the social insurance system and slowing down the decrease in the numbers of working age. Temporarily, however, the mass inflow of 'expelled people' caused various problems for local authorities in terms of finding housing and employment.

The process of integration of 'expelled people' into German society was, therefore, not easy. Problems faced by 'expelled people' were similar to those encountered by people who were granted asylum or by economic immigrants, including a language barrier, discrimination by the local population and the resulting partial social isolation, confrontation with an unfamiliar social structure and lifestyle and frequently a destruction of family structures resulting from emigration of only one or of a few family members. This led the 'expelled people' to face identity problems, which were particularly severe for young people and women.

'Expelled people' arriving in the Federal Republic of Germany during the 1980s, irrespectively of whether emigration was accepted by the Polish authorities or whether they came with a tourist visa only, were initially directed to transit camps. In some cases, only one representative of a family arrived in the camp while other family members stayed with their relatives or friends or in hotels. The stay in the camp was necessary to deal with formalities of registration and the issue of basic identity documents. The real difficulties began after leaving the transit camp. 'Expelled people' with a poor knowledge of the language either selected, or were directed to, a *Land*. From the mid-1980s local authorities at various levels increasingly encountered difficulties in finding them jobs and accommodation. The main barrier to rapid integration into employment was poor language knowledge, meaning that those who found a job were mainly engaged in low-skilled manual work.

'Expelled people' generally remained politically inactive, isolating themselves from political life and lacking their own representation, but they did integrate into a community via religion. The church was a place not only for praying but also one that offered the chance to meet people of similar origin. Thus 'expelled people' evolved a bi-cultural, or bi-national, Polish-German identity. They felt that they simultaneously belonged to Poles and to Germans, to Polish and to German cultures.

Structures that had been created in earlier decades to facilitate the integration of 'expelled people' into German society had dwindled by the end of the 1980s as financial resources were cut. During the 1990s, conditions for receiving and assisting 'expelled people' deteriorated further following German reunification and the enormous outlays on structural adjustment in Eastern Germany. This coincided with a dramatic decrease in the number of 'expelled people' arriving from Poland in the mid-1990s, caused to a considerable extent by changes in German policy. The Law on Termination of War Consequences, enacted on 1 January 1993, was based on the assumption that there was no persecution of people of German descent in Poland and that there was no pressure for their expulsion. 'Expelled people' arriving in Germany after 1993 could not be granted the 'expelled person' status and they were referred to as 'late expelled people' (Trzcielińska-Polus 1997: 131–2).

German diplomatic posts were instructed to check the language knowledge of applicants. At the same time, the applicants were required to prove that they had suffered discrimination as a result of 'considering themselves to be German'. It was then necessary to await the decision of the Federal Administration Office in Cologne on confirmation of German citizenship at home, meaning in Poland. 'Late expelled people' status was rejected for people whose relatives had arrived in Germany before 1993 and obtained this status. Children born after 31 December 1992 could not be considered 'expelled people'. This law, it should be added, applied to Germans from Central and Eastern European countries, but not to those from the former USSR (Bartz 1995a: 60–6).

The German minority in Opole Silesia

The political transformation of 1989 was followed by a revival of the German minority in Silesia which needs to be interpreted against the background of the development of the Silesian identity, or identities, as outlined above. An indication of the extent of the change was the fact that the option of proclaiming German nationality became, for Silesians, a means of gaining local status as representatives of a minority from a big neighbouring nation. Their views were considered socially important and their cultural distinctiveness won recognition (Szmeja 1997: 116).

The previous isolationism of the local population led to assertiveness from the German minority movement. The mechanism was simple. The local population lacked its own identity, had a low level of participation in public life and did not receive any satisfactory compensation in exchange as its material situation worsened (Kurcz 1997). Its identity was hidden deep in individual communities in isolation from broader structures and processes, on the fringes of social life. In the new reality, this hidden identity sought an external point of reference and this was broadly understood as 'Germanism'.

The German minority had requested recognition several times during the 'thaw' of 1956. The same happened in the mid-1980s, late 1980s and early 1990s. However, during the period of real socialism, Silesians were denied the right to demonstrate their Germanism. It was assumed that they were a historically Polish population with a Polish folk culture. However, they had not revealed their German roots in some cases for fear of reprisals. Silence increased prospects of travel to the Federal Republic of Germany and of material assistance for the region.

The first sign of organisational rebirth was the establishment of German friendship circles in 1988, which started activity without legal registration (Matelski 1999: 293). The systemic changes after 1989 enabled them to manifest openly their Germanism. As a result, nearly all Silesians living in the Opole region of Silesia sought to prove their links with the German nation. They had historical arguments in the 200 years of belonging to Prussia and the German Reich and legal arguments from Article 116 of the German Constitution. German television programmes were received in the Opole region via satellite, and the people were able to see movies and to listen to news in their preferred language. At the same time, changes in the foreign policy of the Federal Republic of Germany, in the form of a shift from immigration facilitation to financial assistance to the minority provided they remained in Poland, encouraged formal organisation of the German minority. In 1990, the Social and Cultural Association of the Germans in the Opole Region of Silesia (*Towarzystwo Społeczno-Kulturalne Niemcóów na Śląsku Opolskim*, henceforth TSKN) was formed.

This did not meet with general social approval. Minority activists collected 250,000 signatures on lists of people of German descent in 1989, but the local press questioned the German descent of Silesians and pointed out that the population had accepted the national verification of the late 1940s and early 1950s, which was taken as confirming their pro-Polish attitude. Apprehension was caused by the strong manifestation of distinctiveness by the German minority and the publicly manifested feeling of having suffered harm, persecution and discrimination. Poles, in turn, manifested distrust of Germans and expressed their apprehension that the German minority could become a 'fifth column' in Poland, that the region could be German-dominated and that the people who had been expelled from Polish eastern territories in 1945,

largely moving into western areas with previously substantial German populations, would have to leave their homes in favour of returning Germans
(Berlińska and Madajczyk 1998: 93).

The German minority had practically unrestricted freedom to organise
itself and protect and develop its own culture. Its most important aims were
teaching the German language, promoting German culture, active participation in local self-government, participation in public life and cooperation
with the German state in order to improve living conditions (Berlińska 1991:
35–6). The minority achieved local autonomy in the cultural sphere while
gaining power to influence the economic and social development of municipalities, thanks to assistance from both the German and the Polish sides
(Berlińska and Madajczyk 1998: 105). Thus the marginalisation of Silesians
gave way to participation in political life via the German minority movement.

Voting regulations were changed by removing the requirement of the
5 per cent minimum of votes for minority groups for participation in administration. This enabled the German minority to make its presence felt on the
political scene for the first time during elections to the Senate in February
1992. One of the minority leaders gained 126,000 votes, and this mobilisation
of the electorate strengthened arguments over the size and strength of the
population considering themselves German. Ethnic tensions peaked at that
time, as manifested in anti-German slogans, such as 'Germans back to
Germany', 'Polacken raus' (Poles out) and 'Poles, do not vote for a Kraut',
during election rallies and in the local media.

The mood changed a few months later during the first democratic local
administration elections. Candidates representing the German minority cam-
paigned around the slogan 'We want to deal with our problems ourselves',
while also declaring a willingness to cooperate and to build a friendly coexistence with Poles. In the subsequent parliamentary election campaign, the
emphasis was on the multicultural character of the region and on the need for
the friendly coexistence of Germans and Poles. Support for the TSKN fell
from 33 per cent of the Opole vote in 1990 to 22 per cent in Senate elections in
1997, but there was a solid support base. Part of the electorate appreciated
the achievements of minority representatives in local self-government. However, German minority leaders continued to express dissatisfaction with the
constitutional and legal guarantees of the freedom of association and with the
law on the educational system. They pressed for a law on national minorities
as one of their most important aims.

German identity has been based to a considerable extent on the social
memory of the oldest generation and does not offer an attractive proposition
of identity formation for younger generations (Berlińska 1999: 339). Thus
support for the German minority movement among Silesians has gradually
weakened. Many of those active in German minority structures see themselves
clearly as Germans. They are mainly representatives of the older generation.
Others operate within several cultures, identifying themselves as Silesian. It
is difficult to make a clear and simple division, as members of these groups

have been strongly integrated with each other for a long time. An unambiguous allegiance to a German identity merges with the mixed identity that
characterises the Silesian ethnic group.

Dual citizenship of Silesians

An important reason for the local Silesian population, including the German
minority, to remain in their country of origin is the possibility of obtaining German citizenship without moving to Germany. The German author
Thomas Urban (1994: 25) maintains that, according to the German authorities' estimates, the number of people in Poland, mainly in Upper Silesia, with
passports of both countries lies between 300,000 and 700,000. Various Polish
sources point to 120,000 people with dual citizenship (Heffner and Solga
2001).

German regulations mean that acceptance of foreign citizenship in the past
does not mean the loss of German citizenship. Nor is it required to renounce
another citizenship when applying for German citizenship. This means that
Germany allows de facto the institution of dual citizenship, although it is not
provided for in German legislation. Similarly, Polish legislation has no provisions concerning dual citizenship, but also no legal consequences for a Polish
citizen possessing citizenship of another state.

The extent of dual citizenship suggests that the region of Opole Silesia
provides a potential source of further migration of people seeking temporary
or permanent jobs in Germany or in other EU countries. This, combined
with the fact that these people maintain their permanent residence in the
Opole region, points to lasting links with Germany in the form of continuing
movement of people in connection with various social contacts (family,
friends, education, social services) and short-term migration in search of
work.

The dual citizenship of part of the Opole population has been of a pragmatic nature. Those with two passports can move to Germany, or to other
EU countries, and find a job legally. There are many job adverts in the local
press, while the Polish radio in Opole runs a daily programme, *Radio Labour
Exchange*. It should be added that both the radio and the press adverts are
addressed mainly to people with German passports and speaking German.
This has led to a differentiation in the economic status of inhabitants, with an
impact also on individuals' social positions. However, the divisions are not
primarily social, relating rather to an ethnically determined segmentation of
local societies.

Finding a job abroad appears as a rational utilisation of chances and possibilities opened for this group by German legislation. Disregarding these
chances of earning abroad would mean a waste of an opportunity to better
oneself and one's family, in the face of prevailing unemployment and hard
living conditions. A kind of 'migration professionalism' has emerged in
which finding a job abroad has become a way of life. Thus the opportunity to

gain dual citizenship has meant that one of the basic EU freedoms, the free movement of people, already applies in the Opole region.

Dual citizenship provides the formal basis, but the functioning of the process is dependent on a dynamic and developed network of family relations that was shaped between the Opole inhabitants and Germany as a result of the migration movements from the end of the Second World War. Networks of migration, similar to those of the Opole region, have emerged in other parts of the country. None are as developed and diversified as those of Opole Silesia.

References

Bartz, B. (1995a) *Exodus i integracja wysiedleńcóów jako wyzwanie dla polityki społecznej RFN*, Tarnobrzeg: Historica.

Bartz, B. (1995b) 'Niemiecki model państwa opiekuńczego w okresie wzmożonej imigracji', *Przegląd Zachodni*, 3.

Berlińska, D. (1991) 'Procesy demokratyzacyjne w Polsce a mniejszość niemiecka na Śląsku Opolskim', *Przegląd Zachodni*, 2.

Berlińska, D. (1999) *Mniejszość niemiecka na Śląsku Opolskim w poszukiwaniu tożsamości*, Opole: Stowarzyszenie Instytut Śląsk.

Berlińska, D. and Madajczyk, P. (1998) 'Mniejszość niemiecka w Polsce', in B. Berdychowska (ed.), *Mniejszości narodowe w Polsce: Praktyka po 1989 roku*, Warszawa: Wydawnictwo Sejmowe.

Grundgesetz für die Bundesrepublik Deutschland (2006), http://www.aufenthaltstitel.de/gg.html (accessed 27 March 2007).

Heffner, K. (1994) 'Die regionale Entwicklung des Oppelner Schlesiens', in Hans van der Meulen (ed.), *Anerkannt als Minderheit: Vergangenheit und Zukunft der Deutschen in Polen*, Baden-Baden: Nomos Verlagsgesellschaft.

Heffner, K. and Solga, B. (2001) 'External migration and labour flows: contemporary social and economic determinants (Opole Silesia case)', in M. Koter and K. Heffner (eds), *Changing Role of Border Areas and Regional Policies*, Łódź/Opole: University of Łódź, Silesian Institute in Opole and Silesian Institute Society.

Jaźwińska, E., Łukowski, W. and Okólski, M. (1997) *Przyczyny i konsekwencje emigracji z Polski*, Warszawa: ISSUW.

Johannes, B. (1996) 'Podwójne obywatelstwo – szansa czy bariera we współpracy polsko-niemieckiej?', in P. Bajda (ed.), *Obywatelstwo w Europie Środkowo-Wschodniej: Materiały z konferencji Prawo do posiadania obywatelstwa w Europie Środkowo-Wschodniej (Jabłonna, 15–17.XII.1995)*, Warszawa: Forum Europy Środkowo-Wschodniej przy Fundacji im. Stefana Batorego.

Kurcz, Z. (1997) 'Mniejszość niemiecka w Polsce', in Z. Kurcz (ed.), *Mniejszości narodowe w Polsce*, Wrocław: Wydawnictwo Uniwersytetu Wrocławskiego.

Łempiński, Z. (1988) 'O niektórych prawidłowościach emigracji z Polski do RFN', *Zaranie Śląskie*, 3–4.

Lis, M. (1991) *Polska ludność rodzima na Śląsku Opolskim po II wojnie światowej*, Opole: Instytut Śląski w Opolu.

Łodziński S. (1997) 'Obywatelstwo polskie – przyczynek do problematyki granic etniczności i obywatelstwa w społeczeństwie polski', in M. Kempny, A. Kapciak and S. Łodziński (eds), *U progu wielokulturowości: Nowe oblicza społeczeństwa polskiego*, Warszawa: Oficyna Naukowa.

Matelski, D. (1999) *Niemcy w Polsce w XX wieku*, Warszawa/Poznań: Wydawn. Naukowe PWN.

Rauziński, R. (1996) 'Wpływ migracji zagranicznych na sytuację demograficzną Śląska Opolskiego w latach 1945–1995', *Śląsk Opolski*, 2.

Szczepański, M. (1999) ' "Inni swoi": Szkic do socjologicznego portretu mniejszości narodowych w Polsce', in D. Berlińska and K. Frysztacki (eds), *'Inni swoi': Studia z problematyki etnicznej*, Opole: Instytut Śląski w Opolu.

Szmeja, M. (1997) 'Dlaczego Ślązacy z Opolszczyzny nie chcą być Polakami', in Z. Kurcz (ed.), *Mniejszości narodowe w Polsce*, Wrocław: Wydawnictwo Uniwersytetu Wrocławskiego.

Trzcielińska-Polus, A. (1997) *'Wysiedleńcy' z Polski w Republice Federalnej Niemiec w latach 1980–1990*, Opole: Instytut Śląski w Opolu.

Urban, T. (1994) *Niemcy w Polsce: Historia mniejszości w XX wieku*, Opole: Instytut Śląski w Opolu.

Part IV

Issues in regional and local development

11 Transport and economic development

Comparisons and contrasts in theory, policy and practice between Poland and the UK

Eamonn Judge

The debate about the relationship between transport and economic development has been a continuing feature of transport, regional and urban economics and associated discussions of policy and planning in many countries in recent years, not least in both post-communist Poland and the UK.

In Poland the debate took off as the country emerged from its communist past and began to update plans for motorway development that had been originally sketched out in the 1970s. Government studies published in 1993 included summaries of extensive but unpublished research on the expected economic impact of the proposed motorway system. These studies provided the basis for frequent claims by the post-communist socialist governments of the mid-1990s that the new system would bring unparalleled economic benefits, especially to peripheral regions. The subsequent era of the Polish Motorways Agency, toll motorway concessions, and the lack of perceptible progress in motorway construction has been the subject of much debate, notably by enraged sections of the Polish press, as successive Polish governments since the mid-1990s have taken contrasting views on the relation between transport and economic development. What was remarkable about these to-and-fro debates was that they took place largely in an aspatial context: the regions that would gain and lose by a new motorway system were not discussed at all and, with some exceptions, there was a relative lack of any new domestic research on the topic.

In the UK the contemporary debate had begun in the early 1960s with the re-emergence of the 'regional problem' in its peripheral areas. Thereafter there was much research but, up to the 1980s, most studies failed to show a strong relationship – or often any relationship at all – between inputs of transport infrastructure (especially motorways) and increments in regional economic growth. In the 1990s, however, the debate widened with the emergence of studies of transport infrastructure development, analysed within the context of the New Economic Geography (NEG), whereby it was possible to cogently argue for the existence of additional economic benefits over and above direct transport benefits (though they were empirically difficult to prove). This in turn opened up a new area of research and reappraisal of past results, the consequences of which are still being worked through in terms of theory, practice and policy. Over the period considered, however, it would be fair to say that the issues were debated in the UK, unlike in Poland, in a framework that was relatively politically neutral.

The next section of this chapter will provide a brief overview of comparisons between discussions of transport and regional development in the UK over the period of approximately 1955–2005 and in Poland in the approximate period 1990–2005. It will also introduce a number of sub-themes which will be taken up in the subsequent discussion. The third and fourth sections will then consider developments in the UK and Poland respectively, followed by a fifth section on recent research on the relationship between transport and regional development in Poland.

Transport and regional development in the UK, 1955–2005, and in Poland, 1990–2005: a comparison

In the 1960s, UK governments were absorbed with a persistent regional problem. The idea that transport investment might help regional development started to be tied in with the new motorway programme which had developed from the late 1950s (Judge and Button 1974). The possibility that the programme could be 'tweaked' to accelerate road construction in certain regions, and hence reduce unemployment, was first expressed in the Toothill Report on Central Scotland (HMSO 1963a) and the Hailsham Report on the Northeast (HMSO 1963b). At the same time, the gradual approach of motorways into urban areas generated anti-road protesting and concern with environmental evaluation techniques. There was thus a coming together of the consideration of the environmental and developmental effects of road construction and the question of direct user costs and benefits in the 'General Appraisal Framework' put forward by the SACTRA Report in 1977 (HMSO 1977). This concluded that it was hard to find convincing evidence of development effects, and if they were to be argued for the justifications would need to be strong.

The bringing together of the environmental and economic development effects of transport into a single evaluation framework in the 1977 SACTRA Report took place without any recognition or awareness that the economic development and environmental impacts of transport growth could be in direct conflict with one another at an aggregate level. This came a decade later with the growing debates about sustainable development, and subsequently there gradually emerged in policy terms the drive for 'non-transport-dependent economic growth'.

At one level, this might have seemed an easier objective to achieve than it turned out to be. If research showed that there was not a strong relationship between transport investment and economic growth, then it could be argued that road construction could be cut back to protect the environment, without any cost to economic growth.[1] However, it was not that easy. Policy objectives became increasingly diffuse, and the role of transport in complex policy packages became increasingly hard to disentangle. But, more significantly, the theoretical context had changed. The late 1980s saw the development of the 'New Economic Geography' (Vernon Henderson 2005). Developed initially by Krugman (1992), this new approach, using dynamic analysis methods, suggested that, under certain conditions, transport investment could produce gross benefit outcomes which would exceed the direct user benefits conventionally calculated in a cost–benefit analysis. This seemed to reopen many areas of argument which had been considered as settled. As the early 1990s progressed, with a New Labour government committed to introducing an integrated transport policy and reining in road construction, the conflict between the environmental and developmental effects of road investment seemed as strong as, or stronger than ever. The result was a further study on roads and the economy (SACTRA 1999), the 1997 interim version (SACTRA 1997) of which settled matters sufficiently for the government to safely publish its White Paper on Integrated Transport (HMSO 1998).

Meanwhile, with the opening up of the newly marketised Eastern European economies after 1989, there was a rush to catch up with Western Europe in terms of vehicle ownership and all its appurtenances, including motorways. Poland is particularly interesting here because, in contrast to some of the other CEE countries which joined the EU in 2004, it was a country which historically had much stronger links to Western Europe. For example, even under communist rule, up to a million Poles a year travelled abroad. There was thus a sharp awareness of intellectual developments abroad and a desire to tap into them. The same arguments about transport, economic development and environment started to emerge quickly as in the West (as did the corresponding problems on the ground), but there was a difference in context (Judge 2000, 2002).

Thus the situations of the UK and Poland are sufficiently similar in some ways, and very different in others, to form the basis for realistic and interesting comparisons. An interesting issue is the differing political significance of the relation between transport and development in the two countries and the way in which this has been influential. Whereas the question has not been a highly contentious party political issue in the UK (Vigar 2002), in Poland the arguments were often highly political and reflected fault lines carried forward from the communist era (Judge 2002; Judge *et al.* 2004b). Before 1989, environmental issues had been used in Poland as a way of attacking the communist government (Hicks 1996), and have remained a differentiating feature between the main political blocs since then.

More specifically in relation to the theme of this chapter, a major area of political debate has focused on the question of whether an economic boost to the economy could be expected from motorway development. Solidarity-based groups have included several environmental activists with a knowledge of Western research in this area, and they have used it when out of power to attack socialist governments which have promoted vigorously the expected economic boost from motorway development. However, the political arguments in Poland on this issue have had a different character from those in the UK: the pro-motorway arguments have tended to be expressed in general terms, and which region would be helped by which motorway was never spelt out. This reflected the expectation that the pattern of construction (from west to east) would be more likely to help the better-off regions of the country first, and being more specific about who benefited would only draw attention to this. To an extent, this aped the situation of the UK. Although the political parties in the UK held similar views (unlike in Poland) it was still the case that the early development of the motorway system was in the most prosperous regions. Arguments concerning regional development issues only came later (Judge and Button 1974), and subsequent research demonstrated that it was in fact the more prosperous areas which received the greatest jobs boost from the motorway system and not the less prosperous ones (Botham 1983).

Transport and economic development in the UK: developments in policy, practice and research, 1990–2005

After the SACTRA Leitch Report in 1977 (HMSO 1977) there were few major developments in this area in the 1980s. Then in 1997 an interim report of SACTRA (SACTRA 1997) was issued and a White Paper on integrated transport was published. The government argued that integrated transport would not have to be paid for by fewer jobs and reduced economic activity.

This was followed by the publication of the full SACTRA report of 1999 (SACTRA 1999). This was a milestone, reflecting the output of three years' work from its initiation in 1996. It took on board all the new work which had been developed during the previous decade in the area of the New Economic Geography. Generally it stated that in a perfectly competitive economy standard cost–benefit analysis will capture all relevant effects and there will be no 'additional' benefits to count. However, if the economy is imperfectly competitive, or if there are productivity gains to be captured by increases in agglomeration, or scale economies made possible by the transport improvement, then there is the possibility that total benefits could exceed (or in certain circumstances be less than) the measured direct benefits. The report acknowledged that economic growth could be associated with transport growth but that the two could be decoupled by appropriate pricing and management policies, and there could be situations where this might actually produce gains. It noted that the distributional effects of transport were the critical ones to assess. It recommended that, where a proposal was of a scale for it to be relevant, then an 'economic impact report' (EIR) should be conducted to take account of potential additional benefits. However, it cautioned: 'generalisation about the effects of transport on the economy are subject to strong dependence on specific local circumstances and conditions' (SACTRA 1999: 3). It also recognised that the Department for Transport (DfT) would have to undertake further research to provide the basis for the new EIRs. One particular recommendation for further research was that a computable general equilibrium (CGE) model be set up (CGE models being the practical implementation of NEG theory). The government in its response was lukewarm (DfT 1999), citing the tremendous data and technical requirements that would be necessary. Such views were not uncommon:

> The [CGE] models are, however, highly technical, and it can be difficult for non-specialists to understand their basic structure, and even for technical economists to get a feel for how far particular conclusions are dependent on specific assumptions made in the construction of particular variants of the models.
>
> (Dodgson 1999: 7)

Accordingly, the period since then has seen the commissioning of a number of research studies, plus the development of guidelines for EIRs. The latter (Steer Davies Gleave 2003; Ove Arup 2005) are much more wedded to assessing local impacts in labour and property markets, assessing job creation, and keeping to accessible data sources and analytical methods which are at a scale which can reasonably be undertaken by competent project teams. Clearly, the lack of a generalised modelling framework makes such studies more focused on distribution and less able to say something about whether the overall evaluation has underestimated or overestimated total benefits. On the other hand, the distributional issues are more likely to be of interest to local policy makers. The DfT subsequently commissioned a study to look at CGE models from the RAND Corporation (DfT 2005a), but still maintained a wary stance.

Among examples of the research undertaken were studies of the impact of rail access and employment in London (Gibbons and Machin 2003) and of the link between agglomeration effects and productivity (Graham 2005). This and other research fed into the production of a consultation draft report by the Department for Transport (DfT 2005b) on assessing the contribution to GDP of transport projects, and offered detailed but not very technical approaches to doing this. The CGE models were thus an ideal to be aspired to but, in practice, technical difficulties and problems with data mean their usefulness is limited in the immediate future.

One of the problems with CGE models, and also with certain types of impact research, is that there is sometimes a confusion between predicting what additional effects are likely to be, and actually observing them *ex post*. There is a wide range of values of the likely size of total benefits in relation to direct benefits in GDP terms, though there seems to be an average of 1.4 emerging from a range of studies (e.g. Quinet and Vickerman 2004). It is often not clear whether this is a theoretical estimate derived from running the model with given parameters, or from making a prediction and seeing if what is actually observed is significantly different. Even an often quoted study such as that by Dodgson (1974) was a prediction, not an actual measurement, of the effect of the M62 Lancashire–Yorkshire motorway based on a cross-sectional estimate of the relationship between employment growth and accessibility, and we are often warned about the problems of making time series predictions from cross-sectional relationships. But the problem with CGE models, apart from their complexity, is that they lack statistical diagnostics (Preston and Holvad 2005), and they have not been developed for long enough to be fitted to an existing situation before the start of a programme such as the British motorway programme and then run in forecasting mode and compared with the actual out-turn.

Transport and regional development issues in Poland, 1990–2005

Most of the discussion of comparable issues in Poland has taken place in relation to motorway development.[2] Figure 11.1 illustrates the network of 2,600 kilometres of private tolled motorways that was first proposed in 1993, consisting of two main east–west routes (A2 and A4) and two north–south routes (A1 and A3), plus a few other sections. In addition, it was proposed to develop an extensive network of expressways (existing roads upgraded to a high standard) which would be publicly financed. For many reasons, however, implementation of the system as originally envisaged soon became unrealistic. In particular there were substantial financing problems, which meant that only limited construction was started in the next few years (except on the A4, which was not financed from tolls). Since then policy has moved away substantially from wholly toll-based financing.

The problems of initiating construction may be considered alongside developments in national transport policy and the debate over economic development versus environmental issues. As indicated earlier, unlike the situation in the UK (Vigar 2002), in Poland there was a dispute over these questions, in some senses reflecting the splits of the pre-1989 period. There have been five elections since the end of communist rule: 1989, 1993, 1997, 2001 and 2005, and political power has changed hands each time. The 1989 and 1997 governments were Solidarity-based coalitions with a strong environmental protection emphasis and, in transport terms, they were rather anti-motorway and pro-public transport (MTGiM 2001). The 1993 and 2001 governments were socialist-based coalitions with a much stronger economic development orientation, arguing for the boost that motorway and road construction would give to the economy (MTGiM 1995; Ministerstwo Infrastruktura 2002).

Thus, *ab initio*, it was expected by the first post-1989 socialist government that the development of the motorway system would make a big contribution to Polish national and regional economic development. The basis for this expectation was provided by work carried out by the Institute for Research on Roads and Bridges (IBDM 1992), which forecasted increasing employment in construction firms, as well as a growth in jobs in businesses established along routes and in motorway maintenance after construction. The indirect benefits were expressed in aggregate terms for the whole country, with no spatial breakdown, precluding estimates of specific regional development benefits. These results were repeated in many subsequent official publications.

The 1995 paper (MTGiM 1995) supported the motorway system as illustrated in Figure 11.1, whereas the 2001 paper (MTGiM 2001) reduced the A3 to expressway standard, and substantially delayed the construction eastwards of the A2 from Warsaw and the A4 from Kraków. Cynics might say that these decisions reflected simply resource shortages rather than environmental credentials, though they were consistent with the tone of the so-called 'Alternative Transport Policy' published by the Institute for Sustainable Development in Warsaw (ISD 1998a, 1998b). The defeat of the Solidarity coalition and the election of another socialist-led coalition in September 2001 brought an end to this proposal even before it could be ratified, let alone acted upon.

In January 2002 the new government published an infrastructure plan (Ministerstwo Infrastruktura 2002) which more or less reversed the previous one, and proposed accelerating the programme so that, using new financing proposals, 550 kilometres of motorway and 200 kilometres of expressway would be built between 2002 and 2005.

The situation continued to develop, but the change of government in 2005 did not seem to have the impact on transport policy that was usually brought about by a change in government. However, a new slant was put on the motorway debate by a study on spatial strategy generally, begun in 2002 (Węcławowicz *et al.* 2006). The section on transport and motorway development saw a reordering of priorities, which to some extent resurrected debates about whether the previously proposed motorway network (which effectively would fan out from Western Europe to the east) was more oriented to European rather than Polish priorities. New motorway-level links were proposed which strengthened the polycentric Polish urban system much more explicitly than the currently proposed network. As about half of all Polish road construction was financed by Western/EU grants and loans (a varying proportion, but 47 per cent in 2002), the entry of Poland to the EU in 2004 might be thought to tie the country even more securely into the network of European priorities. It remains to be seen how this study, carried out by the Polish Academy of Sciences, will influence priorities. More generally, one could say that the political split was an argument on paper, as there was very little motorway construction anyway.

Recent research on transport and economic development in Poland

The interesting aspect of the to-and-fro of government policy was the way in which Western research was used by both sides to support or oppose the alleged boost the motorway system would give to regional development. The Solidarity-based coalitions said these proposals would both be bad for the environment and not deliver the promised regional benefits. But virtually no research seems to have taken place in Poland on the topic, and only

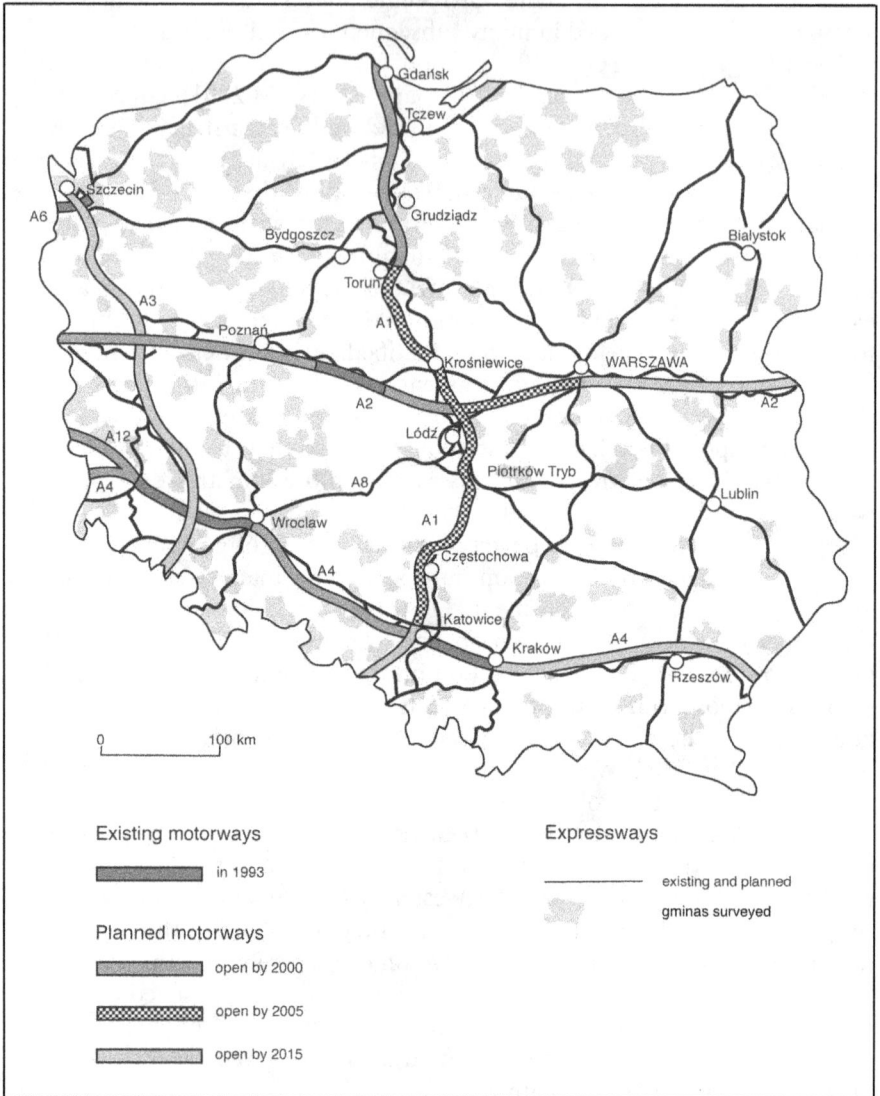

Figure 11.1 Motorway and expressway system as planned in 1993, depicting *gminas* (local authorities) responding to the survey.

Source: Adapted from Figure 1, Judge *et al.* (2004a).

secondary Western research was the basis of the arguments, while there was virtually no discussion of which regions would gain and which would lose from the proposals as they stood.

Much of the debate in Poland using Western research actually was based on research which was becoming progressively out of date. However, there is recent research to draw on in relation to the likely impact of transport investment on regional development which reflects and parallels the sort of research which informed debates in the UK. While this may seem again to be using Western-generated research, in fact there has been a significant involvement of Polish or East European partners.

One area of research has examined the way in which arguments at a political level were reflected in attitudes in the country at large. Content analysis of the Polish press and media suggests that, despite the assertions of environmental pressure groups about economic arguments being pushed by the press to support motorway construction, it was hard to find much discussion at all on the developmental aspects of motorway investment, while much more debate took place on environmental issues (Judge 2002). However, a different approach can be seen in local authority attitudes to government motorway and road plans (Judge *et al.* 2004a, 2004b). A survey of local authorities with populations exceeding 10,000 indicated that, while a high proportion of local authorities expected their areas to benefit economically from the construction of the motorway system, and this proportion increased the closer the local authorities were located to a motorway, the interesting fact was that an even greater percentage of respondents expected significant benefits to accrue from the improvement of the main road or 'expressway' system.[3] This is not surprising, as for a country the size of Poland the motorway network is quite sparse and, for the many local authorities located some distance away from it, local road improvements will be more significant and immediate in improving their locational position and economic prospects. However, the key issue is whether the expectations expressed in the survey are likely to be borne out in reality. To consider this we move on to consider the most recent EU research.

There have been a number of EU-wide transport projects but the most pertinent to this chapter is the IASON project.[4] The IASON model is described as:

> a model of regional socio-economic development . . . applied to different scenarios of further development of the European transport networks in the enlarged European Union plus Norway and Switzerland to answer the question whether infrastructure improvements contribute to the reduction of economic disparities among regions and so the cohesion objective of the European Union.
>
> (Wegener *et al.* 2004: 4)

The IASON (Integrated Appraisal of Spatial economic and Network effects of transport investments and policies) project included in its analyses all the recent entrants to the EU, including Poland, as well as Russia, Belarus, Ukraine, South-East Europe and Turkey. In analysing the impact of trans-European networks on spatial development throughout the EU, the results of the study are presented here as providing evidence on the likely relationship between transport investment and regional development in Poland, as all the motorway routes planned or being constructed in Poland constitute parts of trans-European routes as they pass through Polish territory. Of particular interest is the extent to which the proposed network might lead to advantage for the already developed western regions of Poland and losses to the under-developed eastern regions (the opposite of what one might wish to achieve if pursuing a programme intended to lessen regional disadvantage).

There is a very extensive modelling framework (Bröcker *et al.* 2004), including a CGE model. This would allow the impact of alternative network scenarios on regional economic aggregates (RGDP, employment) to be esti-mated. As far as Poland is concerned the country is modelled on the basis of the new *voivod* structure of sixteen zones. The complex of models covers demographic, economic and transport system variables. It can simulate the economic effects of a wide range of alternative network development patterns (or scenarios) in the EU and new accession states.[5]

Three of the scenarios covering the period 2001–20 are examined here in relation to Poland and nearby states as being most relevant to the theme of this chapter. They were evaluated by reference to a base, or 'do nothing' scenario (Scenario 000), in which no network improvements took place after 2001. It represented *de facto* the actual development of the road, rail and air networks in Europe between 1981 and 2001. The first of the three scenarios is Scenario A1, which is the implementation of all TEN (Trans-European Network) priority projects (of the so-called Essen list) and which was aimed primarily at improving the accessibility of the peripheral regions in the Mediterranean and the Nordic countries. The second is Scenario A3, which is the implementation of all TEN and TINA (Transport Infrastructure Needs Assessment) projects. So it is A1 plus the TINA projects which were defined as the priority transport projects required in the EU accession states of CEE. The third is Scenario A62, which is Scenario A3 plus implementation of rather fewer projects than in the original TINA outline plan. Scenario A62 was one of some additional scenarios elaborated by the Polish Academy of Sciences in Warsaw, representing a more realistic version of Scenario A3 (Komornicki and Korcelli 2003). The scenarios include projects for all modes, so the particular role of road developments cannot be separately indicated, and hence the overall results must be taken as having an indicative relationship to the discussion in the main text.

The results of each scenario are presented in the reports in terms of: (a) accessibility change compared to the reference scenario (000) (the accessibil-ity measures are complex representations of the changes in journey time and operating costs by mode, plus a variety of other factors); (b) change in wel-fare (regional GDP) compared to 000; and (c) change in GDP per capita compared to 000. The combined effects of all mode changes are incorporated in each scenario. The results overall, and for Poland, for each scenario are described in Table 11.1, but graphics are presented only for Scenario A62 and only for Poland and neighbouring states. Figure 11.2 illustrates the road network tested in IASON for Scenario A62. Figure 11.3 illustrates the

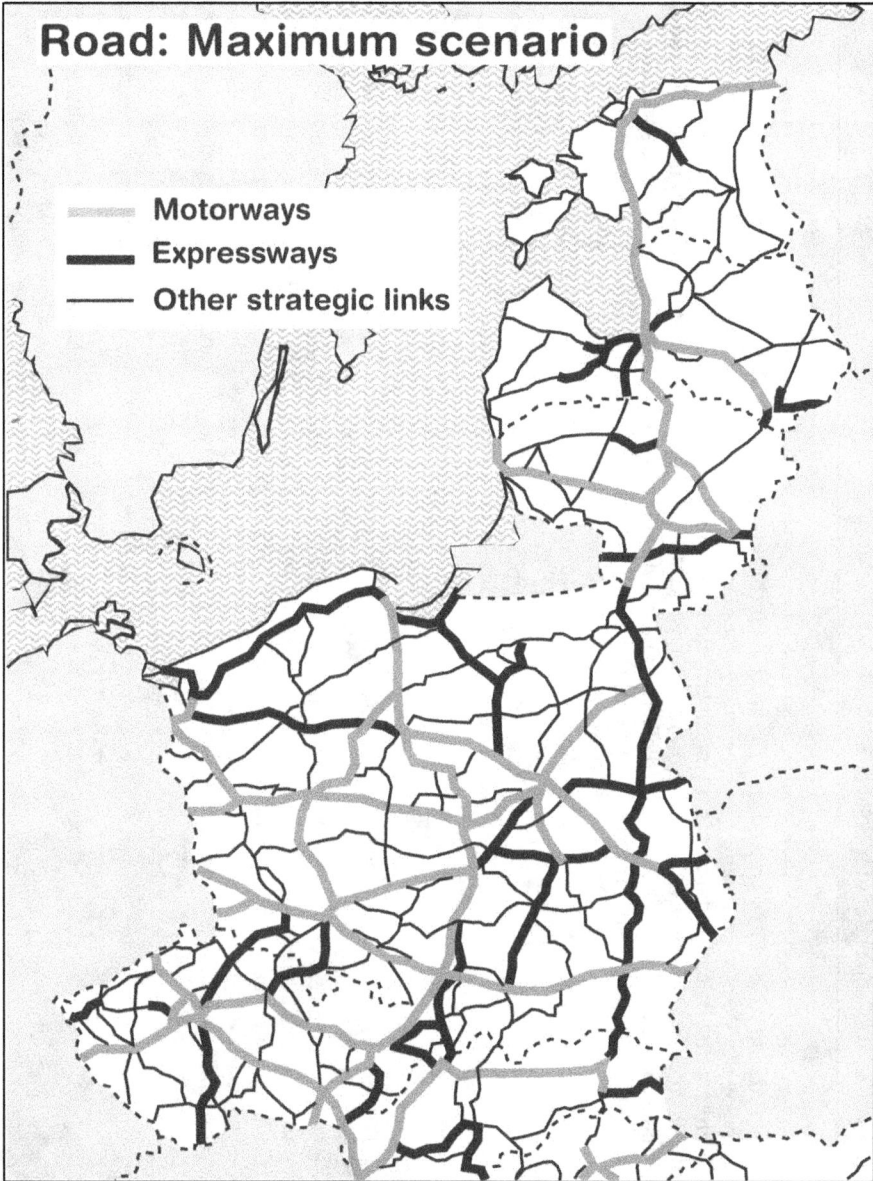

Figure 11.2 Alternative TINA Scenario A62 – roads (extract of Poland and near CEE states).

Source: Tavasszy *et al.* (2004: 130, Figure 57).

Table 11.1 Summary of results of IASON simulations for Poland, 2001–20

Result	Scenario A1	Scenario A3	Scenario A62
Accessibility change	The main impact of A1 was intended to be on the Mediterranean and Nordic states; Poland and the near CEE states would achieve only modest 'knock-on' accessibility benefits in the range 0–10 per cent.	The accessibility change is more generally spread amongst all members, though the Iberian and Nordic peninsulas still show up well. Polish regions benefit either by 10–20 per cent or by 20–30 per cent. The latter are mainly regions along the line of the A1 motorway (slightly), the A2 (more fully) and the A4 (the complete length), plus the Via Baltica to the Baltic states.	The Mediterranean and Nordic countries still benefit significantly, but the changes for the CEE countries are very noticeable, and for the Balkans are quite spectacular. For Poland, all regions will experience accessibility changes of at least 10–20 per cent, though such low-level changes are restricted to the north-west corner of the country, while the rest experience 20–30 per cent change, with a marked band of 30–40 per cent change in the eastern half of the country.
Change in welfare (regional GDP)	GDP benefits clearly flow to the peripheral EU regions, but for Poland and the near CEE states the results are negligible: between 0 and 0.176 per cent over twenty years, or even a negative figure of up to –0.04 per cent. The eastern parts of Poland appear to be less favoured, a not surprising result.	Regional GDP benefits are most marked for the former EU peripheral regions and the CEE entrants. But results for Poland vary significantly within the country. The largest increases in regional GDP seem to be along the lines of the A4 motorway (with the Silesian conurbation particularly noticeable – possibly evidence of agglomeration economies), the A2 motorway, the	The substantial changes in accessibility do not translate into such remarkable changes in regional GDP. However, in this scenario the CEE countries stand out more obviously. The motorway corridors and Via Baltica stand out again and the eastern regions do well, but there are still a significant number of 'cool' spots showing almost zero change. Also noticeable is that the range of changes reaches only halfway up the scale to 0.75–0.87 per cent maximum over the twenty-year period.

Change in GDP per capita			
The Iberian and Nordic peninsulas gain relatively to the rest (up to 3–4 per cent for the former, but only up to 2–3 per cent for the latter). However, Poland loses uniformly from 0 per cent to 1 per cent of regional GDP per capita relative to the EU average.	Via Baltica corridor and partly along the line of the A1 motorway, all of which according to this scenario would be completed by 2020. But in addition the western border regions seem to do quite well, and surprisingly the eastern border regions also record some of the largest increases. However, even the largest increases amount absolutely to only 0.75–0.87 per cent over twenty years. But also noticeable are a number of 'cold' areas, e.g. the two regions south of Ustka on the Baltic coast, which record virtually no change, being well away from main routes and centres.	The main beneficiaries in terms of GDP per capita are the Mediterranean and Nordic areas. There are some 'warm' areas in Eastern Europe, but as far as Poland is concerned the changes are either only mildly positive (0.0 to 1.0 per cent change over twenty years) or actually negative (–1.0 per cent to 0.0 per cent change relative to the EU average). Again, the main beneficiaries are along the lines of the A1, A2 and A4 motorways and Via Baltica.	In terms of GDP per capita, the CEE countries are still doing well, but the area from the Czech Republic down to the Balkans seems to be doing far better than the rest. However, while better than for A3, the results for Poland are mixed. Apart from areas in the southeast and northeast which experience 1–2 per cent change, the rest of the country is in the 0–1 per cent range, while the areas in the northwest are actually in the –1 to 0.0 per cent range. Again, these are gross changes over a 20 year period.

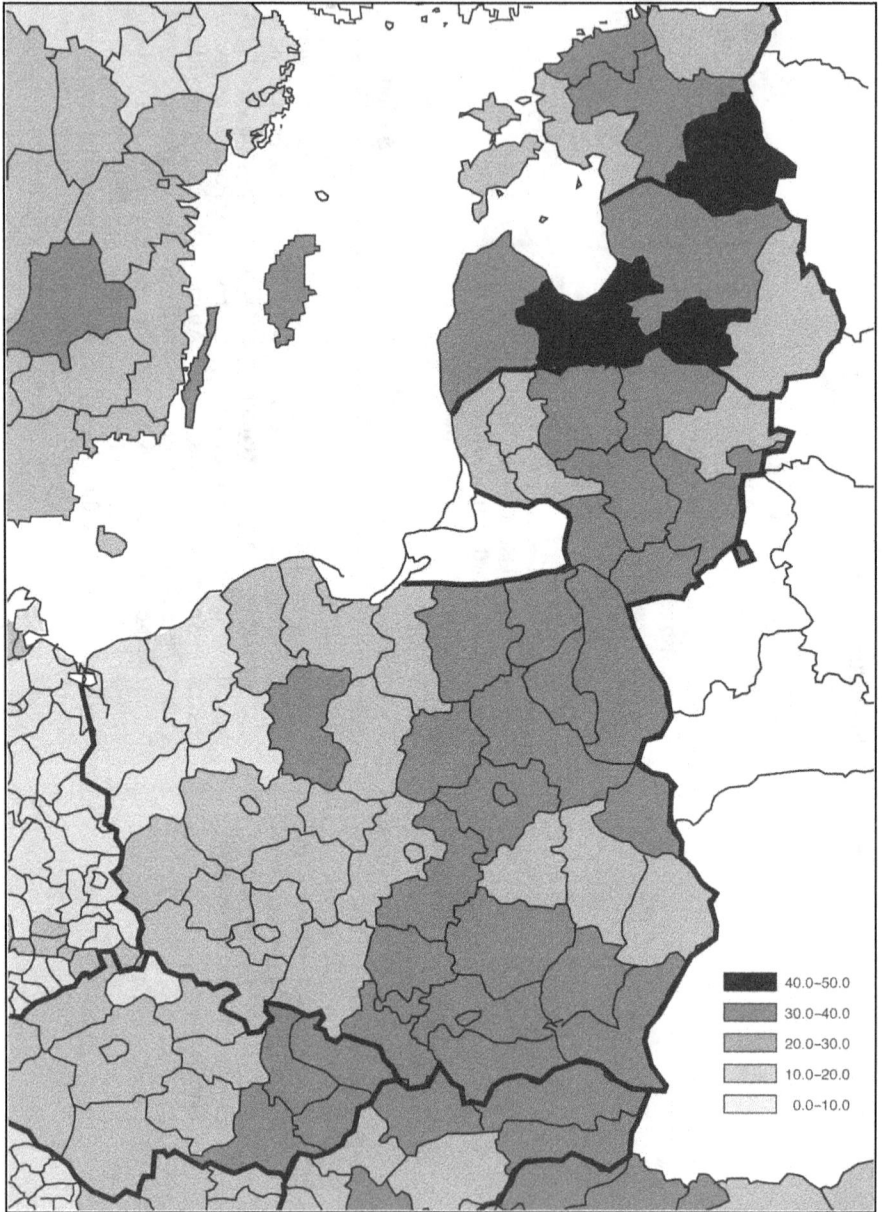

Figure 11.3 Percentage change in accessibility with Scenario A62 (extract of Poland and near CEE states).

Source: Tavasszy *et al.* (2004: 61, Figure 20).

accessibility change generated by these networks, while Figure 11.4 depicts percentage change in welfare, and Figure 11.5 depicts the percentage change in GDP per capita.

Overall, Table 11.1 and the Figures 11.2 to 11.5 indicate that, while A3 and especially A62 show substantial accessibility benefits for Poland, the impacts in terms of change in regional GDP and GDP per capita over twenty years are quite modest. One also has to wonder if changes of the magnitude mentioned are many times smaller than the level of modelling error, and hence swamped by it, for, as Preston and Holvad (2005) note, these models cannot have statistical diagnostics applied to them.

As Wegener *et al.* (2005) have commented (not just on Poland):

> the overall effects of transport infrastructure investments and other transport policies are small compared with those of socio-economic and technical macro trends, such as globalisation, increasing competition between cities and regions, ageing of the population, shifting labour force participation and increases in labour productivity . . . If one considers that under normal economic circumstances the long-term growth of regional economies is in the range between two and three percent per year, additional regional economic growth of less than one or two percent over twenty years is almost negligible.
>
> (Wegener *et al.* 2005: 38)

Thus, even very large increases in accessibility seem to make little difference to regional economic growth.

As far as Poland is concerned, different regions benefit at most between 0.5 per cent and 0.8 per cent in total, and some have negative impacts, in spite of quite large changes in accessibility. These effects over two decades are swamped by other socio-economic trends evidenced by annual regional GDP growth rates of 2–3 per cent. The effects observed in Figures 11.2 to 11.5 give some credence to the view of entrenchment of the pre-existing dominance of the western and southern regions by the transport investment, but it is by no means uniform, and some of the northern and eastern regions (particularly on the line of the Via Baltica) seem to do very well. But the fairly good performance of the eastern border regions is less expected. So there are regional economic effects due to transport investment but they are very modest compared to other factors. Arguably, one possibility is that the number of Poles who have moved to the UK and Ireland since Poland's EU entry in 2004 could already have had a greater impact on regional GDP per head in Poland, for better or worse, than the predicted changes in IASON over twenty years due to transport investment. This is consistent for instance with UK work showing that changes in lorry drivers' hours had a greater effect on employment distribution than investments in the interurban road network (Botham 1983).

The overall conclusions for the whole study area are modified for particular

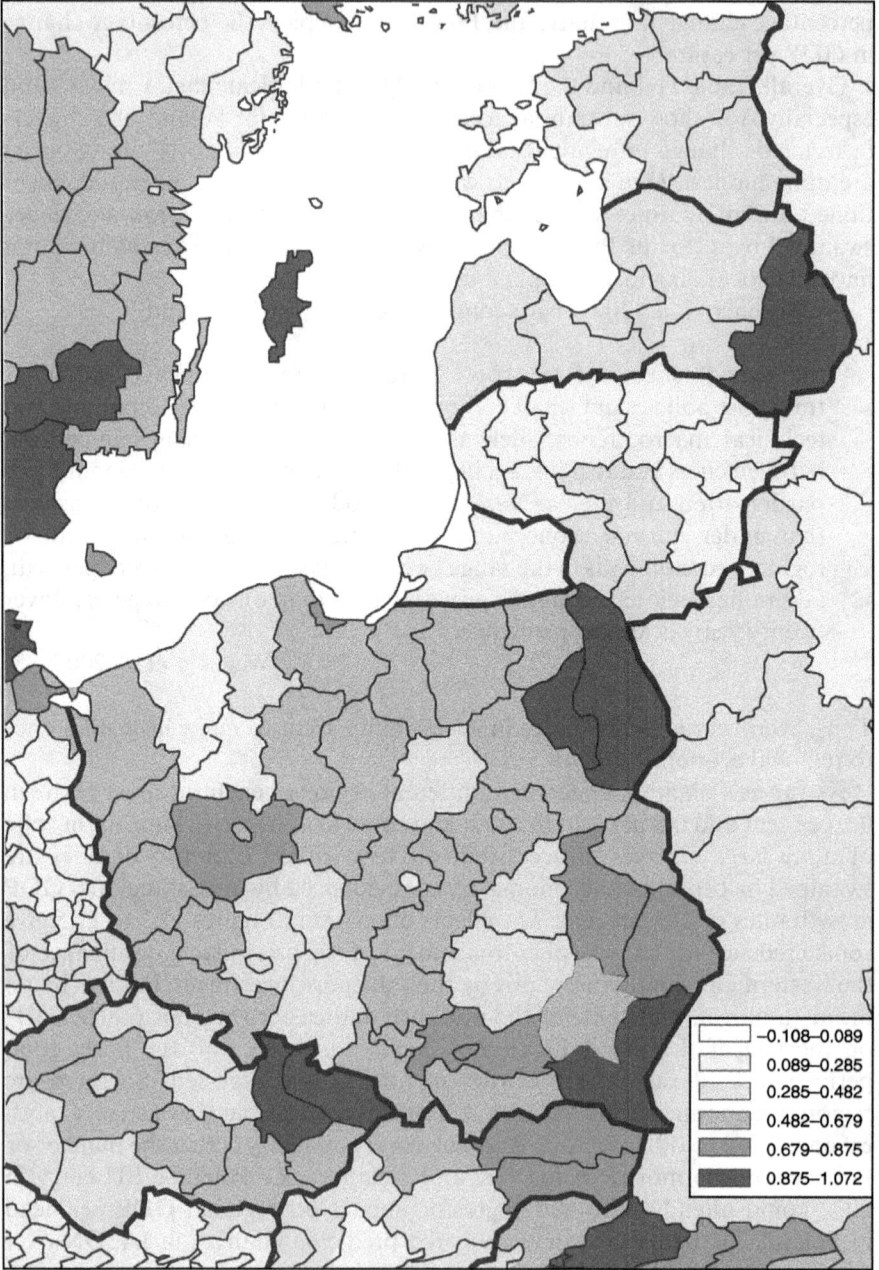

Figure 11.4 Percentage change in welfare (percentage of GDP) with Scenario A62 (extract of Poland and near CEE states).

The legend shows:

☐	−0.108–0.089
☐	0.089–0.285
☐	0.285–0.482
☐	0.482–0.679
☐	0.679–0.875
■	0.875–1.072

Source: Tavasszy *et al.* (2004: 89, Figure 45).

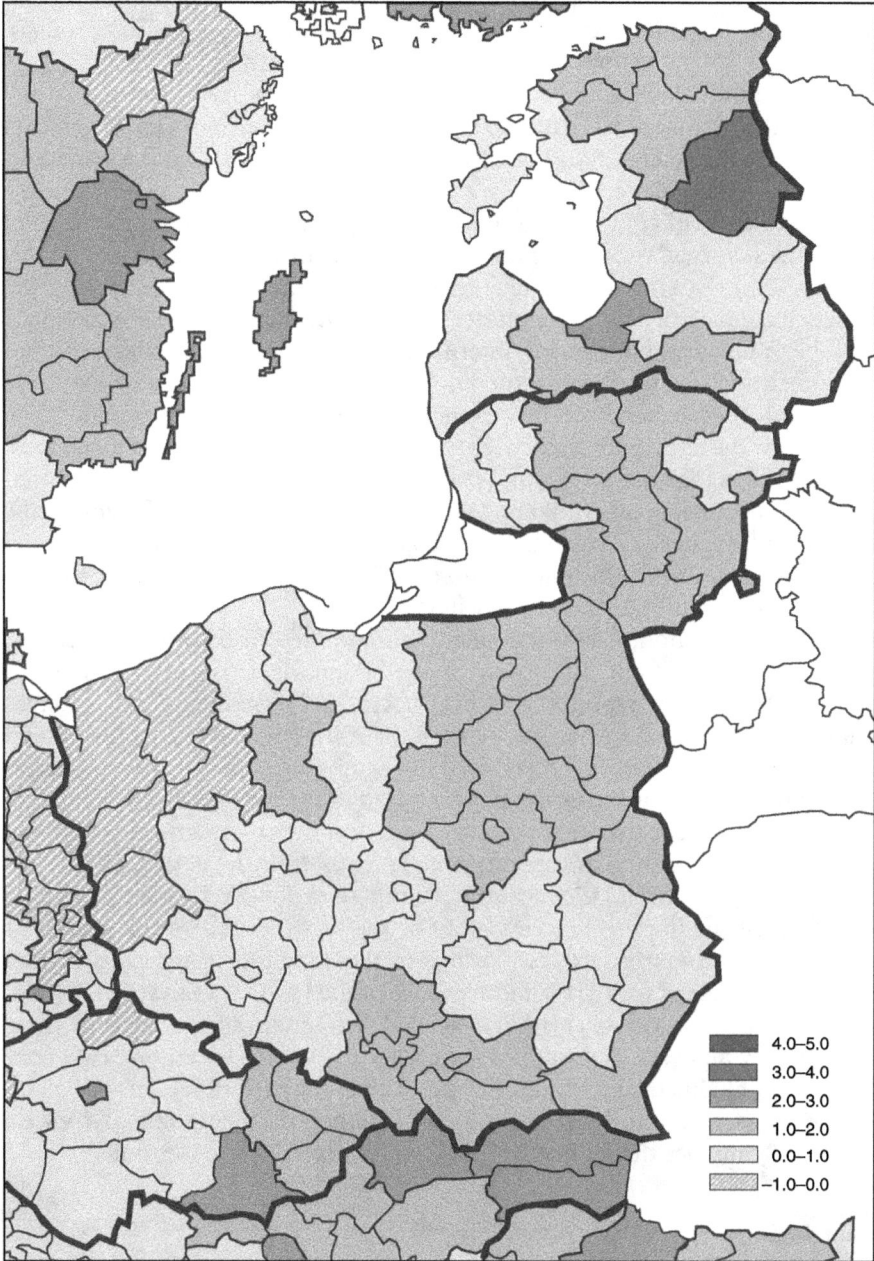

Figure 11.5 Percentage change in GDP per capita (standardised as a percentage of the EU27+2 average to show only distributional effects) with Scenario A62 (extract of Poland and near CEE states).

Source: Tavasszy *et al.* (2004: 69, Figure 29).

regions to the extent that the magnitude of the effect seems to depend strongly on the initial level of accessibility in 2001 (Wegener *et al.* 2005). Thus, for instance, the north-west corner of Poland around Szczecin in 2001 already had excellent connections to the German motorway system, so the incremental change in accessibility from additional transport improvements will only be marginal relative to less well-connected areas, and this shows up in the GDP/GDP per capita analyses.

The difficulty of course is that the results are aggregated for all modes, and the individual roads effect can only be presumed from the dominance of this mode. Also, the sizes of the regions considered are out of kilter with the actual incidence of the likely effects. This is satisfactory if one is taking a European purview, but from an internal Polish perspective the effects of road investment will be to concentrate development in narrow corridors, and the nature and consequence of this cannot be judged from these results. Also, saying that the effects are small over twenty years is not telling one much once one considers that these are small percentages of very large magnitudes concentrated in small areas, and may be yielding decent returns in relation to the scales of investments involved. This would be of key significance to regional policy makers. But of this one has no idea from these results, and this is one of the criticisms of the study locally in Poland.

In this connection, it is worth mentioning the recent research carried out under the aegis of the European Spatial Planning Observation Network (ESPON). A recent report (S&W and RRG 2007) presents data on actual change in potential accessibility by road for 2001–06. The results for Poland and neighbouring states are presented in Figure 11.6. This shows that accessibility improvements have been concentrated in the western areas of Poland, with some areas experiencing up to a 25 per cent improvement, as the impact of road improvements and investments spreads from west to east. Inward investment from abroad is concentrated in these regions. Whether this reflects the effect of the improved accessibility or the fact that the largest and most dynamic urban centres are also located in these regions is not clear. Again, like opinions about the particular relevance of the IASON analyses to Poland, there is some questioning within official Polish circles of the basis of these accessibility analyses. But in terms of earlier discussion based on NEG concepts, it highlights the highly inferior position of the eastern regions of Poland in the short term, and the question of whether the operation of IASON adequately mimics the differential build-up of accessibility over time.

Conclusions

On the issues of transport and the economy, and transport and regional development generally, it is possible to say that a lot more is known than formerly, and it can be concluded that (probably) there is some relationship which needs to be considered, but any claims that boom times are coming in the wake of a particular transport investment should be mistrusted.

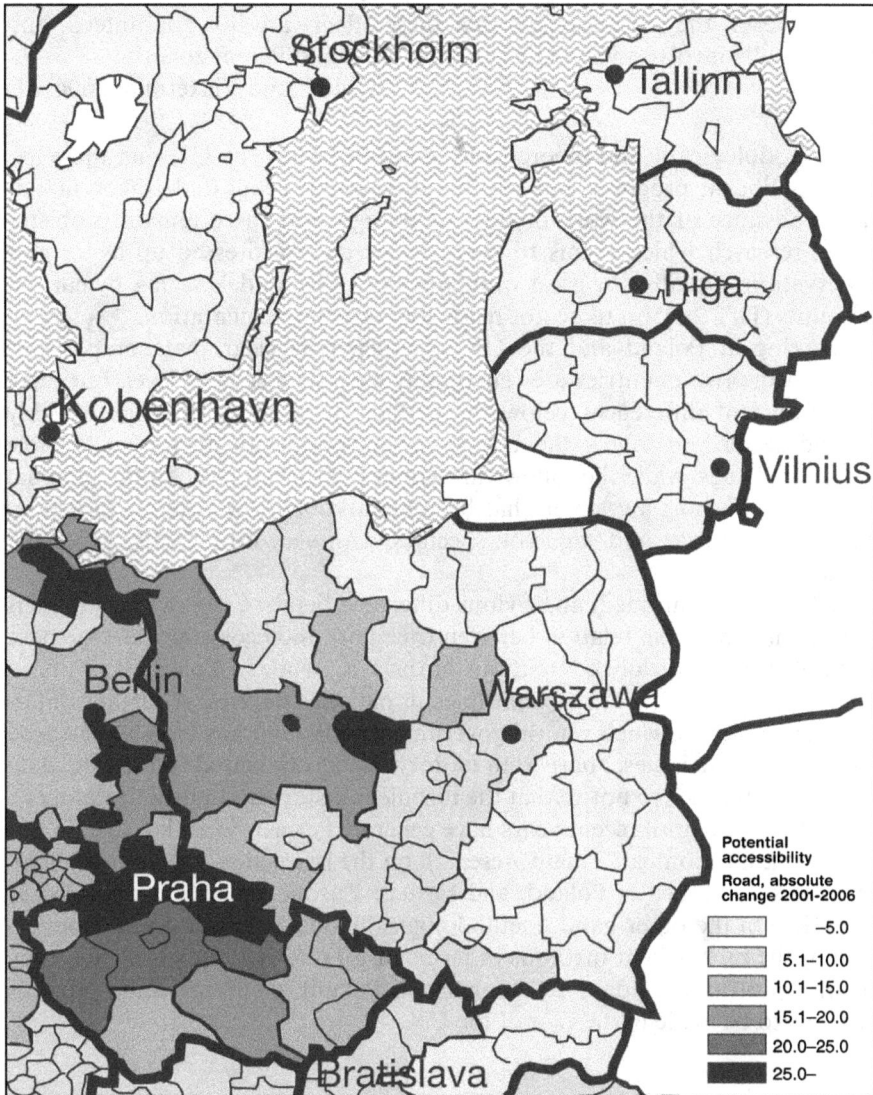

Figure 11.6 Absolute change in potential accessibility by road 2001–06.

Source: Extract from S&W and RRG (2007: 18, Figure 6).

Note: EU-27 absolute average in 2006 = 100.

As Quinet and Vickerman express it very aptly after reviewing a range of studies:

> Taken together these results constitute a substantial body of evidence.
> They provide a certain justification for the frequent claims made by local

politicians in favour of the beneficial effects of transport improvements. However, they also suggest that these effects are not guaranteed, and typically involve some redistribution between different zones.

(Quinet and Vickerman 2004: 51)

Methodologically and theoretically, one can say for the UK that there has been significant progress, and the sort of research being undertaken now is far in advance of the work of forty years ago. But there remain problems about research which seems to be really prediction dressed up as *ex post* observation. Equally, the great white hope of CGE models seems, by current accounts (DfT 2005b), to be not ready for wider implementation.

Looking at Poland and the UK together, it is clear that comparisons between the two countries are remarkably close at a surface level, but there are important differences below the surface. It is interesting how quickly Poland seemed to follow the UK at urban level, with all the sustainable transport issues, while the follow-through at interurban level on the regional effects of transport investment has been remarkably slow in terms of action, strong on rhetoric, and vague on specifics, with very little locally generated research.

As already mentioned, an obvious difference between the two countries is the way in which the relation between transport and economic development has not been politically contentious in the UK, while in Poland it has been strongly associated with the fault lines in national politics. A further difference is the way in which central government in Poland has largely distanced itself from these issues, apart from motorways, as compared to the UK. And it is impossible not to notice that the turbulent history and unstable nature of the Polish state until recent years have generated dimensions that just do not occur in a UK context. Finally, research on the issues discussed in this chapter is less developed in Poland, and Eastern Europe generally, compared to the UK. On the other hand, methodologically one can point to the application of the most recent methods in terms of NEG/CGE models to the study of transport and regional development in Poland, while the same progress remains to be made in the case of the UK.

Acknowledgements

I am grateful to Tomasz Komornicki for useful comments on an earlier draft of this chapter. The usual disclaimer applies. And thanks to Maria Arevena for the graphics.

Notes

1   In fact, environmental lobby groups in Eastern Europe, and especially Poland, using Western research, argued precisely this to counter demands for new motorway networks after 1989 (Judge 1994, 1996).

2　For further more detailed discussion, see Judge (2000, 2002).
3　Of a total of about 400 in all there was a response rate of 67 per cent, or 258 – locations of these are shown in Figure 11.1. The proportion of the total population covered by the responding *gminas* was 35 per cent, or about 56 per cent of the urban population.
4　The specific results of this study as they relate to Poland have been filtered out of the large volume of project reportage (ten reports of 964 pages) to be referred to in the remainder of this section.
5　Many scenarios were analysed: some twenty or so are described, and up to sixty or so were tested (Tavasszy *et al.* 2004). All of them are computed at a general European level, so to some extent it is not possible to consider what the effects separately of the Polish motorway system are, as each scenario operates to some extent on a European basis, and hence overall network effects are in operation. Indeed, none of these scenarios include a simple set of 'Polish motorway' scenarios.

References

Botham, R. (1983) 'The road programme and regional development: the problem of the counterfactual', in K. J. Button and D. Gillingwater (eds), *Transport, location and spatial policy*, Aldershot: Gower Press, pp. 57–81.

Bröcker, J., Meyer, R., Schneekloth, N., Schürmann, C., Spiekermann, K. and Wegener, M. (2004) *Modelling the socio-economic and spatial impacts of EU transport policy*, Kiel/Dortmund: Christian-Albrechts-Universität Kiel and Institut für Raumplanung, Universität Dortmund. Available at www.inro.tno.nl/iason (accessed 4 November 2004).

DfT (1999) *Transport and the economy: government response to SACTRA report*, London: Department for Transport. Available at www.dft.gov.uk (accessed 14 January 2005).

DfT (2005a) *SCGE models: relevance and accessibility for use in the UK*, London: Department for Transport. Available at www.dft.gov.uk (accessed 13 January 2006).

DfT (2005b) *Transport, wider economic benefits, and impact on GDP*, London: Department for Transport. Available at www.dft.gov.uk (accessed 13 January 2006).

Dodgson, J. (1974) 'Motorway investment, industrial transport costs and sub-regional growth: a case study of the M62', *Regional Studies*, 8: 75–91.

Dodgson, J. S. (1999) *Framework for assessing studies of the impact of transport infrastructure projects on economic activity*, London: Department of Environment, Transport and the Regions. Available at www.dft.gov.uk (accessed 14 January 2005).

Gibbons, S. and Machin, S. (2003) *Employment and rail access: evaluation of the wider benefits of transport improvements*, London: Department for Transport. Available at www.dft.gov.uk (accessed 13 January 2006).

Graham, D. J. (2005) *Wider economic benefits of transport improvements: link between agglomeration and productivity, Stage 1 Report*, London: Department for Transport. Available at www.dft.gov.uk (accessed 13 January 2006).

Hicks, B. (1996) *Environmental politics in Poland: a social movement between regime and opposition*, New York: Columbia University Press.

HMSO (1963a) *Central Scotland: programme for development and growth*, Cm 2188, London: HMSO.

HMSO (1963b) *The Northeast: programme for development and growth*, Cm 2206, London: HMSO.

HMSO (1977) *Report of the Advisory Committee on Trunk Road Appraisal* (Leitch Report), Standing Advisory Committee on Trunk Road Appraisal (SACTRA), London: Department of Transport.

HMSO (1998) *A new deal for transport: better for everyone*, Cm 3950, London: HMSO.

IBDM (1992) *Program Budowy Autostrad w Polsce* [Programme of Building Motorways in Poland], Warsaw: Institute for Research on Roads and Bridges.

ISD (1998a) *Instruments of the sustainable transportation policy implementation, information package No. 4 of 'Alternative transport policy in Poland'*, Warsaw: Institute for Sustainable Development.

ISD (1998b) *Options for the development of the transportation system in Poland, information package No. 3 of 'Alternative transport policy in Poland'*. Warsaw: Institute for Sustainable Development.

Judge, E. J. (1994) 'Global environmental aspects of managing the relationship between transport and land use: an Anglo-Polish comparison', in G. Haughton and C. Williams (eds), *Perspectives towards sustainable environmental development*, Aldershot: Avebury.

Judge, E. J. (1996) 'The liberated consumer? Aspects of change in Eastern Europe', *Proceedings of Chartered Institute of Transport*, 5: 24–44.

Judge, E. J. (2000) 'The regional and environmental dimension of Polish motorways policy', *Regional Studies*, 34: 488–93.

Judge, E. J. (2002) 'Environmental and economic development issues in the Polish motorway programme: a review and an analysis of the public debate', *European Environment (Journal of European Environmental Policy)*, 12: 77–89.

Judge, E. J. and Button, K. J. (1974) 'Inter urban roads in Great Britain: perspectives and prospects', *Transportation, Planning and Technology*, 3: 185–94.

Judge, E. J., Werpachowski, K. and Wishardt, M. (2004a) 'Polish gminas' attitudes to government motorway and road plans', *Przegląd Geograficzny* [Geographical review], 76: 125–41.

Judge, E. J., Werpachowski, K. and Wishardt, M. (2004b) 'Environmental and economic development issues in the Polish motorway programme: Some findings on local authority attitudes', *Journal of Transport Geography*, 12: 287–99.

Komornicki, T. and Korcelli, P. (2003) *Alternative scenarios of transportation network development for EU accession countries*, IASON Technical Note IGiPZ PAN 5, Warsaw: Polish Academy of Sciences.

Krugman, P. (1992) *Geography and trade*, Cambridge, MA: MIT Press.

Ministerstwo Infrastruktura (2002) *Infrastruktura – klucz do rozwoju* [Infrastructure – the key to development], Warsaw: Council of Ministers. Available at http://www.mi.gov.pl (accessed 30 June 2002).

MTGiM (1995) *Polityka transportowa: program działania w kierunku przekształcenia transportu w system dostosowany do wymogów gospodarki rynkowej i nowych warunków współpracy gospodarczej w Europie* [Transport policy: a programme of activity to adapt the transport system to the requirements of a market economy and the new conditions of economic cooperation in Europe], Warsaw: Ministry of Transport and Marine Economy.

MTGiM (2001) *Polityka transportowa państwa na lata 2000–2015 dla zrównoważonego rozwoju kraju* [National transport policy in the years 2000–2015 for the sustainable development of the country], Warsaw: Ministry of Transport and Marine Economy.

Ove Arup (2005) *Guide to improving the economic evidence base supporting regional economic and spatial strategies*, London: Office of the Deputy Prime Minister. Available at www.odpm.gov.uk (accessed 13 January 2006).

Preston, J. and Holvad, T. (2005) *A review of the empirical evidence on the additional benefits of road transport investment*, Oxford: Transport Studies Institute, Oxford University. Available at www.tsi.oxon.ac.uk (accessed 14 January 2005).

Quinet, E. and Vickerman, R. (2004) *Principles of transport economics*, Cheltenham: Edward Elgar.

SACTRA (1997) *Transport investment, transport intensity and economic growth: interim report*, Standing Advisory Committee on Trunk Road Assessment, London: Department of Transport. Available at www.dft.gov.uk (accessed 14 January 2005).

SACTRA (1999) *Transport and the economy*, Standing Advisory Committee on Trunk Road Assessment, London: Department of Transport. Available at www. dft.gov.uk (accessed 14 January 2005).

S&W and RRG (2007) *Update of selected potential accessibility measures, draft final report*, Dortmund/Oldenburg: Spiekermann & Wegener Urban and Regional Research (S&W) and RRG Spatial Planning and Geoinformation (RRG). Available at http://www.espon.eu (accessed 1 March 2007).

Steer Davies Gleave (2003) *Guidance on preparing an economic impact report*, London: Department for Transport. Available at www.dft.gov.uk (accessed 13 January 2006).

Tavasszy, L. A., Burgess, A. and Renes, G. (2004) *Final publishable report: conclusions and recommendations for the assessment of economic impacts of transport projects and policies*, IASON Deliverable D10, Delft: TNO Inro. Available at www. inro.tno.nl/iason (accessed 4 November 2004).

Vernon Henderson, J. (ed.) (2005) *New economic geography*, Cheltenham: Edward Elgar.

Vigar, G. (2002) *The politics of mobility: transport, the environment and public policy*, London: Spon.

Węcławowicz, G., Bański, J., Dęgórski, M., Komornicki, T., Korcelli P. and Śleszyński, P. (2006) *Przestrzenne Zagospodarowanie Polski na Początku XXI Wieku* [Polish spatial development at the start of 21st century], Warsaw: Polish Academy of Sciences.

Wegener, M., Komornicki, T. and Korcelli, P. (2004) 'Spatial impacts of the trans-European networks for the new EU member states', Paper to Warsaw Regional Forum Conference, Polish Academy of Sciences, Warsaw, October.

Wegener, M., Komornicki, T. and Korcelli, P. (2005), 'Spatial impacts of the trans-European networks for the new EU member states', in T. Komornicki and K. L. Czapiewski (eds), *New spatial relations in Europe*, Europa XXI, Warsaw: Polish Academy of Sciences, pp. 27–44.

12 EU funds in the Silesia region in the first years after accession (2004–06)

Adam Drobniak

This chapter follows the impact of EU funds on the Silesian region, showing how local authorities reacted to new opportunities arising from EU accession and the initial impact of the subsidies that had become available. This required adaptation to EU practices and conformity with regulations that were, at first, new to actors on the Polish scene. The basic document planning the distribution and utilisation of EU funds in Poland, in the first year after accession, was the National Development Plan (*Narodowy Plan Rozwoju*, NDP) (Ministerstwo Gospodarki i Pracy 2004a), which defined the general directions of Poland's socio-economic development, highlighting aspects aimed at strengthening competitiveness. The goals were further divided into partial objectives concerning improving the levels of employment and education, building the transport and information infrastructure, developing high-value-added sectors and ensuring the participation of all Polish regions in socio-economic development.

The objectives of the NDP became the basis for further socio-economic development planning in the framework of operational programmes which defined in detail how the EU funds should be distributed. In the period 2004–06 there were six main operational programmes. These were sectoral operational programmes for:

- improving the competitiveness of the economy (Ministerstwo Gospodarki i Pracy 2004c), mostly addressed to the business sector, with EU support of €1.30 billion;
- human resource development (Ministerstwo Gospodarki i Pracy 2004b), mainly devoted to the activities of labour offices and training firms in projects for vocational training and practical experience, with EU support of €1.27 billion;
- food sector and rural development (Ministerstwo Rolnictwa i Rozwoju Wsi 2004a), devoted to farmers and rural municipalities, with subsidies to farmers in line with the EU Common Agriculture Policy and total EU support of €1.06 billion;
- fishing and fish processing (Ministerstwo Rolnictwa i Rozwoju Wsi

2004b), allowing direct subsidisation for fishing businesses that gave up or limited their activities, with EU support of €0.17 billion;
* transport (Ministerstwo Infrastruktury 2004), mostly directed to big infrastructure projects such as roads and ports, with EU support of €0.63 billion;
* the Integrated Regional Operational Programme (IROP) (Ministerstwo Gospodarki i Pracy 2004d), supporting public projects and linked to problems of regional inequality, with EU support of €2.86 billion.

Total EU support for Poland in 2004–06 was €7.3 billion, the largest share of which was assigned to the IROP, taking 39 per cent of the total. As a programme for projects from local and regional authorities, it was divided into three priorities:

* Priority 1: Modernisation of the regional infrastructure, receiving 59 per cent of EU support and covering the more costly infrastructure projects.
* Priority 2: Strengthening the development of human resources, receiving only 15 per cent of the EU funds.
* Priority 3: Local development, assigned 26 per cent of the EU support and covering mainly hard investment projects of a local character, unlike the first priority, for which a regional impact was required.

It should be noted that the IROP was a regional development programme prepared mainly by the Polish government and not by the regional authorities. It was applied across all Polish regions despite the diversity of their problems. It nevertheless aroused enormous hopes among local authorities at the levels of the region (*województwo*), city, town with district status and district (*powiat*) and municipality (*gmina*).

Silesia after EU accession

As indicated in Table 12.1, regional differences in per capita GDP in Poland were very large. The differential between the region with highest value of GDP per capita (Mazowieckie) and the region with its lowest value (Lubelskie) was 2.17. The eastern parts of Poland struggled to cope with the problems of high unemployment (up to 35 per cent), a high proportion of employment in agriculture, a lack of industry, an underdeveloped service sector and a poor infrastructure. Silesia (Śląsk, Województwo Śląskie) enjoyed relatively good socio-economic conditions as the most industrialised region in the country (37 per cent of employment was in industry and construction against a Polish average of 25 per cent), well-developed traded services (34.4 per cent of employment in this sector against a Polish average of 30 per cent), relatively low unemployment (13.7 per cent against a Polish average of 15.5 per cent in August 2006), the second-highest population in Poland (4.7 million) and the highest level of urbanisation (about 80 per cent living in cities and towns

Table 12.1 Average per capita GDP in Poland's regions, 2001–03

Region	Per capita GDP, PLN	Regional per capita GDP as % of national average
Dolnośląskie	21,186	103
Kujawsko-pomorskie	18,657	91
Łódzki	18,647	91
Lubelskie	14,469	70
Lubuskie	18,040	88
Małopolskie	17,715	86
Mazowieckie	31,351	152
Opolskie	16,796	82
Podkarpackie	14,766	72
Podlaskie	15,699	76
Pomorskie	20,702	101
Śląskie	22,703	110
Świętokrzyskie	16,096	78
Warmińsko-mazurskie	15,547	76
Wielkopolskie	21,448	104
Zachodniopomorskie	20,198	98
Poland's average	20,560	100

Sources: GUS 2004, 2005.

Note: Regions correspond to the EU's NUTS2 level.

against 61 per cent for Poland as a whole). It also earned an 'A' rank in evaluation of its attractiveness to investors from a prominent research institute (Instytut Badań nad Gospodarką Rynkową 2005) and had a well-developed road, energy, water and sanitation infrastructure, with the highest density in Poland.

The region still had an industrial mono-structure 'label' connected with coal mining and steel. After 1989, employment in coal mining fell from about 200,000 to 100,000. Coal production fell from 200 millions tons to less then 100 millions tons, accounting in 2006 for less than 20 per cent of Silesia's output. FDI in automotive industries, perceived as a 'cure' for the Silesian economy, has created another mono-structure. It seems that Silesia needed more investment in high tech, and further development in culture, science and education.

Within Silesia a major role is played by its central sub-region connected with the Katowice agglomeration. Per capita GDP was 120 per cent of the regional average, as shown in Figure 12.1. It had 44 per cent of the population (2.1 million inhabitants), 45 per cent of the total number of enterprises, 56 per cent of companies' fixed assets, and investment outlays per capita 47 per cent above the regional average. However, it also suffered from environmental damage, caused by mining and heavy industry, from a low birth rate and high level of emigration, from a housing stock in need of modernisation and from social problems associated with long-term unemployment.

ŁÓDZKIE
VOIVODSHIP

Katowice agglomeration
and central sub-region: 120

Southern sub-region: 105

Northern and western
sub-regions: less then 95

kłobucki

częstochowski

CZESTOCHOWA

lubliniecki

OPOLSKIE
VOIVODSHIP

myszkowski

zawierciański

tarnogórski

będziński

gliwicki

rybnicki

KATOWICE

mikołowski

raciborski

RYBNIK

bieruński

ŻORY

wodzisławski

pszczyński

bielski

JASTRZEBIE

BIELSKO
BIAŁA

cieszyński

MAŁOPOLSKIE
VOIVODSHIP

CZECH
REPUBLIC

żywiecki

SLOVAK
REPUBLIC

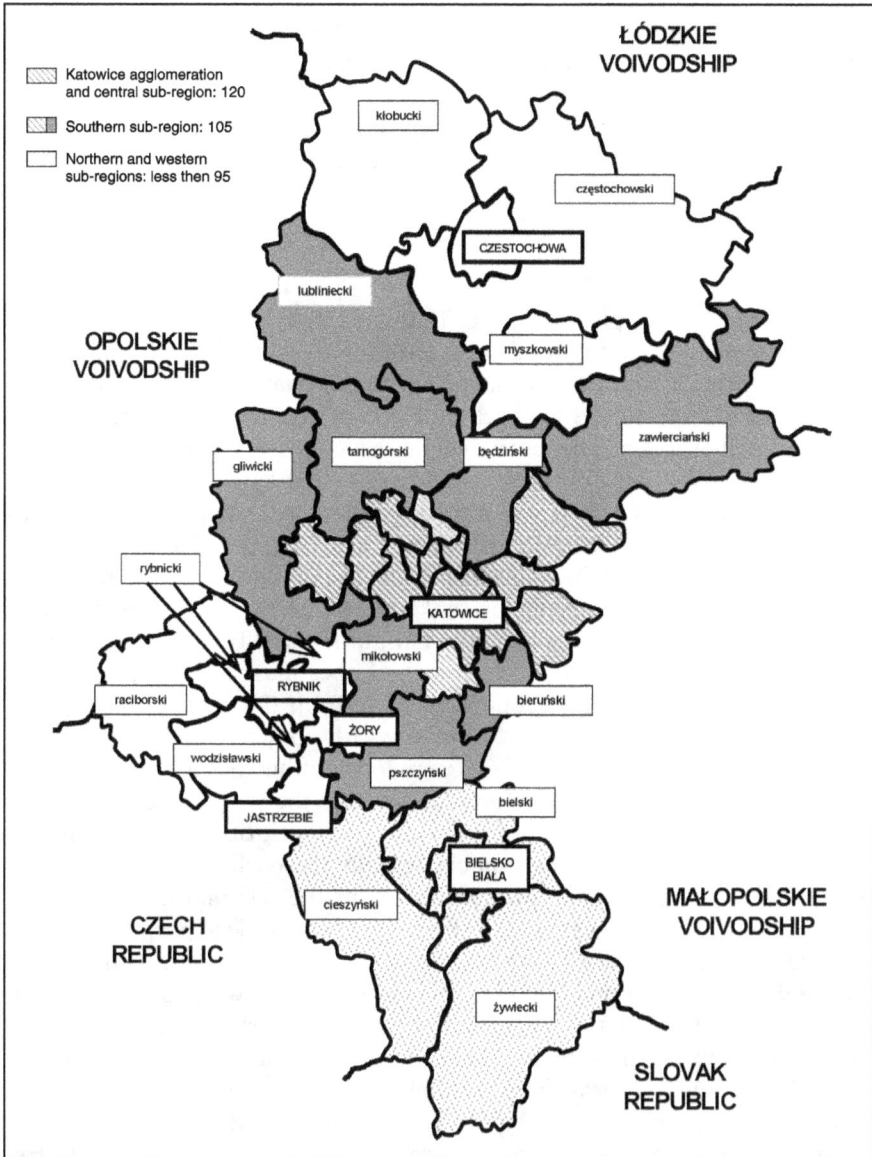

Figure 12.1 Per capita GDP within Silesia as percentage of the regional average, 2001–03.

Sources: GUS 2004, 2005.

The northern sub-region was characterised by a low level of infrastructure in roads and sewage treatment plants, a low potential of SMEs and a pre-dominance of agricultural activities. Its per capita GDP was also the lowest, at only 90 per cent of the Silesian average. The southern sub-region, with the main city Bielsko-Biała, was characterised by a relatively diversified economic structure and great potential of SMEs and tourism connected with the Beskidy Mountains, but a low level of transport infrastructure. Its level of per capita GDP was 105 per cent of the regional average. The western sub-region, formed mainly by the Rybnik agglomeration with 0.5 million inhabitants, was characterised by a low level of development in business services and an economic structure dominated by coal mining.

Applying for funds from the IROP

The procedure for applying for EU funds required proposals prepared by potential beneficiaries, followed by a selection process. This started with a formal verification stage by officials from the Silesian Marshal's Office (the regional authority), aimed at checking the completeness and correctness of project documentation. The second step was a content-related verification by expert panels made up from representatives of big enterprises, universities, local authorities and non-government organisations, using such criteria as the economic impact of a project proposal on Silesian regional development, sustainability and durability and the capacity of the applicant to ensure implementation. Projects were then ranked by a steering committee, made up of experts and representatives of regional authorities. Finally, the Regional Executive Body (the board of directors of the Silesian Marshal's Office) made a selection of project proposals, partly from the rankings and partly from political criteria, that would be granted EU support.

The key beneficiaries of the IROP were local authorities which could gain almost 90 per cent of all the EU funds assigned to the IROP. Table 12.2 shows the full breakdown of applications for the three priority areas, for specific measures within them and the support actually received. Results varied with the priority. For Priority 1, 'Modernisation of the regional infrastructure', local authorities had by mid-2006 presented 157 project proposals worth PLN1.3 billion, but final EU support was only 43 per cent of the value of the proposals. The largest number of proposals within this were for 'Modernisation and rebuilding of the regional transportation system', but the highest success rate was for the 'Regional educational infrastructure', albeit on the basis of only one proposal, from Sosnowiec city and the Silesian University in Katowice for support for building a science and teaching centre. The 'Environmental protection infrastructure' heading also scored well, with EU support for over half the amount applied for. Support for 'Development of tourism and culture' proved the most difficult, receiving only 20 per cent of the amount applied for.

Priority 2, 'Strengthening human resources', included projects for economically disadvantaged students in secondary and tertiary education and for those from rural areas. Projects for 'Regional innovation strategies' were not popular, with only four applications, mostly for Ph.D. students and for entrepreneurship development.

Table 12.2 The number and the value of the Silesian local authorities' project proposals within the IROP

Priority, measure	Number of applications	Value of applications, PLN million	Value of support received, PLN million	Value of support as % of value of applications
Priority 1 Modernisation of the regional infrastructure	**157**	**1,268**	**543**	**43**
Measure 1.1 Modernisation and rebuilding of the regional transportation system	64	615	289	47
Measure 1.2 Environmental protection infrastructure	28	291	148	51
Measure 1.3 Regional educational infrastructure	1	31	31	100
Measure 1.3.2 Regional heath-care infrastructure	7	32	2	6
Measure 1.4 Development of tourism and culture	26	208	43	20
Measure 1.5 Infrastructure of information society	31	90	31	34
Priority 2 Strengthening human resources	**NA**	**NA**	**57**	**NA**
Measure 2.2 Levelling educational opportunities by scholarship programmes	NA	NA	53	NA
Measure 2.6 Regional innovation strategies	NA	NA	4	NA
Priority 3 Local development	**417**	**945**	**263**	**28**
Measure 3.1 Rural areas	169	234	102	44
Measure 3.2 Areas under restructuring	51	128	86	67
Measure 3.3 Degraded urban, post-industrial and post-Army areas	83	275	57	21
Measure 3.5.1 Local education infrastructure	95	250	15	6
Measure 3.5.2 Local health-care infrastructure	19	57	3	5
Total for Priorities 1 and 3	**574**	**2,213**	**806**	**36**

Sources: Urząd Marszałkowski Województwa Śląskiego 2006a, 2006b, 2006c, 2006d.

Note: The total figure for project numbers and project values and the total percentage success rate do not include Measures 2.2 and 2.6.

The largest number and highest total value of proposals came under Priority 3, 'Local development', but EU support matched only 28 per cent of the proposals' value. In some measures, such as 'Local education infrastructure' and 'Local health-care infrastructure', EU support was a tiny fraction of the level applied for. Expectations had evidently been much higher than the level planned within the IROP, reflecting their perception of the scope and scale of problems in those areas.

The average per capita value of project proposals within Priorities 1 and 3 was PLN429 (about €107). Higher-value projects were applied for mainly by local authorities in the northern part of Silesia and in the western and some central and southern parts of the region. These high expectations, from areas with low per capita GDP, were not reflected in high levels of EU support. Indeed, the average per capita value of support in Silesia was only PLN140 (about €35). Among those receiving the highest levels of support were those that applied for the most, such as the towns of Bielsko-Biała, Bytom, Sosnowiec and Żory, and the Częstochowski, Myszkowski, Pszczyński, Rybnicki, Wodzisławski and Żywiecki districts.

Figure 12.2 shows the regional diversity in success in applications. Those districts and cities which applied for EU support on the level of +/−25 per cent of the per capita regional average value also received EU subsidies in the range +/−25 per cent of the regional average. Exceptions are Jastrzębie and the Bieruńsko-Lędziński, Mikołowski and Zawierciański districts. Most of the authorities that applied for EU support at under 75 per cent of the per capita regional average also received EU subsidies below that level. Most of the cities and towns of the Katowice agglomeration neither applied for a high value of projects nor received high levels of EU support.

This may be linked to these cities and towns seeking support from the Cohesion Fund. That implied rather larger financial burdens for the local authorities; projects usually had a value of over PLN60 million, but the scope to refinance reached 80 per cent of eligible project costs, unlike the IROP where the EU subsidy covered only 75 per cent of eligible costs. Analysis of the subsidies from the Cohesion Fund shows that their value was more than PLN1.9 billion, significantly exceeding support from the IROP. Moreover, only about PLN0.9 billion, equivalent to 50 per cent of the value of the subsidies for the Cohesion Fund gained by the Silesian cities and towns, was accessible directly for local authorities. The full picture is indicated in Table 12.3. The greater interest from the larger cities and towns in the Cohesion Fund also reflected the high average value of the Cohesion Fund subsidy, at over PLN140 million, while the IROP subsidy for hard infrastructure projects was merely PLN4.6 million. Thus the IROP supported relatively small projects and was of limited value when set against the scale of challenges facing larger authorities.

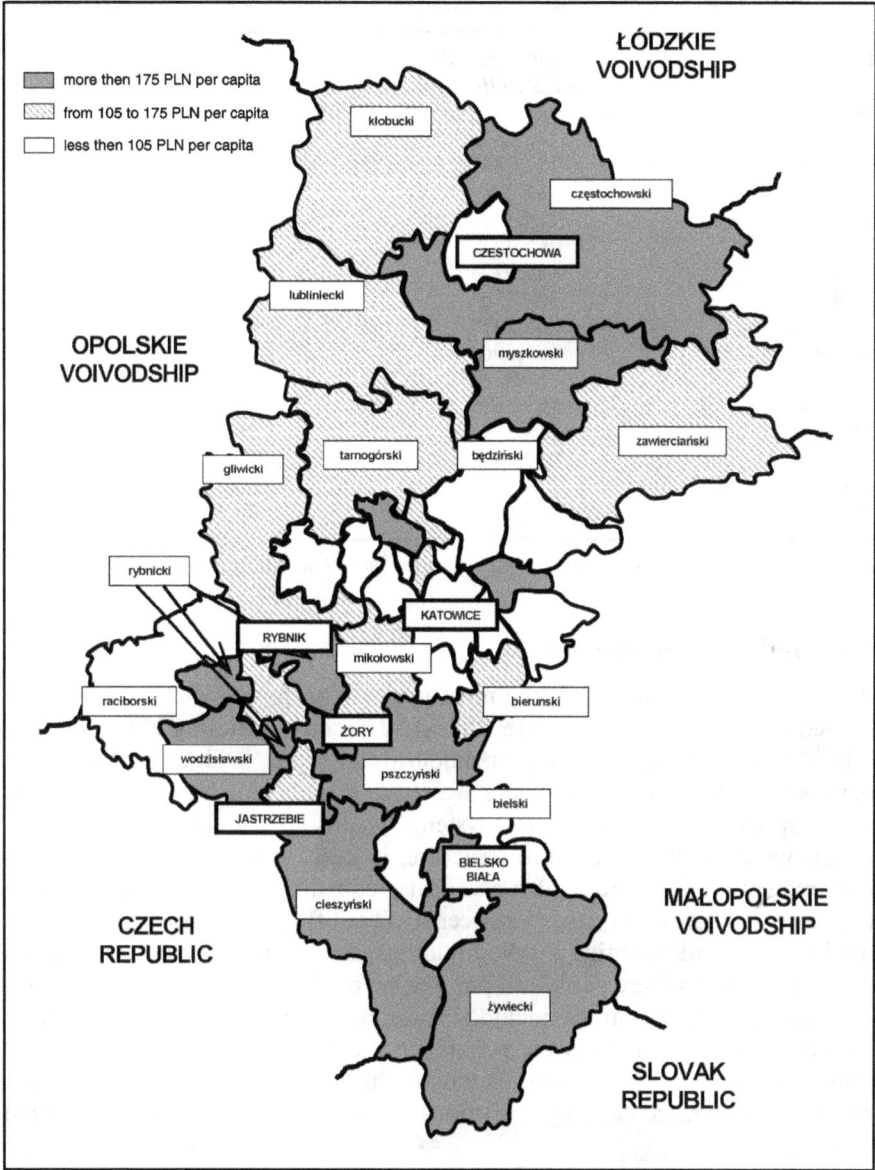

Figure 12.2 Sub-regional diversity in the value of EU funding awarded within IROP in the Silesia region.

Table 12.3 Cohesion Fund subsidies received by the Silesian local authorities, 2004–06

City or town	Estimated value of subsidy, PLN million	Estimated per capita value, PLN
Gliwice	140,757	702
Katowice	121,284	379
Rybnik	285,286	2,012
Ruda Śląska	119,332	810
Sosnowiec	65,422	287
Chorzów	89,072	773
Tychy	300,376	2,284
Racibórz	58,231	517
Bytom	198,396	1,047
Mysłowice	61,834	821
Pszczyna	103,369	993
Jastrzębie	113,889	1,186
Zabrze	233,149	1,211
Zawiercie	75,464	604
Total	1,965,861	902

Source: National Fund for Environmental Protection and Water Management (2006).

An initial assessment of uptake

As indicated in Figure 12.3, the most popular proposals within IROP were related to the road infrastructure: almost 30 per cent, meaning 173 proposals, related to rebuilding, repairing or modernising roads, bridges, roundabouts, pavements and ring roads. There was also a high representation for construction of water and sanitation systems. Nearly 32 per cent of project proposals were for the social infrastructure, broadly defined, including sports and recreational facilities (14 per cent), education (8 per cent), culture (5 per cent) and health care (5 per cent). These frequently covered building, modernising and adapting public buildings, modernising school and sports facilities, creating cycle paths and purchasing medical devices and equipment. Projects related to tourism included modernisation of historical buildings, modernisation of buildings and rooms for tourism information activities and preparing information systems for tourist attractions. A further thirty project proposals concerned clearing post-industrial sites and modernising municipal housing.

Breaking down project proposals by value, as shown in Figure 12.4, produces a similar picture. More than 54 per cent of the value of proposed projects was for activities supporting basic public services supplied by local authorities, meaning transport, water and sanitation. There was also a significant representation for a revitalisation category, accounting for 5 per cent of the total value of project proposals. This included searching for alternative sources of energy, modernisation of churches, clearing landfill sites and recycling waste materials.

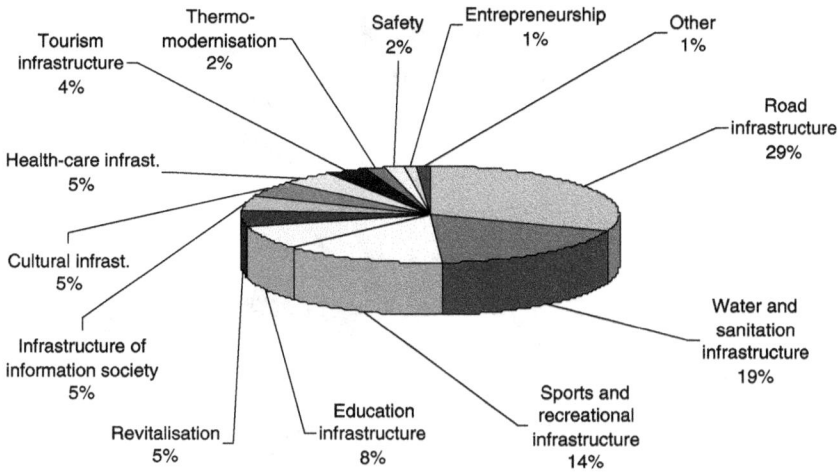

Figure 12.3 Type of project by share in total proposals.

Sources: Urząd Marszałkowski Województwa Śląskiego 2006a, 2006b, 2006c, 2006d.

Note: Measures 2.2 and 2.6 are not included.

The value of subsidies granted from the IROP was only about 26 per cent of the value of the applications. However, the structure of the subsidies granted corresponded, in principle, with the structure of project proposals. Exceptions included proposals for revitalisation, for the infrastructure for an information society and for entrepreneurship, for which the share in subsidies granted was higher than the share in applications, as indicated in Figure 12.5.

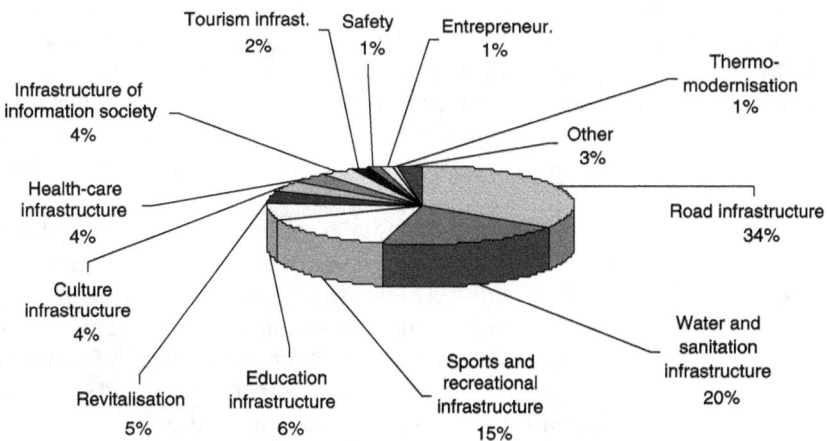

Figure 12.4 Types of projects by share in value of proposals.

Sources: Urząd Marszałkowski Województwa Śląskiego 2006a, 2006b, 2006c, 2006d.

Note: Measures 2.2 and 2.6 are not included.

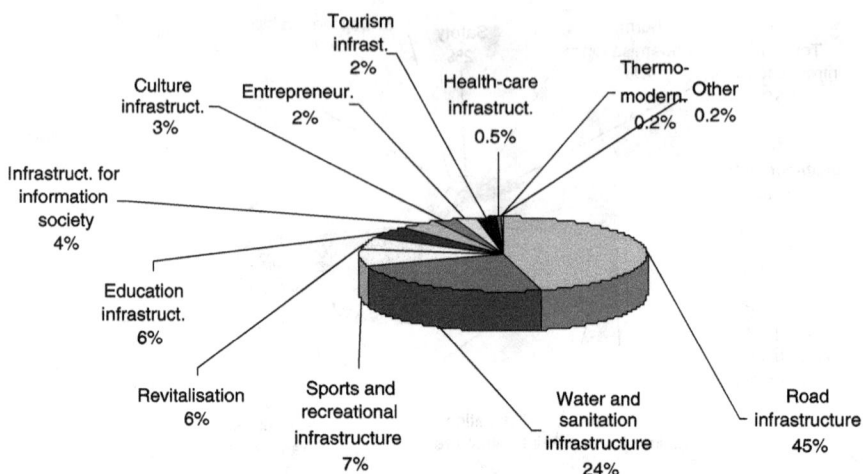

Figure 12.5 Type of project by share in value of subsidies granted from IROP.

Sources: Urząd Marszałkowski Województwa Śląskiego 2006a, 2006b, 2006c, 2006d.

Note: For comparability with Figure 12.4, Measures 2.2 ('Levelling educational opportunities by scholarship programmes') and 2.6 ('Regional innovation strategies') are not included in the total. They would account for 6.1 per cent and 0.4 per cent respectively of the full total.

Against this, the shares in proposals granted for culture and health care were both below their shares in the value of applications.

The comparison between support granted and support applied for indicates that it was most difficult to gain support for the 'Regional heath-care infrastructure' (86 per cent of proposals received no IROP support), 'Local education and sports infrastructure' (85 per cent were unsuccessful), 'Post-industrial and post-Army areas' and 'Development of tourism and culture', for both of which 81 per cent of projects received no IROP support. The most successful were the 'Regional education infrastructure' (all were successful, albeit out of only one application), 'Environment protection infrastructure' (36 per cent unsuccessful) and 'Areas under restructuring' (51 per cent unsuccessful).

The reasons for lack of success for many applications can be followed through the stages of the application process. In many cases the new procedures for applying for EU funds were enough to defeat the local authorities. One proposal in five was rejected because of incomplete documentation, or failure to provide the required documentation, such as financial information, building agreements or environmental assessment reports, and even the absence of more prosaic things such as stamps and signatures of an executive body. Such failings were most prevalent for the 'Infrastructure of information society' category (42 per cent rejected) and the 'Local educational infrastructure' (39 per cent rejected).

Another major reason for rejection at this stage, partly confirming the

Table 12.4 Stage of application process at which proposals for IROP support were rejected

Priority, measure	Total proposals	Percentage rejected in formal verification	Percentage rejected in content-related verification	Percentage of total rejected
Priority 1	**157**	**18**	**23**	**41.4**
Measure 1.1	64	17	25	42.2
Measure 1.2	28	7	25	32.1
Measure 1.3.1	1	0	0	0.0
Measure 1.3.2	7	0	14	14.3
Measure 1.4	26	12	27	38.5
Measure 1.5	31	42	16	58.1
Priority 3	**417**	**21**	**14**	**35.7**
Measure 3.1	169	18	7	24.9
Measure 3.2	51	16	22	37.3
Measure 3.3	83	11	28	38.6
Measure 3.5.1	95	39	7	46.3
Measure 3.5.2	19	21	42	63.2
Total – Priorities I and III	**574**	**21**	**17**	**37.3**

Sources: Urząd Marszałkowski Województwa Śląskiego 2006a, 2006b, 2006c, 2006d.

disproportion between the types of project applied for and the aims of the IROP, was that proposals in 17 per cent of cases did not fit the criteria set in the IROP. Overall, the percentage of proposals rejected because of problems with meeting the formal requirements amounted to 37 per cent of the total. Thus more than one out of three proposals from Silesian local authorities did not even pass the first hurdle for consideration for EU funding.

Table 12.5 shows the ten authorities that benefited the most from the IROP. In terms of the total value of EU funds acquired, Bytom was the biggest winner in the Silesian region, with more than PLN75 million (about €16 million) from the IROP, or almost 10 per cent of the total, although it was actually successful in only two out of ten applications. The first of these, for a ring road round the Upper Silesia agglomeration, was awarded PLN72 million. The second, for modernisation of a building for the Silesia Technical University, received PLN 3.4 million. Żywiecki district, with fifteen municipalities in the southern sub-region, was close behind with EU support of PLN70 million, but in this case there were forty proposals and twenty-one were successful. Those with the highest value included three for water and sanitation systems, receiving in total PLN36 million, and for modernisation of two local roads, which received PLN3.3 million.

Table 12.5 The top ten authorities benefiting the most from the IROP, by absolute value of support received

	Value of the IROP subsidies, PLN million	Share in total value of the IROP support under Priorities 1 and 2 %
Bytom	75.8	9.4
Żywiecki	70.4	8.7
Wodzisławski	43.8	5.4
Sosnowiec	42.7	5.3
Rybnicki	39.3	4.9
Żory	35.1	4.4
Bielsko-Biała	31.0	3.8
Cieszyński	29.8	3.7
Częstochowski	26.4	3.3
Pszczyński	24.1	3.0
Total	418.4	51.9
Total IROP support received	806.5	100.0

Source: Urząd Marszałkowski Województwa Śląskiego 2006a, 2006b, 2006c, 2006d.

The initial impact on investment

The impact of the EU subsidies can be demonstrated by setting them against revenues and investment expenditures by the Silesian authorities in the last year before Poland's accession to the EU in 2003. This can be taken as a base for comparison, although there was already some very small-scale EU financial support. The comparison is restricted to Priorities 1 and 3 and to the Cohesion Fund, because these include subsidies related to investment and also cover more than 93 per cent of the total EU support within the IROP. Support from the Cohesion Fund was also substantial and had an investment character. Figure 12.6 shows the variation in the region in the share of these IROP subsidies in the Silesian local authorities' budget revenues, with an average figure of 7.4 per cent of the total revenues from 2003. Thus the IROP made only a small contribution to local authorities' financial resources, which is in line with earlier conclusions from the analysis of the per capita values of IROP subsidies.

The highest share of IROP subsidies in relation to the budget revenues is found in northern sub-regions and towns, in districts around the Rybnik agglomeration in the western sub-region and in Żywiecki district in the southern sub-region. Detailed analysis also shows examples of local authorities for which the subsidy was equivalent to two-thirds of total 2003 revenues, sometimes even exceeding this value. Examples included Czernichów in Żywiecki district (IROP subsidies of 166.6 per cent of budget revenues from 2003 were for a sewage treatment project); Świerklany in Rybnicki district (IROP subsidies of 153.9 per cent of budget revenues from 2003 for building a sanitation system); and Ślemien in Żywiecki district (IROP subsidy of

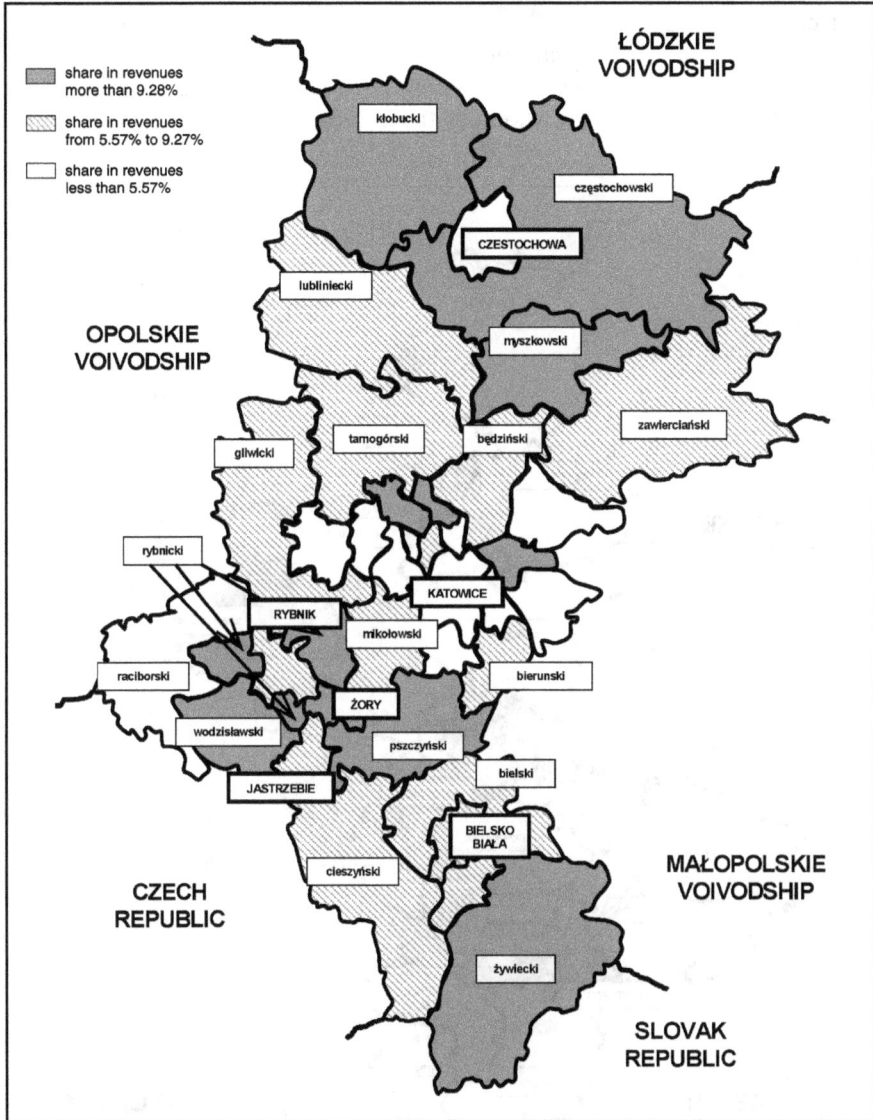

share in revenues
more than 9.28%

share in revenues
from 5.57% to 9.27%

share in revenues
less than 5.57%

ŁÓDZKIE
VOIVODSHIP

kłobucki

częstochowski

CZESTOCHOWA

lubliniecki

OPOLSKIE
VOIVODSHIP

myszkowski

zawierciański

tarnogórski

będziński

gliwicki

rybnicki

KATOWICE

RYBNIK

mikołowski

raciborski

bierunski

ŻORY

wodzisławski

pszczyński

JASTRZEBIE

bielski

BIELSKO
BIAŁA

MAŁOPOLSKIE
VOIVODSHIP

cieszyński

CZECH
REPUBLIC

żywiecki

SLOVAK
REPUBLIC

Figure 12.6 The share of IROP support in budget revenues of the Silesian local
authorities.

112.6 per cent of budget revenues from 2003 for building a sewage treatment
plant and sanitation system).

The IROP appeared to be the most attractive for smaller municipalities,
for which this kind of support was the only one available for co-financing
infrastructure investments. These authorities were in practice excluded from
Cohesion Fund support, which was aimed at big infrastructure projects

with costs of over PLN60 million and with significance for environmental protection.

A similar analysis of variations in Cohesion Fund subsidies, as in Figure 12.7, shows that they were on average equivalent to 22 per cent of the total local authority budget revenues from 2003. Thus the Cohesion Fund

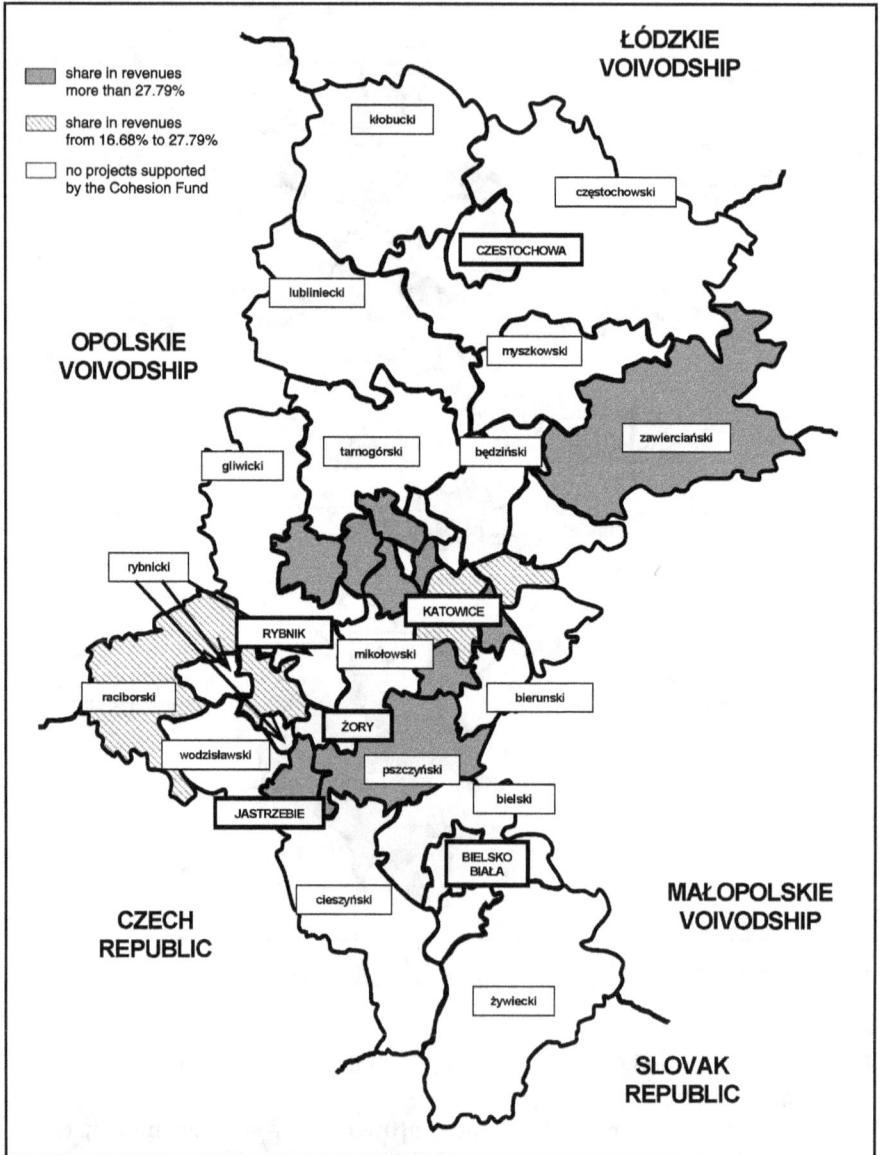

Figure 12.7 The share of Cohesion Fund support in budget revenues of the Silesian local authorities.

appeared to be a very attractive source, particularly for large cities and towns, allowing them to implement complex and costly projects in the water and sanitation systems. For a few large Silesian towns, Cohesion Fund subsidies were equivalent to approximately one year's budget revenues (Tychy: 117.8 per cent; Rybnik: 97.3 per cent).

A different perspective is to compare these IROP subsidies to investment expenditure, as shown in Figure 12.8. They covered 52 per cent of that total from 2003, suggesting a very significant impact. All apart from the cities and towns of the Katowice agglomeration, for which the Cohesion Fund was more important, showed a share of IROP subsidies to investment expenditure similar to the regional average (from 39 per cent to 65 per cent) or even higher (more then 65 per cent). Figure 12.9 shows the combined effect of the two funding sources.

A detailed analysis of the relationship between IROP subsidies and the Silesian local authorities' investment expenditures points to four groupings.

The first is made up of authorities experiencing an 'investment awakening'. Examples include Bytom, in which investment spending grew by 1,255 per cent, and Sosnowiec and Chorzów, in which it grew by 266 per cent and 264 per cent respectively. This implies a significant development of local authority activity, but could also reflect relatively poor investment activity in the past. Thus, in Bytom, investment in 2003 contributed only 1.7 per cent of all expenditure, while in Chorzów the share was 3.0 per cent.

The second group is made up from 'persistent investors'. Here an average, or even low, ratio between EU funding and investment expenditure can be a result of relatively high investment activity in the past. This is the case for Katowice, the regional capital. Investment made up 26.5 per cent of total expenditure, against an average value for Silesia in 2003 of 14.3 per cent. Thus, a high level of EU subsidy appears as only a small proportion of Katowice's investment expenditure (less then 39 per cent and among the lowest for any authority), owing to the high level of the latter.

The third group is made up of authorities experiencing 'investment decay'. The ratio between EU funding and investment expenditure is small, or even zero, as a result of a low level of investment in the past and problems with gaining the funds from the IROP or Cohesion Fund. In Silesia about 30 municipalities out of 167 (18 per cent) did not prepare any project for the IROP or the Cohesion Fund in the period 2004–06. Examples include the municipalities of Wojkowice and Siewierz (Będziński district) for which the ratios between investment expenditure and overall budget expenditures in 2003 were 1.7 per cent and 4.8 per cent. The amount of EU funds received in 2004–06 was zero.

The fourth group is made up of 'self-financing investors', with high investment relative to budget expenditures alongside an unfavourable ratio of EU funding to investment expenditure. These municipalities cover investment from their own sources, or from others not connected with the EU. An example is the Bobrowniki (Będziński district) municipality, for which

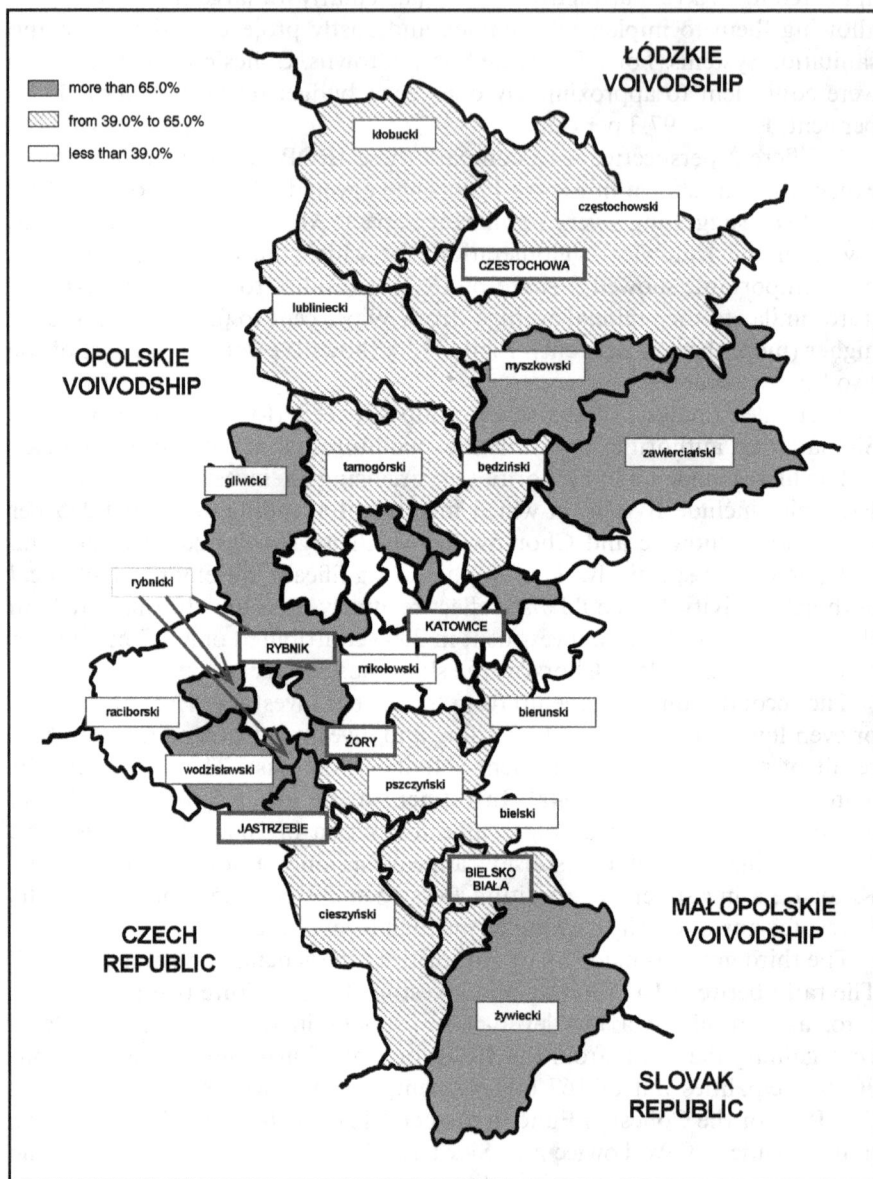

Figure 12.8 The share of IROP support in investment expenditure of the Silesian local authorities.

investment accounted for 34 per cent of expenditure in 2003, but EU support was zero.

Figure 12.9 shows the aggregated support from the IROP and the Cohesion Fund in relation to the investment expenditures. The ratio of this aggregate

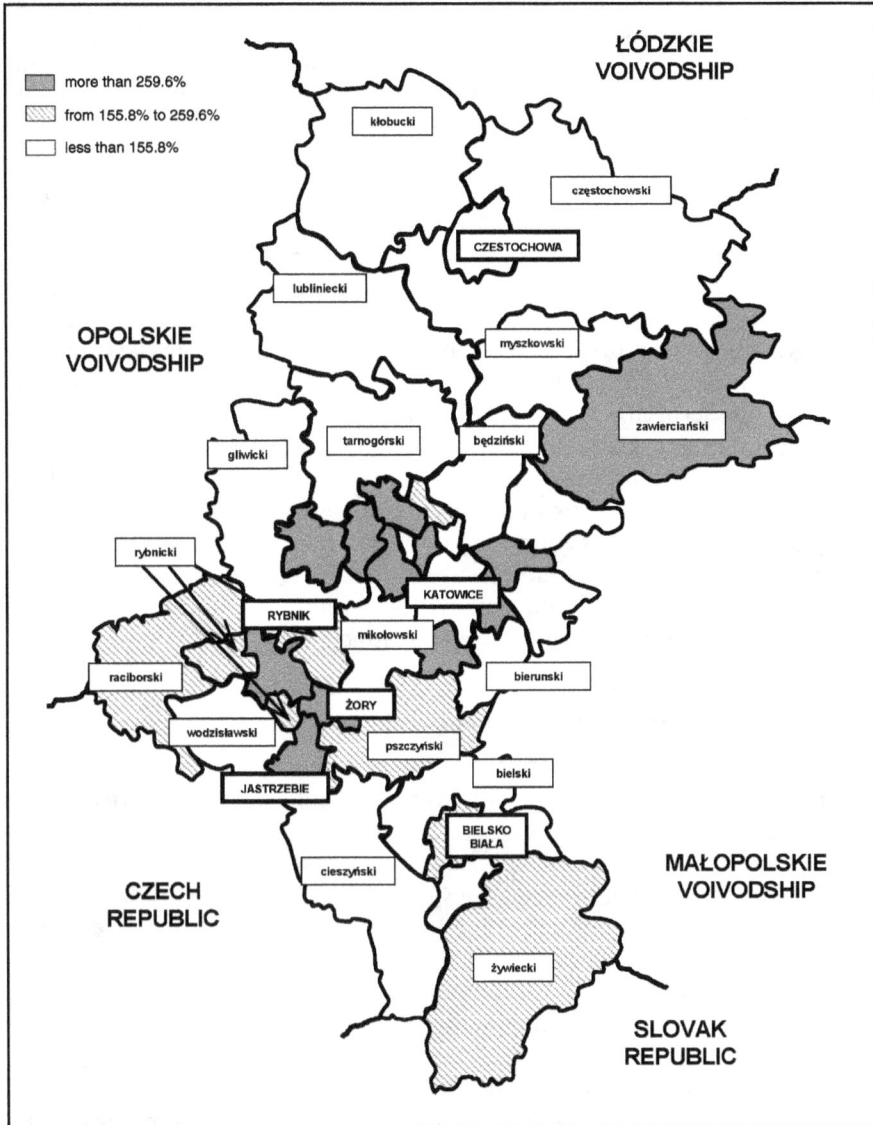

Figure 12.9 The combined share of IROP and Cohesion Fund support as a percentage of 2003 investment expenditures of the Silesian local authorities.

value to the investment expenditure by all Silesian local authorities from 2003 was 207.7 per cent, almost four times the ratio of IROP support alone to investment expenditure. This demonstrates the importance of the Cohesion Fund relative to the IROP and also shifts a large number of the Silesian districts into a group with relatively the lowest level of EU support (less than

155.8 per cent). However, even in this group, the ratio between the support from the IROP and the Cohesion Fund is between 19 per cent and 114 per cent. In only three towns of the Katowice agglomeration is the ratio lower than this (Jaworzno, Siemianowice Śląskie and Świętochłowice), while for one it is only 3 per cent (Dąbrowa Górnicza).

Ranking the Silesian local authorities by the share of IROP support and the Cohesion Fund support in relation to investment expenditure shows up three striking cases. Bytom enjoyed the highest share of EU subsidy, at 4,541 per cent in relation to investment expenditure from 2003, albeit partly reflecting relatively poor investment activity in that year. Only 1.7 per cent of the budget was spent on investment. For Chorzów the share of EU subsidy was 1,742 per cent in relation to investment expenditures, including the Cohesion Fund co-financed sanitation system project and projects supported by the IROP for modernisation of a theatre and revitalisation of post-industrial water resources. For Jastrzębie the share of EU subsidy was 1,156 per cent in relation to the value of investment expenditure. The high value is a result of the Cohesion Fund's co-financed project for environmental projects. For Tychy the EU subsidy was equivalent to 1,005 per cent of investment expenditure from 2003, owing to the largest subsidy in Silesia (more then €100 million) in the form of Cohesion Fund support for development and modernisation of the sanitation system and for sewage treatment plants.

Estimating the impact of EU support

A full assessment of the impact of EU funds in the Silesian region is beyond the scope of this chapter. Data for quantitative indicators of the road, water and sanitation systems would require a detailed survey of the technical documentation of all projects financed from EU sources. Data from official statistics on, for example, the efficiency of the water system, or even growth in per capita GDP, are published with a two-year delay. However, some indication of the significance of EU funds can be derived from an initial quantitative assessment using the unit prices of goods and services delivered by the EU-financed projects. In the case of the IROP these estimations require some assumptions.

Thus, we can assume the construction costs of 1 kilometre of newly built road, with an axle load capacity of 115 kN and a width of 8 metres, to be about PLN4 million. The IROP subsidies assigned to road infrastructure projects (PLN370.0 million), plus the PLN92.5 million co-financing from the Silesian authorities, point to construction of about 115.6 kilometres of new roads, equivalent to 0.8 per cent of the overall network. Alternatively, assuming the approximate costs of modernisation of an existing kilometre of road to be PLN2 million, the EU funds from the IROP will allow for repair of 1.6 per cent of the Silesian road network.

Assuming that construction alone for 1 kilometre of a newly built sanitation system costs about PLN1.1 million, then, taking into consideration the

IROP subsidies assigned to the water and sanitation infrastructure projects (PLN 191.5 million) plus the PLN47.9 million of the authorities' co-financing, that will allow for the construction of 217 kilometres of that kind of network. Taking into account additional EU support in the form of the Cohesion Fund, to the level of PLN1.9 billion plus PLN497.5 million of co-financing from local authorities, 2,200 kilometres of sanitation system could be constructed, equivalent to 32.8 per cent of the existing system.

Similar reasoning points to the scope to construct 73.1 kilometres of cycle routes or five new swimming pools, depending on how sport and recreation funds were allocated. The funding for education could secure modernisation of 1.3 per cent of primary schools or 2.3 per cent of secondary schools.

Conclusion

The first years of Poland's EU membership enabled Silesian local authorities to speed up socio-economic development by utilising EU funds. However, the extent of this acceleration depended on their own activity in preparing projects and applying for EU subsidies. The evidence here shows that there was a positive relationship between the number of projects applied for and the level of subsidies received. Moreover, activity, in terms of the number of project proposals, was not closely related to the size of the municipality. Often small and medium-sized municipalities prepared more proposals than, for example, the big cities of the Katowice agglomeration. However, the total value of proposals was 2.5 times the EU subsidies available within the IROP.

The greatest number of proposals and the highest EU subsidies were linked with basic infrastructure projects (transportation, water and sanitation). Thus, despite the relatively high level of the Silesian infrastructure, the region still tried to make up for its low level of development in the European context. The IROP, as a regional planning document formulated by the central government, appeared able to cope with the specificity of the Polish regions, with their differing economic conditions. However, there were disproportions between the amounts of EU support assigned to the IROP measures and the value of projects applied for by the local authorities in Silesia. In the cases of infrastructure for education and health care and the development of tourism and culture, the municipalities' expectations were significantly higher than planned for in the IROP. For some other measures, such as 'Regional innovation strategies', interest was low.

The IROP did not create scope for complex projects jointly financed and organised by a number of authorities. As a result, a road could be modernised to a high quality in one municipality but not in its neighbour. The lack of coordination in EU subsidies could mean that driving a car through this kind of network could resemble moving on a chessboard. Moreover, despite the appraisal and selection procedures used by the Silesian Marshal's Office (including formal, content-related, multi-criteria assessment and project ranking), the final decision on allocation had a political character, which to some extent negated the assumed rationality of the decision-making process.

Nevertheless, the planning process was transparent. All IROP project documentation was accessible, as were detailed guidelines for project preparation. Formalisation of the application process led to a change in the processes of local and regional development planning. Up to 2004 hardly any municipality had prepared detailed project documentation with financial and socio-economic studies. This changed with EU accession, when such studies were a requirement in funding applications. Thus the first period of Poland's EU membership prompted a rapid learning process.

Competition for project funding increased the entrepreneurial spirit among local authorities, but it also led to a waste of public funds spent on technical and economic documentation for projects that failed to gain EU support. Moreover, thirty-one municipalities opted out of the IROP contests and prepared no project proposals. This implies a further deepening of inequalities within the region.

In all, EU support contributed only a small addition to local authority revenues, about 7 per cent, but there was a more significant contribution to investment, equivalent to about 50 per cent of investment expenditures from 2003. That had a small impact on the overall level of the regional infrastructure, but it varied between authorities. IROP funds were most important to small and medium-sized municipalities, for which the subsidy from the IROP could be comparable to one year's budget revenues.

The IROP was generally not popular among the large cities and towns of Silesia. For them the Cohesion Fund was more relevant, as it supported the bigger projects that were the most relevant to solving their complex development problems. For the region as a whole, the Cohesion Fund, in financial and quantitative terms, had twice the impact of the IROP.

References

GUS (Główny Urząd Statystyczny) (2004) *Gross Domestic Product by voivodships and subregions in 2002*, Katowice: Central Statistical Office and Statistical Office in Katowice.

GUS (Główny Urząd Statystyczny) (2005) *Gross Domestic Products: regional accounts*, Katowice: Central Statistical Office and Statistical Office in Katowice.

Instytut Badań nad Gospodarką Rynkową (2005) *Atrakcyjność inwestycyjna województw Polski 2005*, Gdańsk: Instytut Badań nad Gospodarką Rynkową.

Ministerstwo Gospodarki i Pracy (2004a) *Narodowy Plan Rozwoju 2004–2006*, Warsaw: Ministerstwo Gospodarki i Pracy.

Ministerstwo Gospodarki i Pracy (2004b) *Sektorowy Program Operacyjny – Rozwój Zasobów Ludzkich 2004–2006*, Warsaw: Ministerstwo Gospodarki i Pracy.

Ministerstwo Gospodarki i Pracy (2004c) *Sektorowy Program Operacyjny – Wzrost Konkurencyjności Przedsiębiorstw, lata 2004–2006*, Warsaw: Ministerstwo Gospodarki i Pracy.

Ministerstwo Gospodarki i Pracy (2004d) *Zintegrowany Program Operacyjny Rozwoju Regionalnego 2004–2006*, Warsaw: Ministerstwo Gospodarki i Pracy.

Ministerstwo Infrastruktury (2004) *Sektorowy Program Operacyjny Transport na lata 2004–2006*, Warsaw: Ministerstwo Infrastruktury.

Ministerstwo Rolnictwa i Rozwoju Wsi (2004a) *Sektorowy Program Operacyjny – Restrukturyzacja i Modernizacja Sektora Żywnościowego oraz Rozwój Obszarów Wiejskich 2004–2006*, Warsaw: Ministerstwo Rolnictwa i Rozwoju Wsi.

Ministerstwo Rolnictwa i Rozwoju Wsi (2004b) *Sektorowy Program Operacyjny – Rybołówstwo i Przetwórstwo Ryb*, Warsaw: Ministerstwo Rolnictwa i Rozwoju Wsi.

National Fund for Environmental Protection and Water Management (2006) *List of cohesion fund granted projects approved by the Commission*, www.nfosigw.gov.pl (accessed 6 May 2007).

Urząd Marszałkowski Województwa Śląskiego (2006a) *Aktywność samorządów województwa śląskiego w pozyskiwaniu środków z Europejskiego Funduszu Rozwoju Regionalnego w ramach Zintegrowanego Programu Operacyjnego Rozwoju Regionalnego 2004–2006*, Katowice: Urząd Marszałkowski Województwa Śląskiego.

Urząd Marszałkowski Województwa Śląskiego (2006b) *Mapa dofinansowanych projektów*, http://zporr.silesia-region.pl/mapa/ (accessed 6 May 2007).

Urząd Marszałkowski Województwa Śląskiego (2006c) *Podsumowanie konkursów ZPORR – projekty zgłaszane do dofinansowania ze środków Europejskiego Funduszu Społecznego (Priorytet II ZPORR działanie 2.2 oraz 2.6)*, Katowice: Urząd Marszałkowski Województwa Śląskiego.

Urząd Marszałkowski Województwa Śląskiego (2006d) *Podsumowanie konkursów ZPORR – projekty zgłaszane przez samorządy do dofinansowania ze środków Europejskiego Funduszu Rozwoju Regionalnego (Priorytet I i III z wyłączeniem działań 1.6 oraz 3.4.)*, Katowice: Urząd Marszałkowski Województwa Śląskiego.

13 The role of place marketing in multifunctional rural development

Robert Romanowski

The aim of this chapter is to use the example of Konin region in Poland, the former Konin voivodship, to investigate the use of marketing tools in multifunctional rural development (MRD). The method used is to seek the subjective evaluations of current and potential actors in the process of local development to compare their perceptions of the importance of likely pre-conditions for that development with their perceptions of the level achieved for those preconditions. The investigation uses an adaptation of standard marketing concepts to develop a set of tools appropriate to an investigation of place marketing in rural Poland. These were used as the basis for questionnaire research which pointed to possible policy priorities in different kinds of communes (*gmina*), the smallest self-governing unit in Polish local administration.

MRD is seen as a form of structural state intervention which contributes to the creation of a functioning market mechanism. Generally, MRD means moving beyond 'monofunctionality' (Kłodziński 1997: 41), based on the agricultural production of raw materials. 'Monofunctional' areas, dependent on one main activity, are exposed to crises. Diversification of agricultural production is the simplest form of movement towards multifunctionality, described as an agricultural multifunctionality (Ciechomski 1997: 68). The term MRD can also be used to refer to modification of the rural employment structure, covering more than just agriculture and relating to the whole rural population (Kłodziński 1997: 41; Zarębski 2002: 6). This meaning will be used in the present chapter. Within that, MRD is interpreted as a way of modernising a rural economy by endogenous development, based on the use of resources within the local economy.

Local authorities, also known as self-government in the Polish context, can play a role in stimulating the entrepreneurship of local actors. They are responsible for developing the technical infrastructure and systems of environmental protection and for creating a modern labour force able to adapt to the challenges of the modern, knowledge-based economy. Bringing actors together within a local society is a necessary part of the MRD process, and all levels of government can play a role although, of course, the market mechanisms should not be replaced by an excessive degree of intervention.

Developing from marketing theory

Marketing theory deals with integration and relations between actors, but standard theories require adaptation to apply to place marketing. Marketing a location can be understood as designing a place to satisfy the different needs of inhabitants, entrepreneurs, visitors and investors (Kotler *et al.* 1999: 125). The main actors in place marketing are the self-government (commune) representatives, while other local, regional and national actors also play significant roles.

The core idea of marketing, as developed in the 1960s (McCarthy 1970), is the simultaneous use of four marketing tools – product, price, place (distribution) and promotion, known as the 4Ps – to further an organisation's goals. Over the following forty years, the idea of the marketing mix was modified. The 4Cs framework is an adaptation of the 4Ps starting from the client's point of view: 'price' becomes 'cost', 'promotion' becomes 'communication', 'place' becomes 'convenience' and 'product' becomes 'customer's value'. The 7Ps incorporate the 4Ps plus people, process and provision of service. Each of these marketing-mix ideas can be used to help towards building up an appropriate framework for analysing place marketing, as in Table 13.1.

The appropriate tools for analysing place marketing can be derived from Table 13.1. The 4Ps framework is inadequate because it is mainly developed to relate to the sale of physical goods. Locations offer much more than this. Thus it is immediately appropriate to concentrate on the cost rather than the price mix. The 4Cs framework switches the focus on to the customer's (purchaser's) point of view. It is more natural for place marketers to count all the costs of operating within a territorial unit rather than to settle a price for being a member of it. Moreover, within the 4Cs conception, communication as a bilateral way of informing about the offer becomes more prominent than uni-direction promotion. This points to a further area of inadequacy of the 4Ps framework, as the information feedback loop seems to be an essential part of the process of multifunctional development.

It is difficult to find a place for distribution, appearing within the third of the 4Ps, in place marketing. It is impossible to carry or store a territorial unit.

Table 13.1 Modification of the marketing-mix idea

4Ps and 7Ps	4Cs		Place-marketing mix
Price	→	Cost	→ Cost
Promotion	→	Communication	→ Communication
Place (distribution)	→	Convenience	→ Localisation
Product	→	Customer's value	→ Megaproduct
Provision of service			→ Partnership
Processes			included in participants
People			→ Participants

Sources: Developed from Payne (1997: 44); Mruk *et al.* (1999).

In tourism, for example, distribution processes are used to deliver visitors towards attractive places. However, transporting citizens or local enterprises to communes where they live or earn money takes us beyond the meaning of distribution as usually interpreted in the marketing literature. The term 'localisation' is used to unite the 'place' and 'convenience' terms from the 4Cs framework. Its meaning in practical terms is explained further below.

'Product' in marketing terminology means anything that can be offered to a market for attention, acquisition or consumption, including physical objects, services, personalities, organisations and desires (Cannon 1989: 225). In this case almost everything can be a territorial product, including the investment climate, the system of communication, procedures and even participants and other features. Under different approaches a territorial unit can be treated as one product or as the sum of subproducts, such as the investment product, the tourism product, the educational product, the real-estate product, the social product, the public product and others (Szromnik 1997: 41). For simplicity, the product in place marketing has been treated as infrastructure, meaning technical, social and business support (cf. Gaczek 2005). The complexity of tangible and intangible offerings justifies the use of the term 'megaproduct' for place marketing, as shown in the third column of Table 13.1, incorporating 'product', 'customer value' and more.

The 7P framework has incorporated three further tools that do not correspond to those from the 4Ps model. These are people, processes and provision of service. Provision of service, as a service-marketing tool, has become 'partnership' in place marketing, and it means creating permanent relations among different actors, increasing the value of every subject.

People, when understood as personnel, are required to accomplish marketing tasks and goals. In a service firm, 'personnel' is easy to define, but in a territorial unit almost everyone can carry out marketing tasks. Inhabitants are classified as place buyers (Kotler *et al.* 1999: 75–89), but for tourists they can be guides, informing about interesting people, buildings and other attractions. Even foreign tourists fascinated with an unknown landscape or the hospitality of Polish citizens can promote Poland to their neighbours, friends and relatives, taking on what could be classified as the main task of a sales department. It is therefore meaningless to divide buyer and personnel in place marketing. The assumption here is that 'personnel' can be extended to a broader category of 'participants'. The RAPP framework (Rogoziński 2000: 139), incorporating relations, arena of presentation, product and participants (including personnel and buyers as active subjects in the service-production process), developed for service marketing embodies the assumption that buyers and personnel should be treated as two sides of the product-making process. 'Personnel' then appear as an organisation's human resources, but that concentration on inner factors leads to too narrow a meaning for present purposes. 'Participants' therefore appears as the appropriate variable.

Thus, from the preceding discussion of different marketing frameworks, six groups of tools appear appropriate for an empirical study of place marketing.

These are the megaproduct, participants, partnership, localisation, costs and communication, as shown in Figure 13.1, with 'participants' as the central variable to which others can be assumed to relate.

The framework for research

This provided the framework for an empirical study in which each group of tools was ranked according to the type of respondent and then set against the level of multifunctional development of a commune. The method involved ranking both by the perceived importance of the factor to local development and by the perceived level of provision, allowing for measurement of any gap between the two.

The megaproduct was represented as a group of technical infrastructure elements (motorways, gas and electricity facilities, sewage system and others), ten features of business support organisations and four elements of social infrastructure. Partnership was reduced to relations of residents and inhabitants to the process of decision making in a territorial unit. The role of 'participants' in MRD was measured by estimating the quality of self-government activities (seven features were used, namely honesty, courteousness, willingness to help, competence, efficiency of administrating affairs,

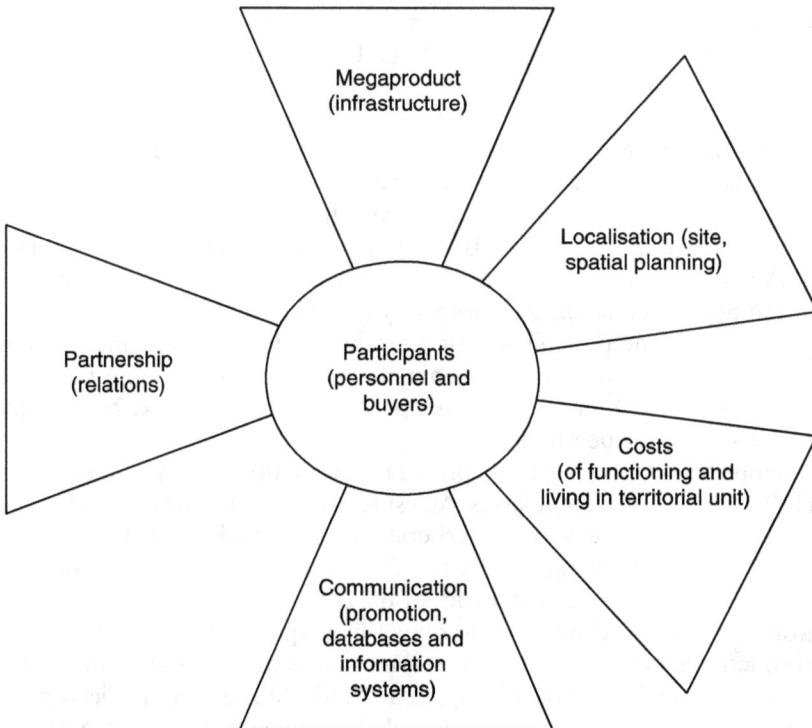

Figure 13.1 The place-marketing mix.

capacity to communicate with enterprises from within the locality and capacity to communicate with enterprises from outside the locality), the entrepreneurial mentality of inhabitants and the qualification level of the labour force, including managers.

Localisation was interpreted as meaning the allocation of functions to the area (Budner 2004: 22). The commune could have considerable influence over this through spatial planning. The location variable could therefore be planned, changed and controlled. This is therefore an important element in the marketing decisions that influence MRD, and their effects can be investigated by seeking opinions from external and internal customers of the local product.

The investigation of costs and promotion was reduced to one direct question in each case. Partnership was reduced to one measure showing the involvement of inhabitants, enterprises and farmers in decision-making processes. This meaning corresponds to the seventeenth obligatory commune task, as set out in the relevant law from 1989, 'to support and bring into general use the idea of self government' (*Ustawa* 1989; Szulce and Florek 2005: 130–1). Partnership should, it is often argued, be important for the integration of local communities and hence for local development and for cooperation in problem solving and in settling common future goals.

The overall role of place-marketing tools in the MRD was measured in the communes of Konin region. This part of the present Wielkopolska voivodship, following reorganisation in 1998, had a rural population of 325,317 in 2003. It has been classified as a peripheral area with no specific territorial strengths (Wysocki and Łuczak 2002: 503). It has been dominated by backward agriculture, but some mining and energy industry, based on brown coal, also significantly influences the employment structure. Despite the difficulties in undertaking non-agricultural activity in the region, there has been some internal differentiation. In this it is similar to other areas with a predominance of backward agriculture and industry, but there are also some opportunities from the adjacency of the A2 motorway (running Berlin–Poznań–Warsaw–Moscow) and some possibilities for alternative energy development, mainly geothermal and from biomass. Konin region is therefore interesting as an area in which MRD has yet to develop on a substantial scale, but in which there are some clear possibilities.

Previous researchers have interpreted multifunctionality as a category that can be graded into different levels. An established taxonomic typology is used here, derived from very broad criteria, as described by Zarębski (2002: 263–92). These include mainly measurable features of rural areas, such that the types describe the characteristics of the communes. Each rural commune of Konin region was classified into one of five types according to the level of multifunctional development. The region consists of forty-four communes of the old Konin region, thirty-nine lying in Konin sub-region of Wielkopolska voivodship, two in other sub-regions of the voivodship and three in Łódź voivodship. Although these have been separated from the administrative point of view since the end of 1997, the old region is still relevant, because relationships amongst enterprises, farmers and local authorities are long-lasting, and important links have persisted.

The classification became the basis for opinion poll research covering pro-portionally selected populations of 621 inhabitants, 301 farmers and 150 entrepreneurs of the region. Respondents were asked to estimate their satis-faction with thirty-three marketing indicators, or tools, that represented the six themes covered above. The level of multifunctional development was measured by the state of non-agricultural activity and the quality of the workforce in a rural area. The diagnostic indicators, following Łojewski and Iwicki (1999: 19), were:

1   the number of employed persons as a percentage of the working-age population, excluding private farmers;
2   the percentage unemployment level;
3   the number of beds for overnight stays per 1,000 inhabitants;
4   the balance of population migration per 1,000 inhabitants over the years 1990–98;
5   the number of persons with secondary and tertiary education;
6   the number of economic units recorded in the REGON register per 100 inhabitants.

The level of multifunctionality was measured by using a grade-points method incorporating all diagnostic variables. Each of these variables was given a score from 0 to 3 points, depending on its deviation from the regional average. Maximum points were given to communes with the highest values of vari-ables, and minimum points to ones with the lowest values. Each commune in Konin region was ranked by its total score. The higher the total of points, the higher the level of MRD that it indicated. Theoretically, each commune could score anywhere between 0 and 18 points. On this basis, communes were divided into five levels of multifunctional development:

• a very high level of multifunctionality, with a minimum of 9 points;
• a high level, with 7–8 points;
• a medium level, with 4–6 points;
• a low level, with 2–3 points;
• a very low level, with 0–1 point.

The role of place marketing in MRD was measured from the subjective evaluation of the internal customers in the different types of communes. Statistical data describing the social and economic situation could have been used, but the results of self-government activity appear in official statistics only after a delay of several years. Moreover, the subjective evaluations of place-marketing tools themselves reflect the subjective reasons for starting business activity, which is an essential element of MRD. Thus, subjective evaluations were used to assess satisfaction with each factor, or place-marketing tool, on a five-point scale (very good, good, medium, poor, very poor). The same scale was then used to measure assessments of the importance of that tool for changing the structure of employment and hence developing the commune.

Four requirements should be fulfilled by an accurate measure of satisfaction levels (Kozielski 2004: 49–50). First, factors should be important for buyers. Second, the measure of satisfaction should be comparable over time and place and between different divisions of an organisation or strategic business unit. Third, measurement should allow for analysis in terms of market segments, meaning types of clients. Fourth, the measure should be compatible with accepted forms of communication with clients. The measures used here met those requirements.

Using a uniform degree scale of satisfaction and perceived importance made it possible to compare the opinions of inhabitants, entrepreneurs and farmers on different place-marketing tools. The comparison of degrees of importance made it possible to establish a first hierarchy of the importance of the different tools, the direct importance hierarchy (DIH). The uniform scale, across three types of questionnaire and two data series, made it possible to determine a 'quality gap' (Di Piazza and Eccles 2002, quoted from Kozielski 2004: 25), meaning a deviation between values in the two different series. The larger the gap, it is argued, the stronger the case for the self-government body to treat this as a priority area. Some authors refer to a 'market gap' (McDonald and Dunbar 2003: 188) or 'marketing gap'. The idea is used here to show the difference between a level of need (how important respondents consider the factor to be) and a level of satisfaction (how satisfied respondents are with the existing level of provision).

Cross-tables were used to estimate the quality gap, or marketing gap. The two series of data were compared showing place-marketing tool satisfaction and the subjective assessment of the importance of those tools for local development. The two were compared by subtracting the grades, leading to a subtraction hierarchy (SH). This provides the second method of establishing the hierarchy of place-marketing tools' importance. This showed that importance was, in almost all cases, judged to be higher than satisfaction.

The third method of establishing the hierarchy of place-marketing tools' importance was to weight the subjective importance grades by the subjective satisfaction grades, providing the weighted importance hierarchy (WIH). Values of the weighted importance indicator vary from 0.25 to 5 for a five-point scale of grades. The expected value would be unity, which would mean that satisfaction of the need is equal to its perceived importance. Values below unity indicate a better state of the place-marketing tool than is judged to be necessary, in terms of perceptions, in the MRD. The higher the weighted importance indicator, the greater the role of self-government and other place marketers could become in bringing about changes to improve the level of the indicator to bring it into line with views on its importance.

Satisfaction grades for place-marketing tools should indicate which activities dominate in the best multifunctionally developed communes. This could guide the establishment of a hierarchy of the priority that should be accorded to the various place-marketing tools. The highest levels of the tool in the hierarchy mean that that form of marketing activity should be attended to first to increase the level of multifunctional development.

The hierarchy established on the basis of the analysis of the indicators of satisfaction of internal actors was set against the levels of multifunctional development of communes. The sets were compared in every type of commune, which helped modify the primary place-marketing mix from Figure 13.1.

Research results

The grouping of communes showing the different MRD levels was set against the activity of three groups of internal place buyers: inhabitants, entrepreneurs and farmers. Each group was treated as a different sample. Using the principles of stratified sampling, 150 entrepreneurs, 300 farmers and 600 inhabitants who were neither entrepreneurs nor farmers should have been used to represent the opinion of the general rural population of the Konin region. This research was conducted between January and April 2005. Returns deviated slightly from these target figures. There were 150 returns from 165 questionnaires carried out among entrepreneurs, 301 out of 330 carried out among farmers, and 621 out of 660 carried out among the rest of the population. Of these a small number were rejected, including 28 from the 44 village mayors of the Konin region, which represented too small a sample within that special category to provide useful information. In the end, returns from 1,072 internal place buyers were used. The conclusions from this field research were related to the level of multifunctional development of the Konin region communes, using Zarębski's (2002) typology. This approach was necessary to define the role of place marketing in MRD.

The hierarchies of the importance of the place-marketing tools, in the opinions of inhabitants, entrepreneurs and farmers for each type of commune, are presented in Tables 13.2, 13.3 and 13.4 respectively. The subtraction indicator and the weighted importance indicator hierarchies show the relationship between satisfaction and direct importance grades in different ways, but it turned out that the differences were minimal: in other words, both hierarchies were almost identical. However, the analysis of both hierarchies together points to partnership as the most important marketing tool, regardless of the type of commune or the type of place buyer.

The truth is that inhabitants did not treat partnership as a prime sphere of activity for multifunctional growth: it occupies a low position in the DIH, as shown in Table 13.2, indicating that they gave it very low values of subjective direct importance. However, they also pointed to very low levels of effort from self-government to involve internal customers in the local planning

Table 13.2 The hierarchy of marketing tools' importance measured by three methods in the opinions of inhabitants in communes of different levels of multifunctional development, 2005

Place-marketing tool	Level of commune multifunctionality														
	Very low			Low			Medium			High			Very high		
	DIH	SH	WIH	DIH	SH	WIH	DIH	SH	WIH	DIH	SH	WIH	DIH	SH	WIH
Product	2	3	3	4	3	3	4	2	2	3	3	3	2	4	5
Localisation	2	6	6	1	6	6	1	6	6	2	5	5	1	6	6
Participants	1	2	2	2	5	5	2	4	4	1	4	4	2	3	3
Costs	5	4	5	5	4	4	3	5	5	6	6	6	6	5	4
Promotion	4	5	5	2	2	2	5	3	3	5	2	2	4	2	2
Partnership	6	1	1	4	1	1	6	1	1	4	1	1	5	1	1

Note: DIH, SH and WIH are explained in the text. Numbers show the position in the hierarchy such that 1 indicates first place and the highest value for the indicator.

Table 13.3 The hierarchy of marketing tools' importance measured by three methods in the opinions of entrepreneurs in communes of different levels of multifunctional development, 2005

Place-marketing tool	Level of commune multifunctionality														
	Very low			Low			Medium			High			Very high		
	DIH	SH	WIH	DIH	SH	WIH	DIH	SH	WIH	DIH	SH	WIH	DIH	SH	WIH
Product	4	2	2	6	4	3	5	5	4	4	5	5	6	6	6
Localisation	2	5	5	1	3	4	2	4	5	3	6	6	3	4	4
Participants	1	4	4	3	6	6	1	3	3	6	4	4	5	5	5
Costs	5	6	6	5	5	5	6	6	6	1	2	2	1	2	2
Promotion	3	3	3	4	2	2	3	2	2	5	3	3	4	3	3
Partnership	6	1	1	2	1	1	4	1	1	2	1	1	2	1	1

Note: DIH, SH and WIH are explained in the text. Numbers show the position in the hierarchy such that 1 indicates first place and the highest value for the indicator.

Table 13.4 The hierarchy of marketing tools' importance measured by three methods in the opinions of farmers in communes of different levels of multifunctional development, 2005

Place-marketing tool	Level of commune multifunctionality														
	Very low			Low			Medium			High			Very high		
	DIH	SH	WIH	DIH	SH	WIH	DIH	SH	WIH	DIH	SH	WIH	DIH	SH	WIH
Product	6	4	4	3	3	2	6	3	2	5	5	5	5	2	2
Localisation	4	3	3	2	6	6	2	5	5	4	6	6	3	6	6
Participants	2	5	5	5	4	5	4	4	4	1	3	4	2	4	4
Costs	3	6	6	6	5	4	5	6	6	6	4	3	6	3	3
Promotion	1	2	2	4	2	3	3	2	3	3	2	2	4	5	5
Partnership	5	1	1	1	1	1	1	1	1	2	1	1	1	1	1

Note: DIH, SH and WIH are explained in the text. Numbers show the position in the hierarchy such that 1 indicates first place and the highest value for the indicator.

process. It therefore occupied first place in the SH and WIH across all groups of respondents and all levels of multifunctional development (MFD). Localisation lies at the opposite pole, both perceived as important and scoring well on implementation, with the weighted importance value close to unity and a position close to, or at the bottom of, the SH and WIH for the three respondent groups and all levels of MFD. It also appears, from detailed responses, that further activities of local authorities should concentrate more on spatial planning than on improving the commune site in the transportation network.

Divergences of other place-marketing tools grades given by different place buyers of different commune types are so wide that it is difficult to judge unambiguously which activity, apart from partnership, should be given priority. These divergences mean that the commune authority cannot settle on

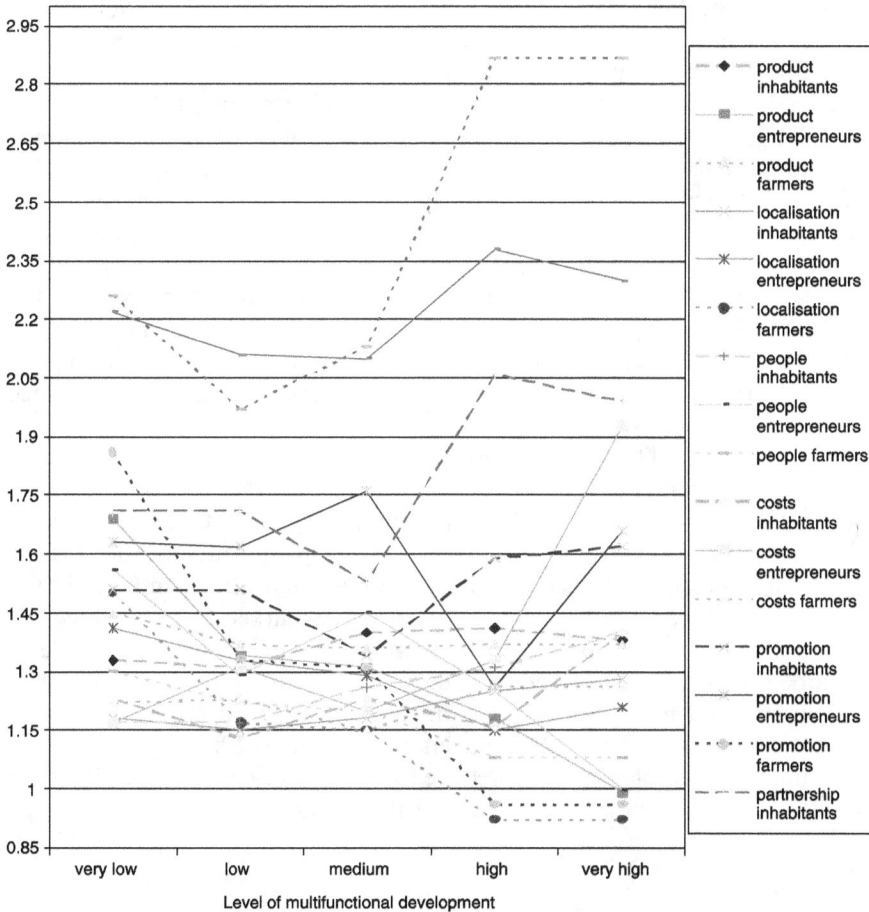

Figure 13.2 Quality gap of place-marketing tools estimated by using the weighted importance indicator for communes with different multifunctional development levels.

a place-marketing mix that fits with the perceptions of both inhabitants and economic actors. It needs to choose one or the other, depending on which target group's opinion it considers most relevant to prospects for growth. Within this, the hierarchies of place-marketing tools for entrepreneurs and farmers were almost the same.

The weighted importance indicator for partnership, as viewed by entrepreneurs and as shown in Table 13.3, is clearly of greater importance in communes with higher levels of MFD. However, for this group, the same indicator shows a downward trend for localisation. Thus, for entrepreneurs in communes with a very high level of multifunctional development, localisation is of less importance. Satisfaction with the product and participants categories is high in communes with high levels of multifunctional development (weighted importance indicators close to unity) and much lower in communes with low levels of multifunctional development. It would therefore appear important for underdeveloped areas to increase the quality of their technical infrastructure and human resources.

However, more advanced activities which enable participation in a local planning process appear more essential for place buyers in highly developed communes. This means that partnership activities can satisfy the hidden needs of internal place buyers in all types of rural areas. Establishing the place in the hierarchy for other place-marketing tools is much more difficult.

The analysis of the importance of different tools points to the hypothesis that partnership is the most important place-marketing tool, setting the conditions for the application of other tools. Their importance in turn varies, depending on the type of the commune. There is a positive relationship between a rising level of multifunctionality and rising weighted importance scores for such marketing factors as partnership, promotion and human resources, measured for farmers and inhabitants. The importance of product, meaning the commune's infrastructure, decreases as the level of multifunctionality rises. In other words, infrastructure is very important in communes of low multifunctionality. These observations lead to a modification of the place-marketing mix to indicate priority policy areas, as shown in Figure 13.3.

Analysing the importance grades of all place-marketing tools allows us to say that, the less developed the commune is, the greater the desirable level of marketing support. Marketing is most important particularly for entrepreneurs and farmers, with a wider range of grades than in the case of the other inhabitants. Internal place buyers in communes with higher levels of multifunctional development appreciate the social infrastructure, while those of underdeveloped ones place more priority on human resources.

Conclusion

The main finding appears to be the need to create partnership relations among local authorities and other local actors. The highest partnership level is required in the best-developed communes. Respondents' opinions suggest

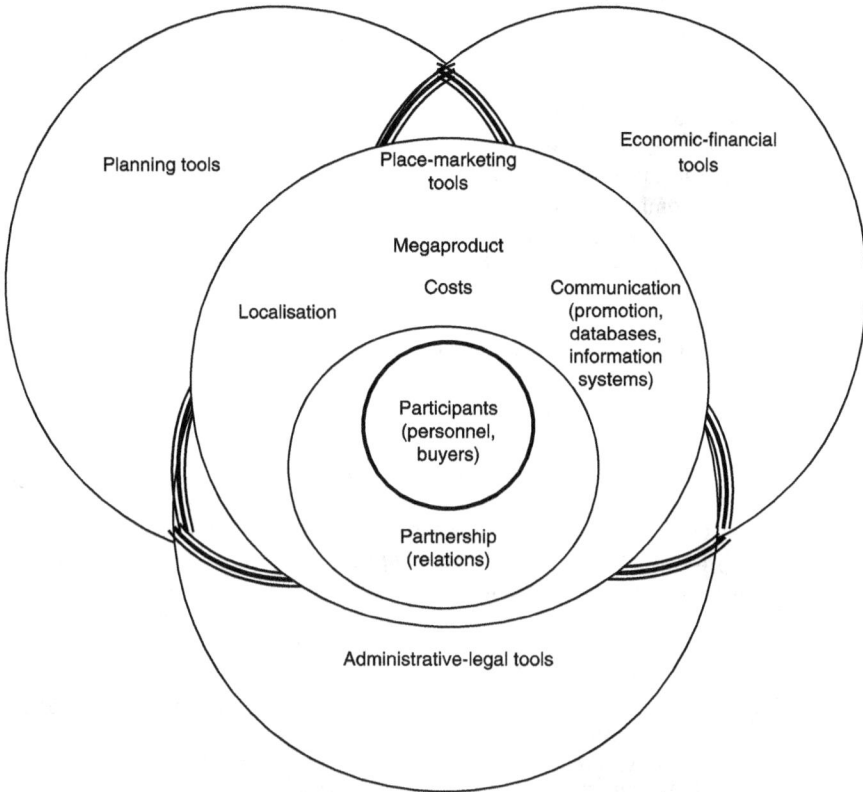

Figure 13.3 Modified place-marketing mix as a basic idea of local development activities.

Source: Conclusions from empirical research plus Frankowski (2000: 22).

that the authorities in the least-developed communes should focus on improving the technical infrastructure, the basic element of the megaproduct. This satisfaction of residents' basic needs is placed ahead of factors that gain in importance as the level of multifunctional development rises, such as participation in the local decision-making process. That is especially clear in the views of entrepreneurs. Professional place marketing from local authorities, together with competence in gaining Structural Funds from the EU, could thus be seen as central factors in local development.

References

Budner, W. (2004) *Lokalizacja przedsiębiorstw: aspekty ekonomiczno-przestrzenne i środowiskowe*, Poznań: Wydawnictwo Akademii Ekonomicznej w Poznaniu.

Cannon, T. (1989) *Basic marketing: principles and practice*, London: Cassell Education.

Ciechomski, W. (1997) *Interwencjonizm państwowy w rolnictwie i obrocie rolnym*, Poznań: Wydawnictwo Akademii Ekonomicznej.

Di Piazza, Jr, S. A. and Eccles, R. G. (2002) *Building public trust: the future of corporate reporting*, New York: Wiley.

Frankowski, Z. (ed.) (2000) *Działalność marketingowa gmin: zarys ujęć marketingu terytorialnego*, Ciechanów: WSH.

Gaczek, W. (ed.) (2005) *Innowacje w rozwoju regionu*, Poznań: Wydawnictwo Akademii Ekonomicznej w Poznaniu.

Kłodziński, M. (1997) 'Istota wielofunkcyjnego rozwoju terenów wiejskich', in M. Kłodziński and A. Rosner (eds), *Ekonomiczne i społeczne uwarunkowania i możliwości wielofunkcyjnego rozwoju wsi w Polsce*, Warszawa: Wydawnictwo SGGW.

Kotler, P., Asplund, C., Rein, I. and Haider, D. (1999) *Marketing places Europe: how to attract investments, industries, residents and visitors to cities, communities, regions and nations in Europe*, Harlow: Pearson Education.

Kozielski, R. (2004) *Wskaźniki marketingowe*, Kraków: E-Oficyna Ekonomiczna.

Łojewski, S. and Iwicki, S. (1999) *Kierunki wielofunkcyjnego rozwoju obszarów wiejskich na przykładzie regionu kujawsko pomorskiego*, Bydgoszcz: ATR.

McCarthy, E. J. (1970) *Basic marketing: managerial approach*, Homewood, IL: Irwin.

McDonald, M. and Dunbar, I. (2003) *Segmentacja rynku: przebieg procesu i wykorzystanie wyników*, Kraków: E-Oficyna Wydawnicza.

Mruk, H., Pilarczyk, B., Sojkin, B. and Szulce, H. (1999) *Podstawy marketingu*, Poznań: Wydawnictwo Akademii Ekonomicznej w Poznaniu.

Payne, A. (1997) *Marketing usług*, Warszawa: PWE.

Rogoziński, K. (2000), *Nowy marketing usług*, Poznań: Wydawnictwo Akademii Ekonomicznej w Poznaniu.

Szromnik, A. (1997) 'Marketing terytorialny – geneza, rynki docelowe i pomiotu oddziaływania', in T. Domański (ed.), *Marketing terytorialny – strategiczne wyzwania dla miast i regionów*, Łódź: Uniwersytet Łódzki.

Szulce, H. and Florek, M. (eds) (2005) *Marketing terytorialny: możliwości aplikacji, kierunki rozwoju*, Poznań: Wydawnictwo Akademii Ekonomicznej w Poznaniu.

Ustawa z dnia 8 marca 1990 o samorządzie gminnym (Dz.U.01.142.1591, art. 7), http://bap-psp.lex.pl (accessed 20 March 2007).

Wysocki, F. and Łuczak, A. (2002) 'Wykorzystanie metod taksonometrycznych i analitycznego procesu hierarchicznego do programowania rozwoju obszarów wiejskich', in W. Poczta and F. Wysocki, *Zróżnicowanie regionalne gospodarki żywnościowej w Polsce w procesie integracji z Unią Europejską*, Poznań: Wydawnictwo Akademii Rolniczej w Poznaniu.

Zarębski, M. (2002) *Bariery i możliwości wielofunkcyjnego rozwoju obszarów wiejskich (na przykładzie regionu konińskiego)*, Toruń: UMK.

14 Business angels in Scotland and Poland

The development of an informal venture capital market

Mike Danson, Ewa Helinska-Hughes, Stuart Paul, Geoff Whittam and Michael Hughes

Introduction

Recent years have seen a greater emphasis across the European Union (EU) on support for small and medium enterprises (SMEs) in the belief that these are the main creators of new jobs, are more innovative, assist the competitive environment, and provide the dynamism for growth within both regional and national economies (CEC 1993). The expectation has been that this focus on SMEs would enhance the competitive position of the EU in the global economy through enhanced innovation and entrepreneurship. As well as seeking to close the job creation gap with the United States (Danson *et al.* 2006), the imperative for a new dynamism and growth in the EU has become even more pressing with its enlargements in 2004 and 2007 through the accession of the Central and Eastern European countries (CEECs).

The EU has given support, predicated on the grounds of market failure, designed to increase the numbers of SMEs. However, the expansions of the EU have prompted significant budgetary reforms, leading to restrictions on the support available to the SME sector. One area of particular significance is the availability of, and access to, equity finance. Exacerbated by changes in the banking sector which have made lending to small enterprises relatively unattractive, raising finance for start-up businesses presents considerable challenges. A potential solution to the problems of raising finance faced by entrepreneurs, at least in part, may be provided by the informal investment markets that exist in a number of countries of the EU.

The finance which sustains these informal investment markets is provided by business angels. These are private individuals (or syndicates of individuals) who supply venture capital to businesses, mainly small start-up firms, in exchange for an equity stake. This chapter presents a preliminary analysis from the first phase of a research project that explores the emergence of business angels in the new EU member states of Central and Eastern Europe. Earlier work (Paul *et al.* 2003; Danson *et al.* 2006) demonstrated that informal investment markets are at different states of development within the economies of the EU. Identification of the factors underpinning the development of more mature markets should allow some exploration of whether these have application in less mature markets. In particular, this chapter examines whether the experiences of establishing a mature market in an economy such as Scotland, which has undergone major industrial restructuring since the 1970s, have a resonance with the challenges facing several of the CEECs (Danson *et al.* 2001). In common with Scotland, a number of accession countries have been attempting to overcome the loss of their traditional industries by pursuing foreign direct investment, whilst simultaneously promoting an enterprising economy. In attempting to create a more entrepreneurial culture, start-up companies in accession countries are faced with the issue of raising capital. It is argued below that business angels are an increasingly important source of finance for new and growing businesses. With the establishment of a national Business Angel Network (BAN) and the development of angel syndicates, Scotland has a mature market for the provision of equity finance, and this mature market provides a good example from which emerging angel markets in accession countries, and Poland in particular, may learn valuable lessons.

The research which informs this chapter focuses on case studies conducted in Poland, and examines the role and function of business angels in the context of a transition economy. A comparison is made with the operation of business angels in the more established informal investment market of Scotland, and policy issues related to the development of a business angel market in Poland are identified in this context. The analysis addresses the important role that business angel networks play at national and international levels in supporting the entrepreneurial process.

The chapter starts with an introduction to the concept of business angels, offering an overview of their role in the venture capital market. Business angels in Scotland are then profiled, followed by an examination of how business angels and their networks have developed in Poland. A comparison of informal investment in Scotland and Poland provides a basis for policy recommendations.

The role of business angels

As economic growth in developed countries has become less dependent on large firms (Storey 1994), entrepreneurial activity which results in the creation of new businesses has increasingly been seen as an important component of economic development (OECD 1998). Promotion of entrepreneurship is high on the political agenda in most developed economies, and a key outcome of such activity is the establishment, survival and growth of new ventures. Continuing the policies established at the extraordinary EU Council summit on employment, economic reform and social cohesion in Lisbon, 2000, the promotion of entrepreneurship within Europe is seen as a priority. This arises out of the acknowledgement that the continued development of the EU internal market and establishment of a knowledge-based economy will not be sufficient to drive innovation, competitiveness and growth. It is argued that this task, in large measure, falls to the continued development of an entre-preneurial climate in which new high-growth businesses can flourish. Such businesses are necessary to exploit evolving market opportunities and develop innovative goods and services through effective and innovative processes. Despite their importance, an area of significant market failure for SMEs has been finance, an area highlighted in the strategy which emerged from the Lisbon summit.

Reflecting an earlier Green Paper (CEC 2003), the Kok Report (2004) argued that there was limited availability of finance for setting up and devel-oping businesses in Europe, a problem exacerbated by the lack of availability of risk capital. Access was particularly difficult for start-up businesses that could not easily meet the demands for guarantees made by traditional finan-cial intermediaries. Moreover, the report argued that any risk capital which was available was often only on a short-term basis; it further highlighted the separation of many funding programmes, making it difficult for SMEs to locate the appropriate funding and opportunities available.

In response to these documents the European Business Angel Network (EBAN) put forward proposals on improving the environment in which busi-ness angels operate. In particular, EBAN (2005) argued that business angels and their networks could help reduce the equity gap experienced by new growth businesses.

In the academic literature, scholars have long argued the centrality of finance to the process of entrepreneurship but have also found its acquisition by new ventures and small, growing companies to be problematic (Oakey 1984; Binks *et al.* 1992; Westhead and Storey 1997; Murray 1999; Paul *et al.* 2007). Capital acquisition for start-up firms commonly begins with invest-ment from personal equity such as personal savings, home equity, sale of personal assets and loans from friends and family (Van Auken and Carter 1989). Where this is not possible, or such sources of capital are insufficient or have been exhausted, entrepreneurs often seek to raise funding from outside their personal networks. However, raising finance for start-ups and early-stage companies from such sources is often difficult. These businesses are typically not yet profitable, often lack tangible assets and are characterised by a high risk of failure. Conventional lenders such as banks are unwilling to invest and, therefore, debt financing is usually not an option (Mason and Harrison 1996; Denis 2004).

Traditionally, venture capital firms were seen as the prime source of equity funds for small and start-up businesses but, in recent years, these firms have increasingly focused on larger deals where transaction costs are compara-tively less (Lerner 1998; Van Osnabrugge 1998; Bank of England 2001). This has contributed to shortfalls in investment funding, with demand from entre-preneurs for finance to start and grow their businesses exceeding the willing-ness of financial institutions to supply funds (Deakins and Freel 2006; Paul *et al.* 2003).

An informal market has developed to meet the unsatisfied demand for finance from new ventures and early-stage companies. In return for equity stakes in the businesses in which they invest, business angels provide the funds that sustain this market. These informal markets are regional, with business angels consistently demonstrating a preference for investing close to their home base (Freear *et al.* 1994; Mason and Harrison 1997; Coveney and Moore 1998). The potential of business angels and the informal venture capital market is enormous, with evidence showing that, across a wide range of developed economies, all forms of informal investment contributed much more capital than venture capitalists, as shown in Figure 14.1. We now turn to a consideration of the operation of business angels in the Scottish economy.

Business angels in Scotland

The largest survey into business angel activity in Scotland was conducted by Paul *et al.* (2003). It found that business angels based in Scotland fit broadly with the age and sex profiles that have emerged in other developed countries, for example Finland (Lumme *et al.* 1996) and Norway (Reitan and Sørheim 2000). A key difference, however, was that angels in Scotland were most likely to have a background in large businesses rather than in small or entrepreneurial businesses. In other countries, research has found that angels typically had business start-up experience or were successful entrepreneurs in their own right (see, for example, Freear *et al.* 1997; Feeney *et al.* 1999). The reason for this difference between angels in Scotland and elsewhere may be attributed to the past industrial structure of Scotland, dominated by a reliance on subsidiaries of multinational corporations and a history of low levels of new firm formation (Scottish Enterprise 2000). Many Scotland-based angels, therefore, only gain their understanding of the realities of small business when they

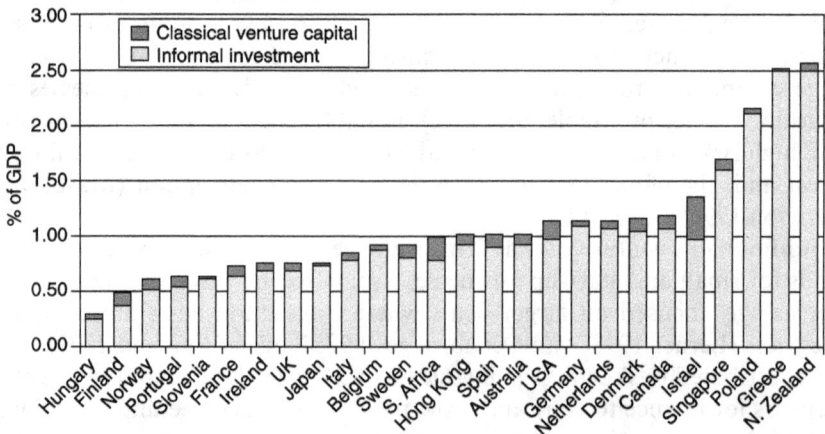

Figure 14.1 Informal investment and classic venture capital as a percentage of GDP.
Source: Bygrave and Hunt (2004).

become angels. Paul *et al.* (2003) quote one experienced angel who formerly had been the managing director of a large manufacturing operation, who commented: 'It has taken me three years to get to a position where I feel I now have a good appreciation of what running a small business is all about.'

The extent to which angel investors have the experience and understanding of small businesses is an important issue, and overcoming this supply-side knowledge shortfall has been identified as a key factor in assisting the effective operation of the informal market (Paul *et al.* 2003).

Paul *et al.* (2003) found that achieving capital growth is the main reason individuals become business angels. However, it should be noted that non-financial reasons are important secondary motivators. These include the concept of 'giving something back', and, while expressions of altruism may be met with a degree of scepticism, Freear *et al.* (1995) found that the expected returns required from an angel investment were lower than those from venture capital funds. The explanation they offer is that angels often consider the non-financial characteristics of their investments and, thus, part of the return is in the form of psychic income. Early research by Wetzel (1983) also indicated that some angel investors were prepared to accept lower returns or assume higher risks when the ventures were expected to, for example, create jobs in their communities or result in socially useful technology. While the prospect of capital growth is the main reason for becoming an angel, Paul *et al.* (2003) point to this being underpinned by a complex 'motivation mix' of secondary, sometimes conflicting, reasons, ranging from financial gain to altruism. They conclude that there exists a reservoir of good will, on the part of at least some business angels, which could be exploited for the public good. One angel encapsulated this mix of motivations neatly: 'Don't get me wrong. I want to make money. But I've done well out of Scotland and I'd like to help others do the same.'

The established literature suggests that angels are active investors, using their business skills and contacts to offer strategic and, in some cases, operational support to the businesses in which they have invested (Wetzel 1983; Harrison and Mason 1992; Freear *et al.*, 1995; Mason and Harrison 2000). Angels in Scotland also fall firmly into the 'hands-on' category. Unlike investors in quoted companies, business angels have little historical data to inform their investment decisions. Facilitated by their preference to invest close to home, the active management of their investments enables angels to mitigate, or at least manage, the risks caused by this shortage of reliable information. A key finding from Scotland is about the type of assistance which angels provide in raising additional funds. Early-stage businesses often require the infusion of several rounds of funding whose magnitude and timing cannot be fully anticipated in advance (Sapienza and Korsgaard 1995). The process of locating additional funding as the business develops can be made easier with help from an experienced outsider and is a task in which an angel can have an important role, especially those who have a well-developed network of business associates.

Scotland has a well-established business angel network called the Local Investment Network Company, usually known by the acronym LINC. It is a public–private non-profit-making partnership which acts as a matchmaker, bringing together business angels with entrepreneurs seeking investment funds. Membership is open to any individual with an interest in becoming a business angel upon payment of a nominal membership fee. LINC provides a focal point for both angels and entrepreneurs and is active in organising events at which they can meet. A key role undertaken by LINC is the screening of potential business investment opportunities to ensure that the entrepreneurs behind a business opportunity are put in contact with appropriate angels.

The UK also has a long history of initiatives based on public expenditure or the tax system, or a combination of both, aimed at filling the equity gap which SMEs confront (see Cressy 2002 for a useful discussion). If more investments between angels and entrepreneurs are to take place, it is important to identify those aspects of the informal market upon which public policy initiatives should focus.

The findings of Paul *et al.* (2003) suggest the need to address not only supply-side but also demand-side deficiencies. On the demand side, it was found that, while angels have funds available, there is a shortage of sufficiently attractive investments and, in this respect, an angel's confidence in the entrepreneur or team behind the project is paramount. Parallels can be drawn with the formal market, where Dixon (1991) found similar evidence, and, as a result of their pan-European study of the investment criteria used by venture capitalists, Muzyka *et al.* (1996) recommended that entrepreneurs seeking funds should concentrate on building the management team and worry less about packaging the financial aspects of their proposals. Paul *et al.* (2003) argue that their findings suggest that the same advice can usefully be given to entrepreneurs seeking funds from business angels. Public policy initiatives should therefore be aimed not just at providing entrepreneurs with help on preparing business plans but also at their presentation skills.

Business angels in Poland

Public policy

This section of the chapter will consider the development of BANs in Poland at both national and regional level, using Silesia as a case study. The analysis begins with some broad background information on public policy issues, and institutional and financial support for entrepreneurial activity. We follow this with a commentary on the development of the contemporary venture capital market before turning our attention to the role, motivation and characteristics of Polish entrepreneurs and business angels.

Privatisation as well as new firm formation has given rise to a large private sector in Poland. The business environment affecting start-ups was significantly changed by Poland's transition programmes, launched on 1 January

1990, which eased regulations, removed many restrictions, liberalised prices and lowered entry barriers for private business. It is clear that new firm formation became crucial for the sustainable economic development of Poland in terms of its contribution to GDP and job creation throughout the 1990s (PAED 2001). The great majority of private enterprises have expanded in terms of the volume of business and employment, with the SME sector providing work for many people who were made redundant by large, state-owned enterprises (Blazyca *et al.* 2002). Not surprisingly, employment trends in the private sector, and especially in SMEs, since 1990 have been mostly favourable (Roberts *et al.* 1997; Koen 1998; PAED 2004; Jackson *et al.* 2005). Many of the new businesses were started by households out of economic necessity to combat unemployment. These new firms required some initial capital that was usually supplied from an entrepreneur's own savings (77 per cent in 1991) or family resources (22 per cent in 1991), and the use of their 'know-how', owing to limited access to and reliance upon the banking sector (Grabowski and Kulawczuk 1992; PAED 2004).

Institutional and financial support

Institutional and financial support encompassed state-sponsored funding schemes, institutional support, training, information services and technology support. In the early stages of transition, most of this activity came from foreign aid, resulting in a host of programmes, schemes, initiatives and institutions (Blazyca *et al.* 2002). However, in Poland the lack of institutional and financial support for small to medium-size private enterprises was especially acute at the beginning of its transition period. Grabowski *et al.* (1992) surveyed 272 private enterprises in three regions of Poland (Gdańsk, Łódź and Kraków) and established that only 16.9 per cent of the firms applied for bank loans. Among the main cited reasons for not using this facility were high interest rates (70 per cent of all firms), uncertainty over future interest rates (37 per cent of firms), high and unrealistic collateral required by the bank (36 per cent of companies), and banks' unwillingness to provide loans for SMEs (12 per cent of respondents). Pawłowicz (1995) assessed the problems that banks face while measuring the creditworthiness and efficiency of potential clients' businesses. Three main criteria were employed: the company's product and its relative competitive position in the market; managerial staff and its experience; and the firm's ability to generate profit. Pawłowicz (1995: 5) observed that 'in classifying particular enterprises as efficient' banks were 'fully aware of the responsibility for the appropriateness and adequacy of their decisions'.

Public sector organisations and business networks which were created to support entrepreneurial developments were to a large extent underfunded. This resulted in frustration among their employees as well as among their potential SME clients. As for EU funding, although Poland received substantial pre-accession funds, the management and administration of these projects

were inefficient. Many programmes were either poorly coordinated or dupli-
cated across regions and institutions. This led to a situation where some
regions were overprovided with programmes and funds while others experienced major shortfalls. As Grabowski *et al.* (1992: 36) stated, 'the greatest
social cost' was the creation of 'a false impression that something is being
done', when in fact very little could be done when 'everything starts and ends
with finances. The rest is just a pretence.'

The levels of support gradually improved, and by the mid-1990s SME
promotion and new firm formation began to gain momentum. At the end of
the 1990s support for SMEs and the private sector had strengthened (Danson
et al. 2001). By 2000, preparations for EU membership meant that the government's position towards entrepreneurial activity and SMEs was further
refocused on emphasising greater private sector involvement. Therefore, by
2002 the majority of small firms were Polish-owned and increasingly financed
from private sources (PAED 2004).

Following EU accession, support for entrepreneurial activity in Poland was
steered by the Lisbon strategy of making Europe the world's most dynamic
and competitive knowledge-based economic area (CEC 2006). As noted at
the time, 'this current year is crucial for the development of new strategies
and priorities for entrepreneurial activity in the next 5–7 years' (Grabowski
2005).

Despite the growing number of institutions encouraging entrepreneurial
activity, finance for SMEs remained an issue, owing to the unrealistic demands
imposed by the banks and by entrepreneurs themselves, who submitted ill-
prepared business plans or provided non-viable projections of their future
profits (Mazurkiewicz 2005).

The development of venture capital

While the number of studies examining venture capital activities in the CEECs
(Poland in particular) has been growing in recent years, the coverage and
understanding of how this market operates remain inadequate (Klonowski
2006). Although Poland represents a relatively new market for venture capital
and private equity institutions, in the context of CEECs it has become pre-
eminent and, therefore, provides an interesting example which may have
wider application for other economies.

At the beginning of the transition process in Poland and at the early
stages of the privatisation of large state-owned companies, venture capital
funds were in their infancy and, therefore, played only a small role in these
processes (Tamowicz 1995). Moreover, the provisions of legislation during
the immediate post-communist transition period were insufficient to promote the functioning of such finance. The first legislative change took place
with the introduction of the Investment Fund Act (IFA) in 1998, which
made some provision for closed-end investment funds. The IFA was further
amended in 2001 and encouraged the development of specialised closed-end

investment funds created by investment fund societies. The process of making venture capital-type finance more readily available was further facilitated by a consolidation of the Polish banking system and the creation of pension funds (Tamowicz 2004).

As the economy began to grow and the private sector developed, Poland became more attractive to large international venture capital companies, with a majority of such funding (in excess of 90 per cent) coming from abroad. By the mid-1990s, twelve companies had conducted venture capital-type activities and managed total capital funds of around $660 million (Tamowicz and Stola 2003). By the end of the 1990s, the Polish venture capital market was attracting such international players as 3TS Venture (with 3i), Baring Communications Equity, and Environmental Investment Fund (Grzywacz and Okońska 2005). At the same time, the government's efforts to stimulate endogenous venture capital were intensifying, and resulted in the creation of the Polish American Enterprise Fund (Tamowicz 2003). In parallel, the Polish government in a 'top-down' approach created a number of other funds, such as the National Investment Funds, and the Agency for Industrial Development (*Agencja Rozwoju Przemysłu*). Although these funds operate along the lines of venture capital, their origin and rationale are different, since they assisted in government-led restructuring and privatisation processes (Tamowicz 1995, 2004).

Despite the expansion of venture capital, indigenous firms have only 3 per cent of the Polish venture capital market and are still reluctant to invest in small start-up companies, owing to a continued perceived high risk in the SME sector (Zwierzchowski 2004). Moreover, venture capital firms set up minimum investment levels which are far too high for start-up firms. Thus, most new small and micro-firms are thrown back upon self-financing sources and find access to credit and capital for growth restricted (PAED 2004). At the beginning of 2000, almost 92 per cent of SMEs were established from an owner's or owner's family's funds. The term 'venture capital' was relatively unknown among Polish entrepreneurs, with only 20.8 per cent of them knowing what it meant (Bobińska 2002).

Business angel networks

The term 'business angel' is relatively unknown in Poland, although the phenomenon of private investors providing funding for business ventures is not a new one and Polish business angels have the same aims as and operate along similar lines to their counterparts in the West. Although their activity is in line with the Lisbon strategy of enhanced entrepreneurship, their functions in Poland are much wider. As mentioned earlier, venture capital and equity markets in Poland remained underdeveloped in the early 1990s, and Polish private entrepreneurs were often either inexperienced or unfamiliar with the way venture capital functions. Therefore, Polish business angels were faced with much greater challenges than their Western counterparts. They also fill an important investment gap for new ventures that still exists in Poland. Polish entrepreneurs seeking funds from banks and similar institutions often face a major obstacle, as banks look for collateral or a guarantee that is equal to the sum of money they wish to borrow (Biernacka and Nowicka 2004).

The potential for the business angels market in Poland is considerable. According to Wojciech Dołkowski (president of PolBAN), there are around 100,000 people in Poland each with PLN1 million in disposable income (Mayer 2004). If only 5 per cent could be persuaded to invest in one or two business ventures this would provide seed capital of between PLN50,000 and PLN500,000 each for around 10,000 firms. However, it is not only start-up funding that entrepreneurs require, and business angels can also provide advice, both strategic and operational, and access to business contacts and networks.

At the national level there were two BANs in Poland: PolBAN and Lewiatan Business Angels (LBA), which operated within the Polish Confederation of Private Employers Lewiatan. PolBAN and LBA had the same aims and objectives as other members of EBAN: namely, to act as honest brokers and a 'marriage bureau' for private investors and entrepreneurs seeking funds for their new ventures. In 2006 a group of entrepreneurs created a web-based business angels network (www.Znajdzinwestora.WP.pl). By 2007 they had over 1,200 names of established and potential business angels and had assisted in two successful investment projects. At the regional level a network of business angels in Silesia called SilBAN was established in 2006. The major features and activities of these organisations at national and regional levels are examined below.

PolBAN was established in December 2003 by Wojciech Dołkowski and three friends, who have funded fifteen Polish entrepreneurs. It is a member of EBAN and, therefore, has access to its contacts and range of networks.

It is a non-profit organisation, and its activities were by 2006 funded from a variety of sources: sponsorships (companies and private individuals), membership fees, and commission from PolBAN-led projects. The organisation had an office in Bydgoszcz but also operated through a network of representatives across Poland. Its main aim was 'to inform the wider public about business angels' activities, seek potential investors and promote interesting projects' (Pietrzak 2005: 88). In 2005, PolBAN was associated with twenty business angels. In June 2005 it concluded its first project (Morawiecka 2005).

LBA was established in April 2005, with 85 per cent of its funding coming from EU sources. It collaborated with a number of organisations, such as Innovation Funds-FIRE and American, German and Irish Chambers of Commerce. However, as a constituent part of the Polish Confederation of Private Employers, it could operate at a regional level by using an existing network of their offices in a number of cities across Poland. In 2006 LBA operated as a non-profit organisation but was set to start charging for its services in 2007. In the early stages of the investment process, it was a 'hands-on' organisation, focusing on project selection prior to preparing a summary document which it then passed to potential investors. Once the initial meeting between an entrepreneur and an angel had taken place, LBA 'took a back seat'. However, according to LBA's project manager Michał Olszewski (interviewed by one of the authors in January 2006, Warsaw), projects had to meet several criteria in order to attract business angel investment, especially those that were to be brokered by national or regional BANs. First, potential products or processes had to be innovative. Second, the managers who were going to be involved in the implementation of the project had to be competent and enthusiastic. Third, a project in question had to meet the criteria of a 'start-up' and had to be competitive.

This approach was successful, and LBA was instrumental in facilitating start-up funds for a network of coffee bars, an indemnity company and a software company. There were fifty business angels associated with LBA, with thirty projects under active consideration. LBA was intending to focus on the information technology, renewable energy and mass media sectors.

The Silesian BAN (SilBAN) was established in April 2006 by three government-sponsored organisations (Fundusz Górnośląski SA, Górnośląskie Towarzystwo Gospodarcze, and Górnośląska Agencja Przekształceń Przedsiębiorstw SA). Its aim was to link angels with investment projects in Silesia. In order to register as a business angel within the network in Silesia, an investor needed to have PLN50,000 to invest (equivalent to €13,000). As this network was only recently created, it is too soon to make any substantive comments about its operation, achievements or failures.

Drawing upon our field work in Silesia in October 2004 and January 2006 during which a number of business angels were interviewed, we examine in the next section the role of entrepreneurs and business angels in Poland, and Silesia in particular.

Polish entrepreneurs and business angels

There are various studies pertaining to the emergence and formation of an entrepreneurial class in Poland throughout the post-communist transformation period. One premise is that, owing to an underdeveloped class of large-scale capitalists in Central and Eastern Europe, the entrepreneurial class carries the responsibility for the progress of capitalism during the transformation process (Osborn and Slomczynski 2005). Developing entrepreneurship and risk taking stimulated the economy and helped it to achieve strong economic growth between 1990 and 2000. However, it is claimed that Polish entrepreneurs still face significant impediments to successful activity, owing to excessive bureaucratic and fiscal constraints from government, and the competitive shock resulting from EU membership (Wyżnikiewicz 2003).

Biographical accounts (Osborn and Slomczynski 2005) confirm the view that many conventional features of entrepreneurial activity dominant in capitalist systems were also important in the formation of the 'new' Polish entrepreneurial class and in the emergence of a growing number of angels.

However, there were also some uniquely Polish conditions that stimulated entrepreneurship, such as foreign contacts and networks, as well as specific government incentives and tax holidays.

Polish entrepreneurs and business angels were better educated than the national average and better off with respect to ownership or access to economic assets. EU membership brought with it new opportunities but also major challenges for entrepreneurs and sustained small business growth. As Wyżnikiewicz (2004) notes:

> However, it seems that the mental preparation of entrepreneurs for open competition in the single market . . . is actually more important than the timely preparation of a legal and economic infrastructure. In my opinion, in the initial period of Poland's presence in the EU, Polish entrepreneurs will have to take lessons in integration, and for many these lessons may prove painful.

Until the mid-1990s business angels were a relatively unknown phenomenon in Poland. With the development of a free market and private sector during the first phase of transition, the demand for private investment intensified, but the investment gap described earlier remained considerable. Although business angels tend not to like publicity and are notoriously difficult to locate, it is estimated that there are a thousand or more potential business angels in Poland who are ready to invest from PLN50,000 up to several million PLN in each project, that is from €12,000 to about €250,000 (Domańska 2005).

The characteristics of Polish angels and their investment practice (based on interviews with business angels in Silesia) are similar to those of the Scottish angels. Typically, they are male (we could find no female business angels in Poland), between 40 and 60 years of age, and have had experience of running a firm. They prefer to invest in a business that is known to them personally or in an industry or sector in which they have prior knowledge and experience. Throughout the first phase of the project (or longer in some cases) the link with the project's management team remains close and very 'hands on'. The following quote illustrates how one of the interviewed angels described the relationship with projects in which he became involved:

> We give advice on organisation or other business and support the universities as well so we could probably be recognised as facilitators and business advisers. We sit the three of us over here and talk to these people and agree on a business plan for next year or next month and this person performs together with us, with our involvement from time to time.
>
> (Interview with business angel, Katowice, October 2004)

Geographical distance (as in the case of Scottish angels) is also important, with Polish angels preferring to invest in close proximity to the place where they live and work. As one of the interviewed angels put it: 'Let's say a distance of 50 kilometres or 50 miles, not far so we can go and visit the guy, visit the business. Easy. That's our experience' (interview with business angel, Katowice, October 2004).

It is apparent that Polish angels are wary of banks and various public bodies. This is how one of them describes his experience in working with the bank:

> I tried to do many things with banks. They offered some loans and sometimes they are free or very cheap. But loans can be complicated because they vary. In some cases you can employ people and keep them for five years. We cannot plan this. How come? Five years? It's like a million years for us.
>
> (Interview with business angel, Katowice, January 2006)

Although angels have some spare cash, they are cautious when it comes to investment. As for the return on investment, it varies depending on the project according to another business angel, who said: 'You can successfully and safely invest with investment partners and collect 15 per cent easily. Or interestingly with the same involvement, it can go up at least four times in four years with the minimum risk' (interview with business angel, Katowice, January 2006).

Silesian angels who were interviewed for this project have developed a unique relationship with local authorities in a town adjacent to where they live, owing to networking and prior involvement in other projects. Networking and personal contacts seem to be a key factor in the success of these angels. Over the last few years they invested in several businesses which were subsequently sold, making a considerable profit. The accumulated profit, as well as a newly acquired business acumen, allowed them to diversify and move on from the IT sector to real estate and more recently to the leisure sector.

Conclusion

Business angels and BANs are comparatively new arrivals in the venture capital investment markets in CEECs. Our interviews with angels in Poland and Scotland lead us to conclude that their characteristics and modus operandi have many similarities. Their activities are important for the development of an entrepreneurial culture, since small companies cite problems with access to capital, credit and bank loans as major obstacles to formation and growth of their business.

It is interesting to note the extent to which both well-founded capital markets and transition economies have a high dependence upon micro-economic features of small business formation. The micro-enterprises in Poland employed 3.2 million people in 2003, which represented 20 per cent of all employees (Grzywacz and Okońska 2005).

Similarities extend to include reliance on family assets, human capital, and specific demographic features of individuals. Clearly, a financial gap is a shared feature for small business start-up and growth processes, and this creates similar responses from formal and informal sources of capital. However, in the case of Poland, banks seem to put ever more stringent conditions (collateral amongst others) upon SMEs which are difficult to meet. Thus, the negative experiences associated with applying for bank loans are shared by many Polish entrepreneurs (Chudzik 2006).

The differences in the experiences of Scotland and Poland are more related to the speed of change in the transition economies, and the capacity for national informal venture capital to gauge its response to demand. For Poland, the majority of new capital has arrived from foreign investors as buyouts of large firms and privatisation, or as greenfield-site investments. In the second half of the 1990s, the venture capital market in Poland expanded further with new funds such as the National Investment Funds (NIFs) that emerged from the programme of mass privatisation (Tamowicz and Stola 2003). However, the situation of Polish SMEs changed during the pre-accession phase, as they became a subject of the more focused governmental policy and funding dictated by the preparations for EU membership (Bednarczyk 2004).

Our study highlights the recent involvement and importance of business angels and that this activity and involvement in the SME sector is becoming more prominent. This is evident in current initiatives by three Polish multi-millionaires who established another BAN, the Business Angel Seedfund (Morawski 2007)

Thus policy recommendations for the Polish economy should take into consideration some key elements of this initial exploration of the nature and role of business angels. First, given the problems of access to capital for start-up firms, incentives could be built into the tax structure for business angels that might mirror those afforded to (large) foreign corporate investors. Major economic development targets, such as regional development, regeneration and rural economic sustainability, could be linked to investment incentives in the SME sector and encouragement of rural entrepreneurial activity to a much greater degree than under existing policies. Second, family-sourced finance for small business is a dominant feature of start-up firms. Therefore family-focused incentives to support SMEs through tax credits on investments would acknowledge and reward this major source of finance. Third, job creation is a major element of economic policy and firmly linked to the success of new business ventures and their survival. Business angels play a key role in this process that needs to be better understood and incorporated into the policy arena in Poland in order to capture the full potential of this source of finance.

References

Bank of England (2001) *Financing of technology-based small firms*, London: Bank of England.

Bednarczyk, M. (2004) *Małe i średnie przedsiębiorstwa w Polsce a integracja europejska*, Kraków: Wydawnictwo Akademii Ekonomicznej w Krakowie.

Biernacka, M. and Nowicka, M. (2004) 'Firmy chcą funduszy', *Puls Biznesu*, 17 June.

Binks, M. R., Ennew, C. T. and Reed, C. V. (1992) 'Information asymmetries and the provision of finance to small firms', *International Small Business Journal*, 11: 35–46.

Blazyca, G., Heffner, K. and Helinska-Hughes, E. (2002) 'Poland – can regional policy meet the challenge of regional problems?', *European Urban and Regional Studies*, 9: 263–76.

Bobińska, M. (2002) 'Kredyt z EBOR-u dla malych firm', *Gazeta Prawna*, 5 April.

Bygrave, W. D. and Hunt, S. A. (2004) *GEM 2004 Financing Report*, Wellesley, MA: Babson College and London Business School.

CEC (Commission of the European Communities) (1993) *Growth, competitiveness, employment: the challenges and ways forward into the 21st century*, White Paper, Brussels: CEC.

CEC (Commission of the European Communities) (2003) *Green Paper on entrepreneurship in Europe*, Brussels: CEC.

CEC (Commission of the European Communities) (2006) *Report on the implementation of the entrepreneurship action plan*, Brussels: CEC.

Chudzik, J. (2006) 'Venture capital jako forma pozyskiwania środków inwestycyjnych', in R. Hanisz (ed.), *Niekonwencjonalne źródła i formy finansowania przedsiębiorstw*, Dąbrowa Górnicza: Wyższa Szkoła Biznesu w Dąbrowie Górniczej.

Coveney, P. and Moore, K. (1998) *Business angels: securing start up finance*, West Sussex: Wiley.

Cressy, R. (2002) 'Funding gaps: a symposium', *Economic Journal*, 112: F1–F16.

Danson, M., Helinska-Hughes, E. and Whittam, G. (2001) 'SMEs and regeneration: a comparison between Scotland and Poland', in G. Blazyca (ed.), *Restructuring local economies: towards a comparative study of Scotland and Upper Silesia*, Aldershot: Ashgate.

Danson, M., Helinska-Hughes, E., Hughes, M., Paul, S. and Whittam, G. (2006) 'An analysis of business angels in Scotland and Poland', *Zagreb International Review of Economics and Business*, Special issue: 61–79.

Deakins, D. and Freel, M. (2006) *Entrepreneurship and small firms*, 4th edn, London: McGraw-Hill.

Denis, D. J. (2004) 'Entrepreneurial finance: an overview of the issues and the evidence', *Journal of Corporate Finance*, 10: 301–24.

Dixon, R. (1991) 'Venture capitalists and the appraisal of investments', *International Journal of Management Science*, 19: 333–44.

Domańska, J. (2005) 'Anioły biznesu Lewiatana', *Życie Warszawy*, 1 November.

EBAN (2005) *The contribution of business angels to delivering the Lisbon strategy, the EU Entrepreneurship Action Plan and CIP, 2007–2013*, White Paper, www.eban.org (accessed 23 May 2007).

Feeney, L., Haines, Jr, G. H. and Riding, A. L. (1999) 'Private investors' investment criteria: insights from qualitative data', *Venture Capital*, 1: 121–45.

Freear, J., Sohl, J. E. and Wetzel, Jr, W. E. (1994) 'Angels and non-angels: are there differences?', *Journal of Business Venturing*, 9: 109–23.

Freear, J., Sohl, J. E. and Wetzel, Jr, W. E. (1995) 'Angels: personal investors in the venture capital market', *Entrepreneurship and Regional Development*, 7: 85–94.

Freear, J., Sohl, J. E. and Wetzel, Jr, W. E. (1997) 'The informal venture capital market: milestones passed and the road ahead', in D. L. Sexton and R. W. Smilor (eds), *Entrepreneurship 2000*, Chicago, IL: Upstart, pp. 47–69.

Grabowski, M. (2005) 'Dobre złego początki – nowe programy wspierania przedsiębiorczości w Unii i w Polsce', *Rzeczpospolita*, 29 June.

Grabowski, M. and Kulawczuk, P. (1992) *Odbudowa sektora małych przedsiębiorstw-analiza i rekomendacje*, Gdańsk: Gdańsk Institute for Market Economics.

Grabowski, M., Kulawczuk, P. and Sak, W. (1992) *Pionierzy Kapitalizmu*, Gdańsk: Gdańsk Institute for Market Economics.

Grzywacz, J. and Okońska, A. (2005) *Venture capital a potrzeby kapitałowe małych i średnich przedsiębiorstw*, Warsaw: Szkoła Główna Handlowa.

Harrison, R. T. and Mason, C. M. (1992) 'International perspectives on the supply of informal venture capital', *Journal of Business Venturing*, 7: 459–75.

Jackson, J. E., Klich, J. and Poznanska, K. (2005) *The political economy of Poland's transition: new firms and government reforms*, Cambridge: Cambridge University Press.

Klonowski, D. (2006) 'Venture capital as a method of financing enterprise development in Central and Eastern Europe', *International Journal of Emerging Markets*, 1: 165–75.

Koen, V. (1998) 'Privatisation as the key to efficiency', *OECD Observer*, 213, August/September, www1.oecd.org/publications/observer/213/spotlight.htm (accessed 21 February 2006).

Kok, W. (2004) *Facing the challenge: the Lisbon strategy for growth and employment*, Report from the High Level Group chaired by Wim Kok, Luxembourg: Office for Official Publications of the European Communities.

Lerner, J. (1998) ' "Angel" financing and public policy: an overview', *Journal of Banking and Finance*, 22: 733–83.

Lumme, A., Mason, C. and Suomi, M. (1996) 'The returns from informal venture capital investments: an exploratory survey', *Journal of Entrepreneurial and Small Business Finance*, 5: 139–58.

Mason, C. M. and Harrison, R. T. (1996) 'Informal venture capital: a study of the investment process, the post-investment experience and investment performance', *Entrepreneurship and Regional Development*, 8: 105–25.

Mason, C. M. and Harrison, R. T. (1997) 'Business angel networks and the development of the informal venture capital market in the UK: is there still a role for the public sector?', *Small Business Economics*, 9: 111–23.

Mason, C. M. and Harrison, R. T. (2000) 'Influences on the supply of informal venture capital in the UK: an exploratory survey of investor attitudes', *International Small Business Journal*, 18: 11–29.

Mayer, B. (2004) 'Aniołowie przedsiębiorczości', *Gazeta Giełdy Parkiet*, 29 April.

Mazurkiewicz, P. (2005) 'Szukam Aniołów do interesów', *Gazeta Wyborcza*, 6 June.

Morawiecka, A. (2005) 'Anioł biznesu czeka', *Rzeczpospolita*, 5 December.

Morawski, I. (2007) 'Słynni biznesmeni szukają polskiego You Tube', *Rzeczpospolita*, 9 March.

Murray, G. (1999) 'Early-stage venture capital funds, scale economics and public support', *Venture Capital*, 1: 351–84.

Muzyka, D., Birley, S. and Leleux, B. (1996) 'Trade-offs in the investment decisions of European venture capitalists', *Journal of Business Venturing*, 11: 273–87.

Oakey, R. P. (1984) 'Innovation and regional growth in small high technology firms: evidence from Britain and the USA', *Regional Studies*, 18: 237–51.

OeCD (Organisation for Economic Co-operation and Development) (1998) *Fostering entrepreneurship*, Paris: OECD.

Osborn, E. and Slomczynski, M. (2005) *Open for business: the persistent entrepreneurial class in Poland*, Warsaw: IFiS Publishers.

PAED (Polish Agency for Enterprise Development) (2001) *Report on the condition of the small and medium sized enterprise sector in Poland in 1999–2000*, Warsaw: PAED.

PAED (Polish Agency for Enterprise Development) (2004) *Report on the condition of the small and medium sized enterprise sector in Poland in 2002–2003*, Warsaw: PAED.

Paul, S., Whittam, G. and Johnstone, J. (2003) 'The operation of the informal venture capital market in Scotland', *Venture Capital*, 5: 313–35.

Paul, S., Whittam, G. and Wyper, J. (2007) 'The process of angel investing', *Venture Capital*, 9: 107–25.

Pawłowicz, L. (1995) *Financial restructuring of enterprises and banks*, Gdańsk: Gdańsk Institute for Market Economics.

Pietrzak, M (2005) 'Anioły lubią inwestować', *Businessman*, January.

Reitan, B. and Sørheim, R. (2000) 'The informal venture capital market in Norway: investor characteristics, behaviour and investment preferences', *Venture Capital*, 2: 129–41.

Roberts, K., Kurzynowski, T. and Jung, B. (1997) 'Employers' workforce formation practices', *Communist Economies and Economic Transformation*, 9: 87–101.

Sapienza, H. J. and Korsgaard, M. A. (1995) 'Performance feedback, decision making processes and venture capitalists' support of new ventures', in P. D. Reynolds, E. Autio, C. G. Brush, W. D. Bygrave, S. Manigart, H. J. Sapienza and K. G. Shaver (eds), *Frontiers of entrepreneurship research 1995*, Wellesley, MA: Babson College.

Scottish Enterprise (2000) *The Scottish business birth rate 2000*, Glasgow: Scottish Enterprise.

Storey, D. J. (1994) *Understanding the small business sector*, London: Routledge.

Tamowicz, P. (1995) *Fundusze inwestycyjne typu venture capital*, Gdańsk: Gdańsk Institute for Market Economics.

Tamowicz, P. (2003) *Policy towards private equity and venture capital*, www.altassets.com/casefor/countries/2003/nz2875.php (accessed 23 February 2006).

Tamowicz, P. (2004) *Venture capital: kapitał na start*, Warsaw: PAED.

Tamowicz, P. and Stola, D. (2003) *The venture capital/private equity market in Poland*, www.altassets.com/casefor/countries/2003/nz3257.php (accessed 23 February 2006).

Van Auken, H. and Carter, R. (1989) 'Acquisition of capital by small business', *Journal of Small Business Management*, 27: 1–9.

Van Osnabrugge, M. (1998) 'Do serial and non-serial investors behave differently? an empirical and theoretical analysis', *Entrepreneurship: Theory and Practice*, 22: 23–52.

Westhead, P. and Storey, D. J. (1997) 'Financial constraints on the growth of high technology small firms in the UK', *Applied Financial Economics*, 7: 197–201.

Wetzel, W. E. (1983) 'Angels and informal risk capital', *Sloan Management Review*, 24: 23–34.

Wyżnikiewicz, B. (2003) 'Trudno być kapitalistą', *Rzeczpospolita*, 6 December.

Wyżnikiewicz, B. (2004) 'Challenges for the Polish economy', *Warsaw Voice*, 18 January.

Zwierzchowski, M. (2004) 'Pomysł to za mało', *Życie Warszawy*, 16 September.

Index

For Product Safety Concerns and Information please contact our EU
representative GPSR@taylorandfrancis.com
Taylor & Francis Verlag GmbH, Kaufingerstraße 24, 80331 München, Germany

9 780415 674843